D1548587

SOCIAL WORK WITH
AFRICAN AMERICAN MALES

SOCIAL WORK WITH AFRICAN AMERICAN MALES

Health, Mental Health, and Social Policy

Edited by

Waldo E. Johnson, Jr.

OXFORD
UNIVERSITY PRESS
2010

OXFORD
UNIVERSITY PRESS

Oxford University Press, Inc., publishes works that further
Oxford University's objective of excellence
in research, scholarship, and education.

Oxford   New York
Auckland   Cape Town   Dar es Salaam   Hong Kong   Karachi
Kuala Lumpur   Madrid   Melbourne   Mexico City   Nairobi
New Delhi   Shanghai   Taipei   Toronto

With offices in
Argentina   Austria   Brazil   Chile   Czech Republic   France   Greece
Guatemala   Hungary   Italy   Japan   Poland   Portugal   Singapore
South Korea   Switzerland   Thailand   Turkey   Ukraine   Vietnam

Copyright © 2010 by Oxford University Press, Inc.

Published by Oxford University Press, Inc.
198 Madison Avenue, New York, New York 10016

www.oup.com

Oxford is a registered trademark of Oxford University Press.

Library of Congress Cataloging-in-Publication Data
Social work with African American males : health, mental health,
and social policy / edited by Waldo E. Johnson, Jr.
p. cm.
Includes bibliographical references and index.
ISBN 978-0-19-531436-6
1. African American men—Services for. 2. Social work with African Americans—United States.
3. African American men—Social conditions. I. Johnson, Waldo Emerson, 1955–
HV3181.S625 2010
362.84'96073—dc22
2009042638

9 8 7 6 5 4 3

Printed in the United States of America
on acid-free paper

CONTENTS

CONTRIBUTORS

WALTER R. ALLEN, PH.D.
Professor
Department of Sociology
University of California at Los Angeles
Los Angeles, California

M. DANIEL BENNETT, JR., M.D.
Assistant Professor
School of Medicine
Mercer University
Macon, Georgia

VENCE BOHNAM, J.D.
Associate Investigator
Social and Behavioral Research Branch
National Human Genome Research Institute
Bethesda, Maryland

REGINALD CLARK, PH.D.
President
Clark and Associates
Claremont, California

EDDIE COMEAUX, PH.D.
Assistant Professor
College of Education
University of Kentucky
Lexington, Kentucky

CONSTANCE M. DALLAS, PH.D., R.N.
Associate Professor
College of Nursing
University of Illinois at Chicago
Chicago, Illinois

OMARI L. DYSON, PH.D.
Assistant Professor
Department of Teacher Education
South Carolina State University
Orangeburg, South Carolina

ROBERT GAROFALO, M.D., M.P.H.
Deputy Director
Howard Brown Health Center
Chicago, Illinois

ALEXES HARRIS, PH.D.
Assistant Professor
Department of Sociology
University of Washington
Seattle, Washington

JA-NEE JACKSON
Research Analyst
Optimal Solutions Group, LLC
Baltimore, Maryland

SEAN JOE, PH.D.
Associate Professor
School of Social Work
University of Michigan, Ann Arbor
Ann Arbor, Michigan

EARL S. JOHNSON, III, PH.D.
Senior Program Officer
California Endowment
San Francisco, California

WALDO E. JOHNSON, JR., PH.D.
Associate Professor
School of Social Service Administration
University of Chicago
Chicago, Illinois

MARK L. JOSEPH, PH.D.
Assistant Professor
Mandel School of Applied Social Sciences
Case Western Reserve University
Cleveland, Ohio

KAREN KAVANAUGH, PH.D., R.N.
Professor
College of Nursing
University of Illinois at Chicago
Chicago, Illinois

CHARLES E. LEWIS, JR., PH.D.
Assistant Professor
School of Social Work
Howard University
Washington, District of Columbia

MICHAEL A. LINDSEY, PH.D.
Assistant Professor
School of Social Work
University of Maryland, Baltimore
Baltimore, Maryland

SHUNTAY MCCOY, M.S.W.
Doctoral Student
Department of Human Development
    and Family Studies
University of North Carolina
    at Greensboro
Greensboro, North Carolina

FATIMA MIRZA, M.S.W.
Doctoral Student
School of Social Work
University of Maryland,
    Baltimore
Baltimore, Maryland

BRIAN MUSTANSKI, PH.D.
Assistant Professor
Department of Psychiatry
University of Illinois at Chicago
Chicago, Illinois

HAROLD W. NEIGHBORS, PH.D.
Professor
Center for Research on Ethnicity,
    Culture and Health
University of Michigan,
    Ann Arbor
Ann Arbor, Michigan

TORSTEN B. NEILANDS, PH.D.
Associate Professor
Center for AIDS Prevention Studies
University of California at
    San Francisco
San Francisco, California

FINAKE OLUGBALA
Social Worker
Atlanta, Georgia

DAVID J. PATE, PH.D.
Assistant Professor
Department of Social Work
University of Wisconsin-Milwaukee
Milwaukee, Wisconsin

JOSEPH E. RAVENELL, M.D.
Assistant Professor
New York University
New York, New York

BARBARA A. RAY
Principal
Hired Pen, Inc.
Chicago, Illinois

JOSEPH B. RICHARDSON, JR., PH.D.
Assistant Professor
Department of African American
    Studies
University of Maryland, College Park
College Park, Maryland

KEVIN M. ROY, PH.D.
Associate Professor
Department of Family Science
University of Maryland, College Park
College Park, Maryland

SHERRILL L. SELLERS, PH.D.
Associate Professor
School of Social Work
University of Wisconsin-Madison
Madison, Wisconsin

AMY JOHNSON, M.S.W.
Project Director
Howard Brown Health Center
Chicago, Illinois

DEXTER R. VOISIN, PH.D.
Associate Professor
School of Social Service Administration
University of Chicago
Chicago, Illinois

KIMBERLY A. WHITE-SMITH, ED.D.
Assistant Professor
College of Educational Studies
Chapman University
Orange, California

LANCE WILLIAMS, PH.D.
Assistant Director
Carruther's Center for Inner City Studies
Northeastern Illinois University
Chicago, Illinois

SOCIAL WORK WITH
AFRICAN AMERICAN MALES

From Shortys to Old Heads

Contemporary Social Trajectories of African American Males Across the Life Course

WALDO E. JOHNSON, JR.

The social ecology within the life course in which African American males are examined in *Social Work With African American Males: Health, Mental Health, and Social Policy* owes much to the earlier scholarship of social scientists who examine the social statuses of African American males. Sociologist Elijah Anderson's scholarship explores the contemporary nomenclature of African American males within their communal spaces for framing language from an inclusive perspective, which enables the editor and the contributors to this volume to examine African American males' social statuses within contemporary American society. Anderson is among the first of social scientists to articulate and validate the interplay between the historical roles and social positions of older African American men and the contemporary statuses and emerging social identities of urban, young males (Anderson, 1990, 1996). Anderson's ethnographic depiction of the diminishing role statuses of older African American men, due in large part to their narrowly constrained opportunities for success in the evolving service economy and the broader American social structure, is reflected in their lifelong pursuit for respectability within American life, community, and culture in his portrayal of these men as "old heads." He contends that these men often operated at the margins of American society in lower status jobs and professional careers, when available, which yielded far fewer advancement opportunities than their White peers exercised and enjoyed. In lieu of broad access to professional advancement, Anderson draws on the depictions of these African American men by noted sociologist E. Franklin Frazier. Frazier (1957) described these men's overreliance on their participation and leadership in African American community institutions such as the Black church, fraternal societies, and other neighborhood and community engagements. These were the means by which they achieved social elevation within their communities, which was largely denied them in the broader American social structure.

Concurrently, the term "shorty" was initially a lexicon in the contemporary vernacular of African American males and, more specifically, hip hop culture in both urban and rural communities throughout the United States. It is used to describe a child or offspring, especially a kid you do not know, or to distinguish a kid from older family or adults in the social group who have the same name or nickname. The depiction of African American men as "boys" is certainly not unfamiliar in the United States, especially in the Jim Crow South, where the customs of social engagement required African American men (and women) to both greet and reference Whites as "Mister" and "Miss" even when the latter were half their age. However, at best, African American males were called "boy." Familiarity and acquaintance with the individual did not alter the formal greeting or reference; Whites retained their titles, which denoted adulthood, and African Americans were infantilized.

In the contemporary vernacular, the term "shorty" might also describe a buddy, pal, friend, or comrade; a dude or an acquaintance. A shorty might also be your main man who holds all your drugs, guns, and other illegal stuff until the heat is off. He is also your hook-up that buys you all your drugs and holds them for you until you need them. Finally, "shorty" has been a term used by a masculine, gay/bisexual man when referring to a slightly feminine gay/bisexual man. Overtime, it has come to describe newly initiated gang members of either sex, often ranging in age from 14 to 17. The term has been used primarily for males in the context of drug running. If used for a female, it would suggest that she is available for sex to anyone in the gang. Among commercial rappers and increasingly in contemporary hip hop culture, the term has come to describe a female or girl, a girl on the side, or a female casual sexual partner. The constantly changing social context of the term "shorty" is emblematic of the context in which it is examined for the purpose of this chapter. The term "shorty" is used to describe African American boys', pre-adolescents', and even young males' diminutive physical stature but also their relative life experiences given their age and social developmental statuses.

In 1981, Howard University social work professor Lawrence E. Gary, author of *Black Men*, argued that too many studies of African American men were constricted by their narrow focus and limited methodologies, as well as their lack of cultural sensitivity. As a result, Gary contended that social scientists and social work and social welfare practitioners perpetuate "many myths, stereotypes and distortions about African American men" (p. 11). Over time, these "myths, stereotypes and distortions" formed the basis for an evolving characterization of African American men. Aided initially by media portrayals perpetrated by electronic and print media that depict Black men as voluntarily disengaged from work, family, and community concerns but immersed in socially undesirable and criminal activities throughout the nation's urban centers and beyond, the emergence of Black men as indifferent, pathological, and endangered has become firmly rooted in the twenty-first-century American psyche.

Gary's focus in 1981 was on Black *men*. Since he edited the volume *Black Men*, the distinction between African American men, adolescents, and boys has steadily eroded. The social stigmas of indifference, pathological, and contemporaneously, at risk of various physical, psychological, educational, vocational and social maladies attributed to Black men beginning in the 1960s now commonly characterize the plight and statuses of African American boys and teenage males as well as African American men. African American male identity has become increasingly amorphous and subsequently threatening in the eyes of many Americans. Today, for many Americans, young African American males—initially those residing in impoverished urban and inner-city communities but more recently African American males, whether residing in upper-income suburban or sparsely populated rural communities in addition to the urban core—are seen as emblematic of a humanity that is both threatening and undesirable, much in the way African American men were uniquely viewed. Contemporary mass media depictions and popular culture contribute to the blurring of these chronological distinctions among African American males, even amid empirical scholarship by esteemed psychologists Oscar Barbarin who examines the effects of violence and poverty on child development, Margaret Beale Spencer whose path-breaking theoretical modeling cuts across African American boyhood and adolescent and the Reginald Jones' seminal volume, whose in *Black Adolescents* (1989) to carefully examine life cycle perspectives, environmental factors, and structural issues that pose unique challenges for African American boys and adolescents respectively.

The Bleeding of Boys Into Men

Similarly, many of the problems that Professor Gary identified as plaguing Black men in 1981 are pervasive today among African American male youth and adolescents. The ramifications for this "bleeding of boys into men" are seen in contemporary public policies and strategies that fail to address pervasive individual, environmental, and structural factors that plague African American boys' orderly transition into adolescence and adulthood (Johnson, 2007), thus setting them on difficult and often unhealthy trajectories. These trajectories begin with the all-too-frequent failure of public education environments to provide them with the preparation needed to successfully compete with their school-age peers (Polite & Davis, 1999). There is wide disparity in the public high school graduation rates of White and African American students. In 2003, the national graduation rate for White students was 78%, compared with 55% for African American students Schoff Foundation, 2008). In urban centers like Chicago, recent public school graduation data suggest that less than 50% of African American ninth-grade males will graduate with their peers. This disparity is even greater when graduation rates are examined by race and gender. Nationally, about 5% fewer White male students graduate than their female counterparts. While 59% of African American females graduated, only 48% of African American males earned a high school diploma Polite and Davis, 1999.

The increasingly lower high school graduation rate among African American males is believed, by some, to be directly linked to the rapid growth of the number of young African American males whose educational opportunities are truncated in elementary and middle school because of multiple suspensions, expulsions, and referral to special education curricula Polite and Davis 1999. The tracking of African American males into special education curricula and multiple suspensions and expulsions during elementary and middle school are linked to higher rates of drop-out and delinquency, which, in turn, are increasingly linked as the gateway to involvement and/or incarceration in juvenile/criminal systems (Mincy, 2006). In fact, African American males are increasingly more likely to complete their formal education while in juvenile detention and the criminal justice system than in formal education institutions (Western, 2000). Meanwhile, the general equivalency degree (GED) has become a weak proxy for a high school diploma (Holzer and Offner, 2004). Data from urban research suggest that when selecting prospective employees, employers are more likely to discriminate against African American holders of GED degrees and those with criminal records, who are also more likely to reside in eco-nomically distressed neighborhoods (Kirschenman & Neckerman, 1991). Moreover, some have argued that employment and earnings of African American males may be negatively affected by a prior history of incarceration (Western, 2006). Further, high rates of incarceration among African American males may even reduce employment prospects for those African American males with no criminal background (Holzer, Raphael, & Stoll, 2006). Poor educational outcomes, in turn, leave African American males unprepared for sustained entry into the evolving service economy (Johnson, 2000), thus rendering them unable to find individual- and family-sustaining work.

These social markers not only affect African American males' ability to become self-sufficient by making choices about labor force opportunities but also inevita-bly affect their ability to form couple and family relationships. African American males are disproportionately represented among those who father children out of wedlock and into fragile families where the parental relationships between mothers and fathers are weakened, in part, due to their youthful developmental and impov-erished economic statuses. In addition, their social and developmental statuses severely limit their family involvement and also exclude them from various forms of civic engagement critical to their individual and family enhancement as well as the healthy development of the communities in which they reside.

The mandate for enhanced research on the social statuses of African American males has never been in greater demand. Multiple indicators of health and well-being suggest that African American males are confronted with a host of psychoso-cial challenges throughout the life course. African American males tend to fare poorly with regard to social indicators of health and well-being regardless of age. Recent studies indicate that African American infants and young children between 0 and 4 years of age are approximately four times more likely to be a victim of homicide than their White counterparts (Joe, 2006). Moreover, homicide is the leading cause of death for African American males between the ages of 15 and 24. Further, recent data suggest that patterns of homicide offending among African

American male adolescents and young adults are similar to patterns of homicide victimization for this group (Joe, 2006).

The challenges faced by African American males are not limited to violence.

_ African American males are also confronted with a number of challenges related to their physical and mental health statuses. Over the life course, they are considerably less likely than their female peers to have access to health care. Although there is documented evidence that males in general use health-care services, African American males specifically express a general distrust for medical and health-care providers due to historical discrimination and mistreatment in medical care and public health. African American males' inability to maintain medical- and health-care continuity is due in large part to their poor access to medical and public health services over the life course. As boys entering adolescence, except those who participate in school sports, African American males generally do not transition from pediatric to family or urological health care in ways comparable to their female peers, who routinely receive continuity in health care via gynecological health services after transitioning from pediatric care. Adult African American males who are either unemployed or underemployed without health insurance generally cannot access health-care services as impoverished non custodial fathers, in contrast to the mothers of their children, who can access maternal health programs. In contrast to their female peers, African American and other disadvantaged males, from late childhood through adulthood, are more likely to receive their health care via emergency room service under crisis situations. For example, African American males have the highest prostate cancer incidence and mortality rates in the world (Platz et al, 2000). Moreover, they die from prostate cancer at a rate 2.3 times that of White men. In addition, African American males have also been found to be at an increased risk for hypertension (Hill et al, 1999), diabetes (National Diabetes Clearinghouse, 1998), heart attack, and stroke (Haveman, 2001). Early detection via health screening could significantly lower the incidences of these health problems and mortality. Consequently, African American males have a life expectancy of 65.8 years compared to 76.5 years for all U.S. population groups (Smedley, Stith & Nelson, 2002).

Mental health is another area of challenge for African American males. The onset of chronic stress, depression, somatization, and other forms of mental illness may be linked to particular social circumstances, including but not limited to experiences with racism/discrimination, homelessness, incarceration, poverty, and substance abuse (National Alliance on Mental Health [NAMI], 2006).The aforementioned conditions may be further exacerbated by *(1)* cultural bias against mental health professionals due to prior experiences with historical misdiagnoses and inadequate treatment, and *(2)* limited access to, and availability of, culturally competent service providers. Only 2% of psychiatrists, 2% of psychologists, and 4% of social workers in the United States are African American (NAMI, 2004). These lowered representations within these intervention disciplines and professions uniquely affect both the frequency and quality of experiences of African American males who utilize mental health services (Joe, 2006).

The indifference often attributed to African American males today encompasses more than failure as fathers to assume provider and protector roles for themselves, their children, and their extended families and communities. Contemporary characterizations and depictions suggest that African American males harbor a lifelong disregard for their own personal development and a lack of commitment to their loved ones and society in general. This perceived indifference, widely held by many Americans, emerges initially from what is often viewed as poor academic performance and the blatant rejection of scholarly achievement among African American males. This perception is associated with African American males' primary and secondary school completion rates, as well as postsecondary education, training, and preparation for vocational and career development. Historically, however, African Americans, like other American citizens, have viewed educational attainment and achievement as a pathway to reaching individual self-sufficiency, building and sustaining couple relationships and family development, and, subsequently, civic involvement and community engagement. African American males' demeanor, often interpreted by their mere physical presence, speech, and attire, contributes to the perceived indifference to otherwise socially sanctioned expectations and pathways to individual and societal success.

African American males' failure to adapt in ways that support and achieve orderly growth and development also results in their characterization as both pathological and dangerous. No other racial or ethnic group, male or female, in American society is so pervasively identified with the negative images of popular culture in which gratification for fast money, hypersexuality, intimidation, and wreckless disregard for life is pursued at any and all costs. Perhaps this is due, in part, to the overrepresentation of African American males in popular culture characterizations in which these images and pursuits are glorified. The commercialization of hip hop as a multibillion-dollar industry in which young African American males are routinely depicted as a cultural paradox: seeking fame and fortune by describing the ghetto life as inescapable yet portraying the very negative aspects of this impoverished existence (e.g., thug life) as authentic and providing credibility. Their White urban and suburban male peers may be among the largest consumers of these mass media representations (Kitwana, 2005), but African American males personify these representations and often seek association to enhance their credibility as artists, athletes, and consumers (Kitwana, 2002). Their active and perceived acceptance of the nexus between their lived experiences and these media characterizations further distinguishes them in ways that create tension within their families and communities in addition to other spheres of society. Increasingly, their presence induces discomfort and fear in both public and private spaces.

The above characterizations often evoke varied and sometimes extreme responses from those who view African American males as personally responsible for their current plights and statuses and those who believe that such depictions unfairly target African American males as a group. Although varying perspectives exist regarding who is responsible for the contemporary status of African American males, many believe that African American males represent an endangered species, a contention that begin to gain national attention in the mid to late 1980s. Agreement, however, regarding the basis for their alleged endangered status is divided. Those who adhere to a personal responsibility perspective charge that the blame for African American males' outcast state falls squarely upon their shoulders. However, those who adhere to a linked fate perspective contend that African American males are not totally responsible for their plights and are often unfairly targeted by individuals and institutions alike. Among those who embrace the linked fate perspective, efforts to rescue, enhance, and preserve African American males' presence in American society are urgently needed. There exists a nuanced intersection among these perspectives, which holds that African American males must assume some responsibility for their plights, but the distinction often lies in the weight placed on personal responsibility.

Those who adhere to a weighted personal responsibility perspective contend that African American males must reject negative behaviors and stereotypes, embrace an engaging concern for themselves and others, and maintain strict adherence to socially acceptable lifestyle choices. They contend that only such personal commitments will save African American males from their current dire straits (McWhorter, 2000). In response to the negative characterization of African American males as indifferent and pathological, others contend that African American males are often caught up in a web of unfortunate circumstances shaped largely by their environments, which in turn often frame their perception of a limited opportunity structure in society for achieving individual success. Those within this camp also bemoan the breakdown of institutional structures that traditionally supported the socialization of youth into socially acceptable roles (Johnson, 2001). In addition, they frequently espouse an alarmist perspective, which charges that the transformation of some and creation of new social institutions, bolstered by historical patterns of racial discrimination and gendered disregard in tandem, have contributed to the weakened social statuses of African American males and their communities. This perspective recognizes that African American males are not sole targets of racial and gender discrimination in the United States but hold that the effects on African American males are indeed unique. They further argue that African American males are victimized in ways that fail to fully acknowledge and value them as citizens deserving of support from the institutional systems of social welfare (Johnson, 2001).

While some African American males fail to assume appropriate responsibility for their personal development and the welfare of their loved ones, African American males, in general, are undeniably viewed with suspicion and mistrust in American society. Their motives are often misunderstood and misconstrued as both calculating and insincere. Again, the bleeding of boys into men is such that the characterizations that formerly depicted African American men a quarter of century ago are now descriptive of African American boys and adolescents as well. From both public and social policy perspectives, the distinct chronological and/or developmental markers that distinguish African American boys from African American adolescents and subsequently from African American men continue to diminish over time. Collectively, African American males across the life course are held with similar disdain and fear. The chronological and developmental differences that formed the basis for earlier malleable and rehabilitative institutional frameworks for intervening on problem behavior in boyhood and adolescence are currently considered intractable. They often result in across-the-board policies, laws, and practices that increasingly apply adult sanctions for often youthful offenses.

It is critical to utilize both social work research and practice to articulate these and other challenges that adversely impact the physical, mental, and social health and well-being of African American males. Intervention strategies and practices that fail to consider historical inequities, racial/ethnic and gender discrimination and even access to treatment and services also fail to provide equitable service and opportunity for all who demonstrate need and seek support. The origin and development of social welfare policies and service provisions in the United States is fraught with the aforementioned concerns regarding the status of men and their access to services. In addition, demographic and technological changes have resulted in societal shifts that have affected individuals, families, and communities in ways such that the provision of common human needs mandate a reassessment of those to whom assistance should be available as well as the circumstances under which it is offered. As a result, historical perspectives that support the existence of "an undeserving" group of individuals are complicated by contemporary expectations of self- and family-sufficiency and the recognition that environmental factors may impinge upon African American males' ability to achieve self-sufficiency and support their families. Original reports of evidence-based social work practice and intervention, as well as the development and validation of social work assessment methods that convey direct applications to social work practice with African American male populations, are sorely needed.

Social work as a professional endeavor aims to investigate and treat with material aid the underprivileged and maladjusted in society. Its methods, services, and activities aim to create a social scientific approach to helping individuals, families, and communities. For example, as the largest provider of mental health services to the poor in America, social work has historically provided frontline intervention to those in need. Historically, social work and social welfare responses to men in American society reflect an often weak, estranged relationship. Social work is also guided by American values of rugged individualism, the core of which purports that the male species triumphs over human adversity and is expected to be physically and emotionally detached from environmental circumstances that might otherwise trample them. Thus, social work as a profession and attendant social welfare responses such as human services, medical, and public health domains in American society historically have been less attentive to the public provision of material and psychological needs of men, given their perceived undeserving status as beneficiaries of public support. As a result, this undeserving status that is routinely attributed to men in generally fails to address the historical and contemporary disadvantaged statuses of African American men in comparison to their white male peers. While it is arguably inaccurate to assume that all white males enjoy privileged statuses in American society that disqualify them as the beneficiaries of the profession, African American adult males and increasingly African American boys and adolescents collectively do not enjoy such privileged statuses.

In contrast, men are expected to be self-sufficient and largely undeserving of such institutional and governmental assistance (Hofstadter, 1944) except in time-limited periods of natural or national disaster. This perspective places African American males in a decidedly disadvantaged position because as men, they too, generally embrace American society's historical notions of male self-sufficiency. Collectively, they also struggle to uphold contemporary perspectives of male personal responsibility and self-sufficiency as an indication of their gender identity despite their historical mistreatment, which legally characterized them as 3/5 of a person in America. African American men endured hundreds of years of servitude as chattel slaves and even during the post-slavery, Jim Crow and civil rights movement of the 1960s, they were denied the full rights of American citizenship, which remains elusive even today. The impact of these historic institutional arrangements has not diminished for the generation of African American males most visibly affected today. In fact, the vestiges of U.S. slavery, Jim Crow, and the twentieth-century manifestations of discrimination are highly visible in practically every domain of African Americans' lives. Perhaps the most damaging effect of this historic mistreatment is the loss of hope among the current generation of African American males. This hope and ambition for a better tomorrow clearly characterized the beliefs, actions, and legacy of their forefathers (Whitaker, 2005). Earlier generations of African American males held steadfast to the belief that social advancement and achievement, despite their historic and present social statuses, were indeed possible—perhaps not for their generation but for their children and the generations to come. Unlike their ancestors, grandfathers, and even fathers of the mid-twentieth century, a disproportionate percentage of African American males today do not articulate or share this belief for either their own personal achievement or the advancement of their progenies today and generations to come.

Instead, as members of a racial group that is disproportionately poor and disadvantaged, due in part, to historical conditions experienced by Africans in America and contemporary vestiges and current conditions facing African Americans in general, African American males are often viewed as absent from both the familial (Johnson, Levine, & Doolittle, 1999; Mincy, 2006; Wilson, 1987, 1996) and community contexts through which social work and social welfare could legitimately engage them. The actual and perceived detachment of African American males from the family and community invokes the continuation of an organizational and institutional framework in which social science research, public policy, and intervention practice are devoid of their presence, discourage their engagement, and diminish their historical, contemporary, and evolving roles and responsibilities within these institutions. In perpetuating such practices, we as American citizens actively and passively participate and contribute to the demise of African Americans and the eventual death of the American society.

Gary observed that African American men are the social fabric of this country. At minimum, they are interwoven into America's social fabric. This volume, *Social*

Work With African American Males: Health, Mental Health, and Social Policy, proposes to provide readers theoretical and conceptual insights supported by empirical data on the African American male experience in dimensions heretofore only addressed in limited scope of papers, seminar discussions, and workshops. It remains mindful of the pioneering scholarship that preceded it. However, in the quarter of the century since Gary's seminal volume on African American males was published, the circumstances and issues confronting African American males have changed dramatically. Ideally, this volume will challenge us all to remember that.

The Chapters in This Volume

This volume, *Social Work With African American Males: Health, Mental Health, and Social Policy* is organized into five parts, which are described briefly in the text that follows.

I. African American Males' Individual and Family Roles

The socially contested roles of African American males in family and community are examined in Part I. Coauthors Constance M. Dallas and Karen Kavanaugh explore similarities and differences between pregnancy-related behaviors that adolescent fathers and their families expect from the young fathers and their actual behaviors in Chapter 2, "Making Room for Daddy: The Unmarried Adolescent Fathers' Role in Pregnancy." Unwed fathers who participate in the prenatal care for the mothers of their children are more likely to remain involved with their children. The extant research literature suggests that little is known about what it might mean for an unwed, low-income, African American adolescent father to be involved during pregnancy and how that involvement might influence his transition to a sustaining fatherhood role. Dallas and Kavanaugh interviewed unwed, low-income, African American adolescent fathers in order to obtain their perspectives of the father's role during pregnancy. They employed the kinscripts conceptual framework developed by Linda Burton and Carol Stack to examine data drawn from a longitudinal, descriptive case study of paternal involvement. Furthermore, they used a convenient sample of kinship systems, which included unmarried, low-income, African American adolescent fathers, the mothers of their children, and at least one parent or parent surrogate for each adolescent parent. Study subjects are interviewed when their children are 1, 6, 12, 18, and 24 months old.

Few studies have acknowledged the reciprocity that may emerge between adult children and their aging parents. In particular, we know little about relationships between older mothers and their adult sons. Several earlier studies on adolescent African American fatherhood suggested that young fathers growing up in fatherless, mother-headed households shaped their parental role engagement (Johnson, 2001). In Chapter 3, "Intergenerational Support and Reciprocity Between Low-Income African American Fathers and Their Aging Mothers," Kevin M. Roy, Omari

L. Dyson, and Ja-Nee Jackson employ a modified grounded theory approach to code and analyze field notes and life history interviews with low-income African American men in fatherhood programs in Chicago ($n = 40$) and Indianapolis ($n = 40$) and a pedifocal perspective that locates child care at the center of a network of reciprocal kin relationships. The authors briefly examine how men are socialized at early ages into parenting behavior, and the roles that their mothers play in "teaching" them to be fathers. The authors then address unfolding reciprocity between aging mothers and their adult sons, with a focus on shared residency and household responsibilities; kin work, through care offered by paternal grandmothers, which helps to secure involvement of nonresidential fathers; and exchange of financial, emotional, and social support. The authors conclude with implications for family policies and work with African American fathers in community-based programs and interventions.

David J. Pate provides insight into the complexity of noncustodial African American fathers' day-to-day existence and their perspectives on the child support system in Chapter 4, "Life After PRWORA: The Involvement of African American Fathers With Welfare-Reliant Children and the Child Support Enforcement System." The data in this chapter are drawn from the ethnographic component of the Wisconsin Works (W-2) Child Support Evaluation Study conducted by the Institute for Research on Poverty at the University of Wisconsin-Madison. The ethnographic component was designed to provide a deeper understanding of and perspective on the life experiences of noncustodial African American fathers living in the city of Milwaukee in the context of social welfare generally, and specifically in light of welfare reform implemented through PRWORA, including changes in child support policies and distribution rules. The topics examined in this ethnographic analysis include noncustodial fathers' understanding of the child support system and of welfare reform, their capacities for employment, and their conception of their role and responsibilities. Field data were collected via semistructured interviews with African American noncustodial fathers whose children were recipients of W-2 payments from April 1999 thru April 2001. This study employs a grounded theory approach, and the sampling strategy was unique in that the majority of the sample participants were randomly selected from an administrative data set. The data from the transcripts of three men with children were analyzed using content and narrative analysis techniques. The larger ethnographic study is comprised of 36 men.

Although an emerging body of scholarship explores the growing phenomenon of the African American grandmother as an almost "heroic figure" in family preservation by assuming custody of grand- and even great-grandchildren to prevent them from becoming wards of the state, minimal scholarship exists on the role of nonbiological fathers as forms of social capital and social support within African American families. How social capital is produced within poor African American families and accessed by families within the communities in which they reside is an evolving area of study. The co-parenting collaborative relationships that nonbiological fathers, particularly African American uncles, play as additional sources of social capital and social support for at-risk children and single-female-headed households are indeed promising. In Chapter 5, "The Socially Supportive Role of the African American 'Uncle' in the Lives of Single-Female-Headed Households and At-Risk African American Male Youth," Joseph B. Richardson, Jr. examines the increasing role of the African American "uncle" within extended familial and fictive kinship networks as a primary source of family-based capital and social support for at-risk male youth and single female mothers. He also explores the roles these men play in the prevention of delinquency and serious youth violence within poor African American families and communities. The uncles were primarily maternal kin, but in several cases the uncles were paternal or fictive kin. This study expands the extant research on the role of African American men in building family-based social capital beyond the emphasized nuclear family norm. Eight intensive case studies comprise the ethnographic study and documented the social context of interaction among the African American males from 7th grade through completion of 10th grade, as early adolescence typically marks the onset of violent and delinquent behavior across three contexts: school, community, and the household. Time series and social network charts were created for each sample member. An analysis of family-based social capital, meaning the individuals within immediate, extended, and fictive kinship networks who provide resources, social support, supervision, and strategies for young men to avoid engaging in serious violence and delinquent behavior was performed. Much of what was learned via participation observation and life-history interviews with the young African American males, the single mothers, and the uncles in the study revealed the invaluable roles that these men played in these families.

In Chapter 6, "Academic Achievement, Peer Influences, and Sexual Behaviors Among High School African American Adolescent Boys," Dexter R. Voisin and Torsten B. Neilands report that African American adolescent males are disproportionately infected with HIV compared to their White counterparts. While factors like early sexual debut, sex without condoms, and a higher number of sexual partners may in part account for such disparities, the factors associated with such risk behaviors remain unclear. The literature suggests that parents are critical in keeping adolescents safe. However, there is a dearth of research on African American adolescent males in relation to family constellation and sexual risk behaviors. The authors use a self-administered survey in order to examine family characteristics, parental support, peer networks, and HIV sexual risk behaviors among 171 African American high school males. The study is one of few that empirically examine the relationship between characteristics of African American families and African American adolescent males within those families. Voisin and Neilands' findings suggest that cultural factors may weigh more heavily than family structure, which has been traditionally viewed as the discerning factor in assessing sexual behavior.

II. Educational Issues Facing African American Males

Reginald Clark, Alexes Harris, Kimberly A. White-Smith, Walter R. Allen, and Barbara A. Ray assert that both research scholars and practitioners alike must learn from the experiences of successful African American males. Numerous community-based programs assist African American men and boys in leading meaningful lives. Despite depressing statistics, most African American males lead productive, positive lives. In Chapter 7, "Promising Practices: The Positive Effects of After-School Programs for African American Male Development and Educational Progress," the authors analyze data collected from 28 after-school programs funded under the W. K. Kellogg African American Men and Boys Initiative. The chapter examines the inevitability of massive failure and incarceration of African American males in American society, and it presents systemic evidence of alternative outcomes. The authors examine the role of public policy for expanding existing and new school and community-based after-school centers. They also examine media practices in which disproportionate attention is given to those African American males who go wrong compared to the greater majority of African American males who lead upstanding, decent, and productive lives. Their public policy analyses further address the lack of attention focused on individual and institutions that assist and produce admirable, high achieving African American men and boys and how this neglect magnifies the issues of race and inequality in American society.

In Chapter 8, "Academic Engagement of Black Male Student Athletes: Implications for Practice in Secondary and Postsecondary Schooling," Eddie Comeaux explores the relationship between male student athletes and faculty and the impact of specific forms of student athlete–faculty interaction on academic achievement. The study theoretically conceptualizes critical components in the academic and social development of Black male student athletes in higher education; describes pedagogical practices and ideological constructions that influence their schooling environments; suggests ways of replicating school environments that are having positive results in empowering African American male student athletes; and contributes to a growing body of literature on the relation between the salience of race and exploring identity as an important mediator of learning and school success. Specifically, Comeaux's study examines faculty who frequently interact with and influence Black student athletes' personal and academic development and subsequently develops selected faculty interaction measures of academic achievement among Black student athletes in the revenue-producing sports of men's basketball and football. The data are drawn from the Cooperative Institutional Research Program (CIRP) 2000 Student Information Form (SIF) and 2004 College Student Survey (CSS) sponsored by the Higher Education Research Institute (HERI) at the University of California at Los Angeles (UCLA) and the Graduate School of Education and Information Studies. Data are limited to Black male revenue-generating student athletes attending predominantly White institutions because preliminary data analysis revealed that revenue-generating athletes are different from nonrevenue athletes in graduation rates, National Collegiate Athletic Association (NCAA) infractions, and overall visibility in American culture. Comeaux explores this group within the college community because the faculty population remains predominantly White within degree-granting institutions in the United States. Black student athletes often interact with faculty whose race or ethnicity is different from their own, which may have implications for their learning.

III. Mental and Physical Health Statuses and Challenges to African American Male Development and Social Functioning

Childhood depression is a serious public health concern with estimates indicating 8.3% of adolescents in the general population suffer from depression. Although research indicates that depression is highly amenable to treatment, few children and adolescents with depressive disorders receive care. This is especially true for ethnic minority children and adolescents. In Chapter 9, "What Are Depressed African American Adolescent Males Saying About Mental Health Services and Providers?" Michael A. Lindsey examines barriers and facilitators to engagement in mental health treatment among depressed, African American adolescents. Qualitative interviews were conducted with 18 urban, African American males, ages 14–18, recruited from community-based mental health centers and after-school programs for youth. The interviews included sociodemographic information, questions regarding depressive symptomatology, and open-ended questions derived from the network-episode model, including knowledge, attitudes, and behaviors related to problem recognition, help-seeking, and perceptions of mental health services. Implications for social work and social welfare practice are examined.

Many young African American males live in urban settings where they are subjected to social and environmental stressors that negatively impact prosocial trajectories, attenuate their developmental course, and increase the likelihood for poor social and developmental outcomes. In Chapter 10, "Don't Bother Me, I Can't Cope: Stress, Coping, and Problem Behaviors Among Young African American Males," M. Daniel Bennett, Jr. and Finake Olugbala examine chronic exposure to certain social and environmental stressors—sometimes referred to as urban stressors—and their link to a range of poor outcomes, including but not limited to increased aggression, anxiety, low grade point average, delinquency, depression, and social withdrawal. Given the range of poor outcomes associated with chronic exposure to urban stressors, it appears that for some young African American males, such exposure may elicit maladaptive coping responses. Hence, for many of these young men, the experience of living in an urban environment presents a set of unique challenges that can have a negative impact on their transition to adulthood. As such, urban stress and its related outcomes are important considerations in the study of ethnic minority children and adolescent development. Specifically, this study explores the relationship between experiences with urban stress and coping behaviors among African American male youth. Moreover, this study seeks to better understand the nature and extent of urban stress and identify particular aspects or dimensions of this phenomenon that may increase the likelihood of maladaptive coping responses.

Furthermore, the nature and extent of coping behaviors specific to this population are explored. A cross-sectional, purposive sample of 76 African American male youth and young adults between 10 and 20 years of age is drawn from geographical areas defined as urban by standard population parameters. Exploratory factor analysis (EFA) is conducted to investigate the interrelationships among variables with common underlying constructs or dimensions related to urban stress and coping behaviors. Multiple regression analysis is subsequently conducted to determine the impact of various dimensions of urban stress on coping behaviors among study participants. Findings from this investigation are discussed in terms of their implications for social work research and practice. It is anticipated that these findings may contribute to our knowledge and understanding of stress and coping among African American male youth and ultimately lead to the development of culturally competent and contextually relevant prevention and intervention services.

In Chapter 11, "Health and Young African American Men: An Inside View," Joseph E. Ravenell reviews health and health perceptions among African American men. Young and middle aged African American men (15–45 years old) are disproportionately affected by accidental injury, human immunodeficiency virus (HIV), and cardiovascular disease. These conditions are preventable and are amenable to primary care intervention, yet African American men underutilize primary care health services. Because health-care utilization is strongly dependent on health beliefs among other factors, this qualitative study identifies and explores African American men's perceptions of health and health influences. Ravenell analyzes focus group interviews with select subgroups of African American men, including adolescents, trauma survivors, and HIV-positive men ($n = 30$). Their definitions of health and beliefs about influences on health are elicited. This study provides insight into African American males' general health perceptions, and it may have implications for future efforts to improve health-care utilization and health in this population. Recommendations for future directions to improve African American males' health are explored.

David Williams (2003) presented a broad picture of the health challenges faced by men in the United States. He reported that men are of poorer health relative to women and that certain men were at higher risk for poor health outcomes. In general, Black Americans access the health-care system at disproportionately lower rates than White Americans. Interestingly, Williams lists middle-class Black men among the high-risk groups. Noting that middle-class African American men are understudied, Williams suggests three factors that might play a role in elevating risks for poor health among middle-class Black men: racial discrimination, tenuousness of middle class status, and unfulfilled expectations. Sherrill L. Sellers, Vence Bonham, Harold W. Neighbors, and Shuntay McCoy in Chapter 12, "Health and Health-Care Service Use Among Middle-Class Black Men" examine participation in health-care services among middle-class Black men from a cross-sectional survey of college-educated African American men. The survey was conducted as a series of computer-assisted telephone interviews (CATI) by Michigan State University's Institute for Public Policy and Social Research, Office of Survey Research. A sample of 399 African American middle income men using the SF-12, a commonly used health status survey instrument, provided the basis for the cross-sectional study. The interviews were conducted by African American men to provide for gender and racial affinity between the interviewers and respondents.

At the twenty-fifth anniversary of the first diagnosis of AIDS, men who have sex with men (MSM) account for the largest number of AIDS cases and still account for two-thirds of the new infections among men. Studies in recent years have found that the burden of HIV/AIDS continue to shift from White MSM to younger men of color, particularly young African American MSM. Unfortunately there is an extraordinary lack of preparedness to address HIV risk and prevention among young African American MSM. In Chapter 13, "At the Intersection of HIV/AIDS Disparities: Young African American Men Who Have Sex With Men," Brian Mustanski, Amy Johnson, and Robert Garofalo review the HIV/AIDS epidemiology of young African American MSM and the characteristics that affect prevention efforts within the African American MSM community. The chapter also reviews the racial disparities in the Center for Disease Control and Prevention's Young Men's Survey and reviews findings from another study of young MSM conducted in Chicago (Project Q) that examines the psychosocial and sociodemographic characteristics that underlie racial disparities. Finally, it offers practical policy solutions and implications for social work practice and suggests areas for future research and advocacy.

Suicide among young African American is a considerable emergent public health problem as indicated by the recent Institute of Medicine's report, *Reducing Suicide.* Suicide is the third leading cause of death among African American adolescents and young adults. Males disproportionately share the burden of suicide among African Americans for reasons yet known. Sean Joe examines suicide and suicidal behaviors among African American adolescent and young adult males in Chapter 14, "Suicide Among African Americans: A Male's Burden." This chapter provides an epidemiological framework to understand, intervene, or prevent suicide and suicidal behavior in African Americans. This report presents clinical data on gender differences in the prevalence of and risk factor for suicidal behavior among African American adolescents presenting at an urban pediatric psychiatric emergency service in Pennsylvania. Psychiatric emergency visits of all patients ages 18 years and under from October 1, 2001 to September 30, 2002 were abstracted and coded. Each patient's demographic, Axis I diagnosis, presenting problem, psychiatric antecedents, and pattern of referrals was assessed. Bivariate and logistic regression analyses were employed to analyze data for a sample of 3586 patient visits to document the incidence and patterns of parasuicidal behavior and gender differences among users. This chapter provides social workers with the most recent data on African American youth suicide and background information on the risk and protective factors; it also discusses important implications for social work practice.

IV. Life Chances: Violence and Incarceration Among African American Males

In Chapter 15, "Cultural Interventions for Reducing Violence Among Young African American Males," Lance Williams examines the role that culture plays in youth violence intervention via the Connections intervention program, an African-centered rites-of-passage program developed to address the needs of youth in the West Englewood community of Chicago. Williams delves into the culture of Connections to find out how the staff members and participants perceive the program's mission and its effectiveness. Given that the program uses transitional initiation rites to instill youth with an African cultural social ethos that promotes a sense of purpose and meaning—difficult concepts to measure in a quantitative way—the researcher used qualitative techniques, in particular, an ethnographic/focused interview process. The study used three ethnographic techniques to collect data: *(a)* participant observation, *(b)* in-depth interviews, and *(c)* focus groups. Former and current staff members and 36 youths between the ages of 18 and 28 who participated in the Connections intervention program between 1991 and 2001 were recruited to participate in in-depth interviews and focus groups. All subjects ranged in ages from 18 to 28 and were interviewed. This study presents an excellent opportunity to examine a neglected area in the field of adolescent violence prevention via a culturally specific program designed for African American youth. Williams notes that it is important to examine youth perceptions of violence-related behaviors because these perceptions may be in the causal pathway of violence-related behaviors. Understanding these perceptions may be relevant to the modification of the targeted behaviors that may, in turn, help to guide the development of more effective youth violence interventions.

The huge growth in incarceration rates in the United States during the past three decades has enormous implications for Black communities because of the disproportionate incarceration rates among young Black males. Because of the barriers to research within the criminal justice system, researchers and policy makers are just beginning to evaluate the costs to Black males, their families, and their communities. One obvious place that incarceration may exact a toll is in family formation if women are less likely to marry someone who has been incarcerated. However, isolating a causal link to incarceration and poor outcomes—whether labor market performance or forming relationships—is difficult because some of the poor outcomes can be explained by unobserved characteristics that may have resulted in poor performance even in the absence of incarceration. In Chapter 16, "Incarceration and Family Formation," Charles E. Lewis, Jr. uses data from the first wave of the Fragile Families and Child Wellbeing Study and multinomial logistic regression models, while controlling for some relevant characteristics, to examine the likelihood of young unwed fathers to be married, cohabiting, or in no relationship with the mothers of their children depending on whether the young men had ever been incarcerated at some point in their lives. The sample includes 656 mothers and 524 fathers who were interviewed during the baseline phase.

In Chapter 17, "Understanding the Economic Costs of Incarceration for African American Males," Mark L. Joseph examines the costs of current levels of incarceration for African American men, their families, and their communities and the United States as a whole. Initially, Joseph summarizes the results of his analysis, using the Panel Study of Income Dynamics (PSID), on the earnings gap experienced by ex-offenders, with a focus on my findings regarding African American males. The PSID contains more than 7000 families with a total of almost 65,000 individuals. In addition to OLS and fixed effects estimation, Joseph uses a wage decomposition analysis and subsequently estimates the costs of incarceration to the individual ex-offender, as well as the costs to society. These costs include loss of annual earnings and lifetime earnings foregone. Joseph also estimates the costs for particular age cohorts of African American ex-offenders and the costs to the African American community and society as a whole, which include costs experienced by the families of ex-offenders, lost income in the neighborhoods to which they return, and the costs to society from increased crime and recidivism. Finally, based on the analysis of the causes of the ex-offender earnings gap, Joseph suggests ways that the earnings gap could be reduced.

Conclusion

The aforementioned chapters address the contemporary issues of physical and social statuses facing African American males across the life course. Collectively, the volume explores the state of African American males in the United States today by examining, with both in-depth interviews and larger surveys and data sets, their physical, mental, and spiritual health and emerging family roles. It focuses on challenges and barriers to African American males' developmental transitions, their assumption of various social roles over the life span, and the profound effect of social neglect and incarceration on their own lives and on their families and communities. After presenting original research, the authors also reflect on the policy and practice implications of their findings, with a special eye toward enhancing social work practice with this often overlooked, but essential, population of African American males. The importance of evidence-based practice will remain central in these discussions.

African American males are often overlooked in the dynamics of African American family and community. In fact, African American males are not only absent from households and neighborhoods of their children and families, but they are also ignored as stakeholders in discussions of African American families and communities. Since the publication of *Black Men*, a number of volumes focused on African American males have been published. (An overview of these volumes is provided in Chapter 18.) Like *Black Men*, these volumes have contributed significantly to the development and the framing of *Social Work With African American Males: Health, Mental Health, and Social Policy*. In fact, the contributions of these volumes and countless other publications that have explored the plight of African American males have made the current volume possible.

The unique contribution of *Social Work With African American Males: Health, Mental Health, and Social Policy* lies in the collective contributions of emerging social work and social welfare research scholars examining the social statuses of

African American males. The knowledge base of social work draws on a broad range of disciplinary theories, conceptual frameworks, and professional approaches that guide research endeavors and practice. Among the volume's contributors are social work researcher scholars who examine recurring issues of functioning that have historically shaped social work research and practice, such as mental health issues of stress and depression and parental role functioning. In addition, social work perspectives on suicide and incarceration among African American males are also examined here. Emerging juvenile justice, nursing, family studies, and public policy scholars also contribute cutting-edge empirical studies on African American uncles as a form of family-based social capital. Expanding paternal roles among adolescent fathers, intergenerational support and reciprocity between low-income African American fathers and their aging mothers, and incarceration effects on African American males' future earnings appropriately broaden the perspectives in which social welfare policy and practice affect the developmental and social statuses of African American males across the life course. This broadened social welfare approach to examining the status of African American males results in a fresh, interdisciplinary empirical study.

The volume's title, *Social Work With African American Males: Health, Mental Health, and Social Policy*, appropriately addresses how social work as a professional endeavor of helping via research and practice and within the larger context of social welfare policy and practice has responded to the evolving social status of African American males. In light of their marginal status across virtually every dimension of well-being in American society, the failure of social work as a helping profession, and social welfare as the broader framework in which social work functions to address these problems, implicitly raises gender, racial, and human rights concerns. Does social work and social welfare respond to the problems that plague African American males across the life course? If not, why? If so, have the responses been sufficient? The contributors in this volume address these concerns head on and offer recommendations for redress.

In a 2006 sermon delivered by Rev. Dr. Jeremiah A. Wright, Jr. entitled "What Have We Seen With Our Own Eyes?" Dr. Wright challenges to us to embrace not upon what we have heard (which possibly has been filtered by others) but to reflect upon what has been revealed to us, that which has been manifested before us, and to think carefully about its meaning and impact. While African American males, like their male and female peers in America are not without their individual and collective faults, structural factors and institutional barriers have also contributed to their physical, mental, and social statuses over time. As we witness this deterioration, we can no longer sit idly by without voicing concern. The status of African American males is inextricably linked to the survival and the future development of the African American family, community, and the status of all human beings. The clarion call for redress must be unified and emerge clearly from all humanity. Anything short of this is insufficient.

REFERENCES

Anderson, E. (1990). *Streetwise: Race, class and change in an urban community*. Chicago: University of Chicago Press.

Anderson, E. (1999). *Code of the street: Decency, violence and the moral life of the inner city*. New York: W. W. Norton and Company.

Diabetes in African Americans (1998). National Diabetes Information Clearinghouse. Bethesda, MD: National Institute on Health.

Edelman, P., Holzer, H., & Offner, P. (2006). *Reconnecting disadvantaged young males*. Washington, D.C.: Urban Institute Press.

Frazier, E. (1957). *Black bourgeoisie*. Glencoe, IL: Free Press.

Gary, L. (Ed.). (1981). *Black men*. Beverly Hills, CA: Sage Publications.

Haveman, J. (2001). Heart disease and African American men: Second in a series. *Michigan Chronicle*, April 24.

Hill, M. et al (1999). Barriers to hypertension care and control in young urban Black men. *American Journal of Health*, 12:951–58.

Hofstadter, R. (1944). Social *Darwinism in American thought, 1860-1815*. Philadelphia: University of Pennsylvania Press.

Holzer, H. and Offner, P. (2004). The puzzle of Black male unemployment. The Public Interest, No 154, 74–84.

Holzer, H., Raphael, S. and Stoll, M. (2006). Employers in the boom: How the hiring of less skilled workers change during in the 1990s. *Review of Economics and Statistics*, 88(2), 283–299.

Joe, S. (2006). Explaining changes in the patterns of Black suicide in the United States: An age, cohort and period analysis. *Journal of Black Psychology*, 32(3), 262–284.

Johnson, E. & Doolittle, F. (1998). Low-income parents and the Parents' Fair Share Program: An early qualitative look at improving the ability and desire of low-income, noncustodial parents to pay child support. In I. Garfinkel, S. McLanahan, D. Meyer, & J. Seltzer (Eds.), *Fathers under fire: The revolution on child support enforcement* (pp. xx-xx). New York: Russell Sage Foundation.

Johnson, E., Levine, A., & Doolittle, F. (1999). *Fathers' fair share: Helping poor men manage child support and fatherhood*. New York: Russell Sage Foundation.

Johnson, W. (1999). Work preparation and labor market experiences. In S. Danziger & A. Lin (Eds.), *Coping with poverty: The social contexts of neighborhood, work and family in the African American community* (pp. 224–261). Ann Arbor: The University of Michigan Press.

Johnson, W. (2001). In A. Neal-Barnett, J. Contreras, & K. Kerns (Eds.), *Forging links: African American children–Clinical developmental perspectives* (pp. 147–174). Westport, CT: Praeger.

Johnson, W. (2004). In J. Everett, S Chipungu, & B. Leashore (Eds.), *Child welfare revisited: An Africentric perspective* (pp. 169–196). New Brunswick, NJ: Rutgers University Press.

Jones, R. (Ed.). (1989). *Black adolescents*. Berkeley, CA: Cobb and Henry.

Kirschenman, J. & Neckerman, K. (1991). We'd love to hire them but . . . : The meaning of race for employers. In C. Jencks and P. Peterson (Eds.). *The Urban Underclass*. Washington, DC: Brookings Institution.

Kitwana, B. (2002). *The hip hop generation: Young Blacks and the crisis of African American culture*. New York: Basic Civitas Books.

Kitwana, B. (2005). *Why White kids love hip hop: Wangstas, Wiggers Wannabes and the New Reality of Race in America*. New York: Perseus Books.

McWhorter, J. (2000). *Losing the race: Self*-sabotage *in Black America*. New York: Free Press.

Mincy, R. (Ed.). (2006). *Black males left behind*. Washington, DC: Urban Institute Press.

National Alliance on Mental Illness (2006). African American Community Mental Health Fact Sheet. Arlington, VA: www.nami.org

Polite, V., & Davis, J. (1999). *African American males in school and society*. New York: Teachers College Press.

Platz, E. et al (2000). Prostate cancer: A major health concern for African American men. *Journal of the National Cancer Institute*, 92:2009–17.

Schott Foundation, (2008) *Given half a chance: The Schott 50 state report on public education and Black males*. Cambridge, MA: The Schott Foundation for Public Education.

Smedley, B., Stith, A., and Nelson, A. (Eds.). (2002). *Unequal Treatment: Confronting Racial and Ethnic Disparities in Health Care*. Washington, DC: National Academies Press.

Western, B. (2006). *Punishment and inequality in America*. New York: Russell Sage Foundation.

Whitaker, E. (2005). The plight of African American males. Keynote address, "Social Work and Social Welfare Responses to African American Males."

Wilson, W. (1987). *The truly disadvantaged: The inner city, the underclass and public policy*. Chicago: University of Chicago Press.

Wilson, W. (1996). *When work disappears: The world of the new urban poor*. New York: Alfred Knopf.

PART I

African American Males' Individual and Family Roles

2

Making Room for Daddy

The Unmarried Adolescent Father's Role in Pregnancy

CONSTANCE M. DALLAS AND KAREN KAVANAUGH

Adolescent fathers in poverty are of particular interest to policy makers. Fathers and mothers who live in poverty tend to produce children who live in poverty and require government assistance with basic survival needs (Gadsen, Wortham, & Turner, 2003). Adolescent fatherhood, however, has been studied much less extensively than adolescent motherhood. Researchers generally agree on four primary tasks for fathers: providing emotional support for the mothers of their children and their children, providing care for their children, providing economically for their children, and more recently, establishing legal paternity (Doherty, Kouneski, & Erickson, 1998; Levine & Pitt, 1995). Unmarried adolescent fathers struggle with their ability to sustain supportive relationships with the mothers of their children, nurture their children, and provide economically for their children, regardless of legal paternity. Supporters of President Bush's Healthy Marriage Initiative believe that these first three factors are interrelated and inseparable: promoting marriage between the couples enhances low-income fathers' ability to both nurture and to provide economically for their children. In support of these beliefs, President Bush signed the Deficit Reduction Act of 2005, which reauthorized the Temporary Assistance for Needy Families (TANF) program and included $150 million to support programs designed to help couples form and sustain healthy marriages, one-third of which was dedicated to promoting responsible fatherhood (United States Department of Health and Human Services, 2006). In addition, in its Welfare Reform Law of 1996, Congress stipulated that the TANF program must make efforts to promote healthy two-parent families.

Few would argue that children born into long-term relationships between financially stable couples face fewer risks than those children born to unmarried, low-income adolescents. Yet in the context of adolescents, who often have transitory romantic relationships, it seems more appropriate to focus on how to better support the fathers' ability to nurture and provide economically for their children and less on sustaining a romantic relationship between the couple.

The purpose of this chapter is to describe ideal and expected fatherhood behavior during pregnancy from the perspectives of unmarried, low-income, African American adolescent expectant fathers. It is important to know what these young fathers expect from themselves and how they view their role during the prenatal period because these fathers are often a significant source of support for adolescent mothers (Chen, Tellen, & Chen, 1995; Sullivan, 1993). Johnson (2001) reported that despite high levels of involvement during pregnancy, unwed nonresidential fathers have weaker intentions for future involvement with their children and commitment to fatherhood. The present study contributes to knowledge of the intentions of unwed nonresidential adolescent fathers to provide emotional support, care, and economic support for their children and the mothers of their children.

Risk Factors for African American Adolescent Fatherhood

The rate of births to adolescent mothers increased slightly in 2004 after years of decline (Hamilton, Vemtira, Martin, & Sutton, 2006). Births to non-Hispanic Black adolescent mothers aged 15–19 remained stable at 62.7 per 1000, but they are still above the national average of 41.2 per 1000.

Information on the prevalence of adolescent fatherhood is less readily available and more difficult to monitor than information on teen mothers. Estimates suggest that between 18% and 35% of the births to adolescent mothers are fathered by males younger than age 20 (Landry & Forrest, 1995; Males & Chew, 1996). Yet approximately 40% of the birth certificates of babies born to adolescent mothers do not include the father's age (Landry & Forrest, 1995). The risk of unmarried adolescent fatherhood is highest among African American adolescent males, particularly those in poverty (Lerman, 1993; Summ & Fogg, 1991), who are more than twice as likely as either Caucasians or Latinos to experience fatherhood during adolescence (Elo, King, & Furstenberg, 1999; Lerman, 1993). Xie, Cairns, & Cairns (2001) followed a sample of participants from grade 7 through early adulthood. They reported that African American race, low socioeconomic status, and low academic competence were stronger predictors of parenthood during adolescence for males than females. The ability and intent of unmarried African American adolescent fathers to provide care for their children has significant societal implications, given that males most poorly equipped to assume the provider role of fatherhood are also those most likely to become fathers during adolescence. In the next section, we discuss some of the factors that may uniquely shape the expectations for paternal behavior of African American adolescent fathers during pregnancy.

Influences on Paternal Involvement

The primary tasks of fatherhood remain stable, although societal expectations for paternal behavior are changing, even among married, middle-class adult fathers (Doherty, 1997; Pleck, 1997). First-time adult fathers often struggle to make a successful transition to fatherhood, which may be further exacerbated for unmarried, low-income, African American adolescent fathers by their adolescent developmental stage, low-income status, differences in cultural perspectives from mainstream fathers, and their perceived readiness for the role. Even under ideal circumstances pregnancy and childbirth are usually accompanied by significant social, financial, and emotional changes that require periods of adjustment and adaptation for family members (Cowan & Cowan, 1992). Fathers of all ages struggle against their socialization, history, societal constraints, and complex dynamics within the couple relationship that both encourage and discourage their participation in childrearing (Berman & Pedersen, 1987). Some researchers argue that the transition to fatherhood is generally difficult for all fathers and especially so for low-income adolescent fathers (Belsky & Miller, 1986; Cowan & Cowan, 1992; Dallas, 1995; Elster, 1986). We know generally very little, however, about the expectations for involvement during the prenatal period among unmarried, low-income, African American adolescent fathers. It is unclear, for example, whether the difficulty fulfilling the caregiving and provider roles experienced by low-income adolescent fathers stems from the challenges of poverty or from adolescence itself (Belsky & Miller, 1986). Researchers have been unable to establish links between economic disadvantage and parental function among low-income, African American adolescent fathers, although these links have established for a group of young white fathers (Florsheim, Moore, Zollinger, MacDonald, & Sumida, 2000; Pears, Pierce, Kim, Capaldi, & Owen, 2005). The adolescent developmental stage may be more susceptible to contextual influences than assumed.

The socioeconomic environment in which children grow up can significantly influence the activities of childhood and their preparation for adulthood. Adolescents from economically disadvantaged environments often assume adult responsibilities early in life and may not follow the same linear developmental stages as adolescents from more economically advantaged environments (Burton, 2001). These adolescents are often expected to share in the family's work by assuming some of the markers of adulthood, such as employment and child care, roles that may help to prepare them for the caregiving and provider roles of parenthood. Adolescent males, who might otherwise have few experiences in providing nurturance and affection to children, may experience these roles as part of the family work.

For fathers, the role of breadwinner often predominates, yet there are conflicting views on the importance of the breadwinner role in sustaining father involvement, particularly for African American families. For some of these mothers, a father's ability to adequately fulfill the provider role is essential (Belsky & Miller, 1986; Dallas & Chen, 1998, 1999; Johnson, 2001; Nelson, Clampet-Lindquist, & Edin, 2002; Sullivan, 1993). In contrast, other qualitative research on low-income

African American fathers suggests that some mothers are willing to consider a broader definition of a good father and view spending time with children and expressions of caring as being equally important as providing financial support (Jarrett, Roy, & Burton, 2002; see also Pate, Chapter 4, this volume).

Perceived readiness for the role of father may also influence expectations for the paternal role. Adolescent fathers who report feeling ready for fatherhood are typically more supportive of their partners during pregnancy and more involved after the birth with both mother and child than are fathers who do not feel ready for parenthood (Westney, Cole, & Munford, 1986). Clear, realistic expectations of transition to the parenthood role can enhance the transitional process (Schumacher & Meleis, 1994) and help policy makers and service professionals develop appropriate interventions for adolescent fathers and their families.

In summary, the challenges that are unique to unmarried, low-income, African American adolescent fathers most likely shape their expectations for paternal behaviors. Knowing what these fathers expect to be doing can contribute to more effective and appropriate policies for this group to better promote and encourage their continued involvement with their children.

Study Design

The interviews in this chapter are part of a larger, ongoing, longitudinal qualitative study, Negotiating African American Adolescent Fatherhood (NAAF), which is examining the expectations for paternal involvement, perceptions of actual paternal involvement, and satisfaction with paternal involvement for 25 kinship systems (adolescent father, paternal grandparents, adolescent mother, and maternal grandparents). The NAAF is following a group of unmarried, low-income, African American adolescent parents and their parents from the late prenatal period (at least 28 weeks gestation) to their child's second birthday. We interviewed each participant (111 individuals representing 50 families) at six points: when the adolescent mother was at least 28 weeks pregnant, when the baby was 1 month old, and again at 6, 12, 18, and 24 months. Because we were examining factors that facilitate or inhibit paternal involvement, we included only adolescent parents who reported wanting the father to remain involved. The study reported in this chapter uses data from the prenatal interviews of the 25 adolescent fathers enrolled in the larger study.

A qualitative approach permits researchers to focus on the meanings of the experiences to the subjects and allows for an in-depth examination of the phenomenon of interest (Creswell, 1998). We use a case study design, treating each individual and each kinship system as a case. Case study approach permits us to identify patterns and themes within each kinship system (adolescent father, his parents, adolescent mother, her parents) as an individual case and to look across the cases for additional patterns and themes (Stake, 1995).

To be included, the adolescent fathers had to self-identify as African American, be first-time fathers, be 13 to 19 years of age, and identify at least one parent or parent surrogate who was willing to participate in the study. At the beginning of the study, all of the adolescent fathers lived with at least one person whom they identified as their parental figure, although several occupied more than one residence simultaneously and were members of multiple neighborhoods (Burton, 2001). The majority (75%) of fathers were between ages 17 and 19 (see Table 2.1). Parents or surrogate parents reported household income at enrollment from $0 to $28,000 (mean household income was $14,661).

We used several recruitment methods to ensure the greatest possible variation of ages and family situations for our sample within a large Midwestern city. Our recruitment methods included radio ads, flyers, and presentations at a variety of community sites such as prenatal clinics; Women, Infant, and Children (WIC) sites; community agencies; alternative public schools; and word-of-mouth referrals. The entire kinship system was usually recruited by either the adolescent mother or the maternal grandmother—whomever called our toll-free telephone number first. After obtaining verbal consent from the adolescent mother and at least one parent, we contacted members of the paternal family and repeated the process. Our lengthy and complex recruitment and interview scheduling procedures contributed significantly to establishing rapport with the study participants even before we arrived at their homes for the first interview.

More than 90% of the kinship system members were interviewed in their homes. Whenever possible, we used the same interviewing team, usually composed of two faculty co-investigators and a graduate student, so that each participant could be interviewed in private and individually. Most of the adolescent fathers were interviewed by African American males. The 60- to 90-minute audiotaped interviews were conducted using a semistructured interview guide based on the kinscripts conceptual framework (Burton & Stack, 1993). The kinscripts conceptual framework organizes and interprets qualitative observations of family role transitions, intergenerational transmission of family norms, and the dynamics of negotiation, exchange, and conflict within a historical and sociological context (Stack & Burton, 1993).

The interview guide was revised after preliminary and pilot studies of similar populations (Dallas, 1995, 2004; Dallas & Chen, 1998, 1999; Dallas, Wilson, & Salgado, 2000). We also pilot-tested the interview guide with three kinship systems prior to its use in the larger study (Dallas, Norr, Dancy, Kavanaugh, & Cassata, 2005).

Data for this study were analyzed using content analysis methods (Graheheim & Lundman, 2004; Patton, 1990). Researchers also reviewed individual and kinship

Table 2.1 Ages of Adolescent Fathers at Enrollment, Number in Age Category, and Percentage of Total

Age	14	15	16	17	18	19
No.	1	2	3	3	8	7
%	4%	8%	12%	12%	32%	28%

system case summaries and the actual adolescent father prenatal interviews to ensure that all relevant data were included in this analysis.

Findings

The 25 expectant fathers in this study described three distinct categories of behaviors that they expected to perform for the pregnant mother and their future child: *(1)* being physically and emotionally present, *(2)* providing material and financial support, and *(3)* acting like a father to the unborn baby. Nearly all adolescent fathers (21, or 84%) were able to identify two or more behaviors that they expected to perform during the pregnancy. Almost one-half (48%) were able to describe four or five specific expectations and the ways that they could meet their expectations of the father role.

Only two of the 25 fathers had difficulty identifying any expected behaviors for themselves or for ideal adolescent fathers, even with further inquiry from the interviewers. In response to a question about expected or ideal behaviors for expectant adolescent fathers, one young father asked the interviewer to clarify and then responded, "I have no idea." Both of these adolescent fathers were also unable to describe the father's role during the birth of the baby and reported having no plans to establish legal paternity until biological paternity had been established. This information is consistent with earlier research reporting that the issue of biological paternity often must be resolved before adolescent fathers are willing to take on legal paternity (Sullivan, 1993).

This, however, was not true for every adolescent father who had doubts about biological paternity. Three of the study fathers who had doubts held specific ideas about their role during pregnancy. Unlike Sullivan who reports that the issue of paternity is settled during pregnancy, we determined that the issue of biological paternity is not definitively resolved by the adolescent couple early in pregnancy. We also learned that even adolescent fathers who questioned the biological paternity of their child were involved during the prenatal period and were able to identify specific expectations.

Being Physically and Emotionally Present

Most participants (88%) indicated that the role of the father was to be there physically and emotionally for the adolescent mother and baby, although some thought it was important to be there for the adolescent mothers of their babies, some just for their babies, and some for both mothers and babies. Some of these young fathers emphasized that not only did they expect to be physically and emotionally present during pregnancy, they also expected to continue their presence "for the long run." As one father said, "It's like be there; support her. Let her know that I am still the man I was before it happened." Another reported, "Do everything you can for not only until she has the child but also afterwards."

Adolescent fathers described a variety of ways that they could be present, including providing emotional support, maintaining a romantic relationship with the mother of the baby, attending prenatal visits, and monitoring the well-being of the mother and unborn baby. As one father explained:

> Just be there whenever and pay attention whenever she might need something. Just be there all of the time and stay there constantly. Be there for her to talk to and be there for her emotionally, physically, and stuff like that; financially, like if she needs to go back and forth to the doctor; stuff like that.

Many of these young fathers linked the emotional equilibrium of the adolescent mother to the health and well-being of the baby. They described the importance of providing emotional support by talking to the mother, keeping her happy, and not stressing her. One father-to-be explained:

> Always be there. Never disrupting her in any way to get her stressed out because that can also harm the child. Do things for her when she knows she's not supposed to be walking around. Tell her that you love her every day to make her feel that she's still loved by you, the father of her child. Basically, do everything for her. Do everything you can for her until she has the child and also afterwards.

Although we were unable to find research to further explain or interpret what this might mean, we did find similar advice in a popular book about African American myths of pregnancy (Coleman, 1997). In at least one case, protecting the pregnant mother from physical harm became a physical emergency. The young father proudly described being present when the mother of his baby went into premature labor. He recalled how both the maternal and paternal families later praised him for his presence and his quick thinking in getting the adolescent mother to the hospital.

These fathers also described the importance of giving the adolescent mother extra attention, maintaining a romantic relationship by demonstrating their love and affection, and attending to her physical discomfort. Attending prenatal visits was one way young fathers spent important time with the mothers of their babies while monitoring the well-being of both. As one father revealed: "Just the basics, like visiting and asking questions, knowing things like when are her doctor appointments, how the baby is doing and just the little things that are going to count toward being involved while the pregnancy is going on."

There are two reasons why the theme of involvement may have resonated so strongly for this population: the almost total lack of experience with their own adult fathers and an acknowledgment of the extremely negative view of adolescent fatherhood in this society. Most of these adolescent fathers grew up in homes without a father or father surrogate, and only 11 of the 50 paternal and maternal families enrolled in our larger study included participating fathers or father surrogates for adolescent parents. As this young man says, "Any boy can make a baby, but it takes a man to take care of one."

Also, these young fathers are not growing up in a social vacuum. It is unlikely that they are ignorant of the contempt that much of society holds for poor, unmarried fathers, particularly African American and Latino fathers living in urban areas (Gadsen et al., 2003).

Providing Material and Financial Support

More than one-half of the fathers (60%) expected to provide material and financial support to the adolescent mother and baby, although very few of them lived with the mother of the child. Material and financial support for the adolescent mother included providing food or drink, providing transportation to prenatal visits, and running errands. For some fathers, material support even included midnight feedings, as this young man revealed:

> I make sure I do whatever she wants me to do for her. Like I said the first time, getting her something to eat and fixing her something to eat in the mornings. Getting up in the middle of the night to get her something to drink. I will try to do it.

Fathers who were not employed believed that they should be actively seeking employment, and those who were already employed believed they should work to keep their job secure or look for one with higher pay so they could provide for the baby.

Few of the respondents' earnings allowed them to maintain a separate residence with the mothers of their babies, and none owned a car. A few of the adolescent parents did live with the other adolescent parent and her family either permanently or for a few days or weeks during the pregnancy. Separate residency and limited earning capacity may be the source of the greatest contradiction and conflict for unmarried, low-income adolescent fathers. It is reasonable to assume that the adolescent fathers who lived with or close to the pregnant mothers could give more attention and monitoring than those who lived far enough away to require access to a car or money for public transportation. Unemployed fathers had more time to spend with the adolescent mothers and were available to attend prenatal visits with them, but they had fewer resources to buy food and supplies for the baby once it was born.

Being a Father to the Unborn Baby

A third of the fathers (32%) saw their unborn baby as a reality and could describe the plans they were already making for their child. One young father provided a detailed picture of his plans for future interaction with his child that included developing an emotional attachment, providing direct care (feeding the baby and changing diapers), and monitoring, teaching, and guiding him or her through the challenges and joys of life. Other fathers demonstrated their attachment and support for the baby by asking about its growth and well-being, by talking to the unborn child, attending its birth, and establishing legal paternity.

All of the adolescent fathers except one expected to attend their baby's birth, which was typically an important event, regardless of their feelings or doubts about biological paternity, their reasons for planning to be there, or their decision about establishing legal paternity at the hospital. Even the father who was reluctant to be in the delivery room planned to be present at the hospital. This same father was one of five who had doubts about biological paternity.

As mentioned earlier, adolescent fathers face competing demands on their time. Some of the fathers attending high school or college worried that they might miss their baby's birth unless it occurred on a weekend or on school break. Nevertheless, fathers viewed witnessing the baby's birth as an important event, and one father made plans to have the event videotaped in his absence.

The reasons these adolescent fathers believed that it was important to attend the birth varied widely, and several had more than one reason. A number of fathers wanted to be present to support the mother and to welcome the baby, while another wanted to be present because his own biological father had been present at his birth. Some adolescent fathers reported having specific ideas about their role during labor, while others were vague about or completely unsure of their roles. One father reported that he expected to spend time during labor "holding her hand or even helping her to hold her legs up and talking to her and telling her to breathe and telling her 'Baby, I love you,' and keeping her mind off of all the pain." Another father viewed his attendance at birth as the culmination of his commitment during pregnancy:

> Because that is not something I want to miss out on. I've been here for everything else. I've been here for the morning sickness. I've been here for the yelling [at me]. I'm going to be there for the contractions. I'm going to be there when the baby comes out.

Some fathers wanted to attend their baby's birth because of the expectations of the adolescent mother or their families. As the young father who was unable to identify any expectations for his role reported, "They told me I have to be there because they want me to sign a birth certificate and take a blood test. So I guess I have to go."

The adolescent father's attendance at the birth did not constitute a declaration of biological paternity. In some states, only unmarried mothers can establish legal paternity in the hospital at the time of their baby's birth. A surprising number of fathers were unfamiliar with the process, and a number of them learned about it for the first time in the interview. Nevertheless, the majority were in favor taking advantage of this opportunity to establish legal paternity for their babies. Only five of the fathers (20%) we interviewed wanted documented proof of biological paternity prior to establishing legal paternity. Of these five, some just wanted to obtain advice from their families, while others wanted reassurance of biological paternity prior to making a legal commitment. As one young man explained:

> I want to make sure it's mine before I start signing, really, because you never know, you know what I'm saying? I'm not trying to say it ain't mine, you know, what I'm saying is that I just want to make sure.

In contrast to the negative popular picture of the adolescent father who escapes at the first mention of pregnancy, these fathers share many of the concerns, expectations, and plans of adult married fathers. They recognize the importance of being physically and emotionally present for the adolescent mothers and for their children, and they express love and concern for the mothers and for their babies through both words and behavior.

Conclusions and Implications

The expectant fathers in this study were for the most part excited about the impending birth and were intent on playing a role in the lives of their children. The majority intended to "be there" for both the mother and the child, and 60% hoped to be able to contribute financially, although most faced serious barriers to that goal. What the findings also reveal is that the context of these young men's lives will likely play a significant role in their aspirations and involvement with their children, and perhaps more important, simply focusing on marriage, as current policy proposes, may not be a realistic goal. The number of divorced and never-married adults of every racial and ethnic group in the United States has been slowly but steadily growing since 1990 (U.S. Census Bureau, 2005). By focusing exclusively on marriage relationship skills, policy makers fail to address the fluidity of family roles among low-income African American families in providing care for children (Burton, 1995). Policy makers should look beyond the legality of the relationship between the natal parents and instead focus on skills that enhance caregiving. Up to one-third of the funds for the reauthorized TANF program are earmarked to promote responsible fatherhood. Promoting fatherhood in an appropriate cultural and developmental context may mean including members from the families of the adolescent parents. Policy makers are beginning to acknowledge racial/ethnic differences in fatherhood roles, but they have done little to acknowledge the developmental challenges for unmarried adolescent fathers, many of whom live with their families of origin.

Being physically present for the mother and baby, providing material and financial support, and acting as a father for their unborn child are important components of the ideal and expected roles of paternal involvement during pregnancy from the perspectives of these unmarried, low-income, African American adolescent fathers, even when they question the biological paternity of the child. These young expectant fathers share the concerns of adult expectant fathers, but they face additional challenges in meeting the needs of their children. None of the adolescent fathers described in this chapter live in independent households; they live with their own families of origin or those of the adolescent mother. It is these families who help low-income, African American adolescents meet the challenges of fatherhood by supporting father involvement and sharing the responsibilities of child care (Dallas & Chen, 1998; Merriwether-de Vries, Burton, & Eggletion, 1996; Hunter, Pearson, Cook, Ialongo, & Kellam, 1998; Presser, 1989; Wilson, 1986).

The nuclear family may be the *ideal* model for childrearing, but it may not be the *best* model for childrearing in every situation, particularly among unmarried, African American adolescent parents. Policies, such as the Healthy Marriage Initiative with its focus only on the couple, rather than on strategies to enhance caregiving for the baby, fail to acknowledge the well-documented role of the paternal and maternal families in promoting and encouraging continued father involvement among low-income, African American families (Burton, 1996; Burton & Stack, 1993; Dilworth-Anderson, Burton, & Johnson, 1993; Stack, 1974). These paternal and maternal families join to create a new extended kinship system that represents the commitment of both families to share responsibility for the survival needs of the adolescent parents' baby. Their negotiations to share this responsibility and to shape the adolescent father's role are complex and require the cooperation of both family units (Dallas, 2000).

African American culture allows paternal and maternal grandmothers to choose from a continuum of responses to adolescent fatherhood that are consistent with low-income, African American families' historical need to structure the family around the needs of children rather than along the traditional, nuclear family structure (Burton, 1990; Crosbie-Burnett & Lewis, 1993; Stack, 1974). Paternal and maternal grandmothers can choose from one or a mixture of the following roles: *(1)* surrogate parenting, in which the grandmothers assume the primary caretaking role; *(2)* co-parenting, when grandmothers support their children's parenting roles; and *(3)* individualized interpretations of the grandmother role (Burton, Dilworth-Anderson, & Merriwether-de Vries, 1995; Stewart, 1997). It is inevitable that each of these roles can potentially influence paternal expectations and behaviors of nonresidential adolescent fathers.

That paternal and maternal families influence the paternal involvement of adolescent fathers has been well established (Christmon, 1990; Miller, 1994). The quality of the relationship between the parents predicts continued involvement for adult couples (Johnson, 1999). The relationship between adolescent couples may prove to be less predictive because of the expected transience of their relationship and the additional complexity of the relationships among the paternal and maternal family members. We need research that examines the influence of those relationships on father involvement and the mechanisms that paternal and maternal family members use to promote or inhibit the ongoing involvement of adolescent fathers. We need policy that acknowledges the fluidity of African American family roles and focuses on the well-being of the child rather than the duration and legality of the relationship between the couple.

NOTE

Unlike quantitative approaches, qualitative approaches excel at examining complexities and processes, particularly for phenomena about which little is known (Marshall and Rossman, 2006). Quantitative approaches use strategies to enhance researcher objectivity in order to identify causal relationships that can be generalized to larger populations. Qualitative approaches, in contrast, rests on naturalism, which proposes that the social world should be studied in its natural state without, as far as possible, manipulation or intervention (Blumer, 1969; Charmaz, 2006; Hammersley and Atkinson, 2007: Lincoln and Guba, 1985; Mason, 2007). Consistent with this approach, researchers collect, analyze and interpret data in a manner that permits understanding the essential elements of fatherhood *from persons who have experienced the phenomenon*. This study, therefore, uses a purposive sample in which each participant was specifically selected because of his or her unique experience with the phenomenon (Patton, 2002). This differs significantly from a convenience sample.

REFERENCES

Belsky, J. & Miller, B. C. (1986). Adolescent fatherhood in the context of transition to parenthood. In A. B. Elster & M. E. Lamb (Eds.), *Adolescent fatherhood* (pp. 107–122). Hillsdale, NJ: Erlbaum.

Berman, P. W. & Pedersen, F. A. (1986). Research on men's transition to parenthood: an integrative discussion. In P. W. Berman and F. A. Pedersen (Eds.), *Men's transition to parenthood: Longitudinal studies of early family experience* (pp. 217–242). Hillsdale, NJ: Erlbaum.

Blumer, H. (1969). *Symbolic interactionism: Perspective and method.* Los Angeles, CA: University of California Press.

Burton, L. M. (1990). Teenage childbearing as an alternative life-course strategy in multigeneration black families. *Human Nature, 1,* 123–143.

Burton, L. M. (1996). Age norms, the timing of family role transitions, and intergenerational caregiving among aging African American women. *The Gerentologist, 36,* 199–208.

Burton, L. M. (2001). One step forward and two steps back: Neighborhoods, adolescent development, and unmeasured variables. In A. Booth & A. C. Crouter (Eds.), *Does it take a village? Community effects on children, adolescents, and families.* (pp. 149–159) Mahwah, NJ: Erlbaum.

Burton, L. M. (1995). Intergenerational patterns of providing care in African-American families with teenage childbearers: Emergent patterns in an ethnographic study. In V. L. Bengston, K. W. Schaie, & L. M. Burton (Eds.), *Intergenerational Relations: Effects of Societal Change.* (pp. 79–125). NY: Springer Publishing Company.

Burton, L. M., Dilworth-Anderson, P., & Merriwether-de Vries, C. (1995). Context and surrogate parenting among contemporary grandparents. *Marriage & Family Review, 20,* 349–366.

Burton, L. M. & Stack, C. (1993). Conscripting kin: Reflections on family, generation, and culture. In A. Lawson & D. L. Rhode (Eds.), *The politics of pregnancy: Adolescent sexuality and public policy* (pp. 174–185). New Haven, CT: Yale University Press.

Charmaz, K. (2005). Grounded theory in the 21st century: Applications for advancing social justice studies. In N. K. Denzin & Y. S. Lincoln (Eds.), *The Sage Handbook of Qualitative Research, (3rd ed.),* (pp. 507–535). Thousands Oaks, CA: Sage Publications.

Chen, S. C., Tellen, S., & Chen, E. (1995). Adequacy of prenatal care of urban high school students. *Public Health Nursing, 12*, 52–57.

Christmon, K. (1990). Parental responsibility of African American unwed adolescent fathers. *Adolescence, 25*, 645–653.

Coleman, C. (1997). *Mama knows best: African American wives' tales, myths, and remedies for mothers and mothers-to-be.* New York: Simon & Schuster.

Cowan, C. P. & Cowan, P. A. (1992). *When partners become parents: The big life change for couples.* New York: Basic Books.

Cowan, C. P. & Cowan, P. A. (1987). Men's involvement in parenthood: Identifying the antecedents and understanding the barriers. In P. W. Berman and F. A. Pedersen (Eds.), *Men's transition to parenthood: Longitudinal studies of early family experience* (pp. 145–174). Hillsdale, NJ: Erlbaum.

Cowan, C. P. & Cowan, P. A. (1992). *When partners become parents: The big life change for couples.* New York: Basic Books.

Creswell, J. W. (1998). *Qualitative inquiry and research design: Choosing among five traditions.* Thousand Oaks, CA: Sage Publications.

Crosbie-Burnett, M. & Lewis, E. A. (1993). Use of African-American family structures and functioning to address the challenges of European-American postdivorce families. *Family Relations*, Special Issue on Family Diversity, *42*, 243–248.

Dallas, C. M. (1995). *Concept of fatherhood: Views of unmarried, low-income, black, adolescent fathers and their role-set.* Unpublished doctoral dissertation, University of Illinois at Chicago.

Dallas, C. M. (2000). *Family transitions: Families of African-*American *adolescent fathers.* Paper presented at the Fifth International Family Nursing Conference, Chicago, IL.

Dallas, C. M. (2004). Family matters: How mothers of adolescent parents experience adolescent pregnancy and parenting. *Public Health Nursing Journal, 21*, 347–353.

Dallas, C. M. & Chen, S. C. (1998). Experiences of African American adolescent fathers. *Western Journal of Nursing Research, 20*(2), 210–222.

Dallas, C. M. & Chen, S. C. (1999). Perspectives of women whose sons become adolescent fathers. *American Journal of Maternal Child Nursing, 24*, 247–251.

Dallas, C. M., Norr, K., Dancy, B. L., Kavanaugh, K., & Cassata, L. (2005). An example of a successful research proposal: Part II. *Western Journal of Nursing Research, 27*, 210–231.

Dallas, C. M., Wilson, T., & Salgado, V. (2000). Gender differences in teen parents' perceptions of parental responsibilities. *Public Health Nursing Journal, 17*, 423–433.

Dilworth-Anderson, P., Burton, L. M., & Johnson, L. (1993). Reframing theories for understanding race, ethnicity, and families. In P. G. Boss, W. J. Doherty, R. LaRossa, W. R. Schumm, & S. K. Steinmetz (Eds.), *Sourcebook of family theories and methods: A contextual approach* (pp. 627–649). New York: Plenum Press.

Doherty, W. J. (1997). The best of times and the worst of times: Fathering as a contested arena of academic discourse. In A. J. Hawkins & D. C. Dollahite (Eds.), *Generative fathering: Beyond deficit perspectives* (pp. 217–227). Thousand Oaks, CA: Sage Publications.

Doherty, W. J., Kouneski, E. F., & Erickson, M. F. (1998). Responsible fathering: An overview and conceptual framework. *Journal of Marriage and Family, 60*, 277–292.

Elo, I. T., King, B., & Furstenberg, F. F. (1999). Adolescent females: Their sexual partners and the fathers of their children. *Journal of Marriage and the Family, 61*, 74–84.

Elster, A. B. (1986). Clinical issues in adolescent fatherhood. In A. B. Elster & M. Lamb (Eds.), *Adolescent Fatherhood.* (pp. 141–171). Hillsdale, NJ: Lawrence Erlbaum Associates.

Florsheim, P., Moore, D., Zollinger, L., MacDonald, J., & Sumida, E. (2000). The transition to parenthood among adolescent fathers and their partners: Does antisocial behavior predict problems in parenting. *Applied Developmental Science, 3*, 178–191.

Gadsen, V. L., Wortham, S. E. F., & Turner, H. M. (2003). Situated identities of young African American fathers in low-income urban settings: Perspectives on home, street, and the system. *Family Court Review, 41*, 381–399.

Graneheim, U. H. & Lundman, B. (2004). Qualitative content analysis in nursing research: Concepts, procedures and measures to achieve trustworthiness. *Nurse Education Today, 24*, 105–112.

Hamilton, B. E., Ventura, S. J., Martin, J. A., & Sutton, P. D. (2006). *Preliminary births for 2004.* Atlanta, GA: Center for Disease Control and Prevention National Center for Vital Statistics.

Hammersley, M. & Atkinson, P. (2007). *Ethnography: Principles in practice.* London: Tavistock.

Hunter, A. G., Pearson, J. L., Ialongo, N. S., & Kellam, S. (1998). Parenting alone to multiple caregivers:Child care and parenting arrangements in black and white urban families. *Family Relations, 47*, 343–353.

Jarrett, R., Roy, K., & Burton, L. (2002). Fathers in the 'hood: Qualitative reseach on African American men. In C. Tamis-LeMonda & N. Cabrera (Eds.), *Handbook of father involvement: Multidisciplinary perspectives.* (pp. 211–248). Hillsdale, NJ: Lawrence Erlbaum Associates.

Johnson, W. E., Jr. (1999, April 25). *Young, unwed, African American fathers: Indicators of their paternal involvement.* Paper presented at Eleventh Annual Kent State Psychology Forum.

Johnson, W. E., Jr. (2001). Paternal involvement among unwed fathers. *Children and Youth Services Review, 23*, 513–536.

Landry, D. J. & Forrest, J. D. (1995). How old are U.S. fathers? *Family Planning Perspectives, 27*, 159–171.

Lerman, R. I. (1993). A national profile of young unwed fathers. In R. I. Lerman & T. J. Ooms (Eds.), *Young unwed fathers: Changing roles and emerging policies* (pp. 27–51). Philadelphia: Temple University Press.

Levine, J. A. & Pitt, E. W. (1995). *New expectations: Community strategies for responsible fatherhood.* New York: Families and Work Institute.

Lincoln, Y. S. & Guba, E. G. (1985). *Naturalistic inquiry.* Newbury Park, CA: Sage Publications.

Males, M. & Chew, K. S. Y. (1996). The ages of fathers in California adolescent births, 1993. *American Journal of Public Health, 86*, 565–568.

Marshall, C. & Rossman, G. B. (2006). *Designing qualitative research* (4th ed.). Thousand Oaks, CA: Sage Publications.

Mason, J. (2007). *Qualitative researching* (2nd ed.). Thousand Oaks, CA: Sage Publications.

Merriwether-de Vries, Burton, L. M., & Eggeletion, L. (1996). Early parenting and intergenerational family relationships within African American families. In J. A. Graber, J. Brooks-Gunn, & A. C. Petersen (Eds.), *Transitions through adolescence: Interpersonal domains and context* (pp. 233–248). Mahwah, NJ: Erlbaum.

Miller, D. B. (1994). Influences on parental involvement of African American adolescent fathers. *Child and Social Work Journal, 11*, 363–378.

Nelson, T. J., Clampet-Lindquist, S., & Edin, K. (2002). Sustaining fragile fatherhood: Father involvement among low-income, noncustodial African-American fathers in Philadelphia. In C. S. Tamis-LeMonda & N. Cabreara (Eds.), *Handbook of father involvement: Multidisciplinary perspectives* (pp. 525–554). Mahwah, NJ: Erlbaum.

Patton, M. Q. (1990). *Qualitative evaluation and research methods* (2nd ed.). Newbury Park, CA: Sage Publications.

Patton, M. Q. (2002). *Qualitative research and evaluation methods.* (3rd ed.) Thousand Oaks, CA: Sage Publications.

Pears, K. C., Pierce, S. L., Kim, H. K., Capaldi, D. M., & Owen, L. D. (2005). The timing of entry into fatherhood in young, at-risk men. *Journal of Marriage and Family, 67,* 429–447.

Pleck, J. H. (1997). Paternal involvement: Levels, sources, and consequences. In M. E. Lamb (Ed.), *The role of the father in child development.* (3rd ed., pp. 66–103). New York: John Wiley and Sons, Inc.

Presser, H. B. (1989). Some economic complexities of child care provided by grandmothers. *Journal of Marriage and the Family, 51,* 581–591.

Schumacher, K. & Meleis, A. (1994). Transition: A central concept in nursing. *Image, 26,* 119–127.

Stack, C. B. (1974). *All our kin: Strategies for survival in a black community.* New York: Harper and Row.

Stack, C. B. & Burton, L. M. (1993). Kinscripts. *Journal of Comparative Family Studies, 24,* 157–170.

Stake, R. E. (1995). *The art of case study research.* Thousand Oaks, CA: Sage Publications.

Stewart, J. B. (1997). Back to basics: The significance of Du Bois's and Frazier's contributions for contemporary research on black families. In H. E. Cheatham & J. B. Stewart (Eds.), *Black families: Interdisciplinary perspectives.* New Brunswick, NJ: Transaction.

Strauss, A. L. & Corbin, J. M. (1998). *Basics of qualitative research: Techniques and procedures for developing grounded theory.* Newbury Park, CA: Sage Publications.

Sullivan, M. L. (1993). Young fathers and parenting in two inner-city neighborhoods. In R. I. Lerman & T. J. Ooms (Eds.), *Young unwed fathers: Changing roles and emerging policies* (pp. 52–73). Philadelphia: Temple University Press.

Summ, A. & Fogg, N. (1991). The adolescent poor and the transition to early adulthood. In P. Edelman & J. Lander (Eds.), *Adolescence and poverty: Challenges for the 1990s* (pp. 37–109). Washington, DC: Center for National Policy Press.

Westney, O. E., Cole, O. J., & Munford, T. L. (1986). Adolescent unwed prospective fathers: Readiness for fatherhood and behaviors toward the mother and the expected infant. *Adolescence, 21,* 901–911.

Wilson, M. N. (1986). The Black extended family: An analytical consideration. *Developmental Psychology, 22,* 246–258.

Xie, H., Cairns, B. D., & Cairns, R. B. (2001). Predicting teen motherhood and teen fatherhood: Individual characteristics and peer affiliations. *Social Development, 10,* 488–511.

3

Intergenerational Support and Reciprocity Between Low-Income African American Fathers and Their Aging Mothers

KEVIN M. ROY, OMARI L. DYSON, AND JA-NEE JACKSON

If you've got your mom, it's like, "OK, I've got my ace" . . . I made a lot of mistakes because I had no father around, but they wasn't mistakes because I had moms and my sister. (Lamont, age 28)

African American fathers in low-income urban communities often have been characterized as marginal participants in the lives of their children and families (Allen & Doherty, 1996; Burton & Snyder, 1998; Marsiglio, Amato, Day, & Lamb, 2000). Recent studies have begun to examine paternal involvement and the substantial barriers to these fathers' participation as providers and caregivers. These studies of involvement are often focused on how men's individual attributes and perceptions, or fathers' fragile relationships with children's mothers, may lead to lack of involvement (Carlson & McLanahan, 2004).

In contrast, using a strengths perspective (Barnes, 2001), we can explore a broad range of family strategies and forms of social support that help to establish and maintain fathers' involvement. In this study, we explore men's perceptions of a vital relationship in their lives—the one they have with their own mothers. As paternal grandmothers, these women contribute to children's well-being. Do they help to promote their sons' involvement as well, and if so, how?

Background

Transitory Fathering

Most studies with national survey data on low-income minority fathers support the finding that low-income fathers are challenged to remain involved with their children (Coley, 2001). Results from the Fragile Families study, based on national data from over 4700 unwed couples, show that most fathers were highly involved at the birth of their children and that involvement was enhanced when they had a positive attitude toward fathering, a committed couple relationship, and stable, full-time jobs (Carlson & McLanahan, 2002; Johnson, 2001). Twelve months after the birth of children, however, multiple disruptions—including relationship conflict and financial instability—contributed to union dissolution (McLanahan, Garfinkel, & Mincy, 2001; Waller & McLanahan, 2005). Although some studies indicate that nonresidential fathers make efforts to provide and care for their children (Danziger & Radin, 1990; Stier & Tienda, 1993), they generally lack the resources to successfully fulfill provider and caregiver roles.

Unwed or divorced fathers' involvement with their children decreases when they move out of the household and terminate their relationship (Lerman, 1993; Lerman & Sorensen, 2000; Seltzer, 1991). Nonresidential fathers' involvement is especially enhanced by both quality and quantity of father–child interactions (Amato & Gilbreth, 1999), consistent financial contribution (McLanahan, Seltzer, Hanson, & Thomson, 1994; Mincy, Garfinkel, & Nepomnyaschy, 2005), an amicable relationship with the mother of the child (Coley & Chase-Lansdale, 1999), and voluntary relinquishment of a street-oriented lifestyle (Nelson, Clampet-Lundquist, & Edin, 2002). In Kathryn Edin's (2000) study of marital beliefs, single low-income mothers report that potential partners often are untrustworthy and unprepared to commit to long-term relationships due to sporadic employment and involvement in illegal activities.

However, the assumption of father absence may mask transitions of men in and out of the home, a pattern especially common for young Black families (Mott, 1990). Multiple sets of children complicate men's parenting responsibilities (Manning, Stewart, & Smock, 2003). African American fathers often spend less time living with their biological children and more time with nonbiological children, although some findings suggest that they become more involved with biological children as those children age (Eggebeen, 2002). These patterns point to the centrality of role flexibility in dynamic family relationships, as well as to cycles of engagement and disengagement of low-income African American fathers with their children (Jarrett, Roy, & Burton, 2002).

Support From Paternal Kin Systems

In general, men's involvement in their children's lives can encourage other paternal kin to commit time and money toward children's well-being (Stack, 1974). Recent qualitative studies of fathers in Trenton, New Jersey (Waller, 2002) and multiple urban sites in the South and Midwest (Hamer, 2001) illustrate how kin systems may be resources by which fathers can give meaning to their roles and can secure involvement with their children. In particular, as Richardson shows in Chapter 5 in this volume, fathers may be able to create social capital for their children by connecting them with motivated kin and caregivers (Marsiglio et al., 2000).

Many single, low-income African American mothers struggle to rear their sons and promote their positive development into adulthood (Boyd-Franklin & Franklin, 2001) (see also Chapter 5 in this volume). Paternal kin—especially mothers—may help to set explicit role expectations for fatherhood (Johnson, 1998, 2001; Roy & Vesely, 2009; Stack & Burton, 1993). Paternal grandmothers provide low-income fathers with a safe home base from which to parent in violent and risky communities (Roy, 2004). In interviews with fathers, Hamer (2001) suggests that men "seemed to feel emotionally closer to their mothers than any other women in their lives" (p. 94). In her study, men reported that their mothers held high expectations for their parenting, encouraging them to spend time with children and to serve as role models. Mothers were their sons' primary confidantes about parenting and intimate relationships, and they could provide financial support and job contacts as well.

We know little about how kin members, especially men's own mothers, shape men's parenting roles. Men's mothers, for example, may be particularly effective when men themselves have few resources to secure positive involvement with their children. Moreover, few studies have explored how these relationships evolve and how reciprocity may emerge between adult sons and their aging mothers. In this qualitative analysis, we consider how men's involvement with their children is shaped by the support and expectations of their mothers. We analyze life history interviews with 85 low-income African American fathers in Indiana and Illinois, asking the following questions:

- How do relationships between fathers and their aging mothers unfold over time?
- How does the participation of grandmothers help to secure their sons' involvement as fathers, when so many of these men are challenged by lack of employment opportunities, incarceration, or dissolved relationships with children's mothers?

Methods

Sample and Research Sites

For this analysis, we draw from interviews with 85 low-income African American fathers across three different projects. In each project, the first two authors worked as facilitators of curriculum for parenting programs in addition to serving as researchers. The first author worked in a fatherhood program in a community college in Chicago for 3 years as a caseworker and researcher. While working with more than 400 fathers, he conducted life history interviews with 40 participants. Both authors facilitated weekly life skills workshops for incarcerated men in a work-release facility in northern Indiana. They interviewed 40 participants, 10 of whom were African American fathers. Finally, the second author facilitated programs for young men in a community-based fatherhood program in Indianapolis, where he interviewed 35 African American fathers.

Each participant was considered to be low income on the basis of total income or eligibility of his children for public assistance. Men's efforts to become more involved with their children through parenting classes and co-parent counseling and their desire to access employment training and placement and educational, housing, and drug treatment referrals distinguished them in some ways from their peers. Aside from their interest in these programs, however, the participants were no different demographically from other fathers enrolled in the program or from other low-income African American men in their communities.

Men in this pooled sample varied in age: 46% ($n = 39$) were 24 years or younger (primarily the participants of the Indianapolis program); 28% ($n = 24$) were between 25 and 35 years of age; and 26% ($n = 22$) were 36 years or older. Of the total sample, 49 of the fathers (58%) were incarcerated or formerly incarcerated, and 51 of the participants (60%) had completed high school or earned a general equivalency diploma (GED). Only about one-third of the men were employed in full-time jobs at the interview; the majority were unemployed or underemployed.

More than half of the men in the study (53%, or $n = 45$) lived with their mothers or grandmothers and not with their children. These men tended to be younger fathers, although older fathers also frequently returned to their mothers' households. Well over three-quarters of the participants were noncustodial fathers who did not live with their children on a daily basis. Just under half of the sample (41%, $n = 35$) had only one child, while 28 fathers (33%) had two children, and 22 (26%) had three or four children.

Data Collection and Analyses

Each of the three programs offered voluntary parenting classes on a weekly basis. The research team recruited active participants during these sessions. We explained to fathers that we were conducting research on paternal involvement, and if they agreed to participate, they signed written consent forms.

Multiple methods were used for data collection. First, we took detailed ethnographic field notes of interactions between fathers, children, program staff, and ourselves at the program site. This technique provided data on ecological processes, barriers, and supports for men's parenting and the making of meaning in fatherhood roles spanning many weeks. During 2-hour sessions at the program site, we conducted retrospective life history interviews to gather more insight into men's relationships with extended family members. Interviews were recorded on audiotapes and transcribed, and interview and field note texts were coded using QSR N6 software (QSR International, Cambridge, Massachusetts). Pseudonyms and ages of participants were noted.

Protocol questions addressed the size of their extended families, reciprocity between members, and socialization to fatherhood. Men discussed common interaction with family members and indicated where the interactions occurred. Major life events such as changes in family structure, residential movement, and shifts in paternal involvement across multiple families were plotted on calendar grids using techniques found in Freedman, Thornton, Camburn, Alwin, and Young-Demarco (1988). The grids provided precise documentation of important transitions in father involvement, including family deaths and physical health problems, dissolution of intimate relationships, and the beginning of fatherhood. We also used a range of methods to enhance the trustworthiness of data (Lincoln & Guba, 1985). Credibility and dependability of the data were enhanced by triangulation of multiple sources and methods as well as prolonged engagement in the field. Discussions with individual participants after the interviews were used to validate initial understanding of the influence of kinship systems on men's parenting.

We adapted a constant comparative method of analytic induction from basic elements of grounded theory (Strauss & Corbin, 1998). Although we did not solicit specific information about men's relationships with their mothers, we noted how frequently and extensively participants discussed the past and ongoing influences of their mothers on their own development as adults and as fathers. For this analysis, we paid attention to men's descriptions of childhood and adolescence; early socialization to fathering; the role that their mothers played in child care and negotiations with "babymamas" and maternal kin; and arrangements that allowed adult sons and aging mothers to exchange financial, emotional, and social supports.

Our own backgrounds and experiences influenced each step of data collection and analysis. As a middle-aged White male academic, an African American male graduate student, and an African American female undergraduate student, we were collectively in good positions to debate and check each other's assumptions and interpretations of men's relationships with their mothers. Prolonged time in the field allowed us to build rapport in personal interactions during classes, program celebrations, and home visits. Although we advocated for paternal involvement in the programs, we encouraged men to tell us about their own experiences and perceptions outside the program sessions.

Findings

The Stone: Young Men's Reliance on Mothers

> After my great grandma died, then my grandma was the stone. Now she died, and my mama will be the stone. It passes on. My mama isn't even the oldest one, but all of her sisters say she's the responsible one.
>
> —Bird, age 21

Each of the 85 men in these studies developed distinct relationships with their mothers. We first examined relationships between young men and their mothers during youth and adolescence. Next, we explored how mothers socialized men to be parents prior to the birth of their children and how they promoted their son's roles as fathers after the birth of those children. In the final section, we describe the emerging reciprocity between many younger and middle-aged fathers and their aging mothers. We found generally that more than half the men had stable, consistent interaction with their mothers over time. A little more than one-fourth saw significant change in their interaction, and about one in five had little to no inter-action with their mothers.

Men reported that their own fathers' movements in and out of the household affected early relationships with their mothers. Well over one-third of the men lost their own fathers by the age of 3 to death, divorce, or departure; the majority of participants had longer resided with their fathers by age 13. Only one-third of all men in the sample had fathers who were involved consistently over the course of their lives (Roy, 2006). Their mothers soon became single parents with limited resources to rear their children, and their sons often became the oldest males in the households, repositories of great hope and reminders of their fathers' presence. Joe, a 41-year-old father, had always lived with his mother. After his parents' divorce when he was 25, his presence in his mother's household was reassuring. "I was the oldest, I looked a lot like my father," he said. "She thought I was my dad sometimes. She would do that."

Parents' breakup or divorce led to important changes in men's early lives. Mothers tried to minimize the effects of family transitions on their sons. As Malcolm, a 35-year-old father in Chicago noted, his parents' separation taught him lessons about perseverance through tough times:

> I watched [my mother] go through a lot of financial problems as a single parent. It was my experience of emotional hurt watching my mother, due to separation from my father, that led me to believe that the best thing for a father and mother is to stick together.

Mothers also struggled to stabilize their households on a single income, and when they lost their jobs, they needed to rely on support from family members. Often, men were sent to live with their relatives, usually their grandmothers. Although most men developed close bonds with their grandmothers, this transi-tion proved jarring at times. Remy was an only child and was "real tight with my Mom, but when my grandmother took me, everything started going downhill. I felt like I was taken away from my Mom, like I wasn't accepted, wasn't loved. I was all by myself and everybody was against me."

Men were struck by the dedication of their mothers to extremely demanding and often demeaning jobs. From an early age, many of the men recalled their moth-ers' intensive activity in the kitchen as they helped to "cut up celery, green peppers, or onions for dinner." These single mothers often maintained two or more jobs to pay for their children's needs. Curt, a 39-year-old father from Chicago, recalled how his mother built computer boards for almost 20 years, until the plant closed; she then processed Styrofoam cups for another 25 years. Isaiah recognized both the stressors and limits of his mother's parenting:

> I was 13, running the streets and climbing out of windows. My mother would be asleep because she was working two jobs so she could send us to Catholic school. That's the reason I can't sit around and do nothing with my kids.

With mothers piecing together resources paycheck to paycheck, many men learned survival skills at an early age. Tamal, a 20-year-old father from Chicago, noted that there were always money troubles in the household, but he learned to be a responsible man in the process.

> Living with my mom is more like I know how to hustle and survive. My mom taught me how to take care of a household. If you were down and out, you had to come up with an idea to pay the bills and feed your family.

These lessons in survival, perseverance, and responsibility stayed with men and influenced the ways in which they thought about their own roles as parents. They admired how their mothers persisted through adverse conditions. For example, mothers not only held down employment, but they pursued education. Charles, an older father in the work release facility in Indiana, related, "In my mother's house, it was work or school, one or the other. I remember my mama getting her GED, her nursing license, her working in hospitals in East St. Louis, the VA hospital in Chicago. My parents fell out when my father wouldn't buy her a robe when she graduated from high school." Many mothers provided the men with their only positive role models. Lamont reported, "My mom was the only one that was there, as far as motivation, understanding, discipline, whatever."

Joe saw many of the same traits in his mother. However, he noted that his mother was overburdened as the sole parent in his family. "She emphasized education, even though she didn't know about that. She gave me enthusiasm, a way to be willing to try to achieve and deal with this society in which I live. But the stress of the family got to her." Holding together a strained marriage was one of the sources of mothers' stress, and they often sought relief and distraction from conflict in family and work life. For example, Alfred recognized that "My father was a rolling stone, always in the fast lane with me. My mother used to go out and drink, but I think that she earned that, because she used to work two jobs to take care of us." A small number of men, particularly younger fathers, were not reared by and never knew their mothers. They emphasized how stress drove their mothers away from family life and toward dependence on alcohol or drugs.

The most common experience that men noted in their discussions of growing up was their mothers' efforts to protect them from violence and the influences of street life. Mothers kept their sons physically close to them at young ages. For Muhammed, this meant that "I was a mama's baby, stuck with her, if she had to go to the store or something. When people tried to snatch her purse, I was there, and that was not going to happen." As men became adolescents, their mothers grew more vigilant in keeping them on the path of positive behavior. Isaiah remembered how his mother came to his neighbor's house "to talk, talk, talk to make me come home. She looked like she was going to cry, so I went home. I told her I was smoking cigarettes, but she said she didn't care, just to come home." The presence of gangs outside of the house caused mothers great concern as well. For example, Nelson recalled, "I been around gangs but knew how to get around it. I knew

I couldn't get involved because I loved my mother too much. I remember the Chicago riots in' 68, the snow of' 67. My mother must have kept me away from all of that."

With hindsight as adults, men realized that their mothers took tough stances in their interests. Earl, a young father in Indianapolis, reported, "My mother was the meanest lady on the block. We always had to be home when the streetlights came on. We had chores and had to get good grades. But she wasn't necessarily hard on us, just stern. It taught me responsibility, gave me a work ethic." Men reflected back on these protective relationships, and they found that their mothers were the primary influences on their lives. Chris, a young father in the work-release facility, emphasized how mother–child relationships are unique. He said, "I would go everywhere she went, and I would protect her no matter what. Fathers may come and go, but mothers are always there."

This closeness was tested in adolescence, particularly when young men left their mothers' households. For many mothers, one strategy of protecting their sons was to send them away from dangerous urban communities. When Wesley, a young Chicago father, ran into trouble with local gangs and law enforcement, his mother suggested that he move to the South to live with his sister. "I got into trouble," he recalled, "And she was like, 'You have to leave.' She didn't kick me out, but she said it was best to leave." For other men, the search for independence led them away from their mothers. Akida, a 19-year-old father in Indianapolis, felt that he may have been "too close" to his mother.

> My mama was overprotective of me. Me and her was like brother and sister. I started to run away because I couldn't deal with my mama's rules. I was 15 when I moved out; she wrote me a check for $150 and sent me on my way.

In summary, mothers were usually the most consistent and prominent adults throughout men's childhood and adolescence. Men described the difficult challenges that their mothers faced as single parents carrying multiple jobs; they also noted how mothers tried repeatedly to protect them from violence, racism, and negative influences in urban communities. Men's respect for their mothers grew with hindsight and with their assumption of fathering roles.

Securing Fatherhood Through Kin Work

> I only saw my oldest daughter when my mom would try to bring her down on the holidays, so she could spend some time with me. My oldest daughter always knew who her dad was because my mom has always been there when I wasn't able to be there.
>
> —Remy, age 27

Mothers played a central role in teaching their sons how to be fathers as well as in securing their involvement with their children through support, both emotional and instrumental. In the life history interviews, we asked each participant,

"Who taught you to be a father?" A number of men (41%; $n = 35$) recognized their mothers' efforts to teach them to be fathers. Some men found these lessons in the day-to-day care and responsibility that mothers personified. Bird, a 21-year-old father, grew up in the housing projects in Chicago and struggled to put his gang affiliation and prison record behind him. He recalled how from the time he was age 3, his mother played a central role in his life after the death of his father, a former gang member:

> I would give a Mother's Day and Father's Day gift to my mom. Because that was who was daddy and mama. Even when we was down and out, she loved the shit out of me. That's what love means.

Nelson also believed that his capacity for parenting was "inherited" from his mother. "I love kids, I love people. I think I got all of this father-learning from my mother. My mom showed me nothing but love, and I loved life, but my dad wasn't there."

As overburdened single parents under extreme stress, many mothers relied on their sons, even when they were quite young. Some men were expected to care for younger siblings, which resulted in early socialization to a parental role in their families. Tamal, the young Chicago father, indicated that the "10-year break between me and my little brother and sister" influenced the way that he thought about himself as an adult and potential parent. "I raised them," he stated simply. Jordan, another young father from Indianapolis, explained, "I was the man of the house since I was little. I was watching my little brothers. It was illegal, but I grew up real fast, faster than any normal person. I was cooking, I was doing everything."

With the birth of their own children, men drew on these lessons from being reared by their mothers. More immediately, their mothers became grandmothers—women who, in many ways, assumed responsibility for the intergenerational continuity of their families, not just their daily survival. Randy, an Indianapolis father, recalled this sense of legacy when he recognized the importance of his own grandmother in his life. He said, "She refused to let any child born into our family disappear [outside of the family]."

Paternal grandmothers performed a range of kin-work roles for the well-being of their grandchildren. From the earliest interactions, mothers helped their sons to negotiate relationships with their children. Paternal grandmothers were instrumental in defining paternity for younger fathers. Even in the face of new DNA tests that could establish biological ties between men and their children, the judgment of grandmothers carried weight in family relations. Bird's mother heard rumors that his son had a baby, so she visited the hospital 2 days after the child's birth "to see it on her own." He recalled, "Once she saw the baby, there was no denying it. 'Yea, that's my granddaughter, that's mine.' She knew it." As a gatekeeper for men's paternity, paternal grandmothers gained some control over their sons' pathways to fatherhood. Gerald, a 35-year-old father in Chicago, had a daughter with his girlfriend, who used cocaine. His mother "didn't like my girlfriend at first, and she denied that it was my child." When Gerald was at work, she called child protective services to report her son's girlfriend and take custody of his child. He said, "I was very upset about that. My baby was only 5 months old. But now she looks like my mother, and my mother gets to keep her sometimes."

Paternal grandmothers helped to negotiate conflicts between fathers and the mothers of their children. However, their kin work was focused on promoting the well-being of their grandchildren. As Bird related, "[My babymama] tried to get all tight with my mom, but my mom knows the routine. She's like, 'Ain't nothing to talk about him. You want to talk about this shorty (baby), we can talk.'" Often, animosity between maternal and paternal families led men's mothers to limit involvement. For Marcus, a young father in Chicago, whose girlfriend's family had provided information to police that led to his arrest, "They were the reason I got locked up." He added, "And my family, theirs, everybody was at each others' throats." As a result, he had not seen his daughter in many months. However, the involvement of paternal grandmothers usually helped to diffuse conflict between parents. Joe found that his family had earned the trust of the mother of his son. When his former girlfriend was incarcerated, Joe's mother was chosen to be the child's guardian.

> My son has been with my mom for the last 3 years. His mother knew no other people who would be able to take care of the child to her satisfaction, but she knew me and my family since she was 15 years old. She knew what kind of people we were and she felt safe since I was the father.

Men's mothers also played key roles by monitoring their grandchildren or by relaying information about their well-being. For many men who lived apart from their children due to separation or incarceration, this link was an important family lifeline. Will and the mother of his child were both young parents, and their relationship as co-parents and partners was fragile. He relied on his mother to play go-between, asserting, "I take one step at a time. Her family calls my mother, and my mother relays the message. If they want me to call, I'll call. If they don't ask me to call, I don't." For some men, these channels of family communication are well established. In these situations, paternal grandmothers could be more assertive and actively monitor their grandchildren. For example, Asante had just been released from prison, and he knew that "My babymama is straight, she's calling my mama everyday. Otherwise, my mama would be like, 'Girl, you better tell me about my granddaughter.' They let her know if anything goes wrong, and she'd let me know."

Some paternal grandmothers cared for children and kept them overnight, which was an important resource for both fathers and mothers of children. Usually, paternal grandmothers served as "bridge" care during weekends, between work shifts, or on random days of urgent need. Isaiah's mother helped him to secure the third shift at a local factory.

I have to find daycare for my daughter right now, but my mother will watch her at night. I want to be there to help raise my grandkids, like my mom is there for me, helping me with my daughters now.

Paternal grandmothers were particularly important for young, first-time fathers. Bird kept his daughter for two weeks out of each month. He said, "They (maternal kin) bring my shorty over to my mother's house . . . . My mom works from morning until 6 p.m., then she comes back to let me go outside and get a breath of fresh air." Two older fathers, Nelson and Gerald, both relied on their mothers to keep their children during weekend days. "With the kids back in school," Nelson said, "we go to my mother's house on the weekends. I've been doing this for 3 years, since my wife passed." Gerald did not worry about transportation or arrangements. He noted that "My mother doesn't work on Saturday, and she goes to get April, my daughter. I get over to my mom's, and she's already there."

When paternal grandmothers keep their grandchildren, it also opens up a neutral space for men to visit with their children if they do not keep them independently (Roy, 2004; Roy & Vesely, 2009). When men served time in correctional facilities, their mothers played a pivotal role in keeping fathers involved in children's lives. At the work-release facility, Remy did not see much of his family, who lived in Michigan. He had to rely on his mother to transport herself and other family members to Indiana for visits. Without the support and initiative of their mothers, many men risked falling out of contact with their children over time.

Legal and policy staff members have begun to recognize the importance of paternal grandmothers to their son's involvement as fathers. With men's frequent movement in and out of jobs and their residential instability, child support courts often try to locate men at their mother's residences. When child support courts tried to find Doc, who had never known that he had fathered an 8-year-old daughter, they first contacted his mother. He recalled, "The state came to my mama's house with a warrant. Said they were going to lock me up—scared her to death." Men's mothers served as strong advocates for their sons in custody battles. Oscar's mother supported him during a custody hearing and calmed him down when the court threatened to place his daughter "in the custody of the state." Eventually, she took custody of her granddaughter, moving to Atlanta to raise her among family. Oscar said, "It was the first time when I felt like I really got to know my mom."

It is important to recognize the balancing act that men faced in ceding some control over parenting by asking for their mothers' support and guidance. In some situations, paternal grandmothers decided that their sons endangered fragile family relations and could not offer assistance in taking care of children. When Devon, a 23-year-old father in Indianapolis, decided to move out of his mother's house and marry his new girlfriend, his mother and the children's mother established joint custody and restricted his access to his children. Some men's mothers made financial decisions without their input. When Wesley, a young father in Chicago, left a boot camp program, he was awarded $2200 to establish a new life. When he returned to his mother's house, he found that "she had spent all of the money on baby stuff for my sister's baby. They were looking at me, and I was looking at them. My mama said, real soft, 'I spent that money on the baby.' I said, 'That's OK, Mom,' but I couldn't believe it." For these men, the involvement of paternal grandmothers could curtail their own future as parents.

Reciprocity Between Aging Mothers and Adult Sons

[My mother] caught a bad cold. She was coughing, had fluid around her heart that choked her. If she ever wanted something out of me, she got it. She didn't have to ask questions, I always did it. She could depend on me, and I could always depend on her, no question about it.

—Miles, age 31

Among the 85 low-income African American men in this study, mothers and sons engaged in a dynamic and often mutual exchange of financial, emotional, and social support. Lacking consistent employment, most men were not self-sufficient, which meant that their relationships with partners and their mothers were critical to their day-to-day survival and potential independence. Aging mothers often had secured resources that their sons could not.

For example, mothers' willingness to share residence with their sons gave most fathers a clear "fall back" option. Cory, a 27-year-old father of two boys in Chicago, moved in and out of his mother's house.

I'm living with my mother, been there for 27 years. She's always there; she'd take care of me if something bad happened. I moved out of her house after high school, but I'd go back now and then. I'd stay with my girlfriend, too. I'd find rent money for my girlfriend and for my mom. I'd go back to my mother's if I got into an argument.

Although a shared residence could require men to adhere to their mothers' rules, this safe refuge from gang activity, drug rehabilitation, re-entry from prison or jail, or the pressures of paying rent on little to no income was invaluable to many men.

These arrangements could, however, divide fathers' commitments and strain relations with men's partners and mothers of their children. Donnell, a young father of three sons, had two jobs and recognized this conflict as well. He said, "Adriana, my girlfriend, is jealous of the bond that I have with my family. She feels like she is competing with my family for my attention, especially my mother. I would do anything for my mother. And Adriana, she ain't even my wife." Donnell recognized that his family ties—and his continued relationship with his mother— were concrete and had real impact, whereas his bond with his child's mother seemed ambiguous and was likely to be short lived.

We also explored the flip side of reciprocity: how men supported their mothers as they aged. Sonny spoke directly of a transition in family relationships, when men can embrace adulthood and its responsibilities. "There's a time to branch out from your family, be your own man," he said. "You can't just keep going to mommy and daddy and saying 'Help me out.' You want to go and say, 'I want to help you out, too.'" Being "the stone" for one's mother was difficult, however. Sonny was an unemployed student with eight children, unable to support himself and reliant on his sister to care for his children. Other men were simply unable to be physically present to support their mothers. Charles was "in and out of jails" and could not assist his mother, who owned property in Indiana but suffered from Alzheimer disease. He regretted his incarceration, admitting "I ain't no good to her sitting in here . . . It's fallen to my brother to be the good son, but he put her in a nursing home and ran up credit card debt for her."

Most men started with small gestures for their mothers. After Isaiah's mother gave him some church tapes to listen to, he began to write poetry and wrote a poem for her birthday. He recognized how central his mother's spirituality was to her health. "Every Sunday now I go to church with her, and she goes swimming and I pick her up and take her home," he said. "If she has to go somewhere during the day, I pick her up and drive her around."

After being single mothers for decades, most women continued to work past retirement age. Men realized that their mothers were worn down from years of financial instability and strained relationships. Jordan's mother was still in her thirties, but he lived with her as he tried to stabilize his own life as a young father. He was struck by the heavy burdens that she carried from work to home each day.

> She's been through so much in her life, and she's like permanently depressed, stressed at all times, taking so many medicines. It's hard for me to deal with, but I have to. Sometimes she just comes home and says things, she doesn't mean it. My mother tries to help me, but I don't rely on her too much, because I don't want to put that extra pressure on her.

Some fathers reported that their mothers' depression and stress led to a reliance on alcohol or drugs. The ability to understand and empathize with their mothers made some men the most effective social supports in extended families. For example, Kelvin had three daughters who lived with his wife. He had done time and kicked a drug habit, and he lived with his mother, helping her out as much as he could. "My mom is an addict. I ignore it, don't let it bother me," he said. "She's been all right with me because I have been feeding her and buying her cigarettes. She talks to the air, she cusses people out, but that's OK with me."

As reciprocity developed over time, some men created intergenerational care-giving arrangements. Russell was an underemployed father of a teenage son in Chicago. His mother had helped to raise Russell's son but had fallen ill in recent months. Russell moved his son and mother into the apartment next to his so he could monitor her health and help her out with daily routines. "My father's passed, and she doesn't like to sleep alone," he said. "My son is the first grandson of my parents, and he is my mother's favorite. I had a lot of help with him, and she needs to know where he is. So it works out for everybody."

Ultimately, men's sense of loss at their mother's deaths or the weight of their mother's absence when she was not involved reflects the complexity of mother–son relationships. Keith met his mother for the first time at the age of 20, when he walked into a department store and introduced himself to her. After initial joy and excitement, he realized that he could not retrieve the years without his mother's involvement.

> A lot of things came out . . . why was my grandmother raising me, why had she never tried to contact me if we'd been living in the same town? There was a lot of envy. It all got to me, like I felt I was in a fake relationship with my mother, and it really, really made me angry . . . After we had a cancer scare with her, I started to rethink religion, of how my next day is not promised. I tried to clean up my life. I got to the point of, why should I keep looking for a mother? No longer can she be my mother.

When mothers were active and supportive, their sudden absence could transform their sons' lives. Leon, an older father of three sons in Chicago, recalled that he was quite close to his mother, closer than to his father. When he visited her at her home, she began to look "different, weaker." At the same time that he lost a good job, she died of cancer, and Leon started using drugs. Miles's mother and brother passed away within 4 months of each other. He became careless as a dealer, which he interpreted as a message from his mother.

> When I was selling, I would never get caught. But then it seemed like every time I touched the stuff, I got caught. The police weren't catching me, it was my mama giving me a warning. I am trying to keep it real, she was giving me a whupping. It brought me back to reality.

Men continued to turn—and to return—to their mothers for shelter, emotional, and material support, even in middle age, and mothers grew increasingly reliant on their sons as well as they aged. For some men, the relationship with their mothers was the single most significant bond with any other person, male or female, in their lives. The loss of their mothers, therefore, dramatically changed the lives and identities of many men in this study.

Discussion and Conclusion

In this analysis of life history interviews with 85 low-income African American men, we found that supportive kin systems may be among the most vital resources to promote paternal involvement with children. Men's evolving relationships with their mothers set the tone for their own development, not just as children or adolescents, but as fathers, partners, workers, and middle-aged adults.

Program Implications for Work With Low-Income Fathers

This description and examination of evolving relationships has implications for social work in local programs. A pathological perspective may emphasize risky behavior of individual fathers as gang members or unemployed workers, or gender conflict in couple formation. In contrast, our use of a family strengths perspective locates positive and often overlooked adaptive strengths of African American families. With this more comprehensive view, we can identify how extended families aid each other and support paternal involvement. Among many African American fathers and their families, role flexibility and kin work become salient strategies for crafting family networks (Jarrett et al., 2002). Caseworkers who look behind absent fathers or failed relationships may identify resources in an extensive web of paternal kin members. This study suggests that there may be potential in intergenerational programs that extend parenting classes, counseling, and related supports to paternal grandmothers.

Social workers also should recognize the long-standing nature of these family relationships. With the limited involvement of fathers in many sons' lives, mothers provide the earliest model for parenting. However, mothers' influences do not end with adolescence. Men's bonds with their mothers may become their most consistent lifetime relationship, shaping their adulthood roles as fathers, partners, workers, and caregivers. The relationships are dynamic and complex; as the analyses suggest, there may be negative consequences in mother–son relationships that are close and supportive as well as in those that are distant or nonexistent. If caseworkers promote marital relationships, for example, without also acknowledging and supporting mother–son relationships, paternal involvement may be jeopardized, particularly if paternal grandmothers help to secure men's involvement through care work, advice, and related support.

Finally, these findings suggest that the constraints of local neighborhood are not simply problems in fathers' lives. Men and their mothers faced similar challenges: drug use and dealing, unemployment and underemployment, lack of education, and resulting depression. Moreover, ecological constraints, including gang presence, police patrols, and poverty in general can directly shape capacities in and functions of kin systems over time (Marsiglio, Roy, & Fox, 2005; Roy, 2004, 2006). Social workers who approach these ecological constraints as threats to family relationships may be able to more effectively promote any kind of adult involvement in children's lives.

Policy Implications

There are a range of policy options that would help young African American fathers to gain a foothold in the labor market and, in doing so, contribute to the well-being of their children and even their own mothers. Pilot projects in career and technical education, school-to-work programs, and career academies, as well as a potential national apprenticeship model, would all benefit such fathers (Edelman, Holzer, & Offner, 2006). Poor jobs could be recrafted through raises in the minimum wage,

wage subsidies, and a childless Earned Income Tax Credit (EITC), allowing work to actually "pay" (Edelman et al., 2006).

These recommendations, and other recent reports on poor Black fathers (Mincy, 2006) tend to focus policies on individual fathers and to ignore family contexts for secure paternal involvement. Few social policies promote closer adult–youth relationships among low-income African American young men. Such policies would be critical for men who are embedded in and turn to kin networks as they transition into parenthood and through fragile relationships and short-lived jobs. Intergenerational programs could capitalize on family strengths and bolster interfamily support options (Barnes, 2001) for child care or material assistance.

The participation of the aging mothers of disadvantaged men becomes even more central for policy makers concerned with paternity establishment and child support programs, as well as re-entry guidelines for incarcerated fathers. Innovative social policies that offer long-term investments in intergenerational relationships would enhance the abilities of both mothers and sons to help each other through difficult challenges. For example, community youth systems, such as Youth Opportunity or Harlem Child Zone (Edelman et al., 2006), could offer a range of intergenerational parenting courses for fathers who live in their mothers' households. In effect, the alternative—separation of men from involvement with their children through lack of jobs or incarceration—may place greater strain on all family members, including paternal grandmothers, who become the last available option for caregiving in stressed families.

Many low-income fathers have little to contribute financially to their children, which makes any social capital they can provide even more valuable. In this way, social policy initiatives should recognize the place of paternal grandmothers as central social capital links for low-income fathers and their children. Instead of punitive measures that force young teen mothers to live with their own mothers in order to receive assistance, programs can provide financial or material incentives for the consistent involvement of maternal and paternal grandmothers in the lives of co-parents and grandchildren. Men's mothers may confirm and legitimize men's paternity status. Caregiving and close relations with paternal grandmothers also may contribute to children's well-being and sense of belonging to a family legacy (Roy and Burton, 2007). Perhaps most significantly, paternal grandmothers may be key facilitators of men's involvement with a child or multiple children when fathers attempt to "play the pivot point" and bring together children in different households.

Acknowledgments

This study was conducted with support from the National Institute for Child Health and Human Development under Project No. 5 R03 HD 42074-2 and the Purdue Research Foundation at Purdue University. The authors would like to thank Sherri Brown and Laura DiTizio for assistance in data analyses.

Correspondence concerning this article should be addressed to Kevin Roy, Department of Family Science, University of Maryland, 255 Valley Drive, Room 1142, School of Public Health Building.

REFERENCES

Allen, W. & Doherty, W. (1996). The responsibilities of fatherhood as perceived by African American teenage fathers. *Families in Society: Journal of Contemporary Human Services, 79,* 142–155.

Amato, P. & Gilbreth, J. (1999). Nonresident fathers and children's well-being: A meta-analysis. *Journal of Marriage and the Family, 61,* 557–573.

Barnes, S. (2001). Stressors and strengths: A theoretical and practical examination of nuclear, single-parent, and augmented African American families. *Families in Society: The Journal of Contemporary Human Services, 82,* 449–460.

Boyd-Franklin, N. & Franklin, A. (2001). *Boys into men: Raising our African American teenage sons.* New York: Plume.

Burton, L. & Snyder, A. (1998). The invisible man revisited: Comments on the life course, history, and men's roles in American families. In A. Booth (Ed.), *Men in families: When do they get involved? What difference does it make?* (pp. 31–39). Hillsdale, NJ: Erlbaum.

Carlson, M. & McLanahan, S. (2002). Father involvement in fragile families. In C. Tamis-LeMonda & N. Cabrera (Eds.), *Handbook of father involvement: Multidisciplinary perspectives.* (pp. 461–488). New York: Erlbaum.

Carlson, M. & McLanahan, S. (2004). Early father involvement in fragile families. In R. Day & M. Lamb (Eds.), *Conceptualizing and measuring father involvement.* (pp. 241– 271). Mahwah, NJ: Erlbaum.

Coley, R. & Chase-Lansdale, P. L. (1999). Stability and change in paternal involvement among urban African American fathers. *Journal of Family Psychology, 13,* 416–435.

Coley, R. L. (2001). (In)visible men: Emerging research on low-income, unmarried, and minority fathers. *American Psychologist, 56,* 743–753.

Danziger, S. & Radin, N. (1990). Absent does not equal uninvolved: Predictors of fathering in teen mother families. *Journal of Marriage and the Family, 52,* 636–641.

Edelman, P., Holzer, H., & Offner, P. (2006). *Reconnecting disadvantaged young men.* Washington, DC: The Urban Institute Press.

Edin, K. (2000). What do low-income single mothers say about marriage? *Social Problems, 47,* 112–133.

Eggebeen, D. (2002). The changing course of fatherhood: Men's experiences with children in demographic perspective. *Journal of Family Issues, 23,* 486–506.

Freedman, D. A., Thornton, D., Camburn, D., Alwin, D., & Young-Demarco, L. (1988). Life history calendar: Techniques for collecting retrospective data. *Sociological Methodology, 18,* 37–68.

Hamer, J. (2001). *What it means to be daddy: Fatherhood for black men living away from their children.* New York: Columbia University Press.

Jarrett, R., Roy, K., & Burton, L. (2002). Fathers in the 'hood: Qualitative research on African American men. In C. Tamis-LeMonda & N. Cabrera (Eds.), *Handbook of father involvement: Multidisciplinary perspectives.* (pp. 211–248). Hillsdale, NJ: Erlbaum.

Johnson, W. (1998). Paternal involvement in fragile African American families: Implications for clinical social work practice. *Smith College Studies in Social Work, 68,* 215–232.

Johnson, W. (2001). Paternal involvement among unwed fathers. *Children and Youth Services Review, 23,* 513–536.

Lerman, R. (1993). A national profile of young unwed fathers. In R. Lerman & T. Ooms (Eds.), *Young unwed fathers: Changing roles and emerging policies.* (pp. 27–51). Philadelphia: Temple University Press.

Lerman, R. & Sorensen, E. (2000). Father involvement with their nonmarital children: Patterns, determinants, and effects on their earnings. *Marriage and Family Review, 29,* 75–95.

Lincoln, Y. & Guba, E. (1985). *Naturalistic inquiry.* Thousand Oaks, CA: Sage.

Manning, W., Stewart, S., & Smock, P. (2003). The complexity of fathers' parenting responsibilities and involvement with nonresident children. *Journal of Family Issues, 24,* 645–667.

Marsiglio, W., Amato, P., Day, R., & Lamb, M. (2000). Scholarship on fatherhood in the 1990s and beyond. *Journal of Marriage and the Family, 62,* 1173–1191.

Marsiglio, W., Roy, K., & Fox, G. L. (2005). *Situated fathering: A focus on physical and social spaces.* Boulder, CO: Rowman and Littlefield.

McLanahan, S., Garfinkel, I., & Mincy, R. (2001, December). *Fragile families, welfare reform, and marriage.* (Policy Brief No. 10). Washington, DC: Brookings Institution.

McLanahan, S., Seltzer, J., Hanson, T., & Thompson, E. (1994). Child support enforcement and child well-being: Greater security or greater conflict? In I. Garfinkel, S. McLanahan, & P. Robins (Eds.), *Child support and child well being.* (pp. 239–256). Washington, DC: The Urban Institute Press.

Mincy, R. (2006). *Black men left behind.* Washington, DC: The Urban Institute Press.

Mincy, R., Garfinkel, I., & Nepomnyaschy, L. (2005). In-hospital paternity establishment and father involvement in fragile families. *Journal of Marriage and Family, 67,* 611–625.

Mott, F. (1990). When is a father really gone? Paternal-child contact in father-absent homes. *Demography, 27,* 499–517.

Nelson, T., Clampet-Lundquist, S., & Edin, K. (2002). Sustaining fragile fatherhood: Father involvement among low-income, noncustodial African American fathers in Philadelphia. In C. Tamis-LeMonda & N. Cabrera (Eds.), *Handbook of father involvement: Multidisciplinary perspectives* (pp. 525–553). Mahwah, NJ: Erlbaum.

Roy, K. (2004). Three-block fathers: Spatial perceptions and kin-work in low-income neighborhoods. *Social Problems, 51,* 528–548.

Roy, K. (2006). Father stories: A life course examination of paternal identity among low-income African American men. *Journal of Family Issues, 27,* 31–54.

Roy, K. & Burton, L. (2007). Mothering through recruitment: Kinscription of non-residential fathers and father figures in low-income families. *Family Relations, 56,* 24–39.

Roy, K. & Vesely, C. (2009). Caring for "the family's child": Social capital and kin networks of young low-income African American fathers. In R. Coles & C. Green (Eds.), *The myth of the missing Black father.* (pp. 215–240) New York: Columbia University Press.

Seltzer, J. (1991). Relationships between fathers and children who live apart: The father's role after separation. *Journal of Marriage and the Family, 23,* 79–101.

Stack, C. (1974). *All our kin: Strategies for survival in a black community*. New York: Random House.

Stack, C. & Burton, L. (1993). Kinscripts. *Journal of Comparative Family Studies, 24*, 157–170.

Stier, H. & Tienda, M. (1993). Are men marginal to the family? Insights from Chicago's inner city. In J. Hood (Ed.), *Men, work and family.* (pp. 23–44). Thousand Oaks, CA: Sage.

Strauss, A. & Corbin, J. (1998). *Basics of qualitative research: Techniques and procedures for developing grounded theory* (2nd ed.). Thousand Oaks, CA: Sage.

Waller, M. (2002). *My baby's father: Unmarried parents and paternal responsibility*. Ithaca, NY: Cornell University Press.

Waller, M. & McLanahan, S. (2005). "His" and "her" marriage expectations: Determinants and consequences. *Journal of Marriage and Family, 67*, 53–67.

4

Life After PRWORA

The Involvement of African American Fathers With Welfare-Reliant Children and the Child Support Enforcement System

DAVID J. PATE

Since the 1960s, fathers for children on welfare have been described in various ways. They have been described as "absent" and more recently as "deadbeat dads" for not contributing to the family financially; this newest term recognizes that some of these fathers do not have the financial ability to take care of their children. With welfare reform in 1996, the pursuit of such "deadbeat" dads was made part of the law, with enhanced child support laws and incentives under the Personal Responsibility and Work Opportunity Reconciliation Act (PRWORA). The purpose of this chapter is to examine the effect of these changes in welfare on the role of low-income fathers and their welfare-reliant children. This is accomplished using qualitative data collected from research conducted on low-income fathers of children on welfare in the Wisconsin Child Support Demonstration Evaluation, a rigorous assessment of a state child support program.

This chapter examines how the low-income fathers affected by PRWORA met the basic needs of their children during the early years of welfare reform, which created work requirements for mothers and eliminated the entitlement to cash assistance. In particular, I share testimony from three fathers who discuss their roles as breadwinners, caregivers, and co-parents.[1] I begin with a brief explanation of the welfare reform of 1996 and how it affected the role of fathers with children on welfare.

Welfare Reform of 1996

Since the passage of PRWORA in 1996, policy makers, academics, and philanthropic foundations have been actively engaging in discussions on the role of
divorced or unmarried low-income fathers in the lives of their children. Several
bills on the subject have been introduced in the House of Representatives and the
Senate.[2] Discussions have focused on the emotional and financial role of these
fathers in their children's lives, and much attention has been given to encouraging
marriage. This concern has been based on the presumption that noncustodial
fathers have not been involved in their children's lives. Yet research on low-income
noncustodial fathers over the last 6 years has challenged this assumption, showing
that they are indeed involved with their children. Therefore, basing policy on
the presumption that they are not involved is problematic.[3] Qualitative research
(Edin, Lein, Nelson, & Clampet-Lundquist, 2001; Johnson, Levine, & Doolittle,
1999; Sorensen & Zibman, 2001; Waller & Plotnick, 2001) has shown that many of
these fathers make "informal" child support payments in addition to paying into
the formal child support system. Many live with the mothers of their children,
provide financial support in excess of the monthly child support order, and have
physical and legal custody of their children. Many also face limited employment
opportunities (Edin et al., 2000; Johnson et al., 1999; Sorensen & Zibman, 2001;
Waller & Plotnick, 2001). My own study was based on 2 years of interviews with
low-income noncustodial fathers, examining in detail their involvement in their
children's lives and in the child support system (Pate, 2002).

The research presented here was part of an evaluation of the child support
component of Wisconsin's welfare reform, conducted by the Institute for Research
on Poverty (IRP).[4] This chapter presents findings of an ethnographic study of
African American fathers in Milwaukee, Wisconsin, whose children were receiving
Temporary Assistance for Needy Families (TANF) benefits.[5] The aim is to add to
the limited research concerning the involvement of these fathers with their children
and their children's mothers and to inform policy makers about the extent of the
fathers' knowledge of the current changes in welfare and child support policy. This
chapter presents a picture of three African American fathers as they manage their
day-to-day existence in the context of a new welfare policy.

A major weakness in the U.S. child support system was has been the failure to
establish paternity for children born to unmarried parents. State paternity establishment rates in the late 1980s ranged from a high of 67% in Michigan to a low of
14% in Louisiana and 20% in New York. At that time, more than two-thirds of
nonmarital children of unmarried parents in the United States had no legally recognized father (Dowd, 2000). The legal system regards it as necessary to establish
paternity so that the child has legal access to a father for emotional, physical,
and—more important—financial support.

Moreover, for children on welfare, child support may have very little impact
on economic resources, depending on the state in which the child resides. Most
states retain child support payments to offset the state's financial outlay on cash

welfare. Wisconsin, at the time of this research, provided a full pass-through of current support based on a waiver from federal distribution law.[6]

Since 1980, researchers have sought to identify the effects of increased paternal involvement on children. In most of these studies, researchers have compared the status of children in "traditional" families with that of children whose fathers share in or take primary responsibility for child care (Lamb, 1997). Other researchers have examined the correlates of varying paternal engagement. However, the model of "father as breadwinner" role predominates in most segments of society today (Lamb, 2004).

Historical View of Fatherhood

The social construction of fatherhood has progressed through four phases over during the last two centuries of American social history: *(1)* from colonial times to the period of industrialization, the "moral overseer"; *(2)* during the period of industrialization, the "breadwinner," which remains the most important and defining characteristic of fatherhood, the criterion by which "good fathers" are defined; *(3)* the "sex-role model" from 1930 to the 1940s, brought on by concern with father absence during the Depression and World War II; and *(4)* and the new "nurturant" father in the mid-1970s, encouraged by the feminist movement (Demos, 1986; Pleck, 1997).

Kost (2000) argues that current concerns about fatherlessness and "deadbeat dads" in the social and economic arenas reduce the duties and responsibilities of a father to a one-dimensional identity: the role of breadwinner. The recognition by social scientists of the importance of a father's emotional involvement with his child(ren) is a recent phenomenon. However, society continues to maintain the breadwinner role as the primary role for "successful" fathering in America. For low-income African American fathers, the effects of slavery and institutional racism continue to be a barrier to successful fathering as defined in the United States.

Two ethnographic publications, *Tally's Corner* (1967) and *All Our Kin* (1974), were the first to examine the issues confronted by low-income Black fathers in their day-to-day existence. The author of *Tally's Corner*, Elliot Liebow, was the first to document the myriad barriers confronted by Black men in the urban ghetto. One chapter in particular focuses on the barriers to acknowledging parentage of one's child without the intervention of the legal system (Liebow, 1976, chap. 3). Liebow emphasizes the absence of the father in the father–child relationship, and he cites such other barriers as the father's failure to provide for his family and the quality of the mother–father relationship.

In *All Our Kin*, Carol Stack chronicles the complex nature of the fathering role, the community, and kinship relationships. She notes that the more a father and his kin assist a mother and the child, the more he validates his parental rights (Stack, 1974, pp. 50–57). Both of these insightful books provide information on the patterns that men develop within their communities that work to maintain a relationship with their child(ren).

The majority of the literature on Black fatherhood in low-income communities has characterized it as nonexistent, describing Black fathers as sexual predators, as uninvolved persons, and as "absentee fathers"(Roberts, 1999). Some conservative scholars have used this as a rationale for welfare reform and marriage promotion (Horn & Bush, 1997; Murray, 1994). However, several new authors have documented findings that contradict these stereotypical viewpoints (Johnson et al., 1999; Pate, 2002; Waller & Plotnick, 2001).

Other Qualitative Research Examining the Role of Noncustodial Fathers

In an article on low-income families and child support policy, Waller and Plotnick (2001) provide a summary of seven qualitative studies, four of which interviewed only fathers and are therefore similar to this study.[7] The sample sizes in these studies ranged from 16 to 47, and participants were primarily African American, followed by non-Latino Whites. Two studies gathered information by in-depth interviews, focus groups, and observations; the other two used only focus groups to collect their data. The majority of the studies lasted 2 years and were held in large cities across the United States. Two of them included only unwed fathers with child support orders and children receiving Aid to Families with Dependent Children (AFDC). None of the samples were randomly selected.

Three recent projects have utilized used qualitative methods as a part of their larger longitudinal examination of welfare reform and child well-being, with a special focus on the involvement of fathers: a 4-year study, Welfare Reform and Children: A Three-City Study; a 5-year project in 20 U.S. cities, the Fragile Families and Child Wellbeing Study; and the Urban Change Project, in four of the nation's largest counties, sponsored by the Manpower Demonstration Research Corporation.[8] In all of these studies most of the fathers are African American, followed by Latinos. The primary methods of data collection were focus groups and intensive, semistructured, face-to-face interviews. The picture that emerges from this research is that fathers have very low incomes, the majority being in poverty or just above the poverty line. In most of the studies, fathers expressed dissatisfaction that assigned child support payments (that is, payments required to be assigned to the state by the mother who receives cash assistance) did not actually go to the children.

Three scholars, Dorothy Roberts, Lynn Haney, and Miranda March, discuss the role that welfare plays in the validation of parenthood for men (and women). The new welfare policies penalize poor Black women for failing to marry the father of their child, which some policy makers regard as worsening their families' welfare. According to these scholars, in the African American community "out of wedlock" does not always mean "without a father." Roberts (1999) argues that a multiplicity of family forms, including families headed by single mothers, have successfully raised Black children under harsh social circumstances. Haney and March (2003) discuss the politics that underlay the welfare reform of 1996, deconstructing policy makers' views on what constitutes fatherhood. Their opinions suggest that PRWORA advanced powerful conceptions of fatherhood with the terms "paternal form" and "paternal function." These terms were reached through discourse analysis of fatherhood legislation and interviews with a subsample of the longest-running study of disadvantaged families, the Baltimore Parenthood Study.[9] Paternal form is defined as a biological, institutional, and financial relationship with a child, while paternal function is defined as participation in paternal activities. Paternal function, giving a positive image of fatherhood, is defined as fulfilling paternal responsibilities.

History of Child Support Legislation

In an effort to increase the financial contribution of noncustodial fathers, new policies beginning in the mid-1970s were established to collect child support from noncustodial fathers. Child support laws have gone through three major revisions: first in 1984, then in the Family Support Act of 1988, and most recently in the PRWORA of 1996.[10] Each time the laws were reviewed, the penalties were harsher for those who were not paying child support.

PRWORA allowed state child support offices to institute more stringent practices to increase the number of men for whom paternity has been established and from whom child support is due. A major weakness in the U.S. child support system has been the failure to establish paternity for children born to unmarried parents. State paternity establishment rates in the late 1980s ranged from a high of 67% in Michigan to a low of 14% in Louisiana and 20% in New York. At that time, more than two-thirds of children of unmarried parents in the United States had no legally recognized father (Dowd, 2000). The legal system regards it as necessary to establish paternity so that the child has legal access to a father for emotional, physical, and financial support.

PRWORA also promoted voluntary paternity acknowledgment. These policy changes have been associated with an increased number of paternities established, possibly because of easier process and more available options to voluntarily acknowledgement paternity, as well as policies, default judgments against noncustodial parents, and incentive payments to the states. Moreover, for children on welfare, child support may have very little impact on economic resources, depending on the state in which the child resides. As noted, most states retain child support payments to offset the state's financial outlay on cash welfare. Wisconsin, at the time of this research, provided a full pass-through to the mother of current support based on a waiver from federal distribution law.[11] With a "pass-through," states allow families entitled to child support to retain all of the amount paid on their behalf rather than, as most states do, keeping a portion of the father's child support payment to offset the costs of welfare. Wisconsin's experiment with pass-ing-through all child support to the resident parent was unique among the states in 1996.

Through these efforts the amount of child support paid has increased, but large numbers of families still do not receive any child support. This has encour-aged state and federal policy makers to support punitive measures directed at "deadbeat dads," including basing orders on imputed income (assuming that a father can earn at a certain level, regardless of his actual earnings) and revoking driver's licenses and other professional licenses for those delinquent in their payments.[12]

However, research on the population of fathers who do not pay child support suggests that nonpayers are a very diverse group and that some people lack the capability to meet the court order for child support.[13] In an attempt to address the employment barriers that some noncustodial fathers face, a few modest employ-ment and training efforts have been undertaken in Wisconsin and elsewhere.[14]

Qualitative research into the complex lives of noncustodial fathers (Edin et al., 2001; Johnson et al., 1999; Sorensen & Zibman, 2001; Waller & Plotnick, 2001) has shown that many of these fathers are involved with their children and make "informal" child support payments as well as paying into the formal child support system. Many live with the mothers of their children, provide financial support in excess of the monthly child support order, have physical and legal custody of their children, and face limited employment opportunities. At the same time, other analysts and practitioners no longer believe that fathers fill play a unidimensional role in their families; they find instead a number of significant roles and a variety of reasons for paternal involvement. Most researchers have implicitly assumed that variations in the definition of fatherhood are primarily the product of subcultural and cultural factors, rather than of individual characteristics. As discussed below, most men set goals that reflect their recollection of their own childhood, choosing either to compensate for their fathers' deficiencies or to emulate them. Parental involvement can be determined by personal motivation (Lamb, 1997), skills (Levine & Pitt, 1995), self-confidence in the role of parent, and support, especially support within the family from the mother (Pleck, 2004).

Entry into the child support system occurs when a petition requesting child support is filed by the custodial parent, or the state on behalf of the custodial parent, to obtain income support for the child. The noncustodial father participates in the child support system based on the status of his children in two categories: (1) IV-D[15] or non-IV-D and (2) TANF or non-TANF. In the IV-D category, the noncustodial father has a child whose custodial family has sought child support enforcement services and/or has received TANF services (cash assistance). In the TANF category, the custodial family is receiving TANF (cash assistance) on behalf of the child and is therefore required by law to cooperate with the child support enforcement system and to assign its right to child support to the state. In TANF cases, the state seeks reimbursement from the noncustodial father. Figure 4.1 adds marital versus nonmarital status, because so many children affected by the child support enforce-ment system tend to be in the nonmarital category.

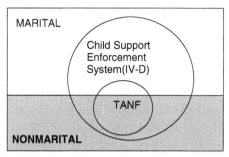

Figure 4.1   Participation in the child support system by category.

This chapter focuses on children receiving IV-D services, represented by the larger circle in Figure 4.1. A large minority of children receiving IV-D services are receiving TANF services and are the result of a nonmarital birth.

The Wisconsin Research

The research discussed here was supported by the Institute for Research for Poverty (IRP), which was awarded a contract grant by the state of Wisconsin to evaluate the child support component of the Wisconsin Works (W-2) program. The research plan of this child support demonstration evaluation (see note 3) included an experimental evaluation, a survey of a sample of mothers and fathers, and an ethnographic component.

The ethnographic component of the Wisconsin study gathered information to complement the research efforts of the overall project. It was designed to provide a deeper understanding of and perspective on the life experiences of noncustodial fathers in the context of social welfare generally, and specifically in light of welfare reform implemented through PRWORA, including changes in child support policies and distribution rules. An ethnographic study can examine and document the complexities of lives in a way that cannot be done by gathering information from survey and administrative records alone (Johnson et al., 1999).

The topics of the ethnographic analysis included noncustodial fathers' understanding of the child support system and of welfare reform, their capacities for employment, and their conception of their role and responsibilities. Two years of fieldwork collected data through face-to-face interviews with African American noncustodial fathers whose children were recipients of W-2 (cash assistance) payments.

This ethnographic research is one of the few qualitative studies to examine the effect of welfare reform on the behavior of fathers. The following three scenarios portray fathers with children on welfare at various stages in their adult development. The first scenario concerns a father in the role of breadwinner, the second in the role of caregiver, and the third in the role of co-parent. These three men were part of the larger study of 36 men with children on welfare in Milwaukee, Wisconsin.

The information was collected in 1999 and 2000. All three were employed, all had had experience with the welfare and child support enforcement systems, all were African American, and all had experienced parenting before the age of 21.

Jimmy

Jimmy is a 23-year-old father of a daughter aged 3 years (see Fig. 4.2). He has a high school diploma and was a prominent school athlete. He lives with his biological mother, and his daughter is at his home 5 to 6 days a week. Jimmy shares in picking up and dropping off his daughter at her child-care center. The mother of the child works the first shift at her job, requiring her to leave for work before the center opens. Jimmy's family (his mother, father, and sister) share in the caregiving for his child. He works as a third-shift security guard at a local company, earning an hourly wage of $9.00. Jimmy's primary child support responsibility has been to pay the lying-in fee (the birthing costs covered by Medicaid). The mother's job does not provide health benefits. Jimmy had just received an active child support order at the time of the interviews. Although he is the primary caregiver for his child at least 5 days a week and provides support informally for his child, his child support order amounted to $97.50 every 2 weeks.

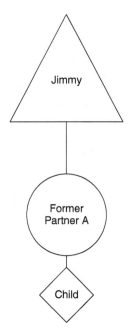

Notes:
———— Indicates the biological relationship of the parents with their children.

Figure 4.2   Jimmy and his child.

R. J.

R. J. is a 32-year-old father of 6 children and is a stepparent to one child of his current girlfriend (see Fig. 4.3). He was raised by his mother and has six siblings: five sisters and one brother. He is currently living with his fiancée of 4 years in a rental house. His share of the rent is $375 a month. She is a student at a local university. R. J. has fathered six children by five women. One woman was the mother of two of these children. At the time of the interview, R. J.'s children ranged in age from 4 to 14 years. He had his first child at the age of 18. He was involved in drug trafficking from the ages of 14 to 22. At the time of the interview, he was self-employed as a barber. He attended technical college for 2 years to obtain a cosmetology degree. His wages fluctuate due to his dependence on clients for weekly work. Four of the mothers of his children have received welfare assistance in the past; therefore, he has four separate child support orders. As a result of his inability to consistently pay the amount stipulated in his child support orders, R. J. was arrested for nonpayment of support and imprisoned. He was later released and charged with four counts of a Class E felony for nonpayment. He was on probation for 5 years. His child support order for all four children amounts to approximately $700 a month.

Robert

Robert Johnson is a 43-year-old father of three children (see Fig. 4.4). He lives with his wife of 10 years, Carol, in Section 8 housing illegally.[16] The current rent is $375

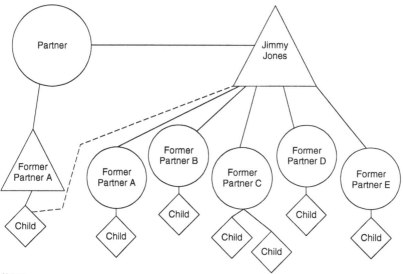

Notes:
– – – Indicates the nonbiological relationship of Joe'D with the children in the household.
——— Indicates the biological relationship of the parents with their children.

Figure 4.3   R. J. and his children.

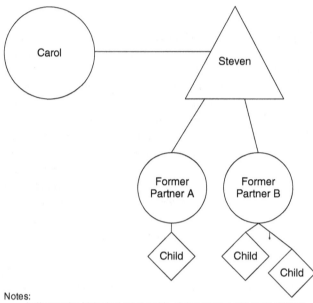

Notes:
——— Indicates the biological relationship of the parents with their children.

Figure 4.4   Steven and his children.

per month. His three children have two different mothers, and they are ages 13, 21, and 27 years. Robert had his first child at the age of 18, his second at age 21, and his third at age 30. He was married to the mother of his 27-year-old daughter for 10 years. Both of the mothers of his children have been long-term welfare users; therefore, he has a long history with the child support and welfare systems. His current child support debt amounts to a total of $63,064. His check is garnished biweekly. He currently works as in-home health-care person on a part-time basis, and he works "off the books" as a tenant manager. Robert's hourly wage at his legitimate place of employment is $7.00 per hour. His off-the-books job provides him with a weekly income of $100.00. His wife had severe asthma problems at the time of our second intensive interview and died a few days afterward. He was forced to leave his home of 10 years because he was living there illegally, and he moved into a shelter for men. Robert's monthly child support order was $50.00.

In the following sections, I discuss the effects of welfare reform on the lives of these three men with regard to their involvement with their children as breadwinners, caregivers, and co-parents.

THE BREADWINNER ROLE   The role of breadwinner for these fathers took the form of maintaining their child support in the formal and informal system.[17] Robert Johnson maintains that his responsibility and that of other fathers is to pay child support in the new welfare system. Robert has been paying child support for

20 years. He had paid off his child support arrears for his first child, but the state, he says, sought child support for his other children as well. However, this time he seems pleased with the results. His total amount of child support arrearages is $63,063.61. He owes $37,673 in past AFDC arrearages, $19,048 interest on the past arrearages (at the rate of 17% annually), $4117 in birth cost fees, and $349 in administrative costs, all of which will reimburse the state for the payment of cash welfare benefits to the mother from the previous welfare system. The remaining amount of $906 is arrearages owed and $843 in interest (at the rate of 12%) from the current welfare system. All arrearages except the part owed to the custodial parent could be forgiven by the state of Wisconsin. Many states have forgiveness program and policies, but Wisconsin does not have a universal forgiveness program. His check is garnished biweekly. I asked him about the father's role in the new welfare system, and he responded as follows:

> *How long have you owed child support? How long have you been paying it?*
> Almost about 20 years.
>
> *So, your first daughter is 27. So you didn't have to pay child support on her [anymore].*
> No.
>
> *So the father's obligation in your opinion is to pay child support. Anything else?*
> Yeah, and to take time out with their kids.
>
> *Is the mother of your youngest child receiving child support?*
> Recently, my kid's mother is getting child support checks now. I called her about a month [ago], she told my daughter to tell Daddy "thank you." I said, "Thank you for what?" She said, "I'm getting child support checks now." Now I'm seeing where my money is going.
>
> *She's getting all of the money that's coming out of your check?*
> Yeah, I was sad about that. I used to couldn't see what was taking my money. She wasn't getting no checks. Now she gets them.
>
> *Does that make a difference in the way she talks to you?*
> Oh yeah! Lots of difference, because she's getting some money now. She's getting child support now. I mean the time I've been paying child support, I've never heard none of the mothers getting any money.

The issue of breadwinner is not as clear-cut for Jimmy. He sees his informal and formal contributions as important to the development of his child. Jimmy has held a job as security guard for several years, but neither he nor the mother of his child has health insurance. They therefore took advantage of the Medicaid program to cover the birth costs of their child. He was surprised to learn that he was being ordered by the state to repay these birth costs.[18]

I paid the hospital fee. . . . .
Oh, you did.

I paid that off. They take that out of my check. . . . .
Okay.

I paid that back . . . $1130. I paid that back like in a year and a half time, there. I forgot how much they were actually taking out of my check. . . . . But I paid that back. You know what I'm saying, I thought that was the only thing I was going to have to pay.
Okay. . . .

Then a year later, . . . [a letter] sent to my house—[said] you gotta pay child support for your daughter. All these payments were coming, I was like I've never been issued to pay child support or anything like that. So we ended up going to court, then the city of Milwaukee . . . I don't know who it was—it was [from], like from the state or something, I forgot what it was, but she said that I recommend you to pay this and that and this and that and—I just didn't understand it. Like [I said], why do I got to pay all this money for my daughter even though she [the mother] caught some assistance for a minute, and I have her [the daughter] every single day. It just didn't make no sense to me, like I was getting, you know what I'm saying—basically screwed in the game. That's how I felt, honestly.

Eventually, Jimmy paid off the birth cost fees, but he was ordered to make biweekly child support payments. He explains:

This guy [lawyer] from the state [said] when I was on the stand, I got to pay all that money [cash assistance] back. See, and it doesn't . . . it doesn't go to the state, it goes to my daughter's mother. I'm giving her money? — Why [am] I [giving] her money and I have my daughter [every day]? She ought to . . . be giving me money, to be honest, but you know what I'm saying, I just think I'm getting [screwed] in the game big time.

In general, these fathers wanted to be seen as responsible parents making their child support payments. They viewed the child support payments as their responsibility, but it left them feeling powerless because their informal child support was not recognized by the courts. In fact, these men were consistent child support payers, either because their employers garnished their child support obligation through income withholding or because they voluntarily paid the monthly amount with a money order.[19] One thing that was common among all of them was the expressed desire for the state to recognize their informal contributions to their children. The next section discusses the overlapping issues of financial contributions and caregiving by these fathers.

THE CAREGIVERING ROLE   These men did not have to overcome significant hurdles to become involved in the lives of their children. They had considerable support from the mothers of their children and from family members in their daily existence. In this group of fathers, family was often their main source of support. In general, the men did have the necessary means to manage their lives and maintain themselves, but the struggle to do so was challenged by their child support order.

R. J. discusses his arrangement with the mother of one of his children and the way that they have worked out their own arrangement of informal "joint custody":

> I get them every summer. Me and their mother have joint custody. We just rotate them from down South to Milwaukee for the summer months.
> *Do you have them through the court system or do you have some papers?*
>
> I don't have no papers. This is just between me and her, because I'm not going to go through the system trying to get joint custody and all this. You got to do what you got to do as far as being a dad. As far as I'm concerned, we cool, she got a good job, her husband got a good job. I like her husband. He likes me. And we got an understanding. So, that is the key thing.
> *Do you have any permanent relationship now where you are involved with somebody else's kid?*
>
> Yeah, I'm involved with somebody else's kid. I've been raising my fiancée's son since . . . I been dating this young lady for 4 years. She about to graduate from college Sunday. She graduates from Marquette and I'm proud of her. Her baby's daddy ain't been doing nothing he's supposed to do, so I guess I'm his daddy. So, everybody asking, you got another son? Yeah, I got another son. I'm helping him, I'm doing whatever I can.[20]

Many of the men equated their manhood with their involvement in their children's lives, and they saw it as their responsibility to be involved. A common theme heard from these fathers was that it was important to remain civil with the mother for the sake of the children.

R. J.'s discussion of the "joint custody" agreement that they have worked out was well intended but was not legally recognized. This is a common way that low-income families adapt to the system, by going through what I term "legislation outside of the system." These families feel disenfranchised in the legal system but have a desire to follow its rules. The rules, however, are determined by their culture and environment. Other members of the group were conducting their daily lives as if they had legal sanction to operate in a particular way. In many cases the paternal grandparents were as supportive as their own resources would allow in facilitating ongoing contact with their grandchildren. The mothers of the noncustodial fathers encouraged and assisted with providing birthday gifts, Christmas gifts, and sometimes housing for their sons' child(ren).

Jimmy also had a working relationship with the mother of his child despite the current involvement of the state.

How are you able to negotiate your relationship with the mother of your child?

That, that's what everyone is amazed by because . . . for me not to have my daugh-ter staying with me, is basically like she is staying with me because she is with me [all the time]. . . . I'd say 80% of the day—cause she don't go home until nine o'clock. When she go home, she's in bed, then the next morning she go to day care at nine o'clock until two and she's right [here] . . . she spen[d]s more time with me than her mother, you know what I'm saying, to be honest, but . . . . [during] the summer months . . . I only have my daughter like four days a week now. But sometimes, five [or] six days. . . . It all depends on how the work week falls [for her mother] . . . but for right now, you know, it's cool.

R. J. discusses the delicate balance between the requirements of paying formal child support (formal support) and continuing to provide informal support. As noted above, R. J. was charged with four counts of a Class E felony for nonpayment of child support.[21] He served some time in prison for that offense and is on 5 year's' probation. He discusses the intersection of his involvement with the child support enforcement system and his involvement with his children. He begins by explain-ing that he was unaware that he was responsible for paying back the state and taking care of his children because they received public assistance.

Far as child support. . . . I always have took care of my kids, but I never knew that I have to take care of them in the system. You know, I thought W-2 was just a program to help mothers out, but come to find out the fathers really got to pay it back. You know, so far as W-2 now, like I talked to all my baby mothers now [and if there is some way] that I can get them out the system and make a better life for my kids, then I [will].

R. J. discusses his length of involvement with the child support enforcement system:

I been in the system now for 16 years. They caught up with me approximately 2 years ago and ever since the 2 years ago, I been taking care of everything I need to take care of. So far, I'm trying to do the best that I can with the type of income I have. With the amount of kids that I have.
Now, when you talk about your child support obligations, what kind of obligations have you had for the past 2 years? How do they approach you? How did you get hooked up into it?

I [was picked up] for a felony warrant . . . for child support. . . . They turn me into a felon because I didn't take care of it [the payment] through the [formal] system. They wanted me to pay back the mother of my child $5000 and instead of [listen-ing to her at court] they did not listen to her at all. She was telling the world, he . . . take[s] care of it [financial responsibilities] through the system but he was taking care of his daughter. They didn't hear me out. They didn't say anything to me.
So the mother intervened on your behalf?

The mother was even there on my behalf, but they wouldn't even listen to her testimony. They said, far as they concerned, I'm a felon . . . [They said] I'm a dead-beat dad. A deadbeat dad is when a dad don't take care of they child, and I take care of my kids as far as clothes, schooling, medical, food on the table, clothes on they back, shoes on they feet. I mean, I even take time out to do my girls' hair, so, I mean, most fathers don't do that much.

What do you think the father's obligation is in this new welfare system?

I think the father's' obligation should [be] to keep these mothers up off the system, period, and let us be a father and take care of our kids. . . .

R. J. expressed a frustration that was shared by Jimmy. They want to be able to take care of their children without the involvement of the state. Both were caring for taking of their children through the child support system both informally and formally, yet their informal contributions were not recognized.

All of these fathers provided what they perceived to be adequate emotional support for their children. They discussed at length the many things they did to be involved in the emotional life of their children. Many played the traditional role of disciplinarian, but they did not rely on corporal punishment. Instead, they were actively involved in discussing problems with their children and usually reverted to corporal punishment as a last resort. They often referred to their children as their "blood" or "a piece" of them, whom they had to look after the best that they could.

THE CO-PARENT ROLE   All three of these fathers were co-parenting their children to varying degrees. They had a workable relationship with the mothers of their children, as was most evident in Jimmy's daily routine of child care and R. J.'s informal "joint custody" role with his son from Mississippi. With the new welfare reform, the men's responsibilities to their children did not change. They still viewed it as their duty to be involved in the daily life of their children.

Robert talks about his relationship with the mother of his youngest child:

How would you describe the relationship with the mother of your child, your son?
It's good.

Do you guys talk often?
Quite often she calls.

Do you and the mother talk about things that the kid needs?
Yeah, we talk about school, when he gets in trouble. [She] calls me to come down there and beat his butt. (*laughs*) [or to] discipline him.

Does he call you Dad? How is he in terms of you being his father?
Yeah, he respects me more than his mother.

How often do you see your son?
Quite often.

Would that mean every week?
Twice a week.
He talks about his relationships with the mothers of his children.

[So] between all five mothers of your [children], it [appears] that . . . you have [a]
working relationship . . . Do you have the privilege to see your kids when[ever] you
want?
I could go pick up my kids when [ever] I want to. I call them [mothers] and say,
[Can I] get my kids? . . . as [long] as it is [within] reasonable hours. I go to all kind
of school events . . . family reunions, every day.

Conclusion

This chapter has explored the effect of changes in welfare on the role of African
American low-income, welfare-reliant fathers and their children, using qualitative
data collected from research in the Wisconsin Child Support Demonstration
Evaluation. This chapter examined in particular the lives of three fathers and how
they met the basic needs of their children during the early years after welfare
reform.

Each of the fathers described in this chapter is representative of the larger
sample of 36 fathers in this study. All of these fathers faced unique challenges
to providing monetary and nonmonetary contributions to their children on a
day-to-day basis. The challenges could be structural or personal. More often,
these challenges were the result of policies that these men were often not able
to negotiate. The men in this study saw the child support enforcement system
as a main source of frustration and pain for them. This was often due to their
inability to obtain legal representation and have an understanding of the laws and
policies of the child support system. For example, two of Robert's children are
27 and 21, and he has two grandchildren who would benefit from his financial
support; however, he continues to pay past due arrears for child support for his
adult children. He is living on a fixed income due to a disability that he obtained
while working.

The new welfare legislation brought with it an increased number of enforcement tools for the collection of child support, along with tougher sanctions and
immediate wage garnishment. The roles of breadwinner, caregiver, and co-parent
for these men were further minimized due to the additional pressure for low-
income fathers with limited resources. The new welfare policy did not change much
for these fathers in terms of social services, but the new tools of child support
enforcement reduced their control over their own lives.

NOTES

1. The roles of breadwinner, caregiver, and co-parent were chosen for the following reasons: The role of breadwinner is a traditional role ascribed to men/fathers in the United States; therefore, it was important to discuss how were these men upholding the "traditional" responsible role of a breadwinner. Furthermore, it was important to discuss the challenges to ascertaining this role as a father. The roles of caregiver and co-parent were selected because they are "nontraditional" roles of African American fathers, and I wanted to explore further the challenges that accompany these roles.

2. Between May and December 2002, the Senate and the House of Representatives introduced fatherhood legislation. The U.S. House of Representatives bill passed on May 16, 2002. *The Personal Responsibility, Work, and Family Promotion Act of 2002*, HR 4737, contains fatherhood legislation entitled "Promotion and Support of Responsible Fatherhood and Healthy Marriage Act of 2002." It is proposed as Title IV-C of the Social Security Act and is sponsored by Representatives Wally Herger (R-CA), Buck McKeon (R-CA), and Benjamin Cardin (D-MD). The Senate bill *Work, Opportunity, and Responsibility for KIDS (WORK) Act of 2002* was approved by the Senate Finance Committee on June 26, 2002. The bill contains fatherhood legislation titled "Noncustodial Parent Employment Grant Program." It is proposed as Title IV-D, section 469C. The most recent fatherhood legislation was submitted by Senators Evan Byah (D-IN) and Barack Obama (D-IL) on June 29, 2006. The Responsible Fatherhood and Healthy Families Act of 2006 (S.3607) removes some of the government penalties on married families and offers support for fathers already trying to do the right thing, while also cracking down on men trying to avoid their parental responsibilities.

3. A city report from the Fragile Families and Child Wellbeing Study, "Baseline City Report," Milwaukee, Wisconsin (October 2001), was based on research conducted in Milwaukee. One of the findings of this research was the proportion of fathers living with their children. The analysis suggests that 43% of the unmarried parents are cohabiting.

4. Under AFDC, states were required to pass through to the family the first $50 per month of child support collected and to disregard this amount in calculating AFDC benefits. Under TANF, states could set their own policies for passing through and disregarding any child support paid on behalf of children on cash assistance and were required only to withhold the federal share of child support collected. Under the new rules, most states chose to pass no money collected to the resident parent. In 1997, Wisconsin received a waiver from federal rules allowing it to pass through the entire amount of current child support collected to the custodial parent and to disregard all child support in calculating TANF cash payments. One requirement of the waiver was to conduct an evaluation of this policy change, the Child Support Demonstration Evaluation (CSDE). A key component of the CSDE was a random-assignment experimental evaluation: although most parents in the state received the full amount of current child support paid on their behalf (the experimental group), a randomly selected group of parents (the control group) received only a portion of what is paid. (See Meyer & Cancian, 2001, Vol. 1.)

5. TANF replaced the former welfare entitlement program, AFDC. Although each state has substantial flexibility in designing its own program, specific work requirements and time limits are mandated.

6. By April 2002, 27 states had opted not to finance a pass-through of child support collected to welfare-reliant families, 5 states had complicated pass-through and disregard policies, while 17 states provided a $50 pass-through to welfare families. Wisconsin provides a full pass-through and disregard of current child support collected. More information is available at http://www.clasp.org.

   Note, however, that even in Wisconsin, families in the control group of the CSDE did not receive all support paid on their behalf. Even in the full pass-through group, amounts paid in excess of the current amount due could accrue to the state rather than the family. As of July 1, 2002, all Wisconsin families were eligible for the full pass-through and disregard of current child support.

7. The four studies are the Young Unwed Fathers Pilot Project, designed by Public/Private Ventures (Achatz & McCullum, 1994); the Parents' Fair Share Demonstration, designed by Manpower Demonstration Research Corporation (Johnson et al., 1999); the Absent Parent Support Program of Kent County, Michigan (Sherwood, 1992); and a study conducted by Mercer Sullivan in New York City, specifically in Harlem, Brownsville, and Queens (Sullivan, 1993).

8. For more information on these studies, go to Welfare, Children, and Families: A Three City Study (http://www.jhu.edu/~welfare/); The Fragile Families and Child Wellbeing Study (http://crcw.princeton.edu/ff.asp); and The Urban Change Project (http://www.mdrc.org/Reports2001/UCImpactDesign/UCImpactDesign.htm).

9. See Furstenberg, Brooks-Gunn, and Morgan (1987).

10. Federal child support legislation has been amended several times since 1975 to broaden its scope and to increase collections. Despite the enhancement of services to include nonwelfare child support payments, the focus of the program remained on welfare collections (Kelly, 1995). Moreover, under the provisions of the Child Support Performance and Incentive Act of 1998 (HR 3130), which were phased in beginning October 1, 1999, a state's annual incentive payment is based on its paternity establishment, support order, current and arrearage collections, and cost-effectiveness performance levels (Fishman, Dybal, & Tapogna, 2000). The most recent changes to the child support enforcement system occurred with the passing of welfare reauthorization or the Federal Deficit Reduction Act of 2005 (S.1932) on February 8, 2006.

11. By April 2002, 27 states had opted not to finance a pass-through of child support collected to welfare-reliant families, 5 states had complicated pass-through and disregard policies, while 17 states provided a $50 pass-through to welfare families. Wisconsin provides a full pass-through and disregard of current child support collected. More information is available at http://www.clasp.org.

   Note, however, that even in Wisconsin, families in the control group of the CSDE did not receive all support paid on their behalf. Even in the full pass-through group, amounts paid in excess of the current amount due could accrue to the state rather than the family. As of July 1, 2002, all Wisconsin families were eligible for the full pass-through and disregard of current child support.

12. The term "deadbeat dads" generally refers to noncustodial fathers who do not pay child support yet can afford to pay the amount assigned by the court.

13. Mincy and Sorensen (1998) showed in their research that a lack of income is a significant barrier to child support payments for a substantial minority of young noncustodial fathers. Heightened efforts to collect from nonpaying fathers, if appropriately targeted, may only push more noncustodial fathers into poverty. See also Sorensen and Zibman (2000).

14. For more on the community-based programs available to noncustodial fathers, see the Department of Health & Human Services Fatherhood Initiative Web site, 2000 (http://fatherhood.hhs.gov/index.shtml). Another report features three Wisconsin programs: that of the Wisconsin Department of Corrections, of the Private Industry Council, and of the Institute for Responsible Fatherhood and Family Revitalization. All of these programs are based in Milwaukee, Wisconsin. See Martinson, Trutko, and Strong (2000).

15. IV-D refers to Title IV, Paragraph D, in the Social Security Act, under which the child support program was created (42 U.S.C. § 651, et al.).

16. He was not listed on the lease as a tenant because this would have increased their rent to an amount that they could not afford.

17. A custodial parent applying for TANF (cash assistance) must assign her past, present, and future right to receive child support from the noncustodial parent to the state. Therefore (with the exception of a few states), the noncustodial parent understands that any money paid through the formal system is subject to and will likely be retained by the state as reimbursement for cash assistance to the custodial parent.

18. In Wisconsin and other states, birth costs of children who receive Medicaid services are charged against noncustodial fathers by the state and collected by the child support agency. Many low-income noncustodial parents in this study and in Wisconsin owe this debt. Even if there is no active child support order (for example, if the parents are married or cohabiting), this debt is owed, and the family income is further depleted by its payment. According to Wisconsin's calendar year 2000 Office of Child Support Enforcement OCSE-34 report, $3,467,007 in birth costs was collected in Milwaukee. The federal government pays 15% of amounts collected for birth costs to the state child support agency.

    The 1996 federal welfare reform law (PRWORA) required that a Medical Child Support Working Group be formed. The working group was composed of advocates, policy makers, employer representatives (including payroll professionals), and sponsors and administrators of group health plans. The working group recommended that state child support enforcement agencies not pursue recoupment of birth-related costs in Medicaid cases. For a copy of the full report, see http://www.acf.dhhs.gov/programs/cse/rpt/medrpt/index.html. The constitutionality of charging lying-in fees solely to noncustodial fathers has been challenged in New York in three separate court cases: *Perry v. Dowling*, 905 F. Supp. 251; *In the Matter of Commissioner of Social Services of Franklin County v. Bernard B.*, (661 N.E.2d 131); and *In the Matter of Steuben County Department of Social Services v. Gregory E. Deats* (560 N.E.2d 760).

19. I defined "consistent" as *at least* nine monthly payments out of the year. Because job prospects can be fragile, I wanted to account for periods of unemployment.

20. See Haney and March (2003) for a discussion of "other fathers'" involvement with intimate partners' children.

21. The charges are based on Wisconsin's state failure to support law [Wis Stat Ann 948.22(2) and (3)].

    948.22(2) Any person who intentionally fails for 120 or more consecutive days to provide spousal, grandchild, or child support which the person knows or reasonably should know the person is legally obligated to provide is guilty of a Class E felony. A prosecutor may charge a person with multiple counts for a violation under this subsection if each count covers a period of at least 120 consecutive days and there is no overlap between periods.

984.22(3) Any person who intentionally fails for less than 120 consecutive days to provide spousal, grandchild, or child support which the person knows or reasonably should know the person is legally obligated to provide is guilty of a Class A misdemeanor.

REFERENCES

Demos, J. (1986). *Past, present, and personal:*
    The family and the life course in American history (pp. xx-xx). New York: Oxford University Press.

Dowd, N. E. (2000). *Redefining fatherhood.* New York: New York University Press.

Edin, K., L. Lein, T. Nelson, and S. Clampet-Lundquist. (2001). "Talking with Low-Income Fathers." Poverty Research News 4(2): 10–12. Chicago: Joint Center for Poverty Research.

Haney, L. & March, M. (2003). Married fathers and caring daddies: Welfare reform and the discursive politics of paternity. *Social Problems, 50*(4), 461–481.

Horn, W. & Bush, A. (1997). *Fathers, marriage, and welfare reform.* Indianapolis, IN: Hudson Institute.

Johnson, E., Levine, A., & Doolittle, F. C. (1999). *Fathers' fair share: Helping poor fathers manage child support and fatherhood.* New York: Russell Sage Foundation.

Kost, K. A. (2000). The function of fathers: What poor men say about fatherhood. *Families in Society: Journal of Contemporary Human Services, 82*(5), 499–507.

Lamb, M. E. (2004). Introduction. In M. E. Lamb (Ed.), *The role of the father in child development* (4th ed., pp. 1–27). New York: John Wiley.

Levine, J. & Pitt, E. (1995). *New expectations: community strategies for responsible fatherhood.* New York: Families Institute.

Liebow, E. (1967). *Tally's corner: A study of negro streetcorner men.* Boston: Little, Brown.

Murray, C. (1994). *Losing ground: American social policy* (10th anniversary ed.). New York: Basic Books.

Pate, D. (2002). An ethnographic inquiry into the life experiences of African American fathers with children on W-2. In D. R. Meyer & M. Cancian (Eds.), *W-2 child support demonstration evaluation, report on nonexperimental analyses, fathers of children in W-2 families, Vol. II., Report to the Department of Workforce Development* (pp. 29–118). Madison: Institute for Research on Poverty, University of Wisconsin–Madison.

Pleck, J. H. (2004). Paternal involvement: Levels, origins, and consequences. In M. Lamb (Ed.), *The role of the father in child development* (4th ed., pp. 227–270). New York: John Wiley.

Roberts, D. (1999). Welfare's ban on poor motherhood. In G. Mink (Ed.), *Whose welfare?* (pp. 152–170). Ithaca, NY: Cornell University Press.

Sorensen, E. & Zibman, C. (2001). *To what extent do children benefit from child support?* Washington, DC: Urban Institute. Available at http://www.urban.org.

Stack, C. (1974). *All our kin: Strategies for survival in a black community.* New York: Harper & Row.

Waller, M. R. & Plotnick, R. (2001). Effective child support policy for low-income families: Evidence from street-level research. *Journal of Policy Analysis and Management, 20,* 89–110.

5

Men Do Matter

The Socially Supportive Role of the African American "Uncle" in the Lives of Single-Female Headed Households and At-Risk African American Male Youth

JOSEPH B. RICHARDSON, JR.

My older brother Tommy comes and gets my sons all the time and he takes them out to the Pocono Mountains or wherever they really want to go with him. He lets them stay with him all the time just about every weekend. And my brother, Timothy, he just got released from prison. He's the one that stays here with me because he is on parole. He takes them out to the movies or dinner all the time. Timothy gets them whatever they want, but I have to tell him all the time: "Don't be giving them everything they want because when you're gone I ain't going to be giving it to them. You know?" (she laughs). But I'm really lucky I guess, that I got my three brothers to help me take care of my sons. I don't know what I would do without them.

—Rhonda Brown, age 40, mother of sample member Clyde, age 13)

This chapter examines the role of nonbiological fathers, specifically the African American "uncle" as a vital but often overlooked source of social support in the lives of African American male youth. Although there is a significant body of literature on the role of the African American grandmother as an almost "heroic" figure in poor, in many instances serving as the primary caregiver and surrogate mother for her grandchildren (Anderson, 1999; Burton, 1997; Pearson, Hunter, Ensminger, & Kellam, 1990), few studies have examined the socially supportive role of men in extended familial networks (i.e., grandfathers, uncles, cousins, and so on) (Jarrett, Roy, & Burton, 2002). Research on the African American grandmother suggests that in the absence of the biological father, many poor single-female headed households often rely on the additional social support and parenting provided by grandmothers (Burton, 1986, 1992, 1993, 1995; Pearson et al., 1990). Extensive data on the inner-city African American family suggest that this collective of women is often left with the task of raising young African American males alone without the assistance of biological fathers. However, the extensive research on the role of women in extended familial networks has left an unaddressed gap in the research on the African American family, specifically the role of men in extended familial networks as surrogate fathers and primary caregivers to single-female headed households. To date, there are no qualitative research studies that examine the role of nonbiological African American fathers within family networks, specifically, the role of the African American uncle as a primary source of social support and social capital within single-female headed households. Data from a recent qualitative research study on social capital in the lives of at-risk African American male youth reveal that single-female headed households often rely on their biological brothers and older male extended family members (i.e., grandfathers and cousins) to serve as father figures for their adolescent boys in the absence of biological fathers.

This chapter will explore the role of these men as fathers in poor inner-city African American families and their successful parenting practices and strategies in preventing delinquency and violent behavior as well as fostering successful adolescent development among at-risk male youth. While the literature on African American fatherhood and young African American males primarily examines the relationship between biological fathers and their sons, the vast majority of the research on African American fatherhood has relatively ignored the relationship between uncles and their nephews. This chapter will examine the relationships between men in extended familial networks (uncles), single-female headed households, and at-risk male youth. This analysis will highlight the significant functions of these relationships such as trustworthiness, social obligations/expectations, reciprocity, information channels, and the social norms that men within these relationships provide to single-female households and at-risk youth to foster prosocial youth behavior and successful adolescent male development. All of these factors are significant determinants of social capital.

This chapter uses data from a 4-year ethnographic adolescent life-course study of social capital and serious violence among a group of eight, early-adolescent African American males and their families living in Central Harlem, New York. These eight case studies were drawn from a larger ethnographic research study of adolescent violence in schools and communities conducted by the Vera Institute of Justice from 1995 to 2000. For the purposes of this discussion, three case studies will be used.

Contemporary Media and the African American Uncle

Ironically, pop culture and not sociological research appears to be the sociological harbinger on other forms of African American fatherhood. Contemporary media has given much more attention to identifying the vital role that uncles play in the African American family and in the lives of African American children. Over the course of the past two decades, television and film have been at the forefront of sociological research on the African American uncle, shedding much needed light on the role of the African American uncle as a primary caregiver and surrogate father figure in African American families. Popular sitcoms and films with predominately African American casts such as *The Fresh Prince of Bel-Air* (1990–1996), *The Bernie Mac Show* (2001–present), and the more recent film *ATL* (2006) have highlighted the role of African American men in extended familial networks as primary caregivers and surrogate fathers within African American families. In each of these sitcoms and films, uncles have served as primary caregivers for the children of their biological sister, often filling the role of surrogate father for their nephews and nieces. Although these sitcoms and films provide great humor and compelling storylines, the sociological "diamond" in the rough within these stories is the valuable role of African American men in extended familial networks who fill the role as fathers and primary caregivers in African American families. Contrary to the traditional research on African American fathers that has focused on the role of the biological father, these sitcoms have highlighted how men within extended familial networks assume the role of fathers in the lives of their nieces and nephews when the biological father is otherwise absent.

Paternal Involvement as a Route to Family-Based Social Capital

James Coleman (1990), a pioneer of social capital theory, defined social capital by its function. Unlike other forms of capital, Coleman (1990) defined social capital as inherent in the structure of relations between actors and among actors. It is productive, making possible the achievement of certain ends that in its absence would not be possible. Thus, the concept of social capital is the value of these aspects of social structure to actors as resources that they can use to achieve their interests (Coleman, 1990). Social capital can therefore be defined as the informal social resources that individuals use to achieve social mobility. Furstenberg and Kaplan (2004) have defined social capital as the stock of social good will created through shared norms and a sense of common membership which individuals may draw in their efforts to achieve collective and personal objectives. Because social capital is inherent within the social networks or the social structures of relationships between actors (individuals), the dimensions of these relationships are of vital importance. The more significant aspects of social capital are based on obligations, expectations, trustworthiness, information channels, effective norms and sanctions among those individuals within the social network. Much of the earlier work on social capital often focused on communities and civic engagement such as Putnam's (1995) seminal work, *Bowling Alone: The Collapse and Revival of American Community*. Putnam (1995) defined social capital as "features of social organization, such as networks, norms, and social trust that facilitate coordination and cooperation for mutual benefit." Although communities and civic engagement are important features of social capital, other pioneers of social capital such as Coleman (1990) and Bourdieu (1973) believed that communities were comprised of families or "collective subjects" that were not just a "simple aggregate of individuals." According to Coleman (1990), families reflected a greater "solidarity of interests," where its members felt required to act as a "united body." Thus, if we were to truly understand the decline of America's communities, we first must understand the decline of the American family.

Much of the earlier work on social capital (Coleman, 1990) analyzed the production of social capital for the social benefit of children by the absence or presence of two parents within families. Single-parent households where men were absent were often perceived as "socially deficient" in social capital, unable to produce the wealth of social capital that would prevent negative outcomes for children, such as dropping out of school. However, few studies of social capital actually addressed how social capital was produced within families regardless of its structure. How social capital is produced within poor African American families is a question that has been more assumed than examined by researchers, although some work is beginning to emerge (Furstenberg, 2001). Much of the discussion on the relationship between social capital and fatherhood within African American families has focused on the presence or absence of the biological father or stepfather. Almost no work has been done on the collaborative parenting relationships that men in extended familial and fictive kinship networks engage in with single mothers. The majority of research on fathers and social capital has been confined to the analysis of the added value of a father's presence in generating social capital. However, Furstenberg (2001) notes, we could ask what effect if any additional parent (grandmother, uncle, or much older sibling) offers when he or she reinforces the values and regulations of a single parent. Thus, fathers may or may not be distinctive in their ability to help generate social capital in the family.

The discussion of fathers as a significant form of family-based social capital is critically important in the discourse on African American families and fatherhood. If we have only begun to scratch the surface of the role of fathers in generating social capital, it is safe to say that the exploration on the role of African American men within extended familial and fictive kinship networks as surrogate fathers is almost nonexistent. It has more often been assumed by family researchers that fatherhood within African American families often does not go beyond the scope of the biological father or stepfather. Furthermore, it is less clear what transpires within African American families to generate larger or lesser amounts of social capital for children, specifically in the study of at-risk adolescent African American males. Part of the explanation may reside in the failure of scholars to intimately examine the role of men in the extended kin and family systems beyond the immediate household. Indeed, over the past two decades one of the most significant areas of research in the Black family literature has concerned the role and functioning of the extended family as informal support networks (Burton & Jayakody 2001; Taylor, Chatters, Tucker, & Lewis, 1990). Similar to the structure of immigrant families, which have used a broader range of kinship ties for social support and capital, kinships systems within African American families also go well beyond the immediate household encompassing grandparents, aunts, uncles, cousins, in-laws, and godparents. Yet there are few studies that qualitatively have documented support exchanges among extended family networks such as cousins or in-laws, not to mention relationships between in-laws, divorce and remarriage chains, and more distal sets of kin.

With the increased discourse on social capital, African American fatherhood, and its influence on youth development, particularly educational success and participation in juvenile delinquency and serious violent behavior among at-risk youth, researchers must begin to address the role of fatherhood beyond the traditional myopic view of fatherhood defined by a biological parent or stepparent. Fatherhood must increasingly become defined by the function and not its traditional associations. Consequently, we have only begun to scratch the proverbial surface regarding how fatherhood is defined and mediated in African American families. We are also just beginning to understand the role that men in extended and fictive kinship networks play in creating mechanisms that foster positive life outcomes; monitor and regulate youth behavior; and simultaneously provide emotional and psychological support for at-risk male youth. This is critically important when examining how systems of social support are produced and accessed within poor single-female headed households. Much of this discussion focuses on the collective parenting relationships between siblings (single mothers and their biological brothers) in the creation of social capital for the social benefit of children. It is vitally important to give attention to these relationships and how factors such as mutual obligation, trustworthiness, expectations, effective norms, and sanctions play in the role of the African American uncle as a surrogate father in these families. But it is even more important to explore how the African American uncle actively engages in the "collective familial body" to monitor and regulate youth behavior. The African American uncle is often a primary participant in the collective and unified body of familial solidarity in the parenting process of at-risk African American male youth.

An Ethnographic Approach to Successful Adolescent Development and the Role of the African American Uncle

This chapter is framed by data collected from a longitudinal ethnographic research study that examined the social context of adolescent violence for eight early adolescent African American males. The research methodology for the study involved in-depth life history interviews and ethnographic participant observations with eight young men and their single mothers over a period of 4 years. The use of ethnography provided thick and rich contextual data that could not be achieved through quantitative analysis. Although quantitative studies can identify the relationship between variables, they cannot fully explicate the range of parenting processes that transpire in real families. However, qualitative research, based on in-depth interviews and participant observations, is particularly suitable for exploring the interaction between individuals and their social environment. Qualitative inquiry highlights the contextual nature of social life, explores subjective perceptions and meanings, and identifies social processes and dynamics. Qualitative studies can describe everyday family life in poor African American neighborhoods, present accounts of how parents and adolescents feel about their lives and their worlds, and how they cope with and create strategies for dealing with poverty. Qualitative studies, particularly ethnographic research, can explain in great detail the nuances of African American family life and the parental activities and behaviors that may account for youth outcomes (Burton, Allison, & Obeidallah, 1996; Jarrett, 1995).

The Study

The ethnographic data used for this chapter were collected over a 4-year period in Soulville, a small subcommunity within Central Harlem, New York. Soulville is predominately poor and almost exclusively African American. At the time of this study, Soulville ranked in the top five neighborhoods in New York City in homicides and robberies. Soulville also ranked first in New York City in per capita rates of tuberculosis infections, infant mortality, and children suffering from asthma. During the period of this study, the Soulville community had also experienced an emerging violent youth gang crisis. Notorious West coast–based youth gangs, specifically the Bloods and Crips, formed in the Soulville community and actively recruited Soulville youth from local schools, neighborhood playgrounds, and street corners. Soulville Junior High, a local junior high school where the young men for this study were selected for the sample group, was the most violent junior high school among the four junior high schools that served the Harlem community. A large number of young men attending Soulville Junior High were members of the Bloods and the Crips. Two of the young men in this study's sample group were members of the Bloods and the Crips and a third member of the sample belonged to the Valley, a local youth gang based in a notoriously violent local housing project.

Life history interviews were conducted every year with sample members and their parents, all of whom were single mothers. When possible, men within extended family networks were also interviewed. When men did participate in life history interviews, the overwhelming majority of these men were typically the older biological brothers of the single mothers. The sample group was comprised of eight early adolescent African American males. The study was initiated in the beginning of the sample group's seventh grade year (approximately age 12, which typically marks the onset of delinquent behavior) and completed at the end of their tenth grade year (age 16, which marks the peak of delinquency). In order to intimately explore the social context of violence and adolescent development for these eight young men, the methodology used for this study was longitudinal, ethnographic, participant observation and intensive case studies. Participant observations were conducted daily across social settings: Soulville Junior High, the local Soulville community, and within households. Although the aim of this study centered on contextualizing adolescent violence in the Soulville community among African American male youth, one of the unexpected findings was the emergence of the African American uncle as a protective resource and surrogate father in the lives of African American male youth. Many of the single mothers in this study were quite candid about the valuable role their brothers played in the collaborative parenting process of her children.

Case Study: Clyde

In many instances, uncles were primary decision makers within single-female headed households. Like the Black inner-city grandmother so often discussed as a primary caregiver within African American families, these men often served similar roles as primary caregivers (Burton, Dilworth-Anderson, & Burton and Synder 1998). In this case study, Rhonda Brown (pseudonym), a young single mother of three African American boys, Clyde (age 13) and his younger brothers Barry (age 10) and Terry (age 6), utilized her brothers as a collective group of surrogate fathers for her children. Taylor et al. (1990) suggest that "having an available pool of relatives, frequent interaction with family members and close familial relationships were predictors for receiving support from extended family." Single mothers such as Rhonda Brown relied on men within her extended familial networks for social support:

> I think for all young men really, they need somebody older in their life. It could be a brother, an uncle, a cousin, anybody. They just need to find a man that is going to show them the right way to go, someone that they can put their trust into. Fortunately for me, those men are my brothers.

In an interview with Rhonda's son Clyde, he echoed his mother's sentiments. African American male youth in this study often looked to older men within their extended family for advice ranging from how to negotiate the street (Anderson, 1999) to issues of intimate relationships with the opposite sex.

> I could go to my mother with my problems but any boy would rather talk to their uncle about a problem or whatever . . . . like getting into beef (disputes on the street) or like girls or whatever. There are just certain things you can't talk to your mom about that you can talk to your uncle or your father about. My uncles understand me better because I'm a boy.

Rhonda Brown enlisted the social support of her three brothers and an older male cousin fictively referred to as "uncle" to collectively engage in raising her three boys. Clyde's three uncles served as surrogate fathers throughout his adolescence.

During the first year of this study, two of Clyde's uncles, Tyrone and Timothy, were incarcerated and a third uncle, Tommy, worked as a bus driver for Greyhound. Tommy resided in the Pocono Mountains in Pennsylvania, about a 90 minute drive from Central Harlem. Every weekend, Tommy would arrange with Rhonda Brown to pick up Clyde and his younger brothers after school to take them to his home for a weekend retreat. Rhonda and her brother Tommy agreed that taking Clyde to his home in such as rural setting provided a necessary social, psychological, and emotional escape from the violent streets of Soulville. Qualitative studies have provided insights on how some poor families create strategies that provide stability for their children in light of neighborhood social disorganization (Anderson, 1990; Jarrett, 1999; Furstenberg, 1993). Some families are able to construct social worlds that limit the impact of the dangers in which their children's lives may be embedded (Jarrett, 1999).

Timothy was released from prison during the second year of the study and was paroled to Clyde's home. It was during his parole that Timothy became instrumental in serving as a surrogate father to Clyde and his two younger brothers, especially after Rhonda resumed permanent employment at the post office. Timothy checked Clyde's homework and monitored his studies. He also attended open school nights and PTA meetings. These social behaviors are often defined as significant measures of social capital (Furstenberg, 2001). Rose and Clear (2002) also acknowledge that incarcerated men often serve as vital forms of social capital within African American families and communities. A growing body of research demonstrates the importance of these men in the collective parenting process. When these men are removed from familial and community settings, via incarceration, their absence often disrupts the collective parenting that often occurs within poor African American families, particularly the supervision of children (Jarrett, 1997a; Rose & Clear, 2002). Consequently, the re-entry of ex-offenders back into supportive familial networks often facilitates successful transitions back into society following incarceration.

Clyde's older cousin Rocky also served as a surrogate father and actively engaged in the parenting process. Although Rocky was Clyde's older cousin, the family considered him fictively an "uncle." This kind of fictive relationship is an adaptive role present in many poor African American families (Jarrett, 1997a, 1999; Stack & Burton 1993). When Timothy and Tommy were not actively engaged in monitoring and supervising Clyde's activities, Uncle Rocky, who was recently discharged from the Army, played an integral role in mentoring and parenting Clyde. In addition, although Tyrone was incarcerated, he still remained active in Clyde's life as well, providing him with sound advice about life and why he should acquire a solid education and employment so he would never end up in prison. Later in the study, Rhonda also started a new relationship with Robert, a local barber and well-known older gentleman in the community. Robert also provided social support for Clyde and his two younger brothers.

Within Clyde's family, uncles provided sound advice on what Anderson (1999) refers to as "the code of the streets." This understanding of how to survive in Soulville was passed down from the uncles to their nephews. In this interview,

Rocky provides keen insights on the code of the streets to his nephew Clyde. When this interview was conducted with Rocky, he was at Rhonda Brown's watching her three sons while she was working a full-time job at the post office.

> As far as the streets go, I tell him that he's going to have to know how to handle himself out there on the streets. I tell him that the police will stop you for anything. So whatever they ask you, just say "yes sir" or "no sir." You have to act like you're giving them respect so they know you're not disrespecting them . . . Cause today man, you can't even move when they stop you, you can't even dig in your pockets. Cause' they think all young Black men are carrying guns but that's not really true. I also tell Clyde how he don't need to be in a gang. I don't even know why people join a gang today anyway, but we got a lot of gangs around here now. I tell Clyde, we got a big family. You know what I'm saying. He's got uncles, a father, and cousins so I tell him anything you have a problem with you can come to us. He's got a lot of role models in his life to look up to. So I don't even see being in a gang in his picture because he knows we would check him on that. I tell him if he has any problems, they can always be handled. He always has me to talk to.
>
> (Rocky, age 38)

Rocky also monitored Clyde's activities while on the streets, thus providing an informal source of social control. Although the neighborhood of Soulville in many respects was socially disorganized, men such as Rocky provided the informal social controls that allowed the neighborhood to regulate itself. Rose and Clear (1998) suggest that social capital is the essence of social control for it is the very force collectives draw upon to enforce order. In this interview with Rocky, he discusses how he monitored Clyde's behavior on the streets of Soulville:

> *So do you ever run into Clyde on the streets?*
> Yeah, most definitely. Sometimes when I walk on the avenue, I will see him. I will call him over and we will stop and talk. The first question I ask him is "Where are you going?" Then I ask, "What time are you going home?" Then I get on the phone and call his mother and I tell her: "Look Rhonda, what do you want me to do with him, do you want me to send him home or what?" Most of the time she's like "As long as he's with you he can stay out." I'm like okay because I don't feel cool unless I know everything is alright.

In many respects, Rocky served as the family's eyes and ears for Clyde while he ventured out on the often volatile streets of Soulville. Jarrett's (1999) research on successful parenting in high-risk neighborhoods suggests that community-bridging parents protect their adolescents from negative neighborhood influences by closely supervising their time, space, and friendships.

Rose and Clear (1998) argue that individual and familial networks are often disrupted by incarceration, which in turn disrupts communities. "It is logical to assume that the loss of criminal males benefits the communities simply because they are seen as residents who are committing crime. When criminals are gone, communities are safer. But if some offenders occupy roles within networks that form the basis for informal social control, their removal is not solely a positive act, but also imposes losses on those networks and their capacity for strengthening families and community life" (p. 458). Clyde's case study touches on the unintended consequences of incarceration and the added social support men contribute to their families once they are released from prison.

Timothy immediately assumed the role of primary caregiver and surrogate father once he was released from prison and paroled to his sister's home. One could also assume that once Clyde's other uncle, Tyrone, who was incarcerated at the time of the study, was eventually released from prison, he too would serve as a primary source of social capital within Clyde's familial network because he had already been doing so while behind bars.

In neighborhoods deficient in social capital, where young men are often left on the streets unsupervised and unmonitored, the presence of older men serves as a deterrent to involvement in serious violent behavior (Anderson, 1999). The collective efficacy displayed by these men in parenting their nephew in many respects refutes popular public opinion about the absence of positive father figures in the lives of at-risk African American male youth in single-female headed households.

It has been assumed that poor communities characterized by single-female-headed households often lack the social capital to encourage children to complete their education, discourage them from engaging in delinquency and crime, and sanction them appropriately in informal and intimate relationships. Clearly, however, even in homes absent biological fathers, other male figures often serve socially supportive roles to these households and children. Currently, we need much more information and research about these networks that are so fundamental to social capital and social control. More importantly, we must learn more about the nature of extended familial networks in poor African American families and their impact on family members and at-risk youth.

Case Study: Jalen

My uncle Rich used to be in jail, my other uncle Ronald was in jail too, and my other uncle, Dickie, is in jail now and so is my father. Two of my cousins, Mark and Tucker, are locked up too. My family got a long record. If people in my neighborhood or the police know you're a Smith, they'll be like oh I know you're going to jail. That's why I don't like being a Smith. I really want to change my last name. You know, I want to change it for emergency situations like say for instance someone gets robbed around here and accuses me of it, if they know I'm a Smith then they'll think I probably had a pretty good chance of doing it. I mean my family just has a bad reputation around here . . . If I had one wish, I just wish I could change my name.

—Jalen Smith, age 13

Jalen has witnessed firsthand the destruction that awaits African American men on the streets of Soulville. Jalen needed to look no further than the men in his family to understand the devastating impact of those streets and the fatal blows they delivered to the lives of men in his family. The majority of men in Jalen's family had extensive criminal histories and had experienced some form of incarceration during their lifetimes. Jalen's father, George Smith, was a career criminal and was in and out of prison for the majority of Jalen's life. The majority of Jalen's paternal uncles and male cousins were either serving prison sentences or had been recently released from prison. Two of his maternal uncles also died on the streets of Soulville. His mother's oldest brother, James, died from a heroin overdose. Her youngest brother, William, was murdered in Soulville, severely beaten by a man with a baseball bat.

The number of men in Jalen's family-based social network lost to the criminal justice system significantly reduced the opportunity for them to monitor and supervise Jalen's social activities. Furthermore, the loss of men to the criminal justice system is symbolic of the enormous aggregate loss of men in the Soulville community who could provide informal social control and social support (Rose & Clear, 1998, 2002).

When this study began, Jalen had few men in his familial network who could offer social support or engage in the collective socialization process. Jalen resided in a household headed by his mother, Valerie Smith, and his paternal grandmother, Grace Moe. Grace Moe was Jalen's primary caregiver and parent. She was the central authority figure, disciplinarian, and decision maker in the Smith household. During much of Jalen's life, he lived with his grandmother in a two-bedroom apartment in a low-income housing tenement. His mother lived several floors below in the same building with Jalen's two younger brothers. Several months following the initiation of this study, Valerie Smith's brother Richard (age 36) was released from prison. "Big Rich," which he was called by his family and neighbors, was a former drug enforcer in the Soulville community. He was well respected and feared by many of the residents of Soulville. Like Clyde's uncle Timothy, when Richard returned to Soulville from prison, he was paroled to his mother's home. Upon re-entry back into the familial setting, Richard immediately assumed the role of Jalen's surrogate father.

Jalen was an avid basketball player who spent most of his leisure time playing in organized leagues. These leagues provided valuable community-based social capital that steered Jalen away from violence and crime. The coaches in these leagues often served as role models and mentors to young men. Few fathers of the young men in the basketball leagues attended the games or engaged in the league activities (i.e., serving as coaches or chaperones). This was often a reflection of the few men in the community who were actively involved in the lives of their sons. This lack of involvement and social interaction between older and younger men in Soulville left a deficit in community-based and family-based social capital, which in turn resulted in fewer forms of informal social controls.

However, Big Rich attended all of Jalen's games, and he often served as a team chaperone when the team traveled to basketball tournaments outside of Soulville. Jarrett (1999) notes that "a commonly used monitoring strategy among poor African American families is chaperonage, or the accompaniment of children in the neighborhood by a parent, family friend or sibling." Through his chaperonage, Rich developed close social ties with the coaches in the basketball leagues. He was also highly respected by men in the local neighborhood and was regarded as a neighborhood celebrity of sorts. His reputation in Soulville served as a protective family feature for Jalen:

> *So do you think Big Rich gets a lot of respect in the neighborhood?*
> Yeah, in my neighborhood and all around really. Every time we walk around here, he stops to talk to someone like on every block. Like at least two people on every block.
>
> *Do you think he's like a celebrity around here?*
> Yeah!
>
> *So how do you feel about that?*
> It's cool because when I'm with him people be like oh that's Rich's nephew so they look out for me and now I'm cool with like almost everybody around here.

Richard's constant involvement in monitoring Jalen's activities and his expansive social networks in the community provided Jalen with additional community-based social capital. Unlike many boys in Soulville, who relied on their crew or gang for back-up in a street disputes, Jalen admitted that he would rely first on an adult, specifically Richard. In the youth culture of Soulville, it was atypical for an adolescent to readily admit that he would rely on their parents or family members for assistance in a dispute, but Jalen bucked that pattern. Young men typically relied on their peers for assistance in street disputes.

By the end of Jalen's last season of junior high school basketball, he was being heavily recruited by numerous high school coaches. During this process, Jalen's older cousin Steven, whom the family fictively referred to as "Uncle Steven," assumed the role of Jalen's informal guardian. Steven, a track coach and gym teacher at Eisenhower High, a basketball powerhouse in New York City, had extensive experience dealing with college basketball recruiters and scouts, who often used desperate measures to recruit young, naïve men such as Jalen into their basketball programs. Confident that Steven would steer Jalen in the right direction, the Smith family collectively decided that Steven should serve informally as Jalen's guardian during his last year of junior high school. Ultimately, the family decided that it would be best if Jalen attended Eisenhower High, where Steven could closely monitor his progress. As time progressed, Steven would eventually assume the role of a father figure and mentor in Jalen's life.

Steven played an instrumental role as a father figure, mentor, coach, confidante, and friend. Steven had an extensive history of working in the Central Harlem community with at-risk children. Consequently, he was skilled in preparing Jalen for all of life's pitfalls. Steven also provided Jalen with temporary escapes from Soulville, utilizing community bridging strategies (Jarrett, 1995) such as trips to visit college campuses, to expose Jalen to a world outside of Soulville. This array of strategies created by the family minimized the exposure to the neighborhood dangers prevalent in the Soulville community. As the track coach for Eisenhower, Steven encouraged Jalen to join the track team, and Jalen would eventually break two long-standing high school track records, ranking third in the city in the triple jump. In this interview with Jalen's mother, she acknowledges the importance of Steven in Jalen's life:

> I don't know what I would do without Steven, especially with things like basketball and track, because I don't know too much about those things, so I'm happy he's here for him. If Steven takes him to play ball or wants to talk to him about condoms, sex, the streets, whatever, I let Steven do whatever he wants with him. Steven tells me that Jalen is a pretty good basketball player. He calls and tells me that Jalen has broken all kinds of school records. See, Jalen won't tell me these things maybe because I am a woman and he does not think I would understand. He's a weird kid. He's the most nonchalant kid I ever met. Nothing fazes him. He broke a 19-year-old and a 10-year-old school record and didn't even tell me. Steven told me that at one of his games, college scouts were watching him. Steven always tells me, "Don't let them scout him too early because you don't know who's who." I told Steven if I get a call or mail from the colleges, I will contact him first because he knows more about this scouting stuff than I do. Steven calls Jalen all the time, they'll be on the phone for hours at a time, I'm glad it's a male figure in my family that can talk to him like that. Even though Darryl (her boyfriend) talks to him, but Darryl's really not a talker, so I'm glad Steven is here for him.

In this case study, two uncles actively participated in collectively parenting Jalen. Uncle Rich served as Jalen's eyes and ears on the street, providing supervision on the street. This form of parental supervision was similar to the role Rocky played in Clyde's life. Rich protected Jalen from the streets and also used his street respect and contacts to provide Jalen with safety while on the streets of Harlem (Borgouis,). Uncle Steven was a crucial source of family-based social capital in Jalen's family network. He understood how to negotiate and "work" the formal institutions and systems in which Jalen was embedded. Steven served as his representative and liaison between the college scouts who aimed to recruit Jalen for his basketball talents. Steven was also Jalen's high school basketball and track coach, another important form of social support and informal social control. It is also interesting that the Smith family had deferred all issues regarding Jalen's academic and athletic college future to Jalen's uncle Steven.

Case Study: Corey

The final case study highlights an extraordinary relationship where an uncle assumed permanent guardianship of his nephew. When I first met Corey, he was 12 years old and lived with his mother and older brother in a renovated tenement building on the south side of Soulville. Corey's father, Curtis Townsend, spent the majority of Corey's childhood in and out of prison before he was murdered when

Corey was 10 years old. There were few organized recreational youth centers in his south side neighborhood and fewer older male mentors. Although this area was much safer than his former neighborhood in Soulville, it lacked the community-based social capital that seemed to be abundant in the central and northern neighborhoods of Harlem. Consequently, the vast majority of the social institutions that provided positive community-based social capital for young men in his community were located more than 20 blocks from Corey's home. In this excerpt from an interview with Corey, he explains the absence of community-based social capital in his neighborhood:

> My neighborhood is boring, it's dull and dead. There's nothing to do around here unless we make something to do like chase kids and beat them up or something like that.

During the first year of the study, Corey's older brother, Darnell, spent a year in prison for robbery. Darnell was also a high school dropout. In this excerpt from an interview with Corey, 1 week before his graduation from Soulville Junior High, he discusses why he so desperately wants to be successful in life:

> People always tell me, don't be like your older brother because he gets into a lot of trouble. I don't want to be like him, with no life and no job. I want to have a future. 'Cause I was realizing that everybody was looking forward to me doing good in school because my brother dropped out. I wanted to make my family proud. So I stopped hanging out with my friends, I left them alone. That's why they're getting left back, getting in trouble and stuff like that and I'm graduating. I left them alone and had to do what I had to do. I'm just solo now. I'm just by myself because you can't trust people. People are backstabbers, they don't want you to get ahead.

While Tina Jackson invested much of her time in creating positive pathways for her youngest son Corey, her oldest son Darnell, 19, spent the majority of his time getting into trouble hanging out on the streets of Soulville. As Darnell moved further into a life of crime, Tina focused more of her efforts and energies on keeping Corey from following the same self-destructive path.

> *As Corey gets older do you have any serious concerns about him?*
> Definitely, especially about being with the right people and going in the right direction. His brother, Darnell, is getting into a lot of trouble being with the wrong crowd. He's 19, and I'm about to kick him out of the house because he's not doing anything with his life but hanging with the wrong people, you know the "do nothing crowd." So you can understand by seeing that, I don't want Corey with the wrong crowd and especially not to hang out on the corners around here. All of my family is so spread out, so we are basically down here alone and it's rough down here. The ghetto is a rough place for a young Black man. There are a lot of policemen doing dirty things to young Black boys around here. They're just looking for young boys to harass and lock up, like they did my older son. He was arrested for

a mistaken identity for a robbery and had to go to jail for a year. That was the most terrible and miserable thing I've ever been through. I don't want that to happen to either one of my boys again. That's why I will always send Corey to some type of after school activity, something to keep his mind busy because it's rough out here.

Corey's mother relied heavily on the advice and support of her family, particularly her brother Melvin, to assist her with rearing her two boys. The Jackson family—Tina's mother-in-law, Eldoise Townsend, Tina's brother Melvin, who lived in Dallas, and her sister Janice—collectively engaged in resolving all family problems and disputes. They shared a consensus and connection to the rules, rituals, and values they instilled in Corey. When families act as a united body and make choices that reflect a "solidarity and mutuality of interests," they are generally more successful in mobilizing social capital for their children. A system that is high in social capital is one in which its members believe that they are indebted or obligated to respond to the needs of other family members (Furstenberg & Kaplan, 2001).

As Corey moved through his early adolescence, a period often marked by the onset of delinquent behavior, he spent much of his time floating among various peer groups "trying on different hats of social identity" but never really finding one group that provided the right social fit. Early in seventh grade, Corey flirted with the social identity of a "thug," forming a relationship with "Sly," a chronic and serious violent offender and a member of two violent Soulville youth gangs. Their primary activity together was getting into trouble and fights in and around the projects where Sly lived. It was during Corey's brief relationship "hanging out" with Sly that he was involved in two violent incidents.

Within a matter of a couple months, Corey stopped hanging out with Sly. He later formed a relationship with several basketball players, including Jalen. Corey was an above average basketball player, but he did not play in as many leagues as Jalen, and he did not have the same love of the game as most of his peers. Basketball, like many activities in Corey's life, was treated as a fleeting hobby. As Corey approached his first year in high school, he was assigned to Browning High School, one of the worst high schools in the city. It was known for serious violent youth gangs and for high levels of violence. It was also the site of a school shooting.

Although Corey's Uncle Melvin had been consistently involved in Corey's life, it was at this juncture that Melvin decided to assume permanent parental guardianship over Corey and moved Corey with him to Dallas. When monitoring strategies such as intensive supervision and chaperonage become ineffective, some community-bridging parents resort to extreme measures, referred to by some researchers as "exile," to geographically separate teens from their parents to promote conventional development (Jarrett, 1999). As a former resident of Soulville, Melvin knew from intimate personal experience the many pitfalls that young African American males faced in this harsh environment that often impeded their successful adolescent development. Melvin was a Soulville success story. He had climbed out of poverty to become a corporate executive for a Fortune 500 company and was now living in an affluent middle-class African American enclave in a suburb of Dallas. In light of Melvin's middle-class wealth, Corey's mother was initially hesitant about Corey's relocation.

> My brother wants Corey to come and live with him now that he's getting ready to go to high school. He wants to keep Corey down in Texas because he believes that it will be better for him. I'm contemplating letting him go because it's nice down there and it's more of a country environment and Corey likes it down there. He gets to go fishing and ride bikes and all kinds of stuff. But my brother, he is so serious about him coming down there. He wants to make Corey a Texas person, he doesn't want him to be in Soulville anymore. I think my brother wants Corey to change his whole lifestyle and live down there. But I told him, let Corey make his own decision. I don't want my brother to force Corey to stay there, but my brother keeps pushing it and pushing it, calling here every day asking, "When are you sending Corey down to stay with me?" But as a mother I'm not sure if I want him to go.

Eventually, Melvin and Corey's mother collectively decided that it would be best if Corey moved to Dallas. Corey attended a high school in Dallas that emphasized academic excellence, a school in stark contrast to the resource-deprived and gang-controlled Browning High School in New York. While in Dallas, Corey became a solid B student and joined the school's basketball team. Throughout his high school career, Corey stayed completely clear of violence or delinquency. By the end of the study, Tina Jackson had completely changed her once skeptical views of sending Corey to live with her brother:

> I'm happy that I sent him to Texas with my brother. I miss him, but I figure what's good for him is good for me too. I want the best for him. I think he has a better chance down there to achieve his goals. There's a better school system there and from what I saw the teachers put more time into the kids, they seem to care a little bit more. That just seems to be the way of the South you know, people are more caring and sensitive. If he would have stayed here, I really don't know what the situation might have been, but I would have tried as much as possible to keep him out of those situations but it would have been rough. More importantly, he really likes it down there. It's warm all year round and he likes to go fishing a lot with his uncle. He has a basketball court in the back of the house. He fishes on the weekends and he rides bikes with his friends. It's a more easygoing type of environment, you know, country like. I am glad that my brother convinced me to let him go.

In Soulville, parents often sought safe havens for their children. In Clyde's case study, his mother often sent him to stay with his uncle in the Pocono Mountains on the weekends. Similarly, Corey's family utilized Uncle Melvin's home as a safe haven as well. A community-bridging pattern with its supportive adult network offers parents the ability to provide broader opportunities for their children by tapping into extended, often socioeconomically diverse kinship networks (Jarrett, 1995). Social networks that provide additional adults furnish young people with additional care, concern, and resources (Anderson, 1990; Aschenbrenner, 1975; Jarrett, 1992; Jeffers, 1967; Martin & Martin, 1978; Valentine, 1978).

The community-bridging strategies used by Corey's mother were instrumental in his successful adolescent development. More importantly, the social obligations, reciprocity, trustworthiness, and responsibility to family members and their children are variables inherent in social capital theory. Social capital stems from a sense of trust and obligation created through interaction among community and family members and serves to reinforce a set of prescriptive norms (Coleman, 1990; Rose & Clear, 1998). In this study, Corey's uncle exhibited a social responsibility and obligation to his sister and his nephew to remove Corey from an environment in Soulville that was toxic and highly volatile. This context had already disrupted the life of Corey's older brother. Without the support of older men within kinship networks who served as surrogate fathers in the absence of biological fathers, many of these young men would not have been provided the monitoring, supervision, and community-bridging opportunities to be exposed to a world outside of Soulville. However, much of the literature on African American fatherhood has failed to acknowledge the importance of these men in the successful development of young African American males.

Closing Remarks

The original title for this chapter was "The 'Emerging' Role of the African American Uncle as Family-Based Social Capital." As scholars in search of new discoveries to unfold in the sociology of the African American family, we have a tendency to use buzz words such as "emerging" to indicate a finding that organically unfolded during the course of our research. It is as if we give life to a finding that we have determined had no life at all before we discovered it. Yet that is far from the case in regard to the socially supportive role of men in extended and fictive kinship networks in African American families. Historically, a variety of social relationships and networks within African American families have contributed to the successful development of African American children. These heterogeneous forms of family-based capital were the result of familial and cultural adaptations created to cope with the social, economic, and psychological distress faced by poor African American families in a society that oppressed these families via discrimination, marginalization, social isolation, and institutional racism.

African American men within poor families and communities have often faced the most extreme forms of social, economic, and political marginalization. This social and economic marginalization of African American men has often been correlated to high rates of incarceration and the loss of social capital to both communities and families. Rose and Clear (2002) have extensively documented that men within immediate and extended familial networks are significant sources of social capital and collective efficacy for African American families. When these men are removed from communities and families via incarceration, there are significant collateral consequences. One consequence is that fewer men are available to engage in the collective parenting process and supervision of at-risk youth. The implications of successful re-entry for men who have been incarcerated into African American families are integral to both criminal justice and family policy initiatives. These case studies have explored how the successful reintegration of African American men back into familial networks following incarceration strengthened familial social capital, increased collective efficacy, and prevented delinquent behavior among young African American males. It also reduced rates of recidivism among African American men, many of whom resisted engaging in future criminal activities because they were now highly valued commodities in African American families as fathers.

Consequently, the role of men in extended and fictive kinship networks has been greatly valued by African American families, particularly single-female headed households, yet much of the research on the family has utilized a Westernized perspective and analysis of these families. Furstenberg and Kaplan (2004) acknowledge in their work on social capital and the family, "we know relatively little about the operation of the broader kinship systems in the West." These ethnocentric approaches have done little to enhance and increase our knowledge of African American families and the role extended family members play in providing social support to children.

Within the social work research, practice, and policy dialogue centering on the strengthening of families via strengthening the role of fathers particularly in the African American community, this work has significant implications for future social work research, practice, and policy. This chapter opens up the proverbial can of worms by discussing the importance of expanding how we define families, specifically the extended and fictive kinship ties that have been traditionally utilized within the African American community to strengthen families, build social capital, and aid in the successful development of children. As scholars, we have failed in many respects to explore the complexity of relationships and social structures that exists within African American families, particularly among men. Consequently, when we initiate policy discussions on the strengthening of families we need to first ask, What do we mean by families? How are we defining family? Is it the limited Westernized perspective of families that does not take into account the broader kinship systems utilized by African American families?

With so much effort being directed toward bolstering the involvement of the biological father in the African American family and the lives of his children, few programmatic efforts have been created to encourage a broader range of fatherhood involvement that extends beyond the biological father. The strengthening of families must begin to move away from the traditional family structure (i.e., mother, father, and children) to a new cultural and social adaptation of how families are defined in the twenty-first century that encompasses a multitude of social structures and relationships. These variegated social structures now cut across both race and class. Hopefully, this work will lead to broader definitions and characterizations of fatherhood that are not strictly defined by the title of "father" but more by the functions of fatherhood carried out by those individuals who are not necessarily biological fathers.

As scholars on the African American family, it is safe to assume, that in respect to the socially supportive role of the African American uncle in the lives of African American children, Hollywood has done a much better job uncovering and unveiling this relationship to the public than sociological research. This myopic view of what defines fatherhood has perpetuated the sociological myth that the absence of biological fathers in poor African American families implies that children lack a heterogeneous pool of socially supportive men in extended familial networks that are able to fill the fatherhood void. These three case studies cannot make generalized assumptions on the social significance of the African American uncle in the lives of single-female headed households and their children; however, it is a relationship that definitely warrants serious attention. Until then, we will continue to take our cues on the diversity of African American fatherhood from Hollywood.

REFERENCES

Anderson, E. (1999). *Code of the street: Decency, violence, and the moral life of the inner city*. New York: W. W. Norton & Co.

Burton, L. (1997). Ethnography and the meaning of adolescence in high-risk neighborhoods. *Ethos, 25*(2), 208–217.

Burton, L., Allison, K., & Obeidallah, D. (1995). Social context and adolescence: Perspectives on development among inner-city African American teens. In L. Crockett & A. Crouter (Eds.), *Pathways through adolescence: Individual development in relation to social context* (pp. 119–138). Mahwah, NJ: Erlbaum.

Burton, L. M., Obeidallah, D. O., & Allison, K., Ethnographic perspectives on social context and adolescent development among inner-city African American teens, in Essays on ethnography and human development, edited by R. Jessor, A. Colby, & R. Shweder (1996), University of Chicago Press.

Burton, L. M., & Jayakody, R., Rethinking family structure and single parenthood. Implications for future studies of African-American families and children, in Family and child well-being: Research and data needs, edited by A. Thornton (2001), University of Michigan Press.

Burton, L. M., & Snyder, A. R., The invisible man revisited: Comments on the life course, history, and men's roles in American families, in Men in families, edited by A. Booth & A. C. Crouter (1998), Lawrence Erlbaum.

Coleman, J. (1990). *Foundations of social theory*. Cambridge, MA: Harvard University Press.

Furstenberg, F. (2001). Managing to make it: Afterthoughts. *Journal of Family Issues, 22*(2), 150–162.

Furstenberg, F. & Kaplan, S. (2004). Social capital, the family. In J. Scott, J. Treas, & M. Richards (Eds.), *The Blackwell companion to the sociology of families*, (pp. 218–232). Malden, MA: Blackwell.

Jarrett, R. L. (1992). A family case study: An examination of the underclass debate. In J. Gilgun, K. Daly, & G. Handel (Eds.), *Qualitative methods in family research* (pp. 172–197). Newbury Park, CA: Sage.

Jarrett, R. L. (1994). Living poor: Family life among single parent, African American women. *Social Problems, 41*(1), 30–49.

Jarrett, R. L. (1995). Growing up poor: The family experiences of socially mobile youth in low-income African American neighborhoods. *Journal of Adolescent Research, 10,* 111–135.

Jarrett, R. L. (1997a). African American family and parenting strategies in impoverished neighborhoods. *Qualitative Sociology, 20*(2), 275–288.

Jarrett, R. L. (1997b). Resilience among low-income African American Youth: An ethnographic perspective. *Ethos, 25*(2), 218–229.

Jarrett, R. L. (1999). Successful parenting in high-risk neighborhoods. *The Future of Children, 9*(2), 45–50.

Jarrett, R.L., Roy, K., & Burton, L.M., Fathers in the "hood:" Insights from qualitative research on low income African American men, in Handbook on fatherhood involvement: Multidisciplinary perspectives, edited by C. Tamis Le Monda & N. Cabrera (2002), Lawrence Erlbaum Associates.

Martin, E. & Martin, J. (1978). *The black extended family*. Chicago: University of Chicago Press.

Pearson, J., Hunter, A., Ensimger, M., & Kellam, S. (1990). Black grandmothers in multi-generational households: Diversity in family structure and parenting involvement in the Woodlawn community. *Child Development, 61,* 434–442.

Putnam, R.D. 2001. Bowling alone: The collapse and revival of American community. New York: Simon & Schuster.

Rose, D. & Clear, T. (1998). Incarceration, social capital and crime: Implications for social disorganization theory. *Criminology, 36,* 441–479.

Rose, D. & Clear, T. (2002). *Incarceration, re-entry and social capital: Social networks in the balance*. Paper presented at the "From Prison to Home" conference of the Urban Institute in Washington, DC.

Taylor, R., Chatters, L., Tucker, M., & Lewis, E. (1990). Developments in research on black families: A decade review. *Journal of Marriage and Family, 52,* 993–1014.

Valentine, C. (1968). *Culture and poverty*. Chicago: University of Chicago Press.

6

School Engagement, Peer Influences, and Sexual Behaviors Among High School African American Adolescent Boys

DEXTER R. VOISIN AND TORSTEN B. NEILANDS

African American adolescent boys are one of the least-studied populations in the United States, and yet one in which educational disparities, sexual risk behaviors, and associated health outcomes converge in a way that further marginalizes them from the broader society and perpetuates social immobility. For example, African American adolescent boys are almost two times more likely than White boys to drop out of school and have lower grade point averages (GPAs). In addition, by age 13, 44% of African American boys are one or more years below grade level compared to 30% of White boys (U.S. Department of Education, 2006).

In addition to low school academic engagement (e.g., GPAs and student teacher relations, positive expectations towards college) another major problem among this population is that of sexual risk taking. African American boys have their first sexual intercourse at an earlier age, and they report higher rates of sex without condoms and group sex, compared to their male counterparts across other ethnic groups (Centers for Disease Control, 2006). Such behaviors are reflected in rates for some sexually transmitted diseases (STDs) as much as 30% higher than those for boys in other ethnic groups (Centers for Disease Control, 2006). Unfortunately, these low academic trends coupled with high rates of sexual risk taking and STDs have further reinforced the marginalization, stigmatization, and disenfranchisement of African American boys. However, there is growing recognition that risk behaviors are not merely influenced by individual traits but profoundly driven by contextual factors that may influence social (Wilson, 1987) as well as sexual risk trajectories (DiClemente, Salazar, Crosby, & Rosenthal, 2004).

School Engagement and Sexual Risk Behaviors

Numerous studies (with diverse youth including substantial numbers of African Americans) document that school engagement markers (i.e., student–teacher relations, GPA) and sexual risk behaviors (e.g., first sexual intercourse and unsafe sex) are interrelated (for reviews, see Hawkins, Catalano, & Miller, 1992). For instance, Slonim-Nevo, Auslander, Ozawa, and Jung (1996), in a study of 358 African American and White adolescents aged 11–18 in 15 residential centers, reported that educational parameters such as relationships with teachers predicted AIDS knowledge, attitude, and behaviors. One shortcoming of the research, however, is that it failed to examine the impact of race/ethnicity on this relationship. Race/ethnicity is an important consideration given that there is considerable social inequality across racial/ethnic communities. In addition, the nature and type of educational outcomes may differ across neighborhoods, owing, in part, to racial segregation, variations in family structures, and differing resources across communities (Sampson, Morenoff, & Gannon-Rowley, 2002). Therefore we are uncertain whether findings may be different across specific ethnic groups. In addition, Voisin et al. (2005), in a study of 550 detained adolescents boys (White, African American, and Hispanic) found that youth who reported low student–teacher connectedness prior to being detained were twice as likely as their peers who reported high teacher connectedness to be sexually active and engage in risky sexual behaviors.

Results from population-based samples have also substantiated that positive educational factors are associated with lower risk behaviors. For instance, Resnick et al. (1997), using data from the National Longitudinal Study of Adolescent Health (Add Health) on 12,118 adolescents in grades 7–12, found that school connectedness was associated with a delay in first sexual intercourse. No racial differences were reported in this study. In addition, McNeely and Falci (2004), also using Add Health data, found that among a multiethnic sample of 13,579 adolescents aged 12–17, increased teacher support was associated with delayed initiation of sexual intercourse. No ethnic differences were examined in this study.

Peer Influences and Sexual Behaviors

Adolescence is a period of heightened peer influence (for reviews, see DiClemente et al., 2004) and sexual activity among youth (Centers for Disease Control, 2006). Significant research documents that peer influences (i.e., perceived norms and negative peer affiliations) are strongly associated with sexual behaviors among youth (for reviews, see DiClemente et al., 2004). Specifically, with regard to HIV sexual risk behaviors, negative peer norms have been associated with unsafe sexual risk behaviors. Studies have documented that when adolescents believe that their friends are engaging in certain sexual practices (e.g., multiple partners, older partners, anal sex, etc.), they will be more likely to adopt such behaviors (Bachanas et al., 2002; Boyer et al., 2000; Crosby et al., 2000; DiClemente & Wingood, 2000; Millstein & Moscicki, 1995; Voisin, 2003).

Several studies have shown that peer affiliation such as gang involvement is a predictor of first sexual intercourse, unsafe sex, and other problem behaviors (for reviews, see Bjerregaad & Smith, 1993). For instance, researchers have found that adolescents who report being in a gang were 6.5 times more likely than peers not in gangs to be sexually active, they were 3 times more likely to use condoms inconsistently, 3 times more likely to have caused a pregnancy, and nearly 4 times more likely to be high on alcohol or other drugs during sexual intercourse, have sex with a partner who was high, or have sex with multiple partners (Voisin et al., 2004).

School Engagement, Peer Influences, and Sexual Risk Behaviors

Given that peer influences are especially salient for youth, researchers have also attempted to further our understanding of how school engagement in conjunction with such influences is related to sexual behaviors. However, there are several gaps in our current understanding of the interrelationships among school engagement, peer influences, and sexual risk behaviors. For instance, we know from the extant literature that the above variables are correlated. However, it is unclear whether they are interrelated to form a pathway of risk. For instance, Bjerregaad and Smith (1993), examining a multiethnic sample of 969 youth (grades 7 and 8), examined the associations between school engagement markers, negative peer involvement such as gang affiliation, and sexual risks. Findings documented that low expectations for graduating were associated with gang involvement and lower commitment to positive peer norms. In addition, higher rates of risky sex were associated with gang membership. Gang involvement was related to substance use for both boys. However, this study reported only bivariate findings and did not test whether gang involvement or other peer influences mediated the relationship between academic indicators and sexual behaviors. In short, it did not test whether expectations for graduating were indirectly related to higher rates of risky sex through gang involvement. In the absence of gang involvement, no relationship existed between graduation expectations and unsafe sex. Nor did the study examine racial/ethnic differences.

Finally, Kassen, Vaugham, and Walter (1992) investigated causal inferences between academic markers and sexual risk behaviors. They found that among a group of 27,743 multiethnic youth aged 10–17, school bonding was predictive of lower gang membership and rates of alcohol abuse and dependence behaviors over a 5-year period. It is widely accepted that having sex while using drugs increases the risk of unsafe sex (Kassen, Vaugham, & Walter, 1992). Unfortunately, the researchers did not explore any mediators among the observed variables. They also did not explore for ethnic differences.

Collectively, the above studies have provided very useful information. However, there are several gaps in the extant literature, and further research is warranted. There is a dearth of studies that have examined the interrelationships among school engagement, peer influences, and sexual behaviors across the same sample of adolescents using statistical techniques that explore for mediation among observed variables. While there may be direct relationships among any of the variables in this study, identifying mediators will identify a set of variables that exert in direct influence on sexual risk taking.

Furthermore, we need to explore whether explicit dimensions of academic achievement (i.e., student teacher connectedness or GPAs) may be related to specific sexual behaviors (i.e., first sexual intercourse or risky sex) and whether particular dimensions of peer influences (i.e., perceived peer norms or negative peer affiliation such a gang involvement) may mediate this relationship. This information may be useful to the design of culturally relevant interventions for this population. Finally, we need to know whether these factors are interrelated, specifically with regard to African American adolescent boys who report low on school engagement parameters and high on sexual risk behaviors.

The purpose of this study was twofold: First, the study examined whether school engagement, as measured by grades and student–teacher connectedness, is independently related to sexual behaviors, including first sexual intercourse and risky sex (sex with multiple partners, sex without condoms, sex while using drugs). Secondly, the study identified whether peer influences (i.e., safer sex norms, risky sex norms, or gang involvement) mediate these relationships.

Study Design

In April 2006, 20 trained research assistants (masters- and doctoral-level social work students) handed out parental permission forms describing the scope of the study to 673 students who identified themselves as African American (ages 13 to 19) in 25 homeroom classes in a large urban school district. Students were eligible to participate in the study if they self-identified as African American boys between age 13 and 19 and were attending regular high school classes (i.e., not special education). Data collection occurred within a 2-week period. The study achieved an 83% participation rate. The final sample comprised of 219 boys who self-identified as African American.

Students who brought signed parental forms were required to assent prior to completing the self-administered survey. The questionnaire was written at a fifth-grade reading level. Participants were offered $10 for completing the survey, which took no more than 40 minutes, and it was administered in a small school auditorium. Names were recorded on questionnaires, and identifying links were removed once GPA scores were obtained from the central database. No students reported any adverse reactions from answering study questions. Institutional Review Board approval was obtained from the university and the local school council and regional office.

Measures

School Engagement was assessed by current GPA and student–teacher connectedness. We obtained students' combined GPA in their core courses (math, English, social studies, and science) from school records. We assessed student–teacher connectedness with the Student Assessment of Teachers Scale (McNeely & Falci, 2004). Adolescents responded to 10 items, which assessed students' perceptions of teachers as caring, fair, supportive, understanding, invested in teaching, trying to make school work interesting, and feeling safe in school. These items were measured on a 5-point, Likert-type scale, ranging from 1 ("strongly disagree") to 5 ("strongly agree"). An example includes, "Teachers at my school care about me." Higher scores on the scale indicated higher teacher connectedness. The alpha coefficient was .86.

Peer Influences were assessed by the Peer Risk Norm Scale (Voisin, 2003). This scale has been previously validated and used to evaluate perceived negative peer norms among populations of mostly African American youth (Voisin, 2003). We assessed what participants perceived were their current peer norms with three items that evaluated perceived negative attitudes of peers toward condom use and positive attitudes to alcohol and drug use. There is substantial literature documenting that adolescents are more likely engage in these risk behaviors if they perceive their peers are supportive of these norms (for reviews, see DiClemente et al., 2004). Additionally, low condom use and having sex while using drugs and alcohol increases the risk for contracting STDs, including HIV (Centers for Disease Control, 2006). An example of perceived peer norms is, "How many of these people believe that condoms reduce pleasure?" Adolescents responded to these questions on a 7-point scale ranging from "0" to "6 or more times." The alpha coefficient was .72.

There are significant debates in the literature about what constitutes a gang, accompanied by recommendations to employ self-definitions of gang membership (Bjerregaad & Smith, 1993). In addition, it is well documented that affiliation in such groups often depends on adhering to group norms that may sanction risky sex (Petraitis, Flay, & Miller, 1995). In addition, adolescents may move in and out of gangs and may still be influenced by the negative socializing influences of many of those norms, although they are not actively gang members (Bjerregaad & Smith, 1993). Therefore, we assessed gang membership with one item: "Have you ever been a member of a gang?"

Sexual Behaviors were assessed by two variables. A single survey item, "Have you ever had sex?" assessed first sexual intercourse. This was defined as ever having had vaginal or oral sex with the opposite sex. While vaginal sex represents a higher HIV risk category than oral sex, the latter can result in the acquisition of other

STDs, which increases vulnerability for the acquisition and transmission of HIV (Centers for Disease Control, 2006). Risky sexual behaviors within the last 12 months were defined as recently having had one or more of the following experiences: sex without condoms, sexual intercourse with multiple persons simultaneously, sex while high on drugs, and sexual intercourse while under the influence of alcohol or drugs without a condom (0 = none of these experiences; 1 = one or more of these experiences).

Data Analysis

Initial analyses described the characteristics of the sample via one-way frequency tables and measures of central tendency. On the basis of the above hypotheses, we then fit structural equation models (SEM) to the data, in which a latent GPA variable (measured by GPAs in English, math, social studies, and physical science) and the observed student–teacher connectedness variable explain the likelihood of gang membership and risky peer norms. These intermediary variables in turn explain a history of sexual intercourse and HIV sexual risk behavior. Because we measured several of our constructs with single indicators (e.g., gang membership) or previously validated scales (e.g., student–teacher connectedness), we treated these variables as observed rather than latent. On the basis of previous research on the impact of school engagement variables on sexual behaviors among adolescents, we opted to examine first sexual intercourse and HIV high risk behaviors in separate analyses.

We specified the SEMs using M*plus* 4.2 for Windows (Muthén & Muthén, 2006). Owing to the dichotomous nature of gang membership and the sexual behavior outcomes, we used weighted least-squares estimation with a mean and variance adjustment (M*plus* estimator, WLSMV) (Flora & Curran, 2004). We assessed the global fit of the model to the data with a robust chi-square test of exact model fit. Because chi-square tests are often sensitive to trivial data-model fit discrepancies, we also report the following approximate fit indices: Bentler's comparative fit index (CFI; Bentler & Bonnett, 1980), the root mean square error of approximation (RMSEA; Browne & Cudek, 1993), and the weighted root mean square residual (WRMR; Yu, 2002). To attain adequate fit, a model's CFI should meet or exceed .90 (Vandenberg & Lance, 2000), RMSEA should be .06 or lower (Hu & Bentler, 1999), and WRMR should be 1.0 or lower (Yu, 2002). Because these statistics' performance varies in certain circumstance—for example, RMSEA may be inflated in small to moderately sized samples (Curran, Bollen, Chen, Paxton, & Kirby, 2003)—we followed the recommendations of Hu and Bentler (1999), who suggest satisfactory model fit is attained when two or more of the fit statistics meet the recommended cutoff levels.

Owing to the presence of indirect effects in the analysis, we computed confidence intervals via the bias-corrected (BC) bootstrap for asymmetric indirect effect distributions (MacKinnon, Lockwood, Hoffman, West, & Sheets, 2002; MacKinnon,

Lockwood, & Williams, 2004; Shrout & Bolger, 2002). Therefore, for each parameter estimate, we report the unstandardized regression coefficient (B), the bootstrap-based bias-corrected 95% confidence interval of B, and the standardized regression coefficient (β). The number of bootstrap samples was set at 5,000 to ensure sufficient precision of the confidence intervals (Hox, 2002). Confidence intervals that do not include zero imply that the parameter estimate around which the confidence interval is constructed is statistically significant at $p < .05$.

Results

The sample was comprised of 219 boys, the majority of which (55%) lived in female-headed households, with 61% reporting receiving "free school lunch," indicating they were from low-income families. Bivariate correlations appear in Table 6.1. Core subject GPAs were highly intercorrelated, while student–teacher connectedness was not associated with GPA variables. Risky peer norms and gang membership were uncorrelated with GPA variables with the exception of their math GPA, which was weakly negatively correlated with gang membership ($r = -.14$).

Table 6.1 Correlations Among Observed Variables

	1	*2*	*3*	*4*	*5*	*6*	*7*	*8*	*9*
1. English GPA	1.00								
2. Math GPA	.70***	1.00							
3. Social studies GPA	.79***	.70***	1.00						
4. Physical sciences GPA	.79***	.74***	.81***	1.00					
5. Student–teacher connectedness	.12	.09	.08	.11	1.00				
6. Risky peer norms	−.05	−.06	−.08	−.08	−.05	1.00			
7. Gang membership history	−.11	−.14*	−.10	−.11	−.16*	.17*	1.00		
8. First sexual intercourse	−.31***	−.19**	−.31***	−.27***	−.15*	.16*	.15*	1.00	
9. High–risk sex	−.23***	−.14*	−.26***	−.26***	−.15*	.15*	.18**	.81***	1.00

Notes. N = 218 boys; Correlations were estimated using full information maximum likelihood in M*plus* 4 with significance levels determined via the bootstrap with 5,000 replicate samples.
*$p < .05$; **$p < .01$; ***$p < .001$.
GPA, grade point average.

GPA variables and student–teacher connectedness were negatively correlated with the two sexual risk behavior outcomes. GPA measures for social studies, physical sciences, math, and English, were significantly negatively correlated with the two sexual risk behavior outcomes. Risky peer norms were positively correlated with gang membership and risky sexual behavior. Additionally, gang membership was associated with risky sexual behavior.

SCHOOL ENGAGEMENT AND FIRST SEXUAL INTERCOURSE   The SEM examining the impact of school engagement factors on first sexual intercourse for boys was an excellent fit: The chi-square test of absolute fit was not significant (χ^2 [N = 218, DF = 8] = 8.27, p = .08), indicating that the null hypothesis of exact model-data fit was upheld. The approximate fit indices also indicated excellent model fit to the data (CFI = .97, RMSEA = .07; WRMR = .61). Direct effects from this analysis appear in Table 6.2. Higher levels of latent GPA were negatively associated with

Table 6.2 Sexual Intercourse: Direct Effects From Structural Equation Models

			Boys		
DV	IV	LCL	B	UCL	β
English GPA	Latent GPA	1.00	1.00	1.00	0.89
Math GPA	Latent GPA	**0.69**	**0.82**	**0.97**	**0.79**
Physical science GPA	Latent GPA	**0.96**	**1.07**	**1.20**	**0.90**
Social studies GPA	Latent GPA	**0.93**	**1.05**	**1.18**	**0.90**
Risky peer norms	Latent GPA	−1.38	−0.45	0.51	−0.07
Gang membership	Latent GPA	−0.42	−0.19	0.03	−0.17
Risky peer norms	Student–teacher connectedness	−0.98	−0.24	0.61	−0.04
Gang membership	Student–teacher connectedness	**−0.41**	**−0.22**	**−0.04**	**−0.21**
First sexual intercourse	Achievement	**−0.67**	**−0.41**	**−0.16**	**−0.32**
First sexual intercourse	Risky peer norms	0.00	0.04	0.08	0.18
First sexual intercourse	Gang membership	−0.06	0.22	0.55	0.20
First sexual intercourse	Student–teacher connectedness	−0.40	−0.17	0.06	−0.15

Notes. N = 218 for boys; DV = outcome or dependent variable; IV = explanatory or independent variable; B = unstandardized regression coefficient; LCL = lower 95% confidence limit; UCL = upper 95% confidence limit; and β is the standardized regression coefficient. Confidence intervals that do not include zero are significant at p < .05 and are displayed in boldface type.
GPA, grade point average.

ever having had sexual intercourse. Higher levels of student–teacher connectedness were negatively associated with gang membership. By contrast, none of the indirect effects linking latent GPA or student–teacher connectedness to first sexual intercourse were significant.

School Engagement and Unsafe Sex The fit of second SEM examining the impact of latent GPA on high-risk sexual behavior to the data was not rejected (χ^2 [N = 218, DF = 4] = 8.33, p = .08). Moreover, the approximate fit indices indicated very good model fit to the data (CFI = .97, RMSEA = .07; WRMR = .61). Direct effects from this analysis are shown in Table 6.3. Higher levels of latent GPA were negatively associated with high-risk sexual behavior. Gang membership was positively associated with risky sex. Lower levels of student–teacher connectedness were associated with a higher likelihood of a gang membership. No indirect effects involving GPA reached statistical significance, but student–teacher connectedness was negatively associated with risky sex by way of gang membership (B = –.06; 95% CI = –.18, –.004; β = –.05). This result suggests that as high levels of student–teacher

Table 6.3 High-Risk Sexual Behavior: Direct Effects From Structural Equation Models

		Boys			
DV	IV	LCL	B	UCL	β
English GPA	Latent GPA	1.00	1.00	1.00	0.88
Math GPA	Latent GPA	**0.69**	**0.83**	**0.98**	**0.79**
Physical science GPA	Latent GPA	**0.98**	**1.10**	**1.25**	**0.92**
Social studies GPA	Latent GPA	0.94	1.06	1.21	0.90
Risky peer norms	Latent GPA	–1.40	–0.45	0.52	–0.07
Gang membership	Latent GPA	–0.42	–0.19	0.03	–0.17
Risky peer norms	Student–teacher connectedness	–0.98	–0.24	0.61	–0.04
Gang membership	Student–teacher connectedness	**–0.41**	**–0.22**	**–0.04**	**–0.21**
High-risk sexual intercourse	Achievement	**–0.57**	**–0.31**	**–0.07**	**–0.25**
High-risk sexual intercourse	Risky peer norms	–0.01	0.03	0.07	0.16
High-risk sexual intercourse	Gang membership	**0.004**	**0.26**	**0.57**	**0.24**
High-risk sexual intercourse	Student–teacher connectedness	–0.36	–0.15	0.06	–0.13

Notes. N = 218 for boys; DV = outcome or dependent variable; IV = explanatory or independent variable; B = unstandardized regression coefficient; LCL = lower 95% confidence limit; UCL = upper 95% confidence limit; and β is the standardized regression coefficient. Confidence intervals that do not include zero are significant at $p < .05$ and displayed in boldface type.
GPA, grade point average.

connectedness is associated with lower rates of gang membership, and lower incidences of risky sex for boys.

Policy and Practice Implications

There is a dearth of literature on the relationship between school engagement, peer influences, and sexual behaviors. In addition, few studies have examined the interrelationships among these variables focusing exclusively on African American adolescent boys. Major findings from this study indicate that the higher GPAs are associated with lower rates of sexual début and risky sex. Student–teacher connectedness is also negatively associated with gang involvement, and such involvement is associated with risky sex. In addition, the relationship between student–teacher connectedness and risky sex is linked by gang involvement. These are important and novel findings because they both substantiate and expand knowledge gained from prior studies. For instance, several studies document that both school engagement markers (Slonim-Nevo et al., 1996; Voisin et al., 2005) and gang involvement (Bjerregaad & Smith, 1993; Voisin et al., 2005) are associated with sexual behaviors. However, this study documents that gang involvement links the relationship between student–teacher connectedness with African American boys. There might be several reasons for this finding many of which may resonate with educators, clinicians, and community-based organizations (CBOs) providing services to this population.

According to social control theory (SCT) (Hirschi, 1969) the bond to conventional society is represented by four elements: *(1)* attachment to others, *(2)* commitment to conventional institutions, *(3)* involvement in conventional activities, and *(4)* belief in conventional values. Consistent with one application of this theory, low grades and poor attachment to prosocial "agents" such as teachers is associated with involvement with or recruitment by risky peer groups such as gangs, which endorse unsafe norms. Membership in such peer groups may then reinforce risky norms, such as increased drug use and unsafe sexual behaviors (Petraitis, Flay, & Miller, 1995). Such involvement and diminished prospects for a viable future further undermine the belief in conventional values.

In this study, 30% of boys reported gang membership. This is a disturbing figure and may reflect a host of neighborhood factors that underscore an environment of risk. For instance, as cited elsewhere, boys from this sample report extremely high and disproportionate levels of community violence exposure (see Voisin & Neilands, 2009). Consistent with Wilson (1987), in communities with significant community violence and crime, youth may join gangs as a source of protection or income generation. The high rates of gang membership may also underscore the need that all youth developmentally have the need to belong to something, and they may sadly highlight what viable options are perceived by these boys in this study. Without viable prosocial opportunities for membership in developmentally appropriate groups some youth may drift towards gang involvement.

However, given that the data were cross-sectional, findings cannot infer causality and can only highlight associations. Longitudinal research will be needed to clarify causal ordering. For instance, it is also plausible that gang membership may lead to lower student–teacher connectedness, and sexual risk behaviors. Nevertheless, as these results highlight, it is first important to document the interrelationships among key constructs prior to designing costly and complicated longitudinal studies to clarify causal inferences. These findings provide the basis for such future studies. Another consideration in contextualizing this finding is that this study assessed ever being involved in a gang and not current gang involvement. Nevertheless, as we have discussed earlier, it is feasible that some adolescents, regardless of their current gang status, may still be influenced by the socializing influence of such groups, even though they do not currently belong to them. In addition, youth may also move in and out of such groups throughout adolescence. Future research should examine such assumptions, and qualitative designs are needed to further illuminate reasons for gang membership among this population.

At minimum, these findings suggest that empirically based youth interventions to promote student–teacher connectedness are viable prevention approaches. For example, efforts could be made to hire, train, and support competent teachers, or to ensure that adolescents feel connected to at least one supportive adult at school (McNeely & Falci, 2004; Voisin et al., 2005). Consistent with this recommendation, increasing the number of African American male teachers is important to challenging fallacies that high academic performance is a challenge to African American masculinity (Davis, 2003). The increased presence of supportive and nurturing African American males in the classroom is critical on several fronts given that the majority of African American boys are coming from single-female-headed households (U.S. Census Bureau, 2000). Other measures to promote higher school engagement include providing multicultural curriculum support, eliminating tracking, providing more supports for families, and expanding mentor and internship programs, all of which have shown some promise (Davis, 2003).

Likewise, interventions that prevent gang membership or target current gang members by promoting greater parental involvement in their adolescents' lives or by promoting viable future options such as school completion and employment (Bjerregaad & Smith, 1993; Voisin et al., 2004) are also necessary. According to Hill and colleagues (1999), factors such as early initiation of problem behaviors, poor family management, drug use, and failure to become successfully engaged in school predict gang involvement (Hill, Howell, Hawkins, & Battin-Pearson, 1999). Providing measures to curtail such antecedents may be effective in reducing gang involvement. Although not considered directly here, the above recommendations should supplement, not replace, efforts to enhance knowledge and prevention of sexually transmitted diseases in the school curricula which is lacking in the curricula of some many inner city schools.

REFERENCES

Bachanas, P. J., Morris, M. K., Lewis-Gess, J. K., Sarett-Cuasay, E. J., Flores, A. L., Sirl, K. S., & Sawyer, M. K. (2002). Psychological adjustment, substance use, HIV knowledge, and risky sexual behavior in at-risk minority females: Developmental differences during adolescence. *Journal of Pediatric Psychology, 27*(4), 373–384.

Bentler, P. M. & Bonnett, D. G. (1980). Significance tests and goodness of fit in the analysis of covariance structures. *Psychological Bulletin, 88,* 588–606.

Bjerregaard, B. & Smith, C. (1993). Gender differences in gang participation, delinquency, and substance use. *Journal of Quantitative Criminology, 9*(4), 329–355.

Boyer, C. B., Shafer, M., Wibbelsman, C. J., Seeberg, D., Teitle, E., & Lovell, N. (2000). Associations of sociodemographic, psychosocial, and behavioral factors with sexual risk and sexually transmitted diseases in teen clinic patients. *Journal of Adolescent Health, 27*(2), 102–111.

Browne, M. W. & Cudek, R. (1993). Alternative ways of assessing model fit. In K. A. Bollen & J. S. Long (Eds.), *Testing structural equation models* (pp. 136–162). Newbury Park, CA: Sage.

Centers for Disease Control. (2006). Racial/ethnic disparities in diagnoses of HIV/ AIDS—33 states, 2001–2004. *Morbidity and Mortality Weekly Report, 55,* 121–125.

Crosby, R. A., DiClemente, R. J., Wingood, G. M., Sionean, C., Cobb, B., & Harrington, K. (2000). Correlates of unprotected vaginal sex among African American female teens: The importance of relationship dynamics. *Archives of Pediatrics and Adolescent Medicine, 154,* 893–899.

Curran, P. J., Bollen, K. A., Chen, F., Paxton, P., & Kirby, J. B. (2003). Finite sampling properties of the point estimates and confidence intervals of the RMSEA. *Sociological Methods and Research, 32*(2), 208–252.

Davis, J. (2003). Early schooling and academic achievement of African American males. *Urban Education, 38,* (5), 515–537.

DiClemente, R., Salazar, L., Crosby, R., & Rosenthal, S. (2004). Prevention and control of sexually transmitted infections among adolescents: The importance of a socio-ecological perspective, a commentary. *Public Health, 119*(9), 825–836.

DiClemente, R. J. & Wingood, G. M. (2000). Expanding the scope of HIV prevention for adolescents: Beyond individual-level interventions. *Journal of Adolescent Health, 26,* 377–378.

Flora, D. B. & Curran, P. J. (2004). An empirical evaluation of alternative methods of estimation for confirmatory factor analysis with ordinal data. *Psychological Methods, 9*(4), 466–491.

Hawkins, J. D., Catalano, R. F., & Miller, J. Y. (1992). Risk and protective factors for alcohol and other drug problems in adolescence and early adulthood: Implications for substance abuse prevention. *Psychological Bulletin, 112,* 64–105.

Hill, K., Howell, J., Hawkins, D., & Battin-Pearson, S. R. (1999). Childhood risk factors for adolescent gang membership: Results from the Seattle Social Development Project. *Journal of Research in Crime and Delinquency, 36*(3), 300–322.

Hirschi, T. (1969). *Causes of delinquency.* Berkeley: University of California Press.

Hox, J. (2002). *Multilevel analysis techniques and applications.* Mahwah, NJ: Erlbaum.

Hu, L. T. & Bentler, P. M. (1999). Cutoff criteria for fit indexes in covariance structure analysis: Conventional criteria versus new alternatives. *Structural Equation Modeling, 6*(1), 1–55.

Kassen, S., Vaugham, R., & Walter, H. (1992). Self-efficacy for AIDS preventative behaviors among tenth grade students. *Health Education Quarterly, 19*, 187–202.

MacKinnon, D. P., Lockwood, C. M., Hoffman, J. M., West, S. G., & Sheets, V. (2002). A comparison of methods to test mediation and other intervening variable effects. *Psychological Methods, 7*(1), 83–104.

MacKinnon, D. P., Lockwood, C. M., & Williams, J. (2004). Confidence limits for the indirect effect: Distribution of the product and re-sampling methods. *Multivariate Behavioral Research, 39*(1), 99–128.

McNeely, C. & Falci, C. (2004). School connectedness and transition into and out of health risk behavior among adolescents: A comparison of social belonging and teacher support. *Journal of School Health, 74*(7), 284–292.

Millstein, S. & Moscicki, A. (1995). Sexually-transmitted disease in female adolescents: Effects of psychosocial factors and high risk behaviors. *Journal of Adolescent Health, 17*, 83–90.

Muthén, L. K. & Muthén, B. (2006). *Mplus user's guide*. Los Angeles: Muthen and Muthen, Inc.

Petraitis, J., Flay, B., & Miller, T. (1995). Reviewing theories of adolescent substance use: Organizing pieces in the puzzle. *Psychological Bulletin, 117*(1), 67–86.

Resnick, M. D., Bearman P. S., Blum R. W., Bauman, K. E., Harris, K. M., Jones, J., Tabor, J., Beuhring, T., Sieving, R. E., Shew, M., Ireland, M., Bearinger, L., & Udry, R. (1997). Protecting adolescents from harm: Findings from the National Longitudinal Study on Adolescent Health. *Journal of the American Medical Association, 278*, 823–832.

Sampson, R., Morenoff, J., & Gannon-Rowley, T. (2002). Assessing "neighborhood effects": Social processes and new directions in research. *Annual Review of Sociology, 28*, 443–478.

Shrout, P. E. & Bolger, N. (2002). Mediation in experimental and nonexperimental studies: New procedures and recommendations. *Psychological Methods, 7*(4), 422–445.

Slonim-Nevo, V., Auslander, W., Ozawa, M., & Jung, G. (1996). The long-term impact of AIDS-preventive interventions for delinquent and abused adolescents. *Adolescence, 31*(122), 409–421.

U.S. Bureau of the Census. (2000). *March current population survey*. Washington, DC: U.S. Government Printing Office.

U.S. Department of Education, National Center for Education Statistics. (2006). *Digest of education statistics, 2005* (NCES 2006-030, Table 105). Washington, DC: Department of Education.

Vandenberg, R. J. & Lance, C. E. (2000). A review and synthesis of the measurement invariance literature: Suggestions, practices, and recommendations for organizational research. *Organizational Research Methods, 3*(1), 4–69.

Voisin, D. (2003). Victims of community violence and HIV sexual risk behaviors among African American adolescent males. *Journal of HIV/AIDS Prevention & Education for Adolescents & Children, 5*(3/4), 87–110.

Voisin, D. & Neilands, T. (2009). Community violence and health risk factors among adolescents on Chicago's Southside: Does gender matter? *Journal of Adolescent Health*. DOI is 10.1016/j.jadohealth.2009.11.213.

Voisin, D., Salazar, L., Crosby, R., DiClemente, R., Yarber, W., & Staples Horne, M. (2004). The association between gang involvement and sexual behaviors among detained adolescent males. *Sexually Transmitted Infections, 80*, 440–442.

Voisin, D., Salazar, L., Crosby, R., DiClemente, R., Yarber, W., & Staples Horne, M. (2005). Teacher connectedness and health-related outcomes among detained adolescents. *Journal of Adolescent Health, 37*(4), 337.e17–337.e23.

Wilson, J. (1987). *The truly disadvantaged: The inner city, the underclass, and public policy.* Chicago: University of Chicago Press.

Yu, C. Y. (2002). *Evaluating cutoff criteria of model fit indices for latent variable models with binary and continuous outcomes.* Unpublished doctoral dissertation, University of California, Los Angeles.

PART II

Educational Issues Facing African American Males

7

Promising Practices

The Positive Effects of After-School Programs for African American Male Development and Educational Progress

REGINALD CLARK, ALEXES HARRIS,
KIMBERLY A. WHITE-SMITH, WALTER R. ALLEN,
AND BARBARA A. RAY

Portrayals of Black males, whether in the media or in the research world, often focus on the negative. What is often missed in these portrayals, however, is the fact that many young Black males are succeeding. This is not to ignore the sometimes staggering statistics. Black males today do indeed face many more pitfalls than the average youth or young adult. When prison is the institution that touches Black males more than college or the military, something has gone terribly awry. The challenge facing scholars and practitioners today is to learn from the experiences of Black males who somehow manage to successfully negotiate the too-often treacherous terrain. Once we more clearly understand this "Black box" of resources, opportunities, socialization, and support that directs Black males to pathways of success, we will be better able to design and implement intervention programs that will appreciably impact their lives.

This chapter focuses on one set of resources—after-school programs—that can help youth sidestep potential pitfalls. Well-designed after-school programs can provide structure, mentors, and guidance to youth, and they can offer an alternative to street corners and risky behavior. To lift the curtain on how after-school programs create success, we surveyed 304 youth (primarily African American and male) on a range of topics before and after they had taken part in an after-school program, either community or school based. The survey covered 28 programs nationwide with a variety of goals and serving a broad range of age groups.

Our results show that these programs help to develop important foundations. Youth in these programs spent more time in structured activities and they spent more time with adults and mentors. Both contribute to better school connections, higher educational aspirations, and greater commitment to more positive life choices. We also find that the ratio of youth to volunteers and staff is important on a number of levels. Overcrowded programs limit mentor and adult contact, which has been shown to improve youth attitudes and social connections. In overcrowded programs, youth also are less likely to feel they have benefited from the program. In addition, program administrators in overcrowded programs often face a Catch-22. They are less likely to create strategic outreach plans, either to recruit more volunteers or to sustain or round up additional funding.

Given the study's structure, we cannot say that the after-school program's *caused* the improvement we saw in youths' advances. However, the correlation we find between participation and positive outcomes is nevertheless notable. The findings underscore the importance of after-school programs to youth achievement, especially at-risk youth such as African American males. The results also underscore the need for more funding, staffing, and outreach. Below we outline these findings in detail and place them in the larger context of what we currently know about after-school programs and how they work.

What We Know About After-School Programs for Youth

Formal and Structured After-School Programs

Our previous article provides a detailed, extensive review of published research on after-school programs for youth aged 6–18 (see Clark, Harris, & Allen, 2005). Evidence shows that youth who spend time in formal and structured after-school activities benefit in peer interactions and social adjustment (Bernman, Winkleby, Chesterman, & Boyce, 1992; Marshall et al., 1997; Pettit, Laird, Bates, & Dodge, 1997; Posner & Vandell, 1994) as well as academic achievement (Posner & Vandell, 1994). They also spent more time in adult-guided activities, high-yield literacy-building activities, and constructive learning activities. As a result of such experiences, these youth participants reported greater enjoyment and engagement in educational activities, were less likely to participate in antisocial activities, saw improved academic outcomes, and enjoyed improved relationships with family and peers (Allen & Clark, 1998; Schinke, Cole, & Poulin, 2000; Tierney, Grossman, & Resch, 1995).

Similarly, children who are placed in child-care arrangements with structure and activities benefit more than children who are placed in unstructured programs (Posner & Vandell, 1994; Witt & Baker, 1997). Youth who participate in extracurricular activities and organized sports increase their likelihood that they will remain in school and see improved academic outcomes (Bell, 1967; Gerber, 1996). Youth who participate in extracurricular activities are less likely to engage in deviant behavior, including drug usage, and school- and community-related deviance (Hastad, Segrave, Pangrazi, & Petersen, 1984; Landers & Landers, 1978).

After-School Program Benefits for African American Youth

Ten studies include youth from different racial-ethnic groups in their data samples, and a handful we reviewed explored the different effects of program participation among African American and White students or the effects of program participation in majority African American populations. In an examination of school- and non–school-based extracurricular activities and academic achievement, Gerber (1996) found that the amount of participation in extracurricular activities improved academic achievement. However, this relationship was stronger for White students overall.

Along the same lines, Posner and Vandell (1999) explored after-school activities of African American and White children (grades 3–5) from low-income households. Among key distinctions, African American children spent more time in transit after school (likely owing to the school district's busing policy), and consequently had less time available than White children for after-school activities. By fifth grade, African American children's participation in after-school activities surpassed that of White children (Posner & Vandell, 1999, p. 876). However, both groups saw similar patterns in academic achievement. The African American youth who had greater emotional adjustment, higher academic grades, and less behavioral problems spent less time in unstructured activities (e.g., hanging out, watching television) in fifth grade than did children with poor adjustment scores. Higher academic grades were associated with children participating in extracurricular activities as fifth graders. However, fifth graders reported by teachers as having better emotional adjustment had spent the prior 3 years in non-sport-related extracurricular activities.

Correspondingly, Kahane et al. (2001), in an analysis of after-school programs with an African American student sample, found that almost all programs provide significantly more engaging and sufficient learning and social contexts for students than the school day, according to student surveys. In addition, this finding was particularly greater for African American male youth. Thus, it seems that for African American students, structured, adult-led after-school programs help them develop academically and socially.

It is important to not only identify programs that have been successful in their efforts to work with Black males but also to understand how and why these programs work. An important goal of our cluster evaluation of the African American Men and Boys Initiative was to identify elements, practices, philosophies, and procedures common across programs that are proven to be successful in their work with African American men and boys. In addition, we hoped to identify exemplary examples or programs that represent "best practices" in this area of endeavor. From this specific and concrete information can come models for use in other African American communities across the nation.

Based on our review of the published literature, we developed six research questions:

1. What is the relationship between youths' length of time in the program and their time doing high-yield activities?
2. What is the relationship between youths' perceived support from parents, school, kin, and friends with youths' personal development?
3. What areas of personal development correlate most strongly with educational aspirations and achievement?
4. What is the relationship between variables measuring youths' weekly time in relationships with program volunteers and other caring adults with the youths' personal development?
5. What is the relationship between program leaders' efforts/strategies to acquire money and volunteers with the ratio of youths-to-adults in the program?

Despite depressing statistics, most Black men lead productive, positive lives. Although it is true that African American males have the highest high school and college dropout rates in the country (Braddock, 1990), the findings from this research will serve to demonstrate that the massive failure and incarceration of Black males in American society is not inescapable. Examples, models, and procedures will illuminate specific strategies used to engender alternative outcomes for African American youth. The following text details the design, results, and implications of this study.

Study Design

The African American Men and Boys (AAMB) Initiative is funded by the W. K. Kellogg Foundation to increase opportunities for African American men and boys considered at greatest risk. This $11 million initiative served nearly 17,000 youth in 30 programs in 1996 (this sizeable number for youth served by these programs was mostly attributable to the large weekly audience of the Omega Boys Club "Street Soldiers" radio program). We draw our data from these AAMB programs listed in Table 7.1 and organized by goals. The programs are arranged by procedures for delivery of services listed at the end of the chapter. The primary objective of the Entrepreneurial Leadership Development Village, for example, was to help participants develop job- or business-related skills. The Personal and Academic Leadership Development Village developed participants' life-management and/or literacy skills. The main objective of the Family and Community Leadership Development Village was to develop participants' skills to work effectively with agencies and/or with families in their local communities. This village distinguishes itself from the others by its emphasis on explicitly assisting participants to attain higher standards of living.

Table 7.1 Programs by Village

Geographical Region	Entrepreneurial Leadership Village (n = 7)	Personal and Academic Leadership Village (n = 15)	Family and Community Leadership Village (n = 8)
East Coast	The Club (Boston, MA)	Project 2000 (Washington, D.C.)	Institute for Responsible Fatherhood (Washington, D.C)
	Champs Cookies (Washington, D.C)	National Trust (Washington, D.C.)	National Urban Coalition (Washington, D.C.)
	OIC (Philadelphia, PA)	Ellington Fund (Washington, D.C.)	People's Church (Washington, D.C.)
	Boston Health CREW (Boston, MA)	Bridging Bridges (Cambridge, MA)	
	Project LEEO (Roxbury, MA)	Boys Choir of Harlem (New York, NY)	
South/Southeast	Pathways (Dermott, AR)	Ervin's Youth Club (Clearwater, FL)	Project Alpha (Atlanta, GA)
	Our Family Table (Atlanta, GA)	Piney Woods (Piney Woods, MS)	Federation of So. Cooperatives (Epes, AL)
		Omega Little Brothers (Helena, AK)	
		Keep Hope Alive (Commerce, TX)	
Midwest		Youth Leadership Academy (Milwaukee, WI)	MAD DADS (Omaha, NE)
		University of Kansas (Lawrence, KS)	East End Rites of Passage (Cleveland, OH)
		Athletes Against Drugs (Chicago, IL)	
		No Dope Express (Chicago, IL)	
		Boys to Men (Chicago, IL)	
West Coast		Al Wooten Jr. Boys to Men (Los Angeles, CA)	Omega Boys Club (San Francisco, CA)

Most programs were located in the East, Midwest, or South. Five Entrepreneurial Leadership programs were in East Coast cities and two in Southern cities. Of the 15 Personal and Academic Leadership Village programs, five were in East Coast cities, four were in Southern cities, five were in Midwestern cities, and one was in a West Coast city. Of the Family and Community Leadership programs, three were in East Coast cities, two in Southern cities, two in Midwestern cities, and one in a West Coast city.

This study consisted of three main phases: a pilot study, a pretest, and a post-test. The primary goal of the pilot study was to provide baseline information on program participants. What are the characteristics of program participants? How did they learn about these programs? What attracted them to these programs? What activities and services did the program provide? In what ways did the program affect the participants' lives? Results from this study are summarized in an unpublished report (Allen & Clark, 1998).

In a second phase of our work (Allen & Clark, 1998), we developed a short-form, "Time 1" survey of participants in programs funded by the African American Men and Boys Initiative. From this we could assess program process and participant outcomes (see Clark & Associates Web site—http://www.timeuse.com—for details on time use survey).

For the third phase of our work (Allen & Clark, 1998), we collected pre- and post-"treatment" data on 21 community-based programs working with African American men and boys. Of these programs, 15 had high school populations and 14 had elementary school-aged populations. Eight of the programs had overlapping age groups. Program participants completed the survey at the beginning of the program (September/October 1996) and then again in May/June 1997 after having been involved with the program for between 6 and 10 months.

The first survey collected demographic data from the participants as well as data designed to measure their academic, social, emotional, physical, intrapersonal, and ethical development. (For more details on procedures, surveys, and items, see Allen & Clark, 1998; Clark, Harris, & Allen, 2005.) The second survey assessed students' time-use patterns in the previous 168-hour week (Monday through Sunday from 6:00 a.m. until 11:30 p.m. in half-hour intervals). Students outlined the activities they participated in during a usual week. Twenty-six categories of activities were included, focusing on four major areas of life: learning, health maintenance, work, and leisure (see Web site of Clark & Associates; http://www.timeuse.com). In addition, project directors responded to a survey about their perceptions of each respondent's progress in the key areas. The directors also responded to questions about their own social and educational backgrounds, the number of employees and volunteers working with the youth, recruitment strategies, public relations practices, involvement of parents, and fundraising efforts (Table 7.2). Comparison of results between Time 1 and Time 2 show whether and how programs affect participants' values, activities, life goals, attitudes, and other outcomes over time.

Table 7.2 Variable Description

Variable Name	Description	Coding
Ds14cnt	Directors survey—Variety of recruiting techniques	Interval
Ds19_1	Directors survey—Effort to recruit volunteers	0 = No, 1 = Yes
Ds19totl	No. of strategies	Interval
Ds20@12	Ratio of participants to directly involved volunteers (partic/ds20_1)	Ratio
Ds21	Directors survey—no. of months involved	Interval
Ds25_2sc	Directors survey—no. of times a year a newsletter is published	1 once a year 2 twice a year 3 three or more times a year
Ds30_scl	Directors survey—no. of proposals submitted in 1996	1 0 to 1 2 2 to 3 3 4 to 5 4 6 to 10 5 11 or more
Ds39tot	Directors survey—no. of methods used to contact financial donors	
Ds40ccnt	Directors survey—no. of relationships with service organizations	0 zero contacts 1 up to 8 contacts 2 9 to 12 contacts 3 13 to 15 contacts 4 16 to 19 contacts 5 20 or more contacts
Hlei_2	Sum of total time spent during the week in leisure activities	Interval
Hlrn2_2	Sum of total week learning without school	Interval
Lg5_2	Less than 22.5 hours a week of leisure	0 = No, 1 = Yes
Po1_1v4	Have you participated in community activities?	0 = No, 1 = Yes
Po1_1v5	Have you participated in constructive activities?	0 = No, 1 = Yes
Po15	Educational goals	Categorical: 1= some high school, 7 = Ph.D. or professional
Po19_rc	Trouble since joining the program	0 = No, 1 = Yes
Po1tot	Total activities–post	Interval
Po2_v	Participant rating of progress–post	Categorical 1 = none, 5 = tremendous amount
Po3_1v1	How has life changed—better job?	O = No, 1 = Yes
Po3_1v2	How has life changed—better attitude?	O = No, 1 = Yes

Continued

Table 7.2 Variable Description (*Continued*)

Variable Name	Description	Coding
Po3_1v3	How has life changed—better person?	O = No, 1 = Yes
Po3_1v4	How has life changed—self-aware?	O = No, 1 = Yes
Po3_1v5	How has life changed—culturally aware?	O = No, 1 = Yes
Po3_1v6	How has life changed—school improved?	O = No, 1 = Yes
Po3tot	Total ways that life has changed	Interval
Po4_1v1	Support from parents	O = No, 1 = Yes
Po4_1v10	Support from spiritual	O = No, 1 = Yes
Po4_1v2	Support from siblings	O = No, 1 = Yes
Po4_1v3	Support from extended family	O = No, 1 = Yes
Po4_1v4	Support from friends	O = No, 1 = Yes
Po4_1v5	Support from school staff	O = No, 1 = Yes
Po4_1v6	Support from mentor	O = No, 1 = Yes
Po6_1	Future job first choice	Categorical
Po7_1rc	Do you smoke?	0 = Yes, 1 = No
Po8_3	Have you used alcohol/drugs?	0 = Yes, 1 = No
Pol_1v4	Activities participated in community	O = No, 1 = Yes
Pr30	When participant joined the project	1 = 1995 or earlier (1 year or more at pretest) 2 = 1996 or later (less than 1 year at pretest)
Prcount	Directors survey—no. of times public relations activities done in 1996	Interval
Prdone	Directors survey—no. of times conducted public relations activities	1 0–10 instances 2 11–20 instances 3 21–30 instances 4 31–40 instances 5 41 or more instances
Vol_yr	Total volunteer hours per year	Interval

The current analysis includes 304 youths separated into elementary and high school subsamples. Within the elementary school aged sample (*N* = 131), the youth are primarily African American (96%) and male (82%) and ranged in age from 5 to 15, with the majority (81%) being between age 10 and 14. Within the high school sample (*N* = 173), the youth are again primarily African American (98%) and male (87%). Their ages range from 13 to 25, with the majority (80%) aged 14 to 17.

Study Results: Programs Making a Positive Difference

Building a Solid Foundation

The findings from analyses (Tables 7.2–7.7) show that within the elementary-aged sample, youths' time in the program correlates with fewer community activities ($-.246$, $p < .01$), and with spending fewer than 22.5 hours per week in leisure activities ($-.246$, $p < .01$). Thus, the more time a youth has spent in a program, the less leisure time he or she has. Within the high school population, more time spent in the program is associated with less cigarette smoking ($-.196$, $p < .05$); more time spent on leisure activities ($.197$, $p < .05$); getting more sleep ($-.180$, $p < .05$); and increased cultural awareness ($-.210$, $p < .05$). In sum, there is a positive relationship between youth participation in these community programs and healthy, well-balanced personal development.

Personal development is also affected by perceptions of family and other direct support. Among the elementary age group sample, we found that the support of immediate family is correlated with higher youth ratings of progress ($.214$, $p < .05$) and with likelihood of improved school outcomes ($.269$, $p < .05$). Support of extended family also correlated with perceived school improvement ($.278$, $p < .01$), better attitude ($.194$, $p < .05$), and a perception of improvement in more areas ($.215$, $p < .01$). The support of the school staff correlates with higher educational goals ($.248$, $p < .01$). Spiritual support correlates with the likelihood that respondent says that he or she is more self-aware ($.216$, $p < .05$) and with a perception that improvement has occurred in multiple areas ($.214$, $p < .05$). Perception of mentor support correlates with the number of program activities ($.441$, $p < .01$).

For the high school youth, we found that the support of immediate family (parents) is correlated with likelihood that participants' school performance improved ($.280$, $p < .01$). Support from siblings is correlated with less frequent drug use ($.323$, $p < .05$) and a tendency for a participant to say that he or she is a better ($.201$, $p < .01$), more self-aware ($.190$, $p < .01$) person. In addition, the support of friends/peers correlates with the likelihood that the participant will indicate that he or she is a better person ($.271$, $p < .01$), is more culturally and self-aware ($.323$, $p < .01$, $.317$, $p < .01$), and that he or she is doing a better job ($.223$, $p < .01$). Friend/peer support is also correlated with reported school improvement ($.178$, $p < .05$). Support of mentors correlates with indications that a participant has a better attitude ($.245$, $p < .05$), is a better person ($.239$, $p < .05$), and is more culturally aware ($.284$, $p < .01$). In addition, spiritual support correlates with lower frequency of drug use ($.425$, $p < .05$) and with higher educational goals ($.282$, $p < .01$).

Assuming that participation in community-based programs coupled with support from family and community mentors increases youths' educational aspirations, what in turn is the relationship between youths' educational aspirations and other aspects of their personal development? Within the elementary age group, we found that the variable measuring high educational goals correlates positively with participants' reporting that they have a better attitude ($.208$, $p < .05$). Among the high school sample, a positive correlation was found between youth, the variable

Table 7.3 Elementary Correlation Matrix: Research Questions 1–4

Variable Name	Learn Without Xchool	Trouble	Progress	When Joined Program	Total Activity	Total Leisure Time	Time Hanging Out	Cons-tructive Activity	Support Parents
Learning w/o school (hlrn2_2)	1.000 (131)								
Trouble (po19_rc)	.311** (105)	1.000 (105)							
Progress (po2_v)	−.152 (109)	.081 (84)	1.000 (109)						
When joined program (pr30)	.050 (117)	−.091 (96)	.068 (95)	1.000 (117)					
Total activities (po1tot)	.022 (131)	−.082 (105)	.256** (109)	−.177 (117)	1.000 (131)				
Total leisure time (hlei_2)	−.545** (131)	.020 (105)	.155 (109)	.173 (117)	−.078 (131)	1.000 (131)			
Time hanging out (a19tot_2)	−.389** (131)	.136 (105	.224* (109	.062 (47)	−.015 (131)	.592** (131)	1.000 (131)		
Constructive activities (po1_1v5)	.158 (131)	−.099 (105)	.066 (109)	−.087 (114)	.558** (131)	−.188* (131)	−.246** (131)	1.000 (131)	
Support parents (po4_1v1)	.027 (122)	−.060 (96)	.214* (103)	.025 (110)	.172 (122)	−.074 (122)	−.094 (122)	.142 (122)	1.000 (122)
School improve (po3_1v6)	.173 (120)	−.101 (96)	.132 (101)	−.087 (109)	.309** (120)	−.171 (120)	−.105 (120)	.191* (120)	.269** (120)
Support extended family (po4_1v3)	.031 (122)	.022 (96)	.024 (103)	.016 (110)	.386** (122)	−.138 (122)	−.022 (122)	.190* (122)	.134 (122)
Doing better job (po3_1v1)	−.039 (120)	−.099 (96)	.142 (101)	.147 (109)	.148 (120)	.098 (120)	.015 (120)	.050 (120)	−.057 (120)
Support school (po4_1v5)	.250** (122)	.071 (96)	.061 (103)	−.026 (110)	.192* (122)	−.087 (122)	−.149 (122).	.165 (122)	.194* (122)
Education goals (po15)	.109 (127)	.141 (103)	.022 (106)	−.033 (115)	.088 (127)	−.146 (127)	−.086 (127)	.124. (127)	.231* (119)
Support spiritual (PO4_1v10)	.278** (103)	−.052 (78)	−.027 (103)	−.205 (91)	.298** (103)	−.199 (103)	−.141 (103)	.219* (103)	.106 (103)
Self-aware (po3_1v4)	.000 (120)	.009 (96)	.128 (101)	−.007 (109)	.381** (120)	.128 (120)	−.196* (120)	.091 (120)	.115 (120)
Ways life changed (po3tot)	.030 (120)	−.150 (96)	.158 (101)	.002 (109)	.475** (120)	.107 (120)	.175 (120)	.178 (120)	.144 (120)
Support mentor (po4_1v6)	.080 (104)	.044 (79)	.105 (103)	−.006 (92)	.441** (104)	.051 (104)	−.019 (104)	.437** (104)	.132 (104)
Better attitude (po3_1v2)	−.021 (120)	−.121 (96)	.169 (101)	.124 (109)	.377** (120)	.095 (120)	.130 (120)	.087 (120)	.102 (120)
Community activity (po1_1v4)	−.095 (131)	−.017 (105)	.211* (109)	−.246** (117)	.477** (131)	−.180* (131)	.025* (131)	.017 (131)	−.065 (122)
Leisure time (lg5_2)	.460** (131)	−.007 (105)	−.094 (109)	−.246** (117)	.037 (131)	−.834** (131)	.089 (131)	.136 (131)	.026 (122)

School Improve	Support Extended Family	Doing Better Job	Support School	Education Goals	Support Spiritual	Self-Aware	Ways Life Changed	Support Mentor	Better Attitude	Community Activity	Leisure Time
1.000											
(120)											
.278**	1.000										
(120)	(122)										
.177	.108	1.000									
(120)	(120)	(120)									
.166	.188**	.021	1.000								
(120)	(122)	(120)	(122)								
.057	.200*	−.021	.248**	1.000							
(117)	(119)	(117)	(119)	(127)							
.172	.227*	−.048	.303**	.090	1.000						
(101)	(103)	(101)	(103)	(101)	(103)						
.035	.087	.203*	.087	.112	.216*	1.000					
(120)	(120)	(120)	(120)	(117)	(101)	(120)					
.305**	.215*	.366**	.113	.152	.214*	.806**	1.000				
(120)	(120)	(120)	(120)	(117)	(101)	(120)	(120)				
.104	.166	−.117	.266**	.021	.286*	.076	.019	1.000			
(102)	(104)	(102)	(104)	(102)	(103)	(102)	(102)	(104)			
−.001	.194*	.078	.128	.208*	.100	.501**	.684**	−.003	1.000		
(120)	(120)	(120)	(120)	(117)	(101)	(120)	(120)	(102)	(120)		
.172	.172	.165	.061	−.005	.108*	.156	.276**	−.048*	.242**	1.000	
(120)	(122)	(120)	(122)	(127)	(103)	(120)	(120)	(104)	(120)	(131)	
.099	.087	−.077	.046	.156	.164	−.045	−.085	−.062	−.110	.139	1.000
(120)	(122)	(120)	(122)	(127)	(103)	(120)	(120)	(104)	(120)	(131)	(131)

Table 7.4 Elementary Correlations Matrix: Research Questions 5–6

Variable Name	Ratio of Clients to Volunteers	School Improve	Publish Newsletter	Proposals Submitted	Public Relations Total	Volunteer Hours/Year	Public Relations Done	Relationship With Service Organization
Ratio of clients to volunteers (ds20@12)	1.000 (131)							
School improve (po3_1v6)	−.189* (120)	1.000 (120)						
Publish newsletter (ds25_2sc)	−.450** (84)	−.110 (77)	1.000 (84)					
Proposals submitted (ds30_scl)	−.347** (131)	.157 (120)	−.639** (84)	1.000 (131)				
Public relations total (ds39tot)	−.520** (131)	.028 (120)	−.217* (84)	.260** (131)	1.000 (131)			
Volunteer hours/year (vol_yr)	−.538** (129)	.130 (118)	.612** (82)	.202* (129)	−.100 (129)	1.000 (129)		
Public relations done (prdone)	−.520** (131)	.204* (120)	.208 (84)	.369** (131)	.087 (131)	.409** (129)	1.000 (131)	
Relationship with service organizations (ds40ccnt)	.163 (131)	.053 (120)	.471** (84)	−.173* (131)	−.464** (131)	.312** (129)	.310** (131)	1.000 (131)

Table 7.5 High School Correlation Matrix Questions 1 and 2

Variable Name	Time in Project	Cultural Awareness	Smoke Cigarettes	Total Leisure	Trouble	Future Job	Progress	Leisure
Time in project (pr30)	1.000 (122)							
Cultural awareness (po3_1v5)	−.210* (116)	1.000 (163)						
Smoke cigarettes (po7_1rc)	−.196* (121)	.110 (160)	1.000 (170)					
Total leisure (hlei_2)	.197* (122)	.022 (163)	−.072 (171)	1.000 (173)				
Trouble (po19_rc)	.047 (113)	.103 (158)	.071 (161)	.027 (164)	1.000 (164)			
Future job (po6_1)	.062 (110)	−.043 (151)	.087 (154)	.118 (155)	−.059 (152)	1.000 (155)		
Progress (po2_v)	.244 (54)	−.081 (93)	−.062 (100)	.088 (101)	−.032 (92)	.058 (87)	1.000 (101)	
Leisure (lg5_2)	−.100 (122)	.073 (163)	.046 (170)	−.816** (173)	.042 (164)	−.122 (155)	−.196* (101)	1.000 (173)

Table 7.6 High School Correlation Matrix Question 3

Variable Na,me	Self-Aware	Frequency of Alcohol and Drugs	Support of Family	School Improve	Support of Siblings
Self-awareness (po3_1v4)	1.000 (163)				
Frequency of alcohol and drugs (po8_3)	.020 (43)	1.000 (44)			
Support –of family (po4_1v1)	.126 (162)	.056 (43)	1.000 (166)		
School improve (po3_1v6)	.188* (163)	−.144 (43)	.280** (162)	1.000 (163)	
Support –of siblings (po4_1v2)	.190* (162)	.323* (43)	.242** (166)	.121 (162)	1.000 (166)
Better person (po3_1v3)	.369** (163)	.089 (43)	.025 (162)	.103 (163)	.201* (162)
Support –of friends (po4_1v4)	.323** (162)	.213 (43)	.238** (166)	.178* (162)	.354** (166)
Better job (po3_1v1)	.234** (163)	−.071 (43)	.072 (162)	.205** (163)	.141 (162)
Support of mentors (po4_1v6)	.08198)	.067 (29)	−.029 (101)	−.028 (98)	.054 (101)
Better attitude (po3_1v2)		.206** (163)	−.102 (43)	.085 (162)	.080 (163)	.026 (162)
Cultural awareness (po3_1v5)	.432** (163)	−.055 (43)	.097 (162)	.271** (163)	.058 (162)
Support –spiritual (po4_1v10)	.286** (97)	.425* (29)	.017 (100)	−.137 (97)	.148 (100)
Educational goals (po15)	.020(154)	.498*(42)	−.044(157)	−.130 (154)	.063 (157)

	Better Person	Support of Friends	Better Job	Support of Mentors	Better Attitude	Culturally Aware	Support– Spiritual	Education Goals
	1.000							
	(163)							
	.271**	1.000						
	(162)	(166)						
	.159*	.223**	1.000					
	(163)	(162)	(163)					
	.239*	.110	−.071	1.000				
	(98)	(101)	(98)	(101)				
	.191*	.075	.092	.245*	1.000			
	(163)	(162)	(163)	(98)	(163)			
	.265**	.317**	.227**	.284**	.193*	1.000		
	(163)	(162)	(163)	(98)	(163)	(163)		
	.286**	.267**	.053	.218*	.200*	.195	1.000	
	(97)	(100)	(97)	(99)	(97)	(97)	(100)	
	.013	−.044	−.003	.005	.031	.081	.282**	1.000
	(154)	(157)	(154)	(92)	(154)	(154)	(92)	(164)

Table 7.7 High School Correlation Matrix Questions 4–6

	Educational Goals	Used Drugs or Alcohol	No. Months Volunteers Involved	Volunteer Hours/Year	Better Attitude
Educational goals (po15)	1.000 (164)				
Used drugs or alcohol (po8_3)	.498** (42)	1.000 (44)			
No. months volunteers involved (ds21)	−.076 (161)	−.286 (42)	1.000 (168)		
Volunteer hours/year (vol_yr)	−.102 (160)	−.405** (42)	.487** (167)	1.000 (167)	
Better attitude (po3_1v2)	.031 (154)	−.102 (43)	.209** (158)	.216** (157)	1.000 (163)
Community activity (po1_1v4)	−.017 (164)	−.293 (44)	.360** (168)	.175* (167)	.052 (163)
Ratio of clients to volunteers (ds20@12)	.003 (161)	.191 (44)	.120 (168)	−.188* (167)	.119 (158)
No. of recruitment techniques (ds14cnt)	−.277** (164)	−.133 (44)	.031 (168)	.429** (167)	−.023 (163)
Recruit volunteers (ds19_1)	.070 (164)	.108 (44)	−.351** (168)	.045 (167)	−.240** (163)
Strategies used (ds19totl)	−.285** (164)	−.218 (44)	.205** (168)	.037 (167)	.013 (163)
Public relations (prcount)	−.076 (164)	.120 (44)	.496** (168)	.599** (167)	.198* (163)
Service organizations (ds40ccnt)	−.207** (164)	−.127 (44)	.463** (168)	.279** (167)	.054 (163)

Community Activity	Ratio of Clients to Volunteers	No. Recruitment Techniques	Recruit Volunteers	Strategies Used	Public Relations	Service Organizations
1.000						
(173)						
.103	1.000					
(168)	(168)					
.015	−.152*	1.000				
(173)	(168)	(173)				
−.243**	−.951**	.058	1.000			
(173)	(168)	(173)	(173)			
.086	−.313**	.286**	.442**	1.000		
(173)	(168)	(173)	(173)	(173)		
.235**	.646**	.201**	−.472**	−.166*	1.000	
(173)	(168)	(173)	(173)	(173)	(173)	
.048	.125	−.101	−.018	.453*	.225**	1.000
(173)	(168)	(173)	(173)	(173)	(173)	(173)

measuring youths' educational goals, and their drug use (.498, $p < .01$). Thus, the higher the educational goals, the more likely the youth has not engaged in the use of drugs and alcohol.

Although these findings cannot establish the causal direction between the variables or the effect of one variable on another, we suggest that important foundations are being established through youths' participation in these community-based programs. When youth spend time in these programs, they feel their schoolwork improved, they have better attitudes, and have higher educational and occupational aspirations. In turn, youth with higher educational goals tend to be more committed to positive lifestyles.

Inside the Black Box

The remaining two research questions focus on the structure of the community-based programs, including the relationships between youths' time with program volunteers and other caring adults and their perceived personal development. Within the elementary-aged group, the ratio of clients to volunteers (essentially, a measure of overcrowding in a program) is inversely correlated with the likelihood that youths perceive their schoolwork has improved ($-.189$, $p < .05$). In other words, the less crowded the program, the more likely youth are to say their schoolwork has improved. For the high school group, the two variables the longer the volunteers had been involved and the total volunteer hours per year is positively associated with youths' reports of better attitude (.209, $p < .01$, .216, $p < .01$) and more time spent volunteering in their community (.360, $p < .05$, .175, $p < .05$). Clearly, the structure of the program is important. As Kahane et al. (2001) note, not all programs designed to improve achievement and development of youth provide positive opportunities.

Strategic outreach on the part of administrators is also important. Within the elementary group, we find that the ratio of clients to volunteers (more volunteers than clients) is correlated with efforts to publish newsletters ($-.450$, $p < .01$), proposals submitted for funding ($-.347$, $p < .01$), and public relations efforts ($-.520$, $p < .01$). Likewise, volunteer hours per year are correlated with public relations efforts (.409, $p < .01$), the number of times per year a newsletter is published (.612, $p < .01$), the number of proposals submitted (.202, $p < .05$), and having more relationships with other service organizations (.312, $p < .01$). Results were similar for programs serving older youth. A large ratio of clients-to-volunteers has a negative relationship to recruitment strategies. The higher the ratios, the fewer recruitment techniques ($-.152$, $p < .05$), efforts to recruit volunteers ($-.951$, $p < .01$), and strategies used ($-.313$, $p < .01$). The more volunteer hours per year, the more recruitment techniques used (.429, $p < .01$), more public relations efforts underway (.599, $p < .01$), and a greater web of relationships with other service organizations (.279, $p < .01$). Thus, the more overcrowded a program is, the less efforts are made to publicize the program and solicit funding. Conversely, the more hours volunteers are present in the program, the more proposals are submitted for funding, the more newsletters published, the more the program is marketed, and the greater the collaboration with other service organizations. In summary, when programs are overcrowded (i.e., have a higher clients-to-volunteers ratio), youth perceive fewer benefits and the administration is less able to promote the organization through public relations and in turn receive less attention from potential volunteers or fundraising sources.

Change Over Time

We next conduct t-tests to explore participants' changes in survey responses between Time 1 to Time 2. Among the elementary sample, we found significant increases in time spent in structured academic activities. For example, during an average week, the youth spent 46 additional minutes in tutored lessons ($p \leq .01$), 89 minutes in study time ($p \leq .05$), and 38 minutes in computer time ($p \leq .05$). In addition to increased amounts of time in structured activities, the youth experienced 3:45 more time per week with adults ($p \leq .01$).

We also found increases in high school youths' time in constructive activities. Between Time 1 and Time 2, the youth, on average, spent 2 additional hours in school enrichment activities ($p \leq .000$) and 2 hours performing health activities (excluding sleep) ($p \leq .05$). Similar to the elementary sample, the youth experienced an increase of 2:20 in time spent with adults per week ($p \leq .01$). Although the time increases in structured activities may overlap with the time spent with adults, this overall growth in the amount of time youth spent with adults is viewed as a positive lifestyle change, one that can contribute to the social, personal, and academic aspects of the youths' lives. Combining these results with the above review of past research suggests and reinforces the fact that participating in structured and adult-led community programs can lead to more productive uses of youths' time and better overall outcomes.

Policy and Practice Implications

The evidence is encouraging that community-based programs can successfully assist African American boys in leading meaningful and productive lives. After-school programs that have sufficient resources, adult supervision, and structured curricular supports achieve positive outcomes for their participants (see Cosden, Morrison, Gutierrez, & Brown, 2004; Fashola, 2003; Mahoney, Lord, & Carryl, 2005). They have shown themselves to be effective vehicles for assisting the healthy, constructive development of youth. This study furthers those findings by illuminating the contributions made by the African American Men and Boys Initiative. Given the daily barrage of negative images of Black males, it is important to document the patterns, experiences, and personal relationships that improve the outcomes for youth, and that can showcase the stories of the many African American males who manage to succeed, often against the odds. By presenting the empirical findings on these youths' positive experiences and outcomes, as we have done in this study, we can better identify common themes, challenges, and achievements.

Among the practical lessons learned from this research is that after the school bell rings, youth need more school- and community-based centers where they can feed and foster their own futures. While there are numerous programs already operating, not all programs are equally effective. What is needed are more programs that are well structured, well staffed, and well considered programmatically. The ideal centers would offer structured opportunities to participate in healthy and positive academic and sports-related activities under the mentorship of adults. Youth should be able to choose their activities, but those activities must be well structured with connections made between school and home. The activities should also be developmentally appropriate and fun (Costello et al., 2000). The programs would have low student:staff ratios and staff would be well trained in their program areas. Ideally, each child would be connected to one staff or volunteer based on interests and expertise. Having a place to interact with positive peer and role models and to explore new identities in safe, less formal settings (sometimes beyond the expectations of direct family) is imperative to healthy development.

More funds are also needed to attract experienced and dedicated executive directors to administer and recruit volunteers for these programs. Rarely is human success a solo project. Rather, successful people are usually products of networks of individuals, groups, institutions, and organizations that help them identify, develop, and exercise their capabilities. At their most basic, organizations should ensure that staff understand the organization's mission, and scheduling should ensure adequate programming and some degree of continuity. Staff should have the necessary supplies at their disposal, and budgets should be in place for each program and regularly reviewed. The roles and responsibilities of staff members and volunteers should be clear and both have appropriate support. Staff and volunteers should have opportunities for advancement and to improve their skills. Parents should also be regularly involved (Costello et al., 2000). Ideally, the program would have a method to assess its quality and the time and funding to commit to marketing its services, collaborating with other service organizations, and to continue to seek out and apply for funding opportunities.

James Baldwin (1985) once said that in a racially oppressive country like America, "the wonder is not that so many fail, but rather that so many succeed." The massive failure and incarceration of Black males in American society is not inevitable. The challenge before us is to focus on success stories, understand their underlying processes, and to replicate the models. All stakeholders—Black males themselves, Black families, Black communities, the larger White community, private business and government agencies—must recommit to the goal of achieving viable roles and full citizenship for African American men and boys. If America is to achieve her full promise as a democracy, the persistent crisis of Black males must be solved. For ultimately the status of Black males is but a reflection of the larger crisis arising from the persistent gap between the American Dream of equality and freedom for all and the American Nightmare of stubborn, widening inequality.

How Do the Youth Programs Deliver Their Services?

This section describes the activities and methods used by selected youth programs to help participants build the necessary foundation for success. Note the common threads of responsible adult guidance and encouragement of youths to participate in success-oriented learning activities.

Project Keep Hope Alive

Project Keep Hope Alive, in Commerce, Texas (Dr. Anthony Harris and Ricardo Finley, directors), is a program that promotes personal and academic leadership among Black males from first through sixth grade. The program focuses on both academic and psychosocial aspects of life. Academics are implemented by pairing up each child with a mentor who has previously worked with youngsters. The children are instructed to bring homework with them on a daily basis, and if they have no homework to do, to bring a book to read instead. Writing journals are also part of their academic program. The children are given a topic and instructed to write about that topic for a specified length of time each day. Psychosocial learning is implemented in both formal and informal ways. Children are taken to cultural and social events, such as museums, sporting events, and restaurants. Enrichment activities, such as photography classes, martial arts classes, wrestling classes, art classes, computer training, and choir, are an important part of the daily routine as well. The children are also taught to be effective leaders. The group elects officers and is then taught Robert's rules of order, which is a lesson that has inspired many children to run for student government at their schools.

The program runs throughout the entire school year and then resumes again about 1 month after the end of the school year for the summer. During the school year, the children are at the center from 3 p.m. to 6 p.m., and during the summer they attend from 10 a.m. to 5:30 p.m. Since they are present for a longer period of time each day during the summer, this is when more time can be dedicated to computer work and other enrichment activities, as there is no homework to be completed. A routine day during the school year goes as follows: the children are picked up from school by the center's vans and brought to the center. The first thing they do when they arrive is put their belongings down, gather on the stage, and recite the motto, which is "Be the Best." They then must shake the hands of the mentors who are present. After this, the children begin on their homework with their mentors. The length of time spent on this task varies with the age of the child; first graders will spend less time on homework than sixth graders. Once homework is completed, the children are given a topic and instructed to write about that topic in their journals for a given length of time, usually from 30 to 45 minutes, depending on the topic. Enrichment activities are next, which include the photography classes, art classes, and so on. The children are then taken home by the center's vans. Throughout the day, informal lessons may be brought up and discussed. One example of an informal lesson is how to talk to girls. The children are taught how to introduce themselves, how to open doors for ladies, to let ladies go first, and how to pull out chairs. Other "lessons" may be brought up when the children want to discuss something in particular, for example, the death of a classmate.

Champs Cookies

Champs Cookies, in Washington, D.C. (Ali A. Khan, director), provides a number of services to participants, including counseling services and intergenerational activities. Program directors have worked with community leaders such as police officers, school officials, and professional athletes to plan various high school youth activities in the Washington, D.C. area. As part of the entrepreneurial village, this program also focuses on marketing.

Omega Little Brothers

Omega Little Brothers, in Helena, Arkansas (Walter A. Darnell, director), is a program that deals not only with education of young people but also with their mental health. The program was established when a mental health organization came together with a fraternity that was seeking to become involved with a community service program. The mental health organization provides a full range of mental health or psychiatric services for children and adults, both emergency and outpatient services, as well as day treatment services. The program serves approximately 100 children. Seminars given include teen father programs and other educational programs. Fridays are set aside for recreational, social, and enrichment activities. These activities include taking the children to visit state parks for a weekend, taking them to visit major cities, and trying to find young men who could be positive influences and who would share their experiences with the children. They have implemented a Fitness for Life program in which they train the young people how to become athletic trainers. This develops interpersonal, leadership, group, and thinking skills in the children. The educational aspect of this program is addressed in the tutoring programs. High school juniors and seniors with a grade point average of 3.25 or above are hired as tutors for elementary students. High school students are also hired as peer mentors, facilitating special projects such as awareness and assessment for youth, primarily in the area of drug prevention. The program has a summer day camp where children who do not do well academically get tutoring, special mentoring with peers, and participate in growth programs and awareness sessions on positive choices. The children have the opportunity to participate in volunteer services in the community, where they can earn points that turn into "store money." Community banks volunteer to participate in this program, and they will open savings accounts for the students with their "store money."

Project 2000

Project 2000, in Washington, D.C. (Spencer Holland, director), is a program that takes seventh, eighth, and ninth grade students who are doing well in school and watches their progress carefully to assure that the students continue to do well. Each school has a liason, who is either a counselor or a head teacher. The program directors and the liason keep in close contact throughout the school year, discussing the student's grades, attendance, behavior, and so on. All eighth grade students in the program must go through an interpersonal skills development workshop, which is a 10-week-long seminar. Other seminars are offered to the students, such as leadership development, conflict and anger management, teenage pregnancy prevention, and AIDS awareness. Other programs, such as mentoring by sorority members, assist the students in maintaining their grades. Project 2000 also has programs available during the summer. Students 14 years of age and older work for the city government in the mornings and go to seminars in the afternoons. Those students under 14 years old are not allowed to work and therefore only attend the seminars.

Ervin's Youth Club

Ervin's Youth Club, in Clearwater, Florida (E. Ajamu Babalola, director), is a program whose goals include teaching young children respect for themselves and for their community, as well as instilling in them the responsibility of developing that respect. The program teaches children that they should not be looking for handouts, but rather looking for ways to improve themselves. For example, when the group was going on a trip, the program directors told the children that if they wanted to attend, they had to raise enough money to be able to go. By this they did not mean going out and asking for money, but rather, going out and working to earn the money. The directors believe that you do not help a person by giving them handouts and that you must do things in order to help yourself.

Athletes Against Drugs

Athletes Against Drugs (AAD), in Chicago, Illinois (Stedman Graham and Andre Lanier, directors), is a program whose mission is to build clean bodies and clean minds among children. This is accomplished through sports, education, leadership training, role models, and mentors. The program started out by offering all services needed by the children, such as eyeglasses, counseling, corporate visits, speakers, alternative activities, and special events. The program has grown so much that it now offers a more specialized range of services for the children. The services currently provided by AAD are meant to be a replacement for gangs in children's lives. Gangs fill a void in the lives of their members, and therefore it is not wise to remove that from the lives of the children without replacing it with another means of support. The program believes that simply belonging to something, being a member, will fill that void in the children's lives.

Athletes Against Drugs works with professional athletes who volunteer their time, their likeness, and their images. The program maintains an athlete's resource bank of who is available and what kinds of contributions they are willing to make to the program's activities. Members of the community will also talk to the children about their careers and the different options available to them. These community members are usually successful people who came from the same poor neighborhoods as the children. This activity is meant to inspire the children, enabling them to see that they too can make it out of their neighborhoods and become successful individuals. The program receives considerable funding from the sponsors of the athletes, such as Nike, Gatorade, and Converse.

Children who actively participate in the AAD program take part in sports programs and an in-class curriculum. While children from kindergarten to eighth grade can take part in the program, fourth, fifth, and sixth graders are specifically targeted. Schools must agree to provide classroom time for the program because these programs take place during the day. From September to June, various sports clinics take place, as well as a 16-part curriculum that covers drug prevention education, health and fitness, and career awareness. These programs are usually held once a week. In addition to this, AAD activities are facilitated by teachers and coaches usually once or twice a month. Summer programs are planned as well, but they work with smaller groups than the school year programs do. The children attend summer school from 9 a.m. to 12 p.m. and then programs from 12 p.m. to 3 p.m., followed by special planned activities.

The Youth Leadership Academy

The Youth Leadership Academy, in Milwaukee, Wisconsin (Ron Giles, director), is a program that teaches young boys many lessons in leadership. Admittance to the program is by application, and not all who apply are accepted. The first step involves the school referring a child. After the school has referred a child to the program, it is up to that child whether he wants to apply to the program. If he gets the application in on time, he must then attend two interviews with the program. Those who attend both interviews are then invited into the pledge class, where they will attend six Saturday sessions. During this pledge period, some boys will drop out, but there are still many more applicants than positions available. The determining factor for admittance to the program at this point is how early the boys' applications were turned in. Those who turned in their applications earliest will be accepted before those who turned in their applications later.

The program begins once the application process is complete and the boys have been accepted. There are Saturday sessions that are held throughout the academic year, some after-school tutorial work, and 6 weeks of programs during the summer. Other activities may be planned when the opportunities present themselves. During the summer, the schedule is as follows: physical training, breakfast, and then the boys are broken into small groups for a series of classes that focus on leadership, drill, and ceremony. Other classes are given as well, such as history, culture, and science and technology. All of these courses are designed to help the boys work on the basics of reading, writing, and arithmetic. There are two class sessions held in the morning, followed by lunch and another class session. Recreation takes place from 2:30 p.m. to 4:30 p.m. and tries to get the boys involved in nontraditional athletic programs, such as golf and tennis. The day is over at 4:30 p.m., and the boys are sent home. Wednesdays are field trip days each week during the summer.

The Youth Leadership Academy gives boys an education that is not available in their classrooms. For example, each day some of the students go to a television station across the street to learn about video production. The parent's role in all of this is to support their son's involvement in developing the thought and habits of the Academy. This is something that becomes important to the boys. A ceremony is held each September called "Big Bang," at which facilitators and staff pledge their support to the boys as young men. This support is essential for their success, and it fills the boys with a sense of pride.

Boys to Men

Boys to Men, in Chicago, Illinois (Dr. Nolan Shaw, director), is a program that strives for social, cultural, and educational improvement on the part of youth. The program is led by mentors, reinforced by parents, and is under the guidance of a Council of Elders and school principals. The program accepts boys from sixth, seventh, and eighth grades, and students with leadership ability in particular. Much of the program's success comes from the participation of the school's principals and their willingness to be part of the program. Their participation gives the program legitimacy in each school system. Another reason for the program's success is the fact that the mentors are willing to give more of themselves than they are responsible for. The mentors in the program are the teachers at these schools, many of whom have already had some contact with the boys in the program.

In order for a child to be admitted into the program, he must first be nominated by his principal, parents, school staff, or community leaders. Once the nomination is received, it is then reviewed by the review team, which in turn makes recommendations and passes them on to the Council of Elders, who make the final decision. A child must be enrolled in a public elementary school on the South Side of Chicago to be considered for the program. The child should have demonstrated leadership skills and a desire to participate in the program.

The program runs from September through June, and the mentors meet with the boys 2 to 4 times a week, for 30 to 60 minutes. There are also periodic after-school activities, such as convocations or outdoor activities. These times are meant to be a total gathering of the program's membership. The curriculum for the program is divided into units that focus on self-discovery; cultural heritage in terms of background and the history of the people; the ability to understand rituals, protocols, and ceremonies that are part of ancestral development; spiritual, physical, and economic well-being; preparing the boys to become self-reliant; business and entrepreneurial skills; understanding of assertiveness in leadership (when and where to be assertive), along with how to resolve and reduce conflict; how to become and maintain a leader in the midst of adversity; understanding manhood and womanhood in the African sense; teaching the boys respect for the other gender and a social component that allows them to interact and apply these skills. The curriculum concludes with developing and understanding community service so that students are equipped with the skills they need to do volunteer work in their communities.

Sankofa

Project Alpha (Alpha Phi Alpha Fraternity) sponsors the Sankofa Program (Dr. Zollie Stevenson, coordinator) at 11 sites across the country. Programs are located in New Orleans, Louisiana; Baltimore, Maryland; Washington, D.C.; Detroit, Michigan; Miami, Florida; Cleveland, Ohio; Philadelphia, Pennsylvania; Hollywood, California; Atlanta, Georgia; Jackson, Mississippi; and one unknown city. Male volunteers go into school classrooms and teach students principles of effective living and cultural pride.

The Federation of Southern Cooperatives

The Federation of Southern Cooperatives, in Atlanta, Georgia, and Epes, Alabama (Ralph Parge and Gus Townes, directors), is a group of many smaller programs whose mission is to preserve the history and culture of the area and to develop programs for self-sufficiency and empowerment of people. This is done through four programs: *(1)* history and culture, *(2)* land-use education, *(3)* early childhood education, and *(4)* academic and cultural enrichment. The mission for the academic and cultural enrichment program is to help students enhance their academics, culture, and leadership skills through *(1)* daily tutorial programs, *(2)* Saturday programs, *(3)* 6-week summer programs, which include computer training to better assist students in finding jobs, *(4)* teen leadership programs, which include career building, college directions, and job skills, and *(5)* leadership training. The program works with youth ages 3 to 5, and another age group from seventh grade through twelfth grade.

Entrepreneurship training is emphasized through youth camps that provide an understanding of what's involved in founding and operating a business; assistance is also provided to those who are interested in going into business through acquisition of youth loans. The program operates a commercial kitchen, teaching youth canning practices which can involve food processing and marketing. Youth enterprise and agriculture training, which is a school-to-work type of initiative, is designed to promote continued education as well as encourage youth interest in careers related to rural community development and agriculture. The program begins with a summer camp, which involves all of the abuse centers, Native American education, and school programs. Children (ages 12 to 17) who are identified as being at risk are invited to participate. Computer training is provided through a local university. Workshops of 2 to 3 hours are also offered by professionals and teachers (e.g., staff from vocational schools, health clinics, and drug abuse centers). Field trips to vocational schools are organized so the children can get hands-on experience to see if they are interested in particular careers. Attorneys and physicians also offer onsite workshops. Cultural enrichment activities take place, as well as campfire ceremonies and recreational activities. Throughout the year, cultural enrichment activities take place at least twice weekly. The recreational program is scheduled for Saturdays and includes activities such as swimming, camping, picnicking, and canoeing on the lake. Basic programming focuses on high-risk youth, involving a series of workshops that address personal issues and prospective career paths. The program also incorporates components focused on Black fathers with two concerns: *(1)* the youth's own status as fathers or potential fathers, and *(2)* their relationships with and expectations of their own fathers.

Al Wooten Jr. Boys to Men

Al Wooten Jr. Boys to Men, in Los Angeles, California (Linda Miles, director), is a program that was started by Faye Rumph, a woman whose young son was killed by a gang member in a drive-by shooting. The program was developed to give children a haven where they can enjoy themselves and work together as a group. They can work and develop themselves educationally, work on their homework, and have a safe place to be—away from the gang members and the drug dealers. The goal of the program is to help African American boys make a positive transition from boyhood to adulthood by providing comprehensive intervention services to assist them in developing to their full potential as individuals, as men, and as members of the community.

The boys in the program range in age from 8 to 24. It is the hope of the program directors that once a young boy is in the program, he will stay in the program at least until he is 18 years old. The program consists of tutoring, gardening classes, youth leadership training, community service, career vocational guidance, delinquency prevention, and the Boys to Men class. In this class, an adult mentor takes the boys in two different groups, first the 8–12 year olds, then the 13–18 year olds. They talk about whatever the boys want to discuss or whatever may be on their minds at the time. Tutoring takes places every day after school during the school year, and it is provided by youth counselors. During the summer, two tutors come in on every Monday and Friday for reading and math tutoring. Within the youth leadership training, a youth council is formed, and the boys act as the leaders of the center, electing officers and holding meetings. Community service is required of all of the boys, whether it be picking weeds in the yard of the center or painting over graffiti in the community.

For career vocational guidance, members of the community give various career path workshops, as well as workshops on how to fill out an application and apply for a job. For delinquency prevention, former gang members will come in and talk to the kids about what it was like being in a gang. During the school year, the boys get to the center around 3 p.m. Homework assistance is offered from 3:30 p.m. to 4:30 p.m., and reading tutoring is from 4:30 p.m. to 5:30 p.m. On the days when the Boys to Men classes are scheduled, they take place from 4 p.m. to

5 p.m. for the 8 to 12 year olds and from 5 p.m. to 6 p.m. for the 13 to 18 year olds. The center closes at 6 p.m. During the summer, kids can come at 2 p.m., although many end up arriving earlier. They are given work assignments to do, after which they are free to play pool, play basketball, or play on the computers.

The People's Church

The People's Church, in Washington, D.C. (Lenny and Carmen Smith, directors), is a program in which children are taught the importance of visual arts, drama, and music. Children in the program are between the ages of 6 and 17 and are recruited by referrals from their parents, teachers, and school administrators. The musical theater portion of the program contains an element that they call the peer prevention piece, which is basically structuring the educational theater. This program seeks to build resiliency skills with junior high and high school students. Their musical program takes place on Saturdays. The focus with the younger children is self-esteem and leadership skills, whereas the older children's focus is on life skills, such as career growth and planning. The mentor program invites professionals to talk to the kids about decisions they have made and the consequences that they had to go through as a result of those decisions. During this program, the kids have an opportunity to play out some of their decisions and look at the consequences. The mentor program focuses on the teenagers in the group, and the hope is that the teens will then become mentors for the younger children.

Acknowledgments

Please direct correspondence to Walter R. Allen. The authors acknowledge generous support from the Lumina Foundation.

NOTES

1. The key areas include physical self, the sexual self, the intrapersonal self, the spiritual self, the emotional/feeling self, the ethical/moral self, the mental/cognitive and linguistic self, and the social/intrapersonal self.
2. The two studies that relied on records such as school yearbooks to indicate whether youth participated in extracurricular activities is classified as having low fidelity. These reports were not accurate and do not show the extent of involvement.
3. The motivating purpose of the National Task Force on African American Men and Boys was to contribute to the growth and development of African American men and boys as healthy, positive, contributing citizens. To accomplish this goal, the Task Force encouraged long-term, sustained, comprehensive interventions into the lives of young men and boys who are at risk in American society (Allen & Clark, 1998, p. 24).
4. In terms of physical activity, Allen and Clark (1998) found a slight increase in the Kellogg AAMB program participants' time spent in enrichment activities, including hobbies, organized sports, educational television, and working on the computer.
5. Presumably the reason for this is that in many studies, the subjects were elementary school–aged children. The sexual self includes healthy sexuality, self-examination,

awareness discussions, and exploration/intimacy. Researchers may have assumed that this aspect of children's development was not relevant at this age, or that the programs examined did not affect nor were designed to affect participants' sexual maturity.

6. Six of the studies (25%) make no mention of race or have a sample containing only White youth.

REFERENCES

Allen, W. & Clark, R. (1998). *Repairing the breach: The Kellogg Foundation African American men and boys initiative: A post-test survey of youth and teen/adult participants.* Unpublished manuscript, Department of Sociology, University of California, Los Angeles, CA.

Baldwin, J. (1985). *The evidence of things not seen.* New York: Holt, Rinehart, and Winston.

Bell, J. (1967). A comparison of dropouts and non-dropouts on participation in school activities. *The Journal of Educational Research, 60,* 248–251.

Bernman, B., Winkleby, M., Chesterman, E., & Boyce, W. (1992). After-school childcare and self-esteem in school-age children. *Pediatrics, 89,* 654–659.

Braddock, J. H. (1990). Hearing on the Office of Educational Research and Improvement. Washington, DC: Government Printing Office.

Bredemeier, B. J. & Shields, D. L. (1984). Divergence in moral reasoning about sport and everyday life. *Sociology of Sport Journal, 1,* 348–357.

Clark, R., Harris, A., & Allen, W. R. (2005). After-school youth programs: How they affect youths' educational progress. *Challenge,*

Cosden, M., Morrison, G., Gutierrez, L., & Brown, M. (2004). The effects of homework programs and after-school activities on school success. *Theory into Practice, 43*(3), 220–226.

Costello, J., Barker, G., Pickins, L., Cassaniga, N., Merry, S., & Falcon, A. (2000). *A self-study guide for managers and staff of primary support programs for young people.* Chicago: Chapin Hall Center for Children.

Fashola, O. S. (2003). Developing the talents of African American male students during the nonschool hours. *Urban Education, 38*(4), 398–430.

Gerber, S. (1996). Extracurricular activities and academic achievement. *Journal of Research and Development in Education, 30,* 42–50.

Hastad, D., Segrave, J., Pangrazi, R., & Petersen, G. (1984). Youth sport participation and deviant behavior. *Sociology of Sport, 1,* 366–373.

Huang, D., Gribbons, B., Kim, K. S., Lee, C., & Baker, E. L. (2000). *A decade of results: The impact of the LA's BEST after school enrichment initiative on subsequent student achievement and performance.* Unpublished manuscript, UCLA Center for the Study of Evaluation, Graduate School of Education and Information Studies, University of California.

Kahne, J., Nagaoka, J., Brown, A., O' Brien, J., Quinn, T., & Thiede, K. (2001). Assessing after-school programs as contexts for youth development. *Youth and Society, 32,* 421–446.

Landers, D., & Landers, D. (1978). Socialization via interscholastic athletics: Its effects on delinquency. *Sociology of Education, 51,* 299–303.

Lueptow, L. (1984). Participation in athletics and academic achievement: A replication and extension. *The Sociological Quarterly, 19,* 304–309.

Mahoney, J. L., Lord, H., & Carryl, E. (2005). An ecological analysis of after-school program participation and the development of academic performance and motivational attributes for disadvantaged children. *Child Development, 76*(4), 811–825.

Marsh, H. (1992). Extracurricular activities: Beneficial extension of the traditional curriculum or subversion of academic goals? *Journal of Educational Psychology, 84,* 553–562.

Marshall, N., Coll, C., Marx, F., McCartney, K., Keefe, N., & Ruh, J. (1997). After-school time and children's behavioral adjustment. *Merrill-Palmer Quarterly, 43,* 497–514.

Melnick, M., Vanfosen, B., & Sabo, D. (1988). Developmental effects of athletic participation among high school girls. *Sociology of Sport Journal, 5,* 22–36.

Pettit, G., Laird, R., Bates, J., & Dodge, K. (1997). Patterns of after-school care in middle childhood: Risk factors and developmental outcomes. *Merrill-Palmer Quarterly, 43,* 515–538.

Posner, J. & Vandell, D. (1994). Low-income children's after-school care: Are there beneficial effects of after-school programs? *Child Development, 65,* 440–456.

Posner, J. & Vandell, D. (1999). After-school activities and the development of low-income urban children: A longitudinal study. *Developmental Psychology, 35,* 368–879.

Rehberg, R. & Schafer, (1967/68). Participation in interscholastic athletics and college expectation. *The American Journal of Sociology, 73,* 732–740.

Rosenthal, R. & Vandell, D. (1996). Quality of care at school-aged child-care programs: Regulatable features, observed experiences, child perspectives, and parent perspectives. *Child Development, 67,* 2434–2445.

Scales, A., George, A., & Morris, G. (1997). Perceptions of one after-school tutorial program. *Journal of Research and Development in Education, 30,* 166–181.

Schinke, S., Cole, K., & Poulin, S. (2000). Enhancing the educational achievement of at-risk youth. *Prevention Science, 1,* 51–60.

Tierney, J., Grossman, J., & Resch, N. (1995). *Making a difference: An impact study of big brothers big sisters.*: Public/Private Ventures.

Vandell, D. & Corasaniti, M. A. (1988). The relation between third graders' after-school care and social, academic and emotional function. *Child Development, 59,* 868–875.

Vandell, D. & Ramanan, J. (1991). Children of the national longitudinal survey of youth: Choices in after-school care and child development. *Developmental Psychology, 27,* 637–643.

Witt, P. A. & Baker, D. (1997). Youth development: Developing after-school programs for youth in high risk environments. *Journal of Physical Education, Recreation and Dance, 68,* 18–20.

8

Academic Engagement of Black Male Student Athletes

Implications for Practice in Secondary and Postsecondary Schooling

EDDIE COMEAUX

The gap between intercollegiate athletics and the mission and philosophy of higher education has widened significantly over the past decade (Duderstadt, 2000; Eitzen, 2003). An article in the *Chronicle of Higher Education* (2001) reports that college sports are drifting from their fundamental mission. Instead of enhancing the academic environment, college athletics are clearly denying student athletes who participate in revenue-generating sports, such as men's basketball and football, a valuable education. As college athletics become more commercialized and are under increasing pressure to produce winning seasons, universities are challenged with addressing the increasing lack of academic productivity from students in certain team sports. This issue, compounded by the recent National College Athletics Association (NCAA) Academic Reform Movement, requires new strategies and forms of academic engagement to be explored that challenge educational institutions to extend student athletes' competitive spirit beyond the game and into the classroom.

Over the years, several studies have been conducted in an effort to determine significant predictor variables, including demographic and educational criteria of academic achievement for college student athletes (Lang, Dunham, & Alpert, 1988; Sellers, 1992; Simons, Van Rheenen, & Covington, 1999). Few investigators, however, have examined environmental influences, both social and academic, on student athletes' educational outcomes (Comeaux, 2005; Sellers, 1992). The college environment encompasses all that happens to student athletes during the course of their educational programs. In fact, it may affect and influence the desired outcome: to graduate (Astin, 1993a). One potentially important aspect of the environmental experience is student athletes' interaction with faculty members, which all too often influences their educational success in negative ways (Engstrom, Sedlacek, & McEwen, 1995; Sailes, 1993). Unappealing, negative attitudes toward student athletes have endured since organized sports were associated with American higher education (Smith, 1988; Thelin, 1996).

Drawing from a larger project that explores racial differences in student athletes' academic integration patterns on campus (Comeaux & Harrison, 2007), this chapter ascertains the effect of specific forms of student athlete–faculty interaction on academic achievement. Specifically, this study examines selected faculty interaction measures of academic achievement as well as high school grades (grade point average [GPA]), family income and education, the type of institution (public or private), among others. This chapter focuses on Black student athletes in the revenue-producing sports of men's basketball and football.

Data and Sample

The data in this study are from two surveys within the Cooperative Institutional Research Program (CIRP): the 2000 Student Information Form (SIF) and 2004 College Student Survey (CSS). The CIRP is sponsored by the Higher Education Research Institute at the University of California at Los Angeles and the Graduate School of Education and Information Studies. Although the reliability of the instrument has not been formally measured during the past 30 years, the CIRP has generated an array of normative, substantive, and methodological research about a wide range of issues in American higher education (Sax, Astin, Korn, & Mahoney, 1996).

The 2000 SIF was administered to first-time college freshmen during orientation programs. Responses were received from 251,232 students at 494 institutions. The CSS was administered to fourth-year students in the spring of 2004, resulting in 38,964 responses from 161 institutions. Of the total students, 14,975 students filled out both the SIF in 2000 and the CSS in 2004.

The primary purpose of the CIRP is to provide baseline data on entering college freshmen so that they may be followed over time to assess how college contributes to learning and development. The CIRP data set offers an extensive set of longitudinally collected variables with which to answer a variety of questions pertaining to student success and retention patterns in higher education. In addition, a known strength of CIRP is its abundance of student input (demographic and other variables assessed prior to college entry) and environmental variables.

The specific sample used for this study includes Black, male, revenue-generating student athletes attending predominantly White institutions. Because we limit the athletes to those in the revenue-generating sports of men's basketball and football, the results should only be generalized to such individuals on college teams recognized by the NCAA as Division I-A. The author chose to limit the sample to these specific student athletes because preliminary analysis of data revealed that revenue-generating athletes are different from non-revenue-generating athletes in graduation rates, NCAA infractions, and overall visibility in American culture (Coakley, 2003; Eitzen, 2003). The final sample includes 739 Black student athletes attending 4-year colleges and universities.

Research Methods

This study employs the input-environment-outcome (I-E-O) model for studying the impact of college variables on students (Astin, 1993a). "Inputs" refer to the students' entering characteristics. "Environment" is that to which the student is exposed during college (e.g., faculty, peers, diverse views, etc.). "Outcomes" are the students' characteristics after interacting with the environment (Astin, 1993a). The power of the I-E-O model is its ability to allow researchers to measure student change during college by measuring outcomes while controlling for input characteristics.

The study used blocked stepwise regression analyses. Each block of independent variables was included in the sequence in which it may have an effect on student outcome. Within each block, variables (significant at $p < .001$) enter the regression equation in a stepwise fashion. The value of using a stepwise procedures design is that it allows for an examination of how regression coefficients change as each variable enters the equation (Astin, 1993a).

Outcome Variable

The outcome variable in this study is students' self-reported college GPA, a quantitative measure of academic achievement. GPA is scored on a six-point scale (A, A–, B, B–, C, and C– or less). The pretest for this outcome is students' high school GPA (scored on an eight-point scale, from "A or A+" to "D"). The author recognizes that academic achievement encompasses much more than GPA; however, given the variables within the data set, college GPA was the most appropriate measure of academic achievement, coupled with the fact that college GPA is the most common outcome when investigating student achievement in higher education (Astin, 1993a, 1993b).

Independent Variables

Independent variables are blocked in the following sequence: *(1)* students' past achievement, family background, and high school environmental characteristics (inputs); *(2)* institutional type and control (environment); and *(3)* college environmental characteristics (environment). Because the primary focus of this study is the impact of specific forms of student athlete–faculty interaction on academic achievement, independent variables are not limited to those expected to predict a given outcome. Rather, many variables are included because they may shed light on the relation between Black student athletes and faculty. Independent variables can be classified into the following two categories (some variables may qualify for more than one category):

1. Those that previous research has identified as predictive of any of the outcome measures used in this study
2. Those that are included on an exploratory basis because they may mediate the effects of the student athlete–faculty interaction

Input Variables

Student background characteristics (Block 1) include measures of past school achievement, family background, and high school environmental characteristics. The coding scheme for these variables is listed in Table 8.1. Past achievement measure consist of students' self-reported high school GPA. The importance of high school GPA as a control variable when examining college GPA is well documented (Astin, 1993a, 1993b; Sellers, 1992).

Family background measures include socioeconomic status (defined as a composite of mother's and father's educational attainment, as well as students' estimates of their parents' income). It was expected that these family characteristics would influence students' expectations about college, as well as their likelihood of interacting in certain college environments (Sellers, 1992).

Finally, high school environmental characteristics consist of student athlete and teacher relationship measures (see Table 8.1). The significance of incorporating these measures was to eliminate self-selecting students, thereby decreasing the chance of a Type I error (finding a relationship between the environment and the outcome measure when a relationship does not exist). It was impossible to eliminate all possible biasing input variables. However, the goal was to minimize the probability of a Type I error.

Environmental Measures

Measures of the college environment consist of institutional type and control (Block 2) and interaction with faculty (Block 3). Institutional type is defined as a university or 4-year college, whereas institutional control is defined as public or private. Institution-level variables are included to determine whether student athletes are more likely to interact with faculty in universities or 4-year state schools and public or private institutions.

The final block contains the student athlete–faculty interaction variables. These five measures asked students to respond to the following statement: "Faculty provided encouragement for graduate school, faculty provided emotional support and encouragement, faculty provided assistance with study skills, faculty provided negative feedback about academic work, and faculty provided help in achieving professional goals." The importance of student–faculty relationship is well documented as a valuable aspect of the college experience (Astin, 1993a).

Table 8.1 Student Background and Involvement Characteristics

Block	Variables	Measures
Block 1(input)	Background Measures	
	Average high school grades (self-report)[a]	
	Socioeconomic status (SES)	Mother's education[b]
		Father's education[b]
		Parental income[c]
	Interaction With Faculty (high school)[d]	Asked a teacher for advice after class[d]
		Talked with teacher outside of class[e]
Block 2 (environment)	Institutional Type and Control (dichotomous measures)	
	Public	
	Private	
	University	
	4-year college	
Block 3 (environment)	Interaction With Faculty (college)	
		Faculty provided encouragement for graduate school[d]
		Faculty provided emotional support and encouragement
		Faculty provided assistance with study skills
		Faculty provided negative feedback about academic work
		Faculty provided help in achieving professional goals

[a] Eight–point scale: 1 = "D" to 8 = "A or A+."
[b] Eight-point scale: 1 = "grammar school or less" to 8 = "graduate degree."
[c] Fourteen-point scale: "less than $6000" to 14 = "$150,000 or more."
[d] Three-point scale: 1 = "not at all" to 3 = "frequently."
[e] Eight-point scale: 1 = "none" to 8 = "over 20."

Results

Because this study is concerned primarily with selected faculty interaction measures on academic achievement among Black student athletes in revenue-producing sports, the results discussed here focus on the relationship between that environmental measure and the outcome. The effects of precollege variables on the outcome are presented and discussed only when they appear to influence the outcome.

To assess the "effect" of selected precollege variables and environmental measures on academic achievement, the standardarized regression coefficient (Beta-In) was examined at each step in the regression. The Beta-In (as reported in SPSS-X regression results) is the Beta coefficient a variable would receive if it entered the regression equation at the next step; all variables have a Beta-In irrespective of whether they enter a regression.

Table 8.2 provides summary tables of simple correlations for the outcome, as well as Beta-In at each step: *(1)* after controlling for precollege (input) characteristics; and *(2)* after controlling for measures of the environment. The purpose of this section is to examine the relationship between that environmental measure and the outcome by determining how this relationship changes throughout the regression, without addressing specifically *how* or *why* such changes occur.

Relationships Explained by Input and Environmental Effects

While high school grades (input) had a strong positive effect on academic achievement (beta = .31, $p < .001$; see Table 8.2), adding the college environment to the equation led to generally smaller effects in the relationship between faculty measures and college grades. Of course, the relatively smaller "mediating" power of the environmental block was due in part to the natural correlation between inputs and environments; much of the potential "impact" of the environment had already been accounted for by students' high school grades. This suggests that high school GPA had the greatest effect on college grades for Black student athletes. Contrary to past research (Lang et al., 1988), parental status and income, as well as parents' education, had no significant effect on academic achievement.

With respect to environmental factors, only one faculty interaction variable—-faculty provided encouragement for graduate school—had a significant influence on Black student athletes' college GPA for this study (beta = .20, $p < .001$ (see Table 8.2). This finding suggests that Black student athletes who are encouraged to attend graduate school by faculty tend to perform better academically in college. Finally, those attending private schools tend to have higher college GPAs than those attending public institutions (beta = .18).

Discussion

The present investigation provides evidence to support the effects of selected demographic and environmental variables on academic achievement for Black student athletes in this study. We cannot ignore that, consistent with past literature, high school GPA study was the strongest predictor of college GPA at least for students; it is also a predictor of college GPA for Black student athletes in this study (Astin, 1993a). Such a finding is not surprising, since student athletes are a subsample of

Table 8.2 Predicting Academic Achievement (College GPA) Among Black Male Student Athletes in Revenue-Generating Sports

				Beta[a] After Step		
Step	*Variable*	*R*	*r*	*1*	*2*	*3*
Input	Entering:					
1	High school GPA (pretest)	.33	.33	.33	.33	.31
Environment	Entering:					
2	Institutional control	.39	.21	.20	.20	.18
3	Faculty provided encouragement for graduate school	.43	.24	.21	.20	.20
	Not entering:					
	Father's education					
	Mother's education					
	Parental income					
	Asked teacher for advice					
	Talking with teachers outside of class					
	Institutional type					
	Faculty provided emotional support					
	Faculty provided assistance with study skills					
	Faculty provided negative feedback about academic work					
	Faculty provided help in achieving professional goals					

[a] The coefficient for any variable not yet in the equation shows the beta that variable would receive if it were entered into the equation at the *next* step.
GPA, grade point average.
Source. 2000 Freshman Survey (CIRP) and 2004 College Student Survey (CSS), Higher Education Research Institute, UCLA.

college students. Moreover, because Black student athletes tend to matriculate from high schools and environments with inferior academic resources and preparation as compared to their White counterparts, these results are useful insofar as they have implications for dealing with Black student athletes who enter institutions of higher education (Sellers, 1992).

With respect to environmental findings, the academic success of Black athletes in the revenue-producing sports of men's basketball and football is to some extent contingent upon the specific nature of their interaction with faculty. For example, faculty who provided encouragement for graduate school make a strong contribution to Black student athletes' academic success, whereas all other faculty interaction measures were not significant in this study. One possible reason that these faculty measures perhaps did not enter the regression equation, much less influence Black student athletes' academic success, may stem from the ways in which they perceive and respond to the college environment and the fact that they often have limited informal information exchange with White faculty and students (Allen, 1988, 1992). There is usually considerable social distance and alienation from campus life perceived by Black students on predominantly White campuses (Hurtado, 1992; Sedlacek, 1987), and they may feel discomfort from their lack of knowledge and experience interacting with students and faculty different from themselves (Schwitzer, Griffin, Ancis, & Thomas, 1999). An article in the *Chronicle of Higher Education* reports that Black student athletes feel that they are marginalized and are not taken seriously by White professors in the classroom and on campus (Perlmutter, 2003). In many ways, the college experiences of Black student athletes at predominately White institutions are all too often hindered as a result of feelings of social isolation, racial discrimination, limited support, and lack of integration. Thus, Black student athletes may choose to spend as little time as possible with White faculty, who comprise approximately 89% of faculty at predominately White institutions. Instead, they interact and bond with mentors and other support systems off campus, where they feel encouraged and accepted.

Ideas for Change

These findings have important implications for designing program and policies to help Black student athletes enrolled at predominately White institutions improve their academic performance. This study calls for high schools, colleges, and universities to encourage and develop a wide range of academic support and communication that is responsive to the needs of Black student athletes (Redmond, 1990).

When designing such programs, attention should also be given to the practices, processes, and structure of the specific academic support programs at hand and how they can potentially affect Black student athletes in high school or college with differing educational characteristics. It is apparent that programs in high schools should focus on developing the academic talents of Black student athletes for competitive college readiness and also formulating strategies to overcome or circumvent any impediments. Findings from this study indicate that Black student athletes tend to increase the likelihood of college academic success to the extent that they show academic promise and worth (e.g., high GPAs) while in high school. Moreover, since Black students typically enter predominately White institutions with lower GPAs and are less prepared than their counterparts, faculty and student affairs leaders must be well advised to appreciate their situation and work closely with these students in identifying factors that may impede or facilitate their academic development and/or self-identity.

Finally, it is clear that there is a need for much more research to understand the relationship between Black student athletes and non-Black faculty. In the meantime, faculty and others who frequently interact with student athletes could benefit from learning about the types of conscious and unconscious prejudices and discriminatory attitudes directed toward student athletes. Mandatory training workshops that provide insights into the nuances and complexities of race, racism, and cultural sensitivity toward certain groups and that are tailored to the special institutional needs of different campus constituencies and different target audiences are imperative. In that sense, we can begin to work toward improving the college community and contribute to the creation of equitable educational opportunities for all students. Concurrently, Black student athletes could benefit by perpetuating more positive images in a classroom atmosphere by increased participation in classroom discussion, regular attendance, and communicating with faculty members outside of class (Jaasma & Koper, 1999).

Limitations and Future Research

While the present study produced useful findings and has implications for institutional practices pertaining to student athletes, as outlined in the previous section, it is not without limitations. The lack of causal direction among the environmental measures and the dependent variable was another limitation of this study. That is, do student athletes who interact with faculty, depending on the form of interaction, receive higher grades, or is it because those with higher grades are more likely to pursue interaction or contact with faculty? Future qualitative studies that explore Black student athletes' experiences with faculty inside and outside the classroom might be successful in answering such uncertainties. Additionally, the voices of Black student athletes themselves are critical to addressing this issue at both the theoretical and practical level (Benson, 2001).

Lastly, the present study focuses on whether selected faculty measures of academic achievement for Black student athletes, yet it is not known whether faculty members' race/ethnicity, gender, college affiliation, and/or involvement in intercollegiate athletics play a role in the types and magnitude of interaction between Black student athletes and faculty in this study. For example, the fact that Black student athletes feel that they are marginalized by White professors on campus, as discussed earlier, may cause the degree of contact to vary dramatically by race. In future studies, it may be useful to control for faculty characteristics to better understand the impact of specific forms of student athlete–faculty interaction to outcomes of college. This information will be most useful to student affairs leaders and others who are exposed to college athletics in American higher education.

REFERENCES

Allen, W. R. (1988). Black students in U.S. higher education: Toward improved access, adjustment and achievement. *The Urban Review, 20,* 165–188.

Allen, W. R. (1992). The color of success: African American college student outcomes at predominately White and historically Black public colleges and universities. *Harvard Educational Review, 62,* 26–44.

Astin, A. W. (1993a). *Assessment for excellence.* Phoenix, AZ: American Council on Education & The Onyx Press.

Astin, A. W. (1993b). *What matters in college?* San Francisco: Jossey-Bass.

Benson, K. (2001). Constructing academic inadequacy: African American athletes' stories of schooling. *Journal of Higher Education, 71*(2), 223–246.

Coakley, J. (2003). *Sport in society: Issues and controversies.* Boston: McGraw-Hill Companies.

Comeaux, E. (2005, Summer). Environmental predictors of academic achievement among student-athletes in the revenue-producing sports of men's basketball and football. *The Sport Journal, 8*(3) (ISSN: 1543–9518).

Comeaux, E. & Harrison, C. K. (2007, July). Faculty and male student athletes in American higher education: Racial differences in the environmental predictors of academic achievement. *Race, Ethnicity and Education 10*(2), 199–214.

Duderstadt, J. (2000). *Intercollegiate athletics and the American university: A university president's perspective.* Ann Arbor: University of Michigan Press.

Engstrom, C., Sedlacek, W., & McEwen, M. (1995). Faculty attitudes toward male revenue and nonrevenue student athletes. *Journal of College Student Development, 36*(6), 217–227.

Eitzen, D. (2003). *Fair and foul: Beyond the myths and paradoxes of sport.* New York: Rowman & Littlefield Publishers, Inc.

Hurtado, S. (1992). The campus racial climate: Contexts for conflict. *Journal of Higher Education, 63*(5), 539–569.

Jaasma, M. & Koper, R. (1999). The relationship of student-faculty out-of-class communication to instructor immediacy and trust and to student motivation. *Communication Education, 48,* 41–47.

Lang, G., Dunham, R. G., & Alpert, G. P. (1988). Factors related to the academic success and failure of college football players: The case of the mental dropout. *Youth and Society, 20,* 209–222.

Perlmutter, D. (2003). Black athletes and White professors: A twilight zone of uncertainty. *The Chronicle of Higher Education, 50*(7), B7.

Redmond, S. P. (1990). Mentoring and cultural diversity in academic settings. *American Behavioral Scientist, 34*(2), 188–200.

Sailes, G. (1993). An investigation of campus stereotypes: The myth of Black athletic superiority and the dumb jock stereotypes. *Sociology of Sport Journal, 10,* 88–97.

Sax, L. J., Astin, A. W., Korn, W. S., & Mahoney, K. M. (1996). *The American freshman: National norms for fall 1996.* Los Angeles: Higher Education Research Institute, UCLA.

Schwitzer, A. M., Griffin, O. T., Ancis, J. R., & Thomas, C. R. (1999). Social adjustment experiences of African American college students. *Journal of Counseling and Development, 77,* 189–197.

Sedlacek, W. E., (1987). Black students on White campuses: 20 years of research. *Journal of College Student Development, 28,* 484–495.

Sellers, R. M. (1992). Racial differences in the predictors of academic achievement of student athletes of Division I revenue-producing sports. *Sociology of Sport Journal, 1*, 46–51.

Simons, H., Van Rheenen, D., & Covington, M. V. (1999). Academic motivation and the student athlete. *Journal of College Student Development, 40*(2), 151–161.

Smith, R. (1988). *Sports and freedom*. Oxford, England: Oxford University Press.

Thelin, J. (1996). Games colleges play: Scandal and reform in intercollegiate athletics. Baltimore: The Johns Hopkins University Press.

PART III

Mental and Physical Health Statuses and Challenges to African American Male Development and Social Functioning

9

What Are Depressed African American Adolescent Males Saying About Mental Health Services and Providers?

MICHAEL A. LINDSEY

Depression among children and adolescents in the United States is a very serious public health concern. Studies indicate that 1 in 10 children and adolescents in the United States suffers from mental illness severe enough to cause some impairment, and large-scale research studies have reported that up to 3% of children and 8% of adolescents suffer from depression (U.S. Department of Health & Human Services, 1999). African Americans are at particular risk. Studies indicate that African American adolescents experience depression more than adolescents from other ethnic groups (Garrison, Jackson, Marsteller, McKeown, & Addy, 1990; Roberts, Roberts, & Chen, 1997; Wu et al., 1999). Although research indicates that depression is highly treatable (Petersen et al., 1993), both the *Surgeon General's Report on Mental Health* (U.S. Department of Health & Human Services, 2001) and the *President's New Freedom Commission on Mental Health* (U.S. Department of Health & Human Services, 2003) indicate that few African American adolescents receive care.

African American adolescent males are particularly vulnerable. Depression among this group has been linked to their perception of fewer future opportunities (Hawkins, Hawkins, Sabatino, & Ley, 1998), low neighborhood social capital and kinship social support (Stevenson, 1998), and violent behavior in African American adolescent males living in an urban high-risk setting (DuRant, Getts, Cadenhead, Emans, & Woods, 1995). Although their vulnerability to depression has been noted, African American adolescents may experience barriers to identifying and using effective treatments to combat depression. This lack of treatment may underlie and predict their suicidal and homicidal behaviors—two activities in which the rate of increase for African American adolescents males has been double that of White males for every 5-year period since 1980 (Willis, Coombs, Drentea, & Cockerham, 2003). The behavioral presentations of "troubled" urban African American adolescent males are usually linked with delinquency and lead to involvement in the juvenile justice system. Studies indicate that these youth are more likely to be found in corrections than mental health facilities (Cuffe, Waller, Cuccaro, Pumariega, & Garrison, 1995). Their delinquent behavior may be partially the result of a lack of early treatment for depression or other mental health conditions.

The problems of engaging African American youth in mental health treatment have been well documented (Henggeler, Schoenwald, & Munger, 1996; Lindsey et al., 2006; McKay, Nudelman, McCadam, & Gonzales, 1996; Myers, 1989; Singleton. 1989). For example, McMiller and Weisz (1996) found that African American youth have low rates of follow-through on referrals. Studies further indicate that even when African American youth do engage in treatment, the majority of them average only two to three treatment sessions (Cuffe et al., 1995; U.S. Department of Health & Human Services, 2001, 2003; McMiller & Weisz, 1996). McKay and colleagues (1996) identify several other factors, including discouragement from others to seek professional help, parents' negative experiences with helping professionals, race and ethnic mismatch between helping professional and client, obstacles within urban communities (e.g., violence, access to transportation, distance), and experiences with racism that influence young people's willingness to receive services from a "system." Previous negative perceptions and experiences may also reduce the likelihood of seeking care among African American youth (Lindsey et al., 2006).

Although researchers recognize that few African American children and adolescents in need of mental health services receive them (Angold et al., 2002; U.S. Department of Health & Human Services, 2001), there has been little discussion of the attitudes and beliefs that influence how these youths view services and providers, potentially contributing to their underuse of mental health services. It is unlikely that we will increase access to and engagement with services unless we achieve a better understanding of how the youth view their symptoms, service options, and service providers. For example, studies indicate that African American adolescents and adults are less likely than Whites to acknowledge the need for mental health services and are more likely to be skeptical of these services, especially when they feel they may be stigmatized (McKay et al., 1996; Richardson, 2001) or receive inappropriate, inefficient care (Lindsey et al., 2006). African American adolescents and their families are therefore likely to have many negative perceptions of (and experiences with) mental health care that reduce the likelihood of their seeking care even when it is available or of being engaged if they actually access services.

Perceptions of mental illness, mental health services, and mental health providers play an important role in mental health service use. Andersen (1995) argues that perceptions or health beliefs (attitudes, values, and knowledge people have about health and health services) influence people's notions of what constitutes a health need and whether formal services are necessary to address the need. Perceptions of trust, genuineness, quality of treatment setting, level of provider expertise, and mental health problem severity have all been found to affect engagement and therapeutic alliance (prolonged service), primarily among African American adults (Jackson, Neighbors, & Gurin, 1986; Lee, 1999; Neighbors, 1991; Thompson, Bazile, & Akbar, 2004; Thorn & Sarata, 1998). To what extent these perceptions apply to African American youth—males, in particular—requires further study.

Understanding the factors that influence engagement and therapeutic alliance among African American males with depression is essential to improving access to and use of services for this group. Therefore, the purpose of this study was to explore the perceptions of mental health services and providers among depressed African American adolescent males. To better control for variability in disorder type, the study focused on depression in youth. To better understand the factors that facilitate or hinder treatment, respondents included both youth receiving mental health services and youth not in treatment. Findings from this study can inform the design of culturally appropriate intervention and engagement strategies to increase the number of services perceived as acceptable and effective by this underserved group.

Methods

Eighteen respondents ages 14–18 who were already participating in a larger study entitled "Social Network Influences on African American Adolescents' Mental Health Service Use" (Lindsey, 2002) were recruited for this study. Participants were recruited from community-based mental health treatment centers and a mental health practitioner in private practice ($n = 10$), as well as from community-based nonclinical programs for high-risk youth (i.e., a violence prevention program, truancy abatement center, and homeless shelter; $n = 8$). In each setting, all potential participants were individually approached by a therapist or program staff member who explained the study and assessed their participation interest. In addition, flyers were posted at each recruitment site describing the study. Informed consent was obtained for participation from parents or guardians and informed assent from participants.

Participants were selected from the larger study (Lindsey, 2002) based on elevated depressive symptoms as assessed by the Centers for Epidemiologic Studies Depression Scale (CES-D; Radloff, 1977). Of the 69 who participated in the larger study, 18 met this criterion. All 18 who were approached agreed to participate in this study.

Data was collected via a semistructured interview schedule. Questions were derived from the network-episode model (NEM; Pescosolido, 1991), particularly the NEM concept *network content* (i.e., attitudes and beliefs toward mental illness and mental health care). In addition to network content, questions were derived from the literature on help-seeking behaviors among adolescents (i.e., help-seeking pathways engaged in by youth) and the literature on mental health service use by African Americans. Respondents were asked to share their perceptions of and experiences with mental health providers as well as their help-seeking preferences. Table 9.1 lists examples of the questions and follow-up probes used in the protocol. Interviews were conducted in the respondents' homes and a few at mental health centers or community-based organizations. All interviews were conducted in private areas and lasted between 45 minutes and 1 hour, 30 minutes.

The interview covered *(1)* processes and help-seeking patterns and *(2)* attitudes toward mental health care and race/ethnicity of provider. The first author and a trained research assistant (RA) conducted the interviews. They encouraged participants to talk at length about their help-seeking behaviors in relation to their depressive symptoms, with detailed accounts regarding their perceptions of mental illness and formal mental health care. The participants were also asked what provider characteristics were likely to facilitate their successful engagement with formal mental health services.

Interviews were tape-recorded, transcribed in full, and analyzed using inductive coding techniques (Miles & Huberman, 1994). A coding scheme was developed by the first author and a research assistant to reduce data from the transcripts into manageable themes of engagement and therapeutic alliance, including the identification of *individual factors* (e.g., respondents' uncertainty that they had a mental health problem or whether their problem warranted formal care) and *network factors* (e.g., provider characteristics that facilitate or inhibit engagement/ alliance, such as trust or "keeps it real"). A more detailed description of these themes is discussed in the "Findings" section.

As a result of these efforts, a better understanding of the factors and influences on engagement and therapeutic alliance for African American adolescent males with depression was gained—in particular, how this group conceptualizes their

Table 9.1 Sample Interview Questions and Follow-Up Probes

Question	Probes
When you start feeling like something makes you feel sad or hurt inside, what do you do?	• How did you know that you needed to talk with somebody? • Was there anyone who helped you to recognize or identify the feelings that you were having? • Whom did you turn to first for help? • Are there other things you tried to do to help you feel better beyond talking with other people? • How did these other things work?
If you felt you just couldn't handle things going on in your life, where would you prefer to go for help? Why?	• (If therapist/counselor not mentioned) Why wouldn't you go to a therapist/counselor? • What would your friends think if you went to a therapist/counselor? • What about your family?

Reprinted from Lindsey et al. (2006) with permission from the National Association of Social Workers, Inc.

emotional/psychological struggles, views mental health services, and perceives mental health providers as they consider whether formal services would be useful.

Findings

The larger goal of this study was to examine the perceptions of mental health services and providers in depressed African American adolescent males. Several factors emerged as themes that relate specifically to respondents' perceptions of influences on their engagement and therapeutic alliance with mental health services. Figure 9.1 displays the emergent themes from the participant interviews.

Individual Factors

Two individual or personal factors influenced engagement and therapeutic alliance: whether the respondent thought he had a mental health problem, and if so, the severity of the problem as it related to his well-being and functionality.

Do I Have a Mental Health Problem?   There seemed to be quite a bit of uncertainty or second-guessing in this sample as to whether they had a mental health problem. Respondents felt that they could handle their depressive symptoms on their own without formal mental health treatment. When probed further about these symptoms or referred to formal treatment, they disagreed with the

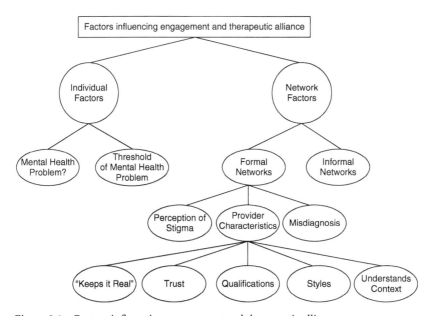

Figure 9.1   Factors influencing engagement and therapeutic alliance.

caregiver or school official about whether formal care was warranted, questioning whether their struggles with depression were even related to problematic functioning. A few passages from interview transcriptions highlight the apparent contradictions between what is real and what is perceived:

So, initially, you were uncomfortable, though, a bit [referring to receiving formal mental health treatment]?

A little.

Why were you uncomfortable?

Because like I hate telling people my problems. Like I think I can handle it all by myself.

———————————

No. Because it was wrong the whole time [referring to formal mental health treatment]. It was a waste of time, honestly. It was an idea to get me a physical. I got a physical. They said my tonsils were huge . . . so what happened is I took a sleep study and they found out it was a physical thing. And the problem was that I was snoring and stopped breathing in my sleep. Not that I had depression. And they say that affected my schoolwork. So once that happened, we got my tonsils taken out. It had nothing to do with my mental health . . .

Well, I wonder. Why did they identify your problem as a mental health–related problem or depression?

Because of the sleepiness . . . I mean I had my bouts like where I would get really upset. I didn't have anyone to talk to. I didn't have many friends. Now I'm just swimming in them. I have friends everywhere. Just by the way that I associate myself.

So the isolation, then?

Yeah. They thought that I had problems with making friends. Therefore, they had many things, many reasons they could call me depressed, I guess.

These perceptions and observations are curious in light of the fact that all of the respondents had high levels of depressive symptoms as determined by their CES-D scores.

THRESHOLD OF MENTAL HEALTH PROBLEM   What constitutes being "bad enough" to receive mental health services also seems to influence factors regarding engagement and therapeutic alliance. At least for those who accessed services, the severity of their depressive symptoms seemed to warrant formal service use and eventual engagement. It is interesting to note that among respondents who believed that they had problems severe enough to warrant service use, there did not seem to be apprehension about service use. The following quotes highlight these points:

> *... if you felt like you just couldn't handle things going on inside, would you feel like you could go to a therapist or counselor?*

> It depends.

> *It depends on what?*

> On how bad I'm feeling.

> _____

> *How about professional help? Would you recommend that?*

> I wouldn't.

> *Okay ... What if the problem was very severe?*

> Well, then I guess you have to go to a professional.

> _____

> *They got you connected with Ms. Deljene. Okay. So would you say it was more your mom's decision for you to come here or was it your decision?*

> I'd say it was my decision because I just had to like talk to someone.

> *So your mom got you into the door, but it was your decision to be—*

> I had to tell her where I was going usually . . .

> *So your mom kind of got you into the door, but you actually took it upon yourself to talk to Ms. Deljene because you knew some things were going on [professional help was necessary]?*

> Yes.

Network Factors

Network influences on help-seeking and perceptions of mental illness, mental health treatment, and service providers were another major focus of inquiry. Influences from both the informal (e.g., family and friends) and formal (e.g., mental health practitioners) networks were examined. Respondents defined informal network influences on perceptions of mental illness and mental health providers/services as those of family and friends. The issue of informal network influences has been extensively discussed elsewhere (see Lindsey et al., 2006) and is not the focus here. However, respondents noted the stigma attached to mental illness and service use in their networks, which fueled their reluctance to seek mental health services for depressive symptoms. Respondents said that it was important to resolve symptoms within the network first or in lieu of a formal service contact. The following quote from a respondent not in treatment captures this point:

> [African American adolescent males] feel as though that—okay, it would be a shame, some of them. It would be a shame to go to a counselor because, like I said before, either people that they're around or them, themselves, should have the answers . . . Rather than taking initial precautions for themselves, they'll just base it off of their friends or who they're normally around, you know, who basically leads them.

When probed further, respondents said that talking to a mental health professional, for some African American adolescent males, meant that they would have to express feelings of sadness or hurt, and that expressing emotions was a sign of weakness.

FORMAL NETWORK   Several themes and subthemes emerged regarding network factors that influence participants' perceptions of and attitudes toward mental health services and providers. These perceptions seemed to directly correspond with the issue of participants' engagement in and therapeutic alliance with formal mental health treatment, as is captured in the following quote from a respondent in treatment:

> The system [formal mental health service delivery system] . . . because I know there's some people that, "Okay, well he's bad." They [mental health clinicians/ practitioners] might bring it up at like the little meetings that they have, because I know they have, because they tell me. I brought—they bring it up, and they're like, "Well, he's ADHD." And they have no choice to go along with it. Not everybody agrees with everybody. Unfortunately, in order for them to keep their job, they got to, "Okay, he's ADHD. We're going to have to put him in the program." They may not agree with it personally, but, you know, job wise they have to go along with [it] because that's what they're doing. That's their profession. So I can't fault all of them for that, but the system is fucked up for real.

Themes such as *perception of stigma, misdiagnosis,* and *provider characteristics* (what does and does not work) provide insight into the issues of engagement and therapeutic alliance, and the difficulty (as reported in *The Surgeon General's Report on Mental Health* and *The New President's Commission on Mental Health*) inherent to mental health service delivery to African American adolescents.

Perception of Stigma   Respondents feared that service providers might stereotype African Americans or fail to understand the subtleties or realities of the African American male experience (e.g., the struggles with being a member of a marginalized and oppressed group). Respondents often perceived that their experiences would *(1)* not be uniquely examined by service providers and *(2)* be based in generalizations regarding the African American male experience. This made them feel unsure about whether they would receive appropriate care. The following quote highlights this theme:

The system, you said?

Like Black. When we go in the system—

What's the system?

Like the law. Like police.

Okay, government . . . the jails or whatever?

Yeah. And mostly Black people, when they go in there it's like we get lost in the system. Like they wouldn't care about us.

. . . mental health people are viewed as people associated with the system?

Yeah.

And the system differentially treats African Americans?

Different.

Really? Better or worse?

Treat them worse than White people.

According to respondents, stereotyping behavior is apparent during diagnosis, when service providers are most likely to form opinions or make judgments that are based partially on media influences and mass perceptions of African American males.

Misdiagnosis   A real or perceived case of misdiagnosis often fueled the perception of stereotyping and mistrust of service providers, and it was reported by respondents to have an influence on their engagement and therapeutic alliance. Some respondents talked very vividly about cases they knew of or were involved in personally in which they or another African American adolescent male was misdiagnosed, often because a provider had categorized or stereotyped them. The following quote captures this perception:

Like this one case that they had. This one dude, he's Black, and they just straight went to him with the Ritalin. Like they didn't want to help him. They didn't want to talk to him. They just went straight to Ritalin . . . [He went to professional help] because his dad died. And he was failing in school because nobody would really help him. I tried to help him, but he was too bad down and I couldn't really help him with the grades and stuff.

So they put him on Ritalin?

Yeah, because he was going wild and crazy. Wasn't wild and crazy. He had anger spells and stuff.

So you think the Ritalin then was inappropriate?

Yeah, they could have helped him. His dad died. It was sad and stuff . . . They could have really helped him.

How?

Talked to him.

Okay. Instead they threw medication at him?

Yeah.

Drugs don't help?

I mean drugs help like Tylenol. That Ritalin slows your mind down.

Slows your mind down. Did they put you on any kind of medication?

Uh-huh [Yes].

Provider Characteristics   Respondents discussed several provider characteristics that were likely to convince them to receive treatment; these included "keeps it real," expertise/qualifications, trust, style, and understands context. In various aspects of treatment delivery, or even instances in which respondents who were not in treatment shared their perceptions of treatment delivery, these provider characteristics appeared to be critical factors ensuring service use.

"Keeps It Real"

This preference was very prominent among respondents, who said that providers who "kept it real" were able to relate to them and provide treatment in ways that were not disconnected from their cultural and contextual background. For example, when providers keep it real, they provide insight that is consistent with what respondents are likely to encounter in their own lives. The following quotes illustrate what this means:

She keeps it real? . . . What do you mean?

She stays upfront with me and my mom. She doesn't like go to the books. She shares her experiences with us, too. She uses those as examples and understandings. And the other lady was using a book.

———————————

Because he [former therapist] could relate to a lot of stuff I was going through. Because he was, he was labeled as a child. He was labeled ADHD because they didn't have a name for it.

He shared this with you then?

Yeah.

Expertise/Qualifications

Respondents, in treatment or not, were very interested in providers who had specialized training in mental health or years of demonstrated success in mental health service delivery. In fact, respondents were likely to say that race and ethnic background were not synonymous with expertise/qualification. The following quotes illustrate this point:

Okay. Are you referring to a mental health counselor or another kind of counselor?

Psychologist . . . And there's a reason for that.

Why?

Well, okay, because like psych, it deals with the mind. And being that they deal with the mind, they know like what's in the mind and what causes stress, so they should be able to have more adequate answers than just a basic counselor. They're—I would actually classify them as a higher level of a counselor.

So you prefer to go to somebody who has particular expertise?

Right. Because they're dealing with life situations, you need to have the best answers that you can get.

———————————

Have you ever had a Black therapist?

No. I can't say it would make a difference at all because it's about getting help. It's about having someone that's there for you to understand what you're going through and to give you advice, to give you encouragement, to help you sort out things that you're going through. So with me, White or Black doesn't really make a difference. What matters is that we're trustworthy of each other.

Trust

African American adolescent males may bring a certain level of mistrust into a therapeutic encounter as a result of living in environments where it is not safe to trust others (e.g., neighborhoods with high criminality). Thus, the way a provider exhibits genuineness and warmth becomes especially important in facilitating therapeutic alliance. Lack of trust was a prominent theme in this sample, as the following quotes indicate:

> *Okay. You didn't mention a therapist or a counselor [regarding getting help with depressive symptoms]. Why wouldn't you go to a therapist or a counselor?*
>
> I don't know. I don't trust them, I don't think . . . Because they get paid to listen to you so they got to do it, but my brother, he don't get paid. He's just listening because he's my brother.

> _____
>
> I couldn't—I don't know. I don't know. I couldn't do that [go to therapy] . . . Because I wouldn't know who I'm talking to. I don't even talk to nobody on the streets if I don't know them.
>
> *What if you all met in the office and then decided that you would go somewhere else to talk, but you don't always have to sit in the office to talk?*
>
> Oh, yeah. From there, I don't—it's hard to trust the person

Style

How providers engaged respondents in treatment, including methods that eased or raised respondents' anxieties regarding sharing intimate details of their lives, was also important to therapeutic alliance for this group. Even among those who were not in treatment, the perception of how the dynamic between the therapist and respondent would play out seemed to influence therapeutic alliance. Respondents reported that they respond favorably when there is some level of self-disclosure from the therapist or when providers use methods that do not seem to be manufactured or highly structured. In other words, how providers present themselves seems to affect whether this population will feel safe enough to relax and share. In their own words,

> *Why is it that you could relate to him?*
>
> Because—it's not because he was Black. It was because he was telling me how—he wasn't talking to me like, you know, like that was his job. He was like talking to me like, "Look man, when I was younger, they labeled me as a cut-up." He would tell me stuff and I could hear what he was saying because of the way he was talking to me. Not because he was Black. Because the shit he was saying, I hadn't told him, but I had to go through the shit that he was talking about. He would remind me of

something that happened to me the other day. That was exactly what I'm talking [about]. I don't care whether they White or Black. As long—don't talk to me like I'm a fucking project.

Okay.

Talk to me like I'm a person just like you . . . The way they sit. You know what I'm saying? Whether they looking at me. You know, when they were doing it, they're sitting there, write down their notepad and they're just asking me questions and I'm like, "What the hell is going on here?"

———————————

My other therapist didn't really care about me or my mom like going there. She always give it the same method. I used to study her every time. I used to study her like every time. She used to do the same method. Well, she does this, then I'll do this. I do this, you'll do that. She does that every time. Then we'd have different things. We'd have different things. She goes with the same method. I'm sitting there thinking, "Man, this is crazy." Then my mom—she treated my mom like, "Just go home and do this and that." And I'm like, what?

Understands Context

Whether a provider understood context was particularly important for respondents. By understanding context, providers convey an appreciation for or a commitment to learning what it means to be an African American male from an urban environment, including how the respondent's social environment shapes or defines him. This was especially true for respondents with a perception that mental health care providers are from suburbia and do not care about or understand urban plight. A respondent in mental health treatment captured it best:

They don't know—they talk to you like they know what you're talking about. They don't know nothing. You ain't grow up in the city. Ain't no one of them motherfuckers grow up in the city. They out in the suburbs and shit. All happy and smiling and shit. Driving around in their nice cars. The dog, and kids, and wife, and husband, and all types of shit like that. Having cookouts. They don't know nothing about being here. You know what I'm saying? They don't know nothing about having to deal with motherfuckers that don't like you just because what you got on. You know what I'm saying? They might have some nice shit on and they don't like what you got on so fuck you. They don't like you. And they don't know about having problems.

Discussion

The young men in this study were similar to those in broader studies of African American adults (Diala et al., 2000; Jackson et al., 1986; Thompson et al., 2004) in their generally negative perceptions of mental health providers and service delivery settings as a result of real or imagined treatment experiences. The African American adolescent males in this study seemed to approach formal service delivery with caution, sensing that the experience would not be warm or encouraging. Franklin (1999) notes that such perceptions among African American men are warranted, given that their skin color and physical features trigger certain thoughts, emotions, and behaviors in other people. Franklin (1999) writes, "Negative responses to these visible attributes are the source of many conflicts, forming barriers to success for black males and triggering intrapsychic consequences" (p. 6). Although many respondents reported that the provider's race does not matter, the issue of race is important as a cultural indicator of what one is likely to experience as a member of a marginalized or oppressed group. Thus, many respondents in this study felt that the formal mental health service delivery system does not understand how to best meet their emotional/psychological needs.

Many respondents felt that they did not need formal mental health care. Respondents seemed to exhibit a bit of machismo and confidence in being able to handle problems without assistance from mental health providers. Part of this can be attributed to what Majors and Billson (1992) described as "cool pose," a self-assured, unflappable psychological and behavioral posturing engaged in by African American adolescent males to ward off emotional or physical vulnerability. Similarly, respondents in this study generally disagreed with others' (e.g., caregivers' or teachers') assessment that they had a problem, or they felt that their problem was not severe enough to warrant formal intervention, primarily because they viewed service use as a sign of weakness, and they were therefore reluctant to engage in treatment. Conversely, those who were engaged believed that their depressive symptoms were severe enough to warrant care. As previously noted, findings regarding problem severity and perception that treatment was not necessary are curious, given that all respondents had clinically assessed high levels of depressive symptoms.

The general sentiment among respondents in this sample was that the formal mental health care system was an extension of the larger "system" (e.g., the government or the legal system) that disproportionately singled out African American males for unfair treatment. In some cases, respondents had actual experiences in which providers seemed to stereotype them or came across as insincere. Respondents reflected that these types of experiences were similar to their interactions with workers from other systems (e.g., police officers), making it difficult for them to connect with providers. Giachello and Arrom (1997) posit that for African Americans, the white middle-class orientation of the formal mental health system is a barrier to service use and engagement and alliance with providers, often leading to communication problems between providers and minority youth of low socioeconomic status.

To improve access to and engagement with a formal mental health system that is predominantly White and middle class in its orientation, respondents wanted providers that "keep it real," understand their context and the experiences associated with being an African American male, offer treatment that is more problem focused than insight oriented, and display trustworthiness through genuine warmth and sincerity. These provider characteristics echo what African American adults in Thompson et al.'s (2004) study identified as important, and they emphasize that these characteristics may be more important than the provider's race.

Limitations of the Study

This study focused strictly on depressive symptoms as an indicator of mental health need. Therefore, it cannot determined how other mental health problems, for example, behavioral disorders (conduct disorder and attention-deficit/hyperactivity disorder) in addition to depressive disorders might differentially or concomitantly affected engagement and alliance with a provider.

Although findings are based on the perspectives of a subgroup of African American adolescent males, this study lays the groundwork for a more extensive investigation of these issues and for the design of an outreach and an engagement strategy for depressed African American adolescents.

Practice Implications

Findings herein have important implications for engagement and therapeutic alliance for depressed African American adolescent males in treatment. Respondents identified the provider's need to (1) increase their understanding of contextual and cultural realities of African American youth and to (2) increase their awareness of how stereotyping affects engagement and therapeutic alliance. As noted elsewhere (Thorn & Sarata, 1998; Wilson & Stith, 1991), providers are encouraged to explore their own preconceptions of African American men and how this may influence treatment. In addition, Cardemil and Battle (2003) note that having open conversations about race and ethnicity is another way for therapists to demonstrate their sincerity and can promote an environment of trust and understanding that will ultimately facilitate engagement and alliance.

Further, giving clients the opportunity to share their reluctance and apprehension about formal mental health care is an important step in building trust and improving service quality. Respondents in this study revealed the need for providers to connect with them via self-disclosure. When possible, providers should explore ways to make connections, using personal examples to clarify a point or to make an insight more real to the lived experience of the client. Respondents in this study agreed that such an approach was an important feature of their engaged treatment experience.

Research Implications

This study highlights the need for more evidence-based engagement strategies targeting African American adolescents referred for mental health care. Examining ethnic match to determine whether clients are more or less engaged or if ethnic match influences clinical outcomes would be worthwhile areas of inquiry for future studies. Future research also is necessary to determine how much the findings in this study reflect the general population of depressed African American males. Finally, findings indicate that traditional therapeutic techniques may not work as effectively with this group. Future research is therefore necessary to confirm which techniques are most appropriate when working with depressed African American adolescents so we can reduce the gap between those who need mental health services and those who receive them.

NOTE

1. Several data display techniques were employed to analyze the meaning of the codes and themes. For example, the first author and a RA developed a final coding matrix to indicate the category and subcategory of themes, a definition clarifying the meaning for each category and subcategory, and corresponding sample quotes that best captured the theme.

REFERENCES

Andersen, R. (1995). Revisiting the behavioral model and access to medical care: Does it matter? *Journal of Health and Social Behavior, 36*, 1–10.

Angold, A., Erkanli, A., Farmer, E., Fairbank, J., Burns, B., Keeler, G., & Costello, E. (2002). Psychiatric disorder, impairment, and service use in rural African-American and White youth. *Archives of General Psychiatry, 59*, 893–901.

Cardemil, E. & Battle, C. (2003). Guess who's coming to therapy? Getting comfortable with conversations about race and ethnicity in psychotherapy. *Professional Psychology: Research and Practice, 34*(3), 278–286.

Cuffe, S., Waller, J., Cuccaro, M., Pumariega, A., & Garrison, C. (1995). Race and gender differences in the treatment of psychiatric disorders in young adolescents. *Journal of the American Academy of Child Adolescent Psychiatry, 34*(11), 1536–1543.

Diala, C., Muntaner, C., Walrath, C., Nickerson, K. J., LaVeist, T. A., & Leaf, P. J. (2000). Racial differences in attitudes toward professional mental health care and in the use of services. *American Journal of Orthopsychiatry, 70*, 455–464.

DuRant, R., Getts, A., Cadenhead, C., Emans, S., & Woods, E. (1995). Exposure to violence and victimization and depression, hopelessness, and purpose in life among adolescents living in and around public housing. *Developmental and Behavioral Pediatrics, 16*, 233–237.

Franklin, A. (1999). Therapeutic support groups for African Americans. In L. Davis (Ed.), *Working with African American males: A guide to practice* (pp. 5–14). Thousand Oaks, CA: Sage Publications.

Garrison, C., Jackson, K., Marsteller, F., McKeown, R., & Addy, C. (1990). A longitudinal study of depressive symptomotology in young adolescents. *Journal of the American Academy of Child and Adolescent Psychiatry, 29*, 581–585.

Giachello, A. & Arrom, J. (1997). Health service access and utilization among adolescent minorities. In D. K. Wilson, J. R. Rodriguez, & W. C. Taylor (Eds.), *Health-promoting and health-compromising behaviors among minority adolescents* (pp. 303–320). Washington, DC: American Psychological Association.

Hawkins, W., Hawkins, M., Sabatino, C., & Ley, S. (1998). Relationship of perceived future opportunity to depressive symptomotology of inner-city African-American adolescents. *Children and Adolescent Services, 20,* 757–764.

Henggeler, S., Schoenwald, S., & Munger, R. (1996). Families and therapists achieve clinical outcomes, systems of care mediate the process. *Journal of Child and Family Studies, 5*(2), 177–183.

Jackson, J., Neighbors, H., & Gurin, G. (1986). Findings from a national survey of Black mental health: Implications for practice and training. In M. R. Mirance & H. L. Kitano (Eds.), *Mental health research and practice in minority communities: Development of culturally sensitive training programs* (pp. 91–116). Washington, DC: U.S. Government Printing Office.

Lee, C. (1999). Counseling African American men. In L. Davis (Ed.), *Working with African American males: A guide to practice* (pp. 39–53). Thousand Oaks, CA: Sage Publications.

Lindsey, M. (2002). *Social network influences on African-American adolescents' mental health service use.* Unpublished doctoral dissertation, University of Pittsburgh.

Lindsey, M.A., Korr, W.S., Broitman, M., Bone, L., Green, A., & Leaf, P.J. (2006) *Help-seeking behaviors and depression among African-American adolescent boys. Social Work, 51,1,* 49-58.

Majors, R. & Billson, J. (1992). *Cool pose—the dilemmas of black manhood in America.* New York: Lexington Books.

McKay, M., Nudelman, R., McCadam, K., & Gonzales, J. (1996). Involving inner-city families in mental health services: First interview engagement skills. *Research on Social Work Practice, 6,* 462–472.

McMiller, W. & Weisz, J. (1996). *Help-seeking preceding mental health clinic intake among African-American, Latino, and Caucasian youths. Journal of the American Academy of Child and Adolescent Psychiatry, 35*(8), 1086–1094.

Miles, M. & Huberman, A. (1994). *Qualitative data analysis: An expanded source book* (2nd ed.). Thousand Oaks, CA: Sage.

Myers, H. (1989). Urban stress and the mental health of urban Afro-American youth: An epidemiologic and conceptual update. In R. L. Jones (Ed.), *Black adolescents* (pp. 123–152). Berkeley, CA: Cobb & Henry Publishing Company.

Neighbors, H. (1991). Mental health. In J. Jackson (Ed.), *Life in Black America* (pp. 221–237). Newbury Park, CA: Sage Publications.

Pescosolido, B. (1991). Illness careers and network ties: A conceptual model of utilization and compliance. *Advances in Medical Sociology, 2,* 161–184.

Petersen, A., Compas, B., Brooks-Gunn, J., Stemmler, M., Ey, S., & Grant, K. (1993). Depression in adolescence. *American Psychologist, 48*(2), 155–168.

Radloff, L. S. (1977). The CES-D scale: A self-report depression scale for research in the general population. *Applied Psychological Measurement, 1,* 385–401.

Richardson, L. (2001). Seeking and obtaining mental health services: What do parents expect? *Archives of Psychiatric Nursing, 15,* 223–231.

Roberts, R., Roberts, C., & Chen, R. (1997). Ethnocultural differences in prevalence of adolescent depression. *American Journal of Community Psychology, 25,* 95–110.

Singleton, E. (1989). Substance use and black youth: Implications of cultural and ethnic differences in adolescent alcohol, cigarette, and illicit drug use. In R. L. Jones (Ed.), *Black adolescents* (pp. 385–401). Berkeley, CA: Cobb & Henry Publishing Company.

Stevenson, H. (1998). Raising safe villages: Cultural-ecological factors that influence the emotional adjustment of adolescents. *Journal of Black Psychology, 24*, 44–59.

Thompson, V. L. S., Bazile, A., & Akbar, M. (2004). African Americans' perceptions of psychotherapy and psychotherapists. *Professional Psychology: Research and Practice, 35*(1), 19–26.

Thorn, G. & Sarata, B. (1998). Psychotherapy with African American men: What we know and what we need to know. *Journal of Multicultural Counseling and Development, 23*, 240–253.

U.S. Department of Health & Human Services. (1999). *Brief notes on the mental health of children and adolescents*. Retrieved on June 11, 2005, from http://www.medhelp.org/NIHlib/GF-233.html

U.S. Department of Health & Human Services. (2001). *Mental health: Culture, race, and ethnicity—a supplement to mental health: A report of the Surgeon General*. Rockville, MD: Author.

U.S. Department of Health & Human Services, New Freedom Commission on Mental Health. (2003). *Achieving the promise: Transforming mental health care in america. Final report*. (DHHS Pub. No. SMA-03-3832). Rockville, MD: Author.

Willis, L. A., Coombs, D. W., Drentea, P., & Cockerham, W. C. (2003). Uncovering the mystery: Factors of African American suicide. *Suicide and Life-Threatening Behavior, 33*, 412–429.

Wilson, L. L. & Stith, S. M. (1991). Culturally sensitive therapy with Black clients. *Journal of Multicultural Counseling and Development, 19*, 32–43.

Wu, P., Hoven, C., Bird, H., Moore, R., Cohen, P., Alegria, M., Dulcan, M., Goodman, S., Horwitz, S., Lichtman, J., Narrow, W., Rae, D., Regier, D., & Roper, M. (1999). Depressive and disruptive disorders and mental health service utilization in children and adolescents. *Journal of the American Academy of Child and Adolescent Psychiatry, 38*, 1081–1090.

10

Don't Bother Me, I Can't Cope

Stress, Coping, and Problem Behaviors Among Young African American Males

M. DANIEL BENNETT, JR. AND FANIKE K. OLUGBALA

Poverty, residential mobility, and population density are important contributors to the social breakdown of many neighborhoods and communities. In turn, this "social disorganization" is thought to be a major factor in the proliferation of a host of social ills (Bursik & Grasmick, 1993; Sampson & Lauritsen, 1994), including drug traffic, gang activity, exposure to violence, high rates of crime, frequent police harassment, residential density, and high ambient noise (Hambrick-Dixon, 2002; Miller, Webster, & MacIntosh, 2002). These social ills ramp up the daily stress among residents, which is thought to be an important factor in psychological outcomes, especially for African American males, who are disproportionately exposed to chronic and high levels of neighborhood stress (Finkelhor & Ormrod, 2003; Foster, Kuperminc, & Price, 2004; McCreary & Slavin, 1996). Chronic exposure to urban stressors such as crime and violence has been linked to increased aggression, anxiety, poor academic performance, delinquency, depression, and social withdrawal (Rasmussen, Aber, & Bhana, 2004; Schmeelk-Cone & Zimmerman, 2003).

Social disorganization can lead to poor outcomes largely because of a neighborhood's inability to effectively self-regulate (Rose & Clear, 1998; Shoemaker, 2000). Weak, unstable social institutions heighten feelings of alienation, distrust, helplessness, and vulnerability among community residents (Bennett & Fraser, 2000; Fagan & Wilkinson, 1998; Shoemaker, 2000). When the organizational structures of neighborhoods deteriorate, residents' ties to one another and to the community become frayed (Rose & Clear, 1998), compromising the social support networks thought necessary to protect children and adolescents from poor social and developmental outcomes (Sampson, Raudenbush, & Earls, 1997).

In the absence of significant social supports, a fragile sense of personal capital predicated on honor, respect, and status, and undergirded by aggression, often becomes the medium for social exchange (Polk, 1996). This is not to say that all individuals who live in socially disorganized communities are themselves disoriented or dysfunctional. In fact, even in high-risk neighborhoods, most residents subscribe to legal, conventional norms and values (Wilson, 1996). Yet given certain contextual and situational factors, some residents may at times be viewed as responding naturally to chaotic social and environmental conditions (Anderson, 1999).

Several studies have demonstrated that what has emerged in many socially disorganized communities is a series of behavioral codes of conduct (Anderson, 1994). Given limited opportunities, weak and unstable local social institutions, and inadequate social support systems, some individuals may create their own standards of conduct and success along variant lines open to them (Anderson, 1990). This gives rise to a "street code" that embraces the concrete utility of violent and aggressive behavior as a building block of social status, honor, and respect (Fagan & Wilkinson, 1998; Massey, 1995). Although some may argue that aggression may at times be warranted (e.g., in self-defense), strict adherence to a code that supports violence and aggression is believed to be a maladaptive coping strategy that increases the likelihood for a range of poor outcomes, including violent victimization and adult criminality. In fact, some believe that the disproportionate rates of crime, violence, delinquency, and substance abuse among young African American males are in fact maladaptive coping responses to chronic exposure to urban stressors (Oliver, 1984).

Coping Strategies for Urban Stress

Social Capital and Adaptive Coping

Given the chronic nature of many urban stressors, children and adolescents must make resourceful and creative adaptations to maintain a healthy level of social functioning (Zimmerman, Ramirez-Valles, & Maton, 1999). These coping strategies and adaptations are thought to be largely a function of social capital. The term *social capital* refers to skills and resources one brings to bear on various situations in an effort to positively affect life circumstances (Rose & Clear, 1998).

Strong kinship support networks; ties to other supportive, caring adults; and relationships with positive peers are examples of social capital that may aid youth in successfully adapting to stressors (Bennett & Fraser, 2000; Printz, Shermis, & Webb, 1999; Stevenson, 1997). Therefore, strong social capital may help to curtail negative behaviors while promoting positive ones. In this way, social capital may function as a protective factor (Carr-Paxton, Robinson, Shah, & Schoeny, 2004; Stevenson, 1997).

However, social capital may not always be sufficient to protect youth from some of the deleterious effects of chronic exposure to urban stressors. The nature and severity of stressors in some neighborhoods and communities are so omnipresent as to render obsolete any protection afforded by social capital. Moreover, not all African American urban adolescents possess the social capital necessary to successfully adapt to the various urban stressors they encounter. Some African American adolescents, particularly males, may instead adopt maladaptive coping strategies (Howard, 1996).

Dysfunctional Compensation and Maladaptive Coping

In an effort to compensate for lack of social capital, some young African American males may respond in ways that are not necessarily related to the actual stressor(s) they encounter. Rather, they may exhibit displacement and acting-out behaviors as a means to cope. Employing such behaviors may further isolate them from potential sources of support and foreshadow poor outcomes (see Richardson, Chapter 5, this volume, for some poignant examples of this). Prior research in this area suggests that psychological distress among urban African American male youth may be related to emotionally distant familial relationships and perceived lack of social support (Fitzpatrick & Boldizar, 1993).

To be sure, behaviors such as aggression, avoidance, distraction, self-criticism, and social withdrawal are examples of dysfunctional, compensatory, maladaptive reactions to stress. These types of reactions are considered asocial or antisocial and may place young African American males at increased risk for poor outcomes, including violence, delinquency, and substance abuse (Dempsey, 2002). Some researchers have argued that dysfunctional, compensatory, maladaptive stress reactions may indicate posttraumatic stress disorder (PTSD; Carr-Paxton et al., 2004; Dempsey, 2002).[1]

Mixed Coping Strategies

Rarely if ever can the coping strategies of an individual be conveniently classified as adaptive or maladaptive. Many young African American males may find it necessary to use both adaptive and maladaptive strategies for coping with chronic exposure to urban stressors, including seeking social support, using emotion-focused and avoidant strategies, and even behaving aggressively (Grant et al., 2000). This would seem to suggest that urban stressors are dynamic in nature—that they vary in duration and intensity over time. Moreover, the response to these stressors likely depends on a host of cognitive, emotional, contextual, and perhaps even situational factors. Furthermore, the dynamic nature of urban stressors may engender coping strategies that are adaptive in the short term given certain contextual and situational factors, but may otherwise be viewed as negative in a broader social context (Dempsey, 2002).

Exploring Stress and Coping Among African American Adolescent Males in an Urban Setting

When one considers the impact of chronic exposure to urban stressors and the variability of stress-buffering resources (e.g., social capital), it is clear that many young African American males who live in urban settings are at considerable risk. Prior research suggests that one's coping ability may function as a mediator between stressors and certain social and developmental outcomes (Dempsey, 2002; Grant et al., 2000). With this in mind, the major aim of this chapter is to examine the impact of exposure to urban stressors on problem behaviors and the extent to which certain coping strategies may mediate this relationship. We were particularly interested in how African American males might differ from non–African Americans (males and females) in exposure to urban stressors, coping strategies, and problem behaviors.

Study Design and Methods

The current study involves data collected as part of a larger study on the continued development, theoretical framework, and utility of the Urban Hassles Index (UHI), which was designed to measure stressors affecting adolescents in the urban environment ($N = 254$).

We drew study participants from two public schools in a large Northeastern city. In each school, students in a health education class participated in the survey. Study participants ranged in age from 10 to 20 years old. The mean age of the sample was 13.76 years (SD = 2.047). The sample was 49% male and 51% female. One-hundred fifty-six (61%) study participants were African American, 17 (7%) were Native American, 1 (0.4%) was Asian or Pacific Islander, 16 (6.3%) were Latino, and 55 (21.7%) were White. Nine (3.5%) participants did not report their racial group membership.

Forty percent ($N = 102$) of study participants reported living in a two-parent household, 35% reported living in a single-female-headed household ($N = 89$), and 3% reported living in a single-male-headed household ($N = 7$). Six percent reported living with grandparents ($N = 14$), 12% reported "other" living arrangements ($N = 31$), and 11% neglected to report their living arrangements.

Measures

Coping Strategies

To measure the participants' coping strategies, we used the *Ways of Coping Checklist* (WCCL), a 68-item scale designed to assess the specific coping efforts of adults (Lazarus & Folkman 1980).[2] Response categories for the WCCL ranged on a scale from "not used," to "used somewhat," "used quite a bit," and "used a great deal."

We include only 38 items from the WCCL in the present study. Problem-focused and social support–seeking behaviors were thought to represent adaptive coping. Avoidant and wishful thinking behaviors were thought to represent maladaptive coping.[3] Wishful thinking, for example, might include thinking about the perfect revenge or finding a million dollars. Avoidance might include keeping things to oneself, not letting on how bad things are, trying to forget the problem, or getting angry with those who are the source of a problem. A composite measure of maladaptive coping was derived from the avoidance and wishful thinking subscales established by Halstead, Bennett-Johnson, and Cunningham (1993).

Urban Stressors

The UHI is a 32-item scale designed to measure adolescents' exposure to common but stressful social interactions in an urban context (Miller & Webster, 1998). Study participants responded either "never," "sometimes," "often," or "very often" to indicate the extent to which they had experienced various urban stressors ($\alpha = .84$). Our findings revealed that the sample as a whole did not report a particularly high exposure to urban stressors. The UHI had a possible range of 0 to 96. In the current study, the mean score was 21, with a range from 0 to 62. This suggests that study participants' exposure to urban stressors was low to moderate. As such, the urban environment of study participants may not necessarily cause constant and elevated levels of stress.

Problem Behaviors

We used 17 items related to conduct disorder and delinquency from the *Adolescent Symptom Inventory* (ASI) to measure problem behaviors. The responses for these items ranged from "never," to "sometimes," "often," to "very often" ($\alpha = .87$). Possible scores on the problem behavior scale can range from 0 to 51. However, our analysis showed scores ranging from 0 to 39, with a mean score of 6, suggesting that the level of problem behaviors among study participants was again low to moderate (see Table 10.1). Recall that the urban stressors are significantly correlated with problem behaviors. Therefore, if study participants reported low to moderate exposure to urban stressors, it makes sense that reports of problem behaviors would be low to moderate as well.

Table 10.1 Descriptive Statistics

	N	Minimum	Maximum	Mean	SD
Problem behaviors	254	.00	39.00	5.4514	5.57598
Maladaptive coping	254	.00	42.00	19.2604	8.41732
Urban stressors	254	.00	62.00	21.4213	12.87764
Valid N (listwise)	254				

Analyses

The above findings are descriptive only. Next we look at the associations between chronic exposure to urban stressors and problem behaviors, as well as the role, if any, that coping plays in mediating problematic outcomes. To do this, we used regression models as described below. But first, we confirmed, using independent *t*-tests (see Table 10.2), that African American males were indeed more likely than other study participants to be exposed to chronic urban stressors. While they were indeed more likely to face urban stressors, they were not more likely to experience problem behaviors than the other study participants (non–African American males and all females). That is, the nature and extent of problem behaviors exhibited by the African American males in the sample were no greater than the problem behaviors exhibited by the sample as a whole. This suggests that the African American males in the study adapted successfully despite greater exposure to stressors. Moreover, it suggests that the coping strategies of African American males may actually moderate the relationship between chronic exposure to urban stressors and problem behaviors.

We should note that the items composing the problem behavior scale represent severe conduct disorder and serious delinquency, including violent acts. Such behaviors are typically limited to a small segment of the adolescent population. The current formulation of items does not acknowledge less serious forms of problem behaviors that may be more prevalent among study participants.

To further explore this association between stress, problem behavior, and coping strategies, we tested a series of regression models to determine whether *(1)* chronic exposure to urban stressors was a significant predictor of problem behaviors, and *(2)* a particular coping strategy mediated the relationship between urban stressors and problem behavior. We examined the potential effect of coping strategy on the relation between urban stressors and problem behaviors using the criteria set forth by Judd and Kenny (1981). To determine the ability of chronic exposure to urban stressors to predict problem behavior, we tested a regression model in which we entered *age* in Step 1 as the control variable, *urban stressors* in Step 2 as the predictor variable, and *problem behavior* as the dependent variable. Additional information that could potentially serve as control variables (e.g., socioeconomic status) was not available in this sample.

Briefly, Judd and Kenny suggest that to establish a mediating factor, one should estimate three regression equations. In the first equation, the mediator should be regressed onto the independent variable. The dependent variable should be regressed onto the independent variable in the second equation. In the third equation, the dependent variable should be regressed onto both the independent and the mediator variables. These regression equations are thought to provide tests of the links within the mediational model (Baron & Kenny, 1986). In the first equation, the independent variable must affect the mediator; in the second equation, the independent variable must affect the dependent variable; and in the third equation, the mediator must affect the dependent variable. Mediation is established if the

Table 10.2 Independent Samples t-Test

Urban Youth	N	Mean	STD	SEM
Urban stressors				
Not African American male (including females)	169	20.230	12.519	.963
African American males	76	23.710	12.651	1.451

	Levene's Test for Equality of Variances			t–Test for Equality of Means					95% Confidence Interval of Difference	
	F	Significance	t	df	Significance (Two-Tailed)	Mean Difference	SED		Lower	Upper
Urban stressors										
Equal variances assumed	.748	.388	-2.006	243	.046	-3.4798	1.734		-6.896	-.0627
Equal variances not assumed			-1.998	143.207	.048	-3.4798	1.741		-6.922	-.0370

effect of the independent variable on the dependent variable is less in the third equation than in the second (Baron & Kenny, 1986).

Prior to testing for the predictive ability of urban stressors and the mediating effect of coping strategies, we performed the Pearson product moment correlation procedure to explore associations among the variables under study. We also included age in this analysis to determine whether it might serve as a control variable. Additional information that could potentially serve as control variables (e.g., socioeconomic status) was not available in this sample. We present the correlation matrix in Table 10.3.

We find that older participants reported significantly more problem behaviors ($r = .130, p < .05$). Urban stressors also were significantly related to problem behavior and to maladaptive coping. We also found a significant relation between coping and problem behavior. The significant correlations among study variables supported further statistical analysis (Baron & Kenny, 1986).

We performed hierarchical regressions to explore the ability of urban stressors to predict problem behavior as well as the possible mediating effect of coping behaviors on the predictive relationship between urban stressors and problem behavior. We tested the initial model separately on the African American males and on the non–African American males and females in the sample. We treated maladaptive coping as the dependent variable. Age (the control variable) was entered in Step 1, and urban stressors were entered in Step 2.

The findings indicate that for African American males, urban stressors contribute a significant portion of the variance in maladaptive coping after accounting for the control variable ($\beta = .36, p = .001$). The overall model was significant ($R^2 = .15, F [2, 73] = 6.453, p < .003$). Once again, after accounting for the control variable, we found that urban stressors contribute a significant portion of the variance in maladaptive coping for the remaining study participants ($\beta = .40, p = .000$). Again, the overall model was significant ($R^2 = .17, F [2, 163] = 16.598, p < .000$). The results of these analyses indicate that urban stressors are significantly related to maladaptive coping (the mediator) and thus meet the first condition of the criteria recommended by Judd and Kenny (1981). We tested subsequent regression models using problem behavior as the dependent variable.

Table 10.3 Correlation Matrix

	1	2	3	4
Age	1.000			
Maladaptive coping	.014	1.000		
Problem behaviors	.130*	.342**	1.000	
Urban stress	−.012	.394**	.441**	1.000

* Correlation is significant at the .05 level (two-tailed).
** Correlation is significant at the .01 level (two-tailed).

Findings

Our findings indicate that for African American males, urban stressors contribute a significant portion of the variance in problem behavior after accounting for age ($\beta = .56$, $p = .000$). That is, those experiencing a higher number of urban stressors were more likely to exhibit problem behaviors. The overall model was significant ($R^2 = .32$, $F[2, 73] = 16.925$, $p < .000$). Again, after controlling for age, we found that urban stressors contribute a significant portion of the variance in problem behavior for non–African American males and all females (Black and White) ($\beta = .40$, $p = .000$). The overall model was significant ($R^2 = .18$, $F[2, 163] = 17.289$, $p < .000$). These findings suggest that urban stressors are a significant predictor of problem behaviors.

We next examined whether maladaptive coping (the mediator) was significantly related to problem behavior and whether the predictive ability of urban stressors was reduced by including the maladaptive coping. We entered age in Step 1 and urban stressors and maladaptive coping simultaneously in Step 2. Once again, we tested the model separately on the African American males and then on the remaining study participants.

Maladaptive coping appears to be significantly related to problem behavior ($\beta = .33$, $p = .001$) and to reduce the relative influence of urban stressors ($\beta = .43$, $p = .000$). The findings suggest that urban stressors and maladaptive coping contribute a greater portion of the variance in problem behavior than do urban stressors alone. The overall model was significant ($R^2 = .40$, $F[3, 72] = 24.302$, $p < .000$).

Maladaptive coping operated in a similar manner for non–African American males and females, in that it appeared to be significantly related to problem behaviors ($\beta = .20$, $p = .014$) and reduced the relative influence of urban stressors ($\beta = .32$, $p = .000$). The overall model was significant ($R^2 = .21$, $F[3, 162] = 13.970$, $p < .000$). These findings suggest that maladaptive coping mediates the relation between urban stressors and problem behavior.

Discussion

Although the current study is based on a sample of urban adolescents, the sample as a whole did not report a particularly high exposure to urban stressors. As such, the urban environment of study participants may not necessarily cause constant and elevated levels of stress. The findings, however, also indicated that African American males were more exposed to urban stressors than other study participants. The reason for this increased exposure is unclear from these analyses. However, prior research has postulated that young African American males are marginalized in society by race, socioeconomic status, and age (Gibbs & Merighi, 1996). This marginalization runs counter to certain gender role expectations and societal appraisals of success and self-worth.

Legitimate paths to success have been historically blocked for low-income urban African American males (Bennett & Fraser, 2000; Gibbs & Merighi, 1996).

As a result, many African American males may pursue masculine roles and strive for success via alternative routes (Anderson, 1990). These routes are typically limited, circumscribed, and risky. Nonetheless, many young African American males may pursue these options to attain a masculine sociocultural role and status within their communities (Anderson, 1999; Fagan & Wilkinson, 1998). The natural drive for self-actualization in the face of limited opportunities may thrust many young African American males into a milieu where they are more likely to encounter a host of urban stressors.

Although African American males were more exposed to urban stressors than the remaining study participants, they were not statistically different from other study participants in terms of problem behaviors. As noted above, this suggests that they successfully adapted to their environment, and perhaps their coping strategies were effective. Of course, the types of problem behaviors we are focusing on here are quite severe—conduct disorder and serious delinquency—and as such are likely less prevalent than other problem behaviors.

Although initial analyses suggest that age is related to problem behavior—the older an individual, the more likely to evidence problem behaviors—the regression analysis did not bear this out. However, age may make joint contribution to problem behaviors, and therefore the importance of age would be underestimated in the regression analysis. In other words, age may have made a strong *joint* contribution in explaining problem behavior, but it did not make a strong *unique* contribution.

Despite reports of low to moderate exposure to urban stressors, stress did account for a statistically significant portion of the variance in the problem behaviors. This may indicate that it is not only exposure to certain stressors that mitigates particular behavioral outcomes but also the response to said stressors. Whether an adolescent views a certain event as stressful depends on a host of cognitive, psychological, and even situational factors. Therefore, it appears that the urban setting may indeed cause constant and elevated stress for a small segment of the urban youth population (Masten, 1994; Zimmerman, Ramirez-Valles, & Maton, 1999).

In the current study, maladaptive coping mediated the relation between urban stressors and problem behaviors; that is, urban stressors along with maladaptive coping contributed a greater portion of the variance in the problem behavior outcome than did urban stressors alone. Thus, it is not only exposure to urban stressors that predicts problem behaviors but also the way in which one responds to such exposure. In this instance, negative or maladaptive responses to urban stressors increase the likelihood of problem behaviors.

Our findings are consistent with prior research that suggests that coping mediates the relation between exposure to stressors and poor outcomes (Berman, Kurtines, Silverman, & Serafini, 1996; Dempsey, 2002). However, in this case, chronic exposure to urban stressors contributes to the use of maladaptive coping strategies that are, in turn, linked to problem behaviors.

Implications for Social Work Research

The complexity of social and developmental outcomes for urban African American adolescents warrants consideration of multiple factors, including race, ethnicity, gender, and culture. Research with this population has not fully addressed the pivotal role of these factors (West-Stevens, 2002). To be sure, it is necessary to closely examine factors such as neighborhood organization, residential mobility, ethnic group segregation, and exposure to urban stressors, including violence, poverty, and school and peer dynamics. However, it is also necessary to explore cultural attitudes, values, and beliefs, including culturally based resources such as religion and spirituality and extended family networks. These factors may affect the response to stressors, coping strategies, and related behavioral outcomes.

A sizable void exists in culturally informed basic research (Jagers, 1997). Therefore, continued research in this area must include culturally sensitive psychometric instruments that are contextually relevant. The use of such instruments may provide information about beliefs, attitudes, and behaviors that contributes to our knowledge and understanding of how urban ethnic minority adolescents evaluate stressors, the coping strategies they employ, and resulting behavioral outcomes. Moreover, the use of ethnographic research methods may yield information about latent processes not otherwise captured by survey methods. This information may then be used to inform social policy as well as to develop intervention strategies that could be evaluated using an experimental research design. Such efforts may ultimately serve to interrupt the negative social and environmental risk processes that affect so many urban African American adolescents.

The Unique Status of African American Males: Implications for Social Work Practice

Although the current study is bound by several limitations, the findings suggest that young African American males encounter more urban stressors than their non–African American male and female counterparts. As a result, young African American males are at increased risk for poor social and developmental outcomes. This seems to highlight the need for culturally sensitive, gender-specific social work practice methods and interventions. One must not assume that all social work interventions are suitable for all groups. Rather, intervention efforts should be sensitive to, and reflective of, the values and traditions of the ethnic group with whom they are used while also acknowledging gender differences in outcomes (Barbarin, 1998). Interventions that recognize the unique status of young African American males are more likely to enhance personal identity and self-esteem and to serve as a form of anticipatory guidance for dealing with urban stressors.

Conclusion

Social work research and practice must continue to explore the impact of contextual factors that attenuate the developmental course for urban African American youth in general and young African American males in particular. It is imperative that future research examine the relationship among macro-level economic factors, neighborhood-level sociocultural factors, and individual-level factors in social and developmental outcomes for this population. These factors may negatively alter the trajectories of people's lives. Therefore, social work research and practice must focus on ways to ease the developmental course for African American youth.

The current study is bound by several limitations. First, the data are cross-sectional. We need longitudinal research to better ascertain how chronic exposure to urban stressors, coping strategies, and problem behaviors is affected by, and changes over, time. This study is also limited by the sole use of self-report measures, which may not yield the most accurate information. Future research should include multiple sources of information.

The standardized format of the WCCL may impose certain limitations as well. We might address this by incorporating items specific to actual stressors (e.g., "What do you do when asked for money by drug addicts?"). Doing so may produce better information to help us understand how adolescents deal with urban stressors. Moreover, research in this area is likely to be enhanced through the use of contextually relevant measures; that is, coping measures should include items that reflect strategies urban adolescents may use.

Future research in the area of stress and coping among urban adolescents could conceivably be enhanced by including items related to the perceived effectiveness of a given coping strategy. Moreover, we could use qualitative methods to gain information about the sequence of coping strategies. Some adolescents may employ presumably maladaptive coping approaches only after repeated attempts with more adaptive methods have failed. Furthermore, particularly for young African American males, items or measures pertaining to self-worth and self-esteem within the context of status at the peer group or neighborhood level may provide insights to their rationale for using certain coping strategies and related behaviors.

NOTES

1. Posttraumatic stress disorder is recognized by the American Psychiatric Association as a condition that occurs as a result of stressors that include *(1)* re-experiencing a traumatic event, *(2)* avoidant behavior, and *(3)* psychic numbing and arousal (American Psychiatric Association, 1987). One may re-experience a traumatic event through dreams, association with certain sounds, or the manner in which one engages in play or recreation. Avoidant behavior is often demonstrated through subdued affect, inactivity, and/or lack of interest in previously enjoyed activities. Psychic numbing and increased arousal may be expressed through startled reactions, sleep disturbances, and aggressive

behavior. Children and adolescents are thought to be more vulnerable to PTSD than adults, particularly when they are exposed to violence (Carr-Paxton et al., 2004; Okundaye, 2004; Oliver, 2000). This suggests that PTSD may mediate the relationship between experiences with urban stress and certain psychosocial and/or mental health outcomes. And while a thorough discussion of PTSD is beyond the scope of this research, it does underscore the need for continued exploration of urban stressors and coping among young African American males.

2. All scales in this study are Likert-type scales. Factor analytic studies of the WCCL with adult populations have yielded a six-to-eight-factor solution (Folkman & Lazarus, 1985; Folkman, Lazarus, Dunkel-Schetter, DeLongis, & Gruen, 1986). However, a four-factor solution (problem focused, seeks social support, wishful thinking, and avoidance) has emerged in studies of the WCCL with adolescent populations (Halstead et al., 1993).

3. One item from the wishful thinking subscale ("Thought about fantastic or unreal things like the perfect revenge or finding a million dollars that made you feel better") and six items from the avoidance subscale ("Kept your feelings to yourself," "Kept others from knowing how bad things were," "Went on as if nothing had happened," "Tried to forget the whole thing," "Felt bad that you could not avoid the problem," and "Got mad at the people or things that caused the problem") were used to create a measure of maladaptive coping ($\alpha = .76$).

REFERENCES

American Psychiatric Association. (1987). *Diagnostic statistical manual of mental disorders* (3rd ed., rev.). Washington, D.C.: Author.

Anderson, E. (1990). *Streetwise: Race, class, and change in an urban community*. Chicago: University of Chicago Press.

Anderson, E. (1994). The code of the streets. *Atlantic Monthly, 273*, 81–94.

Anderson, E. (1999). *Code of the street: Decency, violence, and the moral life of the inner city*. New York: W.W. Norton & Company.

Aneshensel, C. S., & Sucoff, C. (1996). The neighborhood context of adolescent mental health. *Journal of Health and Social Behavior, 37*, 293–310.

Barbarin, O. A. (1998). Integrating service and research on African American youth and families: Conceptual and methodological issues. In V. McLoyd & L. Steinberg (Eds.), *Studying minority adolescents: Conceptual, methodological and theoretical issues*, (pp. 297–326). Mahwah, NJ: Erlbaum.

Barbarin, O. A., McCandies, T., Coleman, C., & Atkinson, T. (2004). Ethnicity and culture. In P. Allen-Meares & M. Fraser (Eds.), *Intervention with children and adolescents: An interdisciplinary perspective* (pp. 27–53). Boston: Allyn & Bacon.

Baron, R. M., & Kenny, D. A. (1986). The moderator-mediator variable distinction in social psychological research: Conceptual, strategic and statistical considerations. *Journal of Personality and Social Psychology, 51*(6),

Bennett, M. D., & Fraser, M. W. (2000). Urban violence among African American males: Integrating neighborhood, family and peer perspectives. *Journal of Sociology and Social Welfare, 27*(3), 93–117.

Berman, S. L., Kurtines, W. M., Silverman, W. K., & Serafini, L. T. (1996). The impact of exposure to crime and violence on urban youth. *American Journal of Orthopsychiatry, 66*(3), 329–336.

Bursik, R. J., & Grasmick, H. G. (1993). *Neighborhoods and crime: The dimension of effective community control.* New York: Lexington Books.

Carr-Paxton, K., Robinson, W. L., Shah, S., & Schoeny, M. (2004). Psychological distress for African American adolescent males: Exposure to community violence and social support as factors. *Child Psychiatry and Human Development, 34*(4), 281–295.

Dempsey, M. (2002). Negative coping as mediator in the relation between violence and outcomes: Inner-city African American youth. *American Journal of Orthopsychiatry, 72*(1), 102–109.

Fagan, J., & Wilkinson, D. (1998). Guns, youth violence, and social identity in inner cities. In M. Tonry & M. H. Moore (Eds.), *Youth violence* (*Vol. 24*, pp. 105–188). Chicago: University of Chicago Press.

Finkelhor, D., & Ormrod, R. (2001). *Homicides of children and youth.* Washington, D.C.: Office of Juvenile Justice Delinquency Prevention.

Fitzpatrick, K., & Boldizar, J. P. (1993). The prevalence and consequences of exposure to violence among African American youth. *Journal of the American Academy of Child and Adolescent Psychiatry, 32*(2), 424–431.

Folkman, S. (1985). If it changes, it must be a process: Study of emotion and coping during three stages of a college examination. *Journal of Personality and Social Psychology, 48*, 150–170.

Folkman, S., & Lazarus, R. S. (1980). An analysis of coping in a middle-aged community sample. *Journal of Health and Social Behavior, 21*, 219–239.

Folkman, S., Lazarus, R. S., Dunkel-Schetter, C., DeLongis, A., & Gruen, R. (1986). Dynamics of a stressful encounter: Cognitive appraisal, coping, and encounter outcomes. *Journal of Personality and Social Psychology, 50*, 992–1003.

Foster, J. D., Kupermine, G. P., & Price, A. W. (2004). Gender differences in posttraumatic stress and related symptoms among inner city minority youth exposed to community violence. *Journal of Youth and Adolescence, 33*(1), 59–69.

Gibbs, J. T., & Merighi, J. R. (1996). Young black males: Marginality, masculinity, and criminality. In T. Newburn & E. A. Stanko (Eds.), *Just boys doing business: Men, masculinities, and crime* (pp. 64–81). New York: Routledge.

Grant, K., O'Koon, J., Davis, T., Roache, N., Poindexter, L., Armstrong, M., et al. (2000). Protective factors affecting low-income urban African American youth exposed to stress. *Journal of Early Adolescence, 20*(4), 388–417.

Halstead, M., Bennett-Johnson, S., & Cunningham, W. (1993). Measuring coping in adolescents: An application of the Ways of Coping Checklist. *Journal of Clinical Child Psychology, 22*(3), 337–344.

Hambrick-Dixon, P. (2002). The effects of exposure to physical environmental stressors on African American children: A review and research agenda. *Journal of Children and Poverty, 8*(1), 23–34.

Howard, D. E. (1996). Searching for resilience among African American youth exposed to community violence: Theoretical issues. *Journal of Adolescent Health, 18*, 254–262.

Jagers, R. (1997). Afrocultural integrity and the social development of African American children: Some conceptual, empirical and practical considerations. In R. Jagers & R. J. Watts (Eds.), *Manhood development in urban African American communities* (pp. 7–34). New York: Haworth Press.

Judd, C. M., & Kenny, D. A. (1981). Process analysis: Estimating mediation in evaluation. *Evaluation Research, 5*, 602–619.

Kubrin, C. E., & Weitzer, R. (2003). New directions in social disorganization theory. *Journal of Research in Crime and Delinquency, 40*(4), 374–402.

Lazaras, R. S., & Folkman, S. (1984). *Stress, appraisal and coping.* New York: Springer.

Luthar, S. S., & Zigler, E. (1991). Vulnerability and competence: A review of research on resilience in childhood. *American Journal of Orthopsychiatry, 61*, 6–21.

Massey, D. S. (1995). Getting away with murder: Segregation and violent crime in urban America. *University of Pennsylvania Law Review, 143*, 1203–1232.

Masten, A. (1994). Resilience in individual development: Successful adaptation despite risk and adversity. In M. C. Wang & E. W. Gordon (Eds.), *Educational resilience in inner-city America: Challenges and prospects* (pp. 3–26). Hillsdale, NJ: Erlbaum.

McCreary, M., & Slavin, L. A. (1996). Predicting problem behavior and self-esteem among African American adolescents. *Journal of Adolescent Research, 11*(2), 216–235.

Miller, D. B., & Townsend, A. (2004). Urban hassles and adolescent mental health: A new look at chronic stressors. Unpublished manuscript, Cleveland, OH.

Miller, D. B., Webster, S. E., & Macintosh, R. (2002). What's there and what's not: Measuring daily hassles in urban African American adolescents. *Research on Social Work Practice, 12*(3), 375–388.

Okundaye, J. N. (2004). Drug trafficking and urban African American youth: Risk factors for PTSD. *Child and Adolescent Social Work Journal, 21*(3), 285–302.

Oliver, W. (1984). Black males and the tough guy image: A dysfunctional compensatory adaptation. *The Western Journal of Black Studies, 8*(4), 199–203.

Paschall, M. J., & Hubbard, M. L. (1998). Effects of neighborhood and family stressors on African American male adolescents' self worth and propensity for violent behavior. *Journal of Consulting and Clinical Psychology, 66*(5), 825–831.

Peterson, R. D., Krivo, L. J., & Harris, M. A. (2000). Disadvantage and neighborhood violent crime: Do local institutions matter. *Journal of Research in Crime and Delinquency, 37*(1), 31–63.

Polk, K. (1996). Masculinity, honour and confrontational homicide. In T. Newburn & E. A. Stanko (Eds.), *Just boys doing business: Men, masculinities and crime* (pp. 166–188). New York: Routledge.

Printz, B., Shermis, M. D., & Webb, P. (1999). Stress-buffering factors related to adolescent coping: A path analysis. *Adolescence, 34*(136), 715–734.

Rasmussen, A., Aber, M. S., & Bhana, A. (2004). Adolescent coping and neighborhood violence: Perceptions, exposure, and urban youths' efforts to deal with danger. *American Journal of Community Psychology, 33*(1/2), 61–75.

Reynolds, L. K., O'Koon, J. H., Papademetriou, E., Szczygiel, S., & Grant, K. (2001). Stress and somatic complaints in low-income urban adolescents. *Journal of Youth and Adolescence, 30*(4), 499–514.

Rose, D. R., & Clear, T. R. (1998). Incarceration, social capital, and crime: Implications for social disorganization theory. *Criminology, 36*(3), 441–480.

Sampson, R. J., & Lauritsen, J. (1994). Violent victimization and offending: Individual, situational and community level risk factors. In J. Albert Reiss & J. A. Roth (Eds.), *Understanding and preventing violence* (*Vol. 3*, pp. 1–114). Washington, D.C.: National Academy Press.

Sampson, R. J., Raudenbush, S. W., & Earls, F. (1997). Neighborhoods and violent crime: A multilevel study of collective efficacy. *Science, 277,* 918–924.

Schmeelk-Cone, K., & Zimmerman, M. A. (2003). A longitudinal analysis of stress in African American youth: Predictors and outcomes of stress trajectories. *Journal of Youth and Adolescence, 32*(6), 419–430.

Shoemaker, D. J. (2000). *Theories of delinquency: An examination of explanations of delinquent behavior* (4th ed.). New York: Oxford University Press.

Stevenson, H. C. (1997). Missed, pissed, and dissed: Making meaning of neighborhood risk, fear and anger management in urban black youth. *Cultural Diversity and Mental Health, 3*(1), 37–52.

West-Stevens, J. (2002). *Smart and sassy: The strengths of inner-city black girls.* New York: Oxford University Press.

Wilson, W. J. (1996). *When work disappears: The new world of the urban poor.* New York: Alfred A. Knopf.

Zimmerman, M. A., Ramirez-Valles, J., & Maton, K. I. (1999). Resilience among urban African American male adolescents: A study of the protective effects of sociopolitical control on their mental health. *American Journal of Community Psychology, 27*(6), 733–751.

11

Health and Young African American Men

An Inside View

JOSEPH E. RAVENELL

African American men arguably have the worst health status of any race-sex group in the United States, evidenced by the highest age-adjusted death rate, shorter life expectancy than almost all other race-sex groups, and the highest rates of premature death (death before the age of 65) (National Center for Health Statistics [NCHS], 2005). The health-related issues facing African American men have rightly been called a "health crisis" (Rich & Ro,). Premature death is the reason African American men can expect to live 6 years less from birth than their White counterparts. The causes that contribute most to premature death disproportionately affect young African American men. Thus, improving the health status of African American men as a whole necessitates a focus on young African American men, a group for whom it is not too late to intervene.

Mayhew Derryberry, a public health pioneer, in writing about improving the health of any given group, suggested that "the problem to be worked on should be selected by [the target group] and be one that a majority of the members of the group feel is important." He later writes, "it is difficult to interest an individual in having a careful periodic medical examination for the protection of his health in the future when he has a throbbing toothache" (Allegrante & Sleet, 2006 p. 270). Implicit in Derryberry's statement is that the first step in addressing health concerns is identifying what concerns matter most to the population of interest. Thus, a critical step in addressing the health of young African American men is elicitation and interpretation of their health beliefs, concerns, and perceptions. This chapter reviews the health and health perceptions of young African American men, and it concludes with a discussion and recommendations for future directions for improving African American men's health.

Health and Health Care Among African American Men

In 1990, a landmark study of mortality in United States by McCord and Freeman found that African American men living in Harlem were three times more likely to die before the age of 65 than White men (McCord & Freeman, 1990). Even more striking, this study also found that African American men living in Harlem were less likely to live to the age of 65 than men living in Bangladesh. This finding was largely due to excess mortality from cardiovascular disease and homicide. More than 15 years later, cardiovascular disease and homicide still contribute to excess and premature mortality in African American men. Currently, homicide is the number one cause of death for African American men aged 15 to 44 years old, followed by accidents, cardiovascular disease, and human immunodeficiency virus (HIV) (National Center for Health Statistics, 2006). The impact of these conditions on the health and longevity of African American men is astounding, and it is considered in more detail in the following section.

Violence and Homicide

For African American men between the ages of 15 and 34, 60% of the deaths are due to homicide or accidents (NCHS, 2006). The homicide rate in 2000 was 5.7 times greater for African Americans than Whites (Williams & Jackson, 2005). According to an analysis of the life expectancy differential between African and White males, homicide is the third leading cause of death contributing to the lower life expectancy in African American men (Centers for Disease Control and Prevention [CDC], 2001). The national homicide statistics for young African American men include homicide due to "legal intervention," defined as "Injuries inflicted by the police or other law-enforcing agents . . . in the course of arresting or attempting to arrest lawbreakers, suppressing disturbances, maintaining order, and other legal action" (Sikora & Mulvihill, 2002). The death rate from homicide at the hands of law enforcement is 10 times higher for African American males aged 20–35 than for the general United States population (Barnett et al., 2001).

Cardiovascular Disease

After homicide and accidents, the next leading cause of death for African American men between the ages of 25 to 44 is cardiovascular disease (NCHS, 2006). Heart disease is the number one cause of death overall in the United States, but for African American men, it is already the leading cause of death by age 35. Heart disease does not become the leading cause of death for White men until they reach the age of 45 (NCHS, 2006). Recent data suggest that 40% of African American men with cardiovascular disease die prematurely (before age 65) compared to 21% of White men (Rich & Ro,). The disproportionate burden of premature cardiovascular death in African American men is largely due to high blood pressure, also known as hypertension (Barnett et al., 2001).

Hypertension is defined as a blood pressure greater than 140/90 (Chobanian et al., 2003), and it is more prevalent and usually more severe in African American men. Hypertensive complications—heart attack, stroke, heart failure, and kidney failure—kill as many young African American men as does homicide. There is now unequivocal evidence that many of these premature cardiovascular deaths can be prevented by controlling hypertension with appropriate physician-prescribed therapy (ALLHAT Collaborative Research Group, 2000). However, young men, who are less likely to have access to quality health-care services than other groups, are less likely to have their hypertension diagnosed, treated, and adequately controlled. In some cases, hypertension can be prevented with lifestyle modifications such as moderate physical activity, intensive dietary salt restriction, and a diet rich in fruits, vegetables, whole grains, and low-fat dairy products and low in saturated fats (Appel et al., 2006; Sacks et al., 2001). Such modifications can be particularly effective at lowering blood pressure in young African Americans (Appel et al., 2006).

Human Immunodeficiency Virus

The leading killer of young African American men in 1999, HIV/AIDS continues to rank among the leading causes of death for African American men between the ages of 25 and 44 (Rich, 2000). Data from the national HIV/AIDS Registry of the CDC indicated that 1333 African American males between the ages of 13 and 24 years were diagnosed in 2003 compared to 639 White males aged 13 to 24 (Rangel, Gavin, Reed, Fowler, & Lee, 2006). Forty-nine percent of HIV infections in African American men result from male-to-male sexual contact, 25% from high-risk heterosexual contact, and 19% from injection drug use. The death rate for African American men aged 35 to 44 is 68 per 100,000 compared to 11 per 100,000 for White men (Rangel et al., 2006).

Therapy for HIV/AIDS has advanced dramatically since the beginning of the AIDS epidemic. However, African Americans have not benefited from the advances as much as other groups. The decline seen in AIDS mortality for Whites over the past decade has not been seen in African Americans. Several large studies have suggested that African Americans are less likely to receive therapy than other groups (Cargill & Stone, 2005). This differential access to HIV therapy could partially explain the wide gap in mortality for African American men compared to White men (Cargill & Stone, 2005).

The aforementioned conditions, which largely account for the higher death rates seen in African American men, are in many cases preventable or amenable to primary care intervention. It has been suggested that the disproportionate burden of preventable death in African American men may be partially due to smaller proportions of minority populations receiving primary care and preventive services (Bliss et al., 2004; Schneider, Cleary, et al., 2001; Schneider, Zasalavsky, et al., 2001). The following section examines the issue of health services utilization in young African American men.

Health Services Utilization Among Young African American Men

African American men are less likely to visit primary care physicians and are also less likely to have any physician contact than other groups (Dunlop, Manheim, Song, & Chang, 2002). Underutilization of primary health-care services is mainly related to access, socioecomonic status, and insurance status, as African American men are twice as likely to be unemployed compared to Caucasians (Brown, Ojeda, Wyn, & Levan, 2000; McCaig & Burt, 2004; Satcher, 2003). Because most Americans obtain health insurance through their jobs, it is no surprise that African American men are more likely to lack health insurance than Caucasian men. African American men who are employed are disproportionately represented among lower-skilled and lower-income jobs, which often do not provide health insurance coverage (Williams, 2003; Williams, Neighbors, & Jackson, 2003). These members of "the working poor" who are not offered insurance from their employers and who cannot afford private insurance on their own are also not eligible for public insurance programs.

Even among insured African American male cohorts, underutilization of primary care services is a significant problem. An analysis of the Medical Expenditure Panel Survey (MEPS) found that Blacks were significantly less likely to have received health care in physicians' offices and outpatient settings compared to non-Blacks, even after controlling for age, insurance status, education, household income, and residence (Bliss et al., 2004). Health services utilization can be thought of as a complex health behavior and has been framed as such in the behavioral model of health services utilization developed by Andersen, Aday, and others (Aday & Andersen, 1974; Andersen, 1995; Phillips, Morrison, Andersen, & Aday, 1998). In the behavioral model framework, health services use is a function of peoples' predisposition to use services, factors that facilitate or impede use, and peoples' need for care. Central to one's disposition to use services is his or her health beliefs. According to Andersen, health beliefs include attitudes, values, and knowledge about health and health services that might influence perceptions of need and subsequent use of health services. Understanding health beliefs of young African American men may be important in developing interventions that seek to improve health services utilization, and ultimately the health of African American men.

The following section describes a qualitative study designed to elicit and explore young African American men's health beliefs. It focuses on the subgroup of young men affected by the health conditions described above.

Young African American Men's Perceptions of Health

A qualitative study was conducted using focus groups to identify and explore African American men's general perceptions of health and health influences. Focus groups offer many advantages that were ideal for our study. These include provision of a protected forum for marginalized voices to be heard, an economical and time-efficient way to probe the perceptions and attitudes of many participants at once, and an opportunity to explore and clarify complex topics through the interaction of the participants with each other in addition to the interaction of the participants with the researchers (Krueger, 1994; Vaughn, Shcumm, & Singaub, 1996). Because the goal of focus groups is to explore and understand a particular group's point of view, it was the ideal vehicle to achieve the goals of our study, which were to explore African American men's health perceptions.

Focus groups were conducted in the Woodlawn community, a low-income neighborhood in Chicago, Illinois, from July 1997 to September 1997. Ninety-five percent of Woodlawn's residents are African American. Sixty-four percent of the Woodlawn community is below twice the poverty line. The all-cause mortality in Woodlawn is 1.5 times higher than in the city of Chicago, while the mortality rate from cardiovascular disease is 35% higher than in the city of Chicago. Deaths from HIV/AIDS occur at three times the rate of the rest of Chicago (Chicago Department of Health, 2004). To ensure that we elicited the views of young African American men, we utilized a purposive sampling strategy. The subpopulations of African American men included adolescents (age 16–18), trauma survivors, HIV-positive men, and men who have sex with men (MSM). Each subpopulation comprised a focus group. Focus groups were moderated by trained, African American male focus group leaders. Group interviews were transcribed and subjected to content analysis. Focused group interviews were conducted over an 8-week period. Each group interview averaged nine participants (range 7–11), and each lasted about 90 minutes. Seventy-one African American men participated in the study, 30 of whom where aged 16 to 44 years old. Health perceptions related to the leading health concerns for African American men described above were elicited. We grouped and categorized responses within each of the three major topic areas of defining health, factors influencing health, and health lifestyle strategies. The latter topic encompassed perceptions on cardiovascular disease prevention; we further examined responses for content specifically related to violence/homicide and HIV.

Defining Health and a Healthy Lifestyle

Categories of responses pertaining to definitions of health included health domains, physical independence, and role functioning. In response to the question "What does being healthy mean to you?" participants cited the absence of physical ailments as an important part of health. However, physical well-being was just one domain of health. Being healthy also included mental and emotional well-being, economic stability, and a sense of spirituality, as one patient summarized:

> Being healthy, if I'm healthy, I'm going to concentrate on being spiritually fit. I want to be spiritually healthy, I want to be mentally healthy, I want to be emotionally healthy, and I want to be economically healthy. But first I got to have a healthy body and a healthy mind to lead me into all of those things.

Health also included being able to fulfill social roles such as holding a job and belonging to a network. The following participants' statements capture the essence of this theme:

> To be healthy . . . means to be able to get up and go to a job, which you like.

> You need to feel wanted, whether it be your family or church members or associates. We need that. Without that, we couldn't make it.

Participants were asked, "What do you do to keep healthy?" to elicit views on healthy lifestyles. Several strategies were employed to maintain health, including healthy behaviors, managing stress, prayer, seeking health care, self-empowerment, and social support.

Healthy Lifestyle and Managing Stress

Adopting healthy behaviors such as eating healthy foods, regular exercise, and abstinence from tobacco, drugs, and alcohol were the lifestyle changes mentioned most often across the groups. One HIV positive participant said,

> I get the proper amount of sleep, take my medication, and eat right, and exercise. I do a lot of walking for my heart. I cut out drugs in my life. So now if I can cut out cigarettes, I can be much healthier. And I try to keep a lot of stress off of me, because stress will tear the body down. So I am trying to reduce stress in my life, get the proper rest, eat, and exercise.

This participant's statement underscored a key point and prevalent theme: managing stress was as important as the other lifestyle changes in maintaining health. Several participants echoed this sentiment. One trauma survivor stated,

> I eat the right foods. Getting my proper rest, exercise . . . it helps physically if I deal with as less stress as possible. If I'm upset or a problem might arise unexpectedly, I have outlets.

Another said,

> As far as staying healthy, I try to keep a good mental picture of things and try not to let stress get to me. Also I try to eat right, try to exercise often.

As this quote illustrates, positive thinking was an important part of stress management and health maintenance. Participants believed that positive thoughts were essential to good health: "If you have that, then you'll always be healthy." One HIV-positive participant expanded on this sentiment: "All you have to do is think positive. If you think negative, you can hurt yourself, and I am sure that nobody wants to do that."

Seeking Health Care

While many of the younger members of the focus groups did not view doctors as having a regular role in health maintenance, the trauma survivors and young men with HIV viewed seeing doctors and following their advice as vital to staying healthy. One healthy adolescent said: "The only time I go to the doctor is when something is really hurting, when I'm injured or something, but otherwise, I don't even know my doctor's name, seriously." In contrast, a trauma survivor said, "As long as I do as my doctor say, I will stay healthy; it ain't too much I can really do to stay healthy but listen to my doctor."

Self-Empowerment

Self-empowerment was frequently mentioned as an important health maintenance strategy and facilitator of health through self-education and being involved in one's own health care. One participant said, "You have to feed your brain, take in knowledge—you'll know how to keep your body healthy and your brain by taking in knowledge." Education was particularly important for the HIV group, since "education is what keeps people from getting infected." Participants also lauded the importance of learning from peers and the elders of the community, "communicating and spreading knowledge to each other."

Social Support

Various forms of social support, including family, friends, and social groups, facilitated health maintenance across the groups. Having positive social interactions was viewed as vital to their health and a meaningful existence. Participants offered the following insights:

> All my family members, even some of my associates, I feel it can help my health a lot. Just them being positive towards you and you being positive towards them.

> You need to feel wanted, whether it be your family or your church members or your associates . . . without that, we basically couldn't make it . . . we need each other to exist.

While all the groups valued being part of a community, the role of membership and social support in maintaining health was valued most by the trauma survivors group and HIV group.

Factors Influencing Health

Responses to the question "What factors influence African American men's health?" fell into two major categories: negative influences and positive influences on African

American men's health. Psychological stress was cited as a dominant negative influence on both physical and mental health. Participants agreed: "Mentally, when you have stress, it affects the body, it affects you physically." Furthermore, stress was felt to influence African American men's health specifically: "In this culture we live in, it's just a stressful society for Black men." Stress was attributed to four major sources: lack of income, experiences of racism, "unhealthy" neighborhoods, and conflict in relationships. Positive influences included a supportive social network and feeling valued by loved ones.

Stress: Lack of Income

Regarding lack of income, participants said, "No income causes high stress because you have lots of bills . . . underemployment and unemployment are great stresses—-clearly that impacts your health." Lack of employment was specifically linked to health through lack of insurance and inability to afford quality medical care. One participant said, "If you are unemployed, you may not have insurance to help your health-care needs."

Stress: Racism

Racism was viewed as a source of stress and therefore a negative influence on health as well as a real obstacle to receiving health care. Participants delineated experiences of racism in distinct settings, including at work, in the community, and portrayed in the media:

> One of the problems of racism that puts a deep mental illness in the community is that we don't know how to deal with it. I think that racism in this country has been so prevalent and we want to act like it's not around and don't know how to confront and deal with it. We see it in the media and we get upset but we don't really know what to do. We see it in our workplaces and we don't know how to respond, and I think that that has caused a lot of mental illness and also it's just not a healthy environment to be in.

Stress: Unhealthy Neighborhoods

Living in "unhealthy" neighborhoods was viewed as a significant source of stress. Neighborhoods were designated as unhealthy because they were unsafe, resulting in the stress of having to look over one's shoulder for fear of being a crime victim or a victim of police harassment. "If you're scared to walk around your neighborhood, that's not good health right there because you in the house a lot." Such neighborhoods were also unhealthy because they were not conducive to healthy habits such as eating healthy food: "The stores that do exist in our neighborhoods . . . only serve foods that are high in salt, high in fat."

Stress: Conflict in Relationships

Stress within intimate relationships was cited as an important health influence. Younger participants in particular felt that "your personal relationship with your significant other has a lot to do with your health . . . if you haven't resolved your problems . . . it brings on stress."

Positive Health Influence: Social Support

Finally, while relationships characterized by stress and violence were viewed as dominant negative influences on health, supportive relationships were cited by all the groups as having a positive influence on health. Supportive and nurturing relationships were felt to impact all aspects of health. As one participant summarized,

> . . . if you have a positive, nurturing, supportive, helpful relationship with whoever, if it's your family, your friends, or your significant other, if those things are going well, then it has a beneficial affect of your physical and mental health. You're going to take better care of yourself because you want to keep enjoying those experiences, you want to get better as time goes on. So it affects how you feel and how you want to feel.

Perceptions Related to HIV and Violence

During the focus groups, several of the participants shared their perceptions related to the top causes of death among young African American men. Since these conditions may be effective targets for intervention to close the health status gap between African American men and other groups, perceptions specifically related to violence and HIV may be particularly instructive. Thus, we analyzed the responses of participants aged 15–44 for content related to these leading health concerns.

Responses related to HIV fell into three categories: disease properties, disease transmission, and disease prevention and treatment. The most important property identified by several of the younger participants was that HIV is a serious health condition with serious health consequences, including death. One of the young HIV positive participants recounted, "I was diagnosed in 1991. Initially it was a shock for me . . . people had to show me that the virus does not mean dying." Another HIV-positive participant said, "A lot of people think that with HIV/AIDS they are just going to pass away, and that's not true." Regarding HIV transmission, two young men with HIV summed up the prevalent beliefs about how HIV infection occurs:

> I had first heard about the virus, I thought gay people got it. But I caught it from my wife; she was a drug user, shooting up.

> I talk to a lot of kids and children, and they ask me if I can catch HIV when I dance because people be out there sweating. I tell them that I can't catch it from sweat . . . So when people in the neighborhood found out that my sister had AIDS, the kids in the neighborhood didn't play with our kids.

For HIV prevention, the message that it is easier to prevent HIV than to treat it was clear and consistent from the young men with HIV. Three strategies for HIV prevention emerged: "practice safe sex," "stick with abstinence," and "don't mess with drugs." Affected participants believed that the key to prevention and treatment is education about the disease and about available social services and support groups.

Responses related to violence identified reasons for violence, possible alternatives to violence during a conflict, and rebirth and awakening after surviving an episode of interpersonal violence. The participants most impacted by violence were the trauma survivors, most of whom had survived gunshots. The most commonly cited reasons for involvement in gun violence included the following: one or more parties involved felt disrespected at some point in the encounter ("He disrespected me, so I felt I had to do what I had to do"); gun violence was the means of choice for conflict resolution ("I wasn't going to let him tell me what to do at that point, gunfire was the next alternative"); or the participant was in the wrong place at the wrong time ("If I wasn't in that neighborhood, it never would've happened"). Participants who survived gunshot wounds reflected on the shooting incident and offered the following insights:

> It could have been handled differently. But instead of me just saying "Alright, forget it," what was on my mind was retaliation.

> To do it all over again, I would've walked away.

These survivors reported an awakening after their brushes with death that resulted in important lifestyle changes. One survivor said, "I feel I got to make a change . . . I don't hang on the streets anymore. Now I'm valuing my life and I'm glad that I still have it, and from this point on I'm going to live it to the fullest the best way I can." Several of the survivors, in addition to leaving the streets, also made changes to improve their health in other ways, as one participant summarized, "I stopped hanging out, stopped drinking, and stopped smoking."

Discussion

Using a sample of African American men in Chicago, we conducted an exploratory qualitative study to understand African American men's perceptions of health. Our findings indicate that young African American men have a very broad and inclusive definition of health that goes far beyond the traditional definition of "the absence of disease." Young African American men appear to subscribe to the World Health

Organization definition, which describes health as "a state of complete physical, mental, and social well-being and not merely the absence of disease or infirmity" (Saylor, 2004). As providers, we must expand our definition of health accordingly, enabling us to improve communication with this group of men who come into our offices all too rarely. Expanding our concepts of health may lead to improved patient satisfaction, an important consideration in long-term health-care utilization (Saylor, 2004).

Participants in our study identified traditional strategies for health maintenance, including diet, exercise, and smoking cessation. These lifestyle changes are vital to cardiovascular risk reduction and disease prevention. Cardiovascular disease is a key target for young African American men, who die prematurely from heart disease more so than any other group in the United States. Equally important targets for improving the health of young African American men are health-seeking behavior and health services utilization. These health behaviors are intricately tied to mortality from cardiovascular disease because hypertension, which begins earlier and is typically more severe in African American men, requires regular health care in a physician's office for appropriate diagnosis and management.

The young men in our study identified self-empowerment through education as an important strategy for HIV prevention. The CDC has recently endorsed an advanced HIV prevention strategy that emphasizes greater access to HIV testing to enhance early diagnosis and reduce HIV-related morbidity, mortality, and disease spread (CDC, 2003). This strategy includes developing models to improve access to HIV testing in nonmedical settings. Despite these new strategies, reducing HIV risk behaviors is still the cornerstone of prevention in African Americans, who comprised over half of the incident cases of HIV in 2001 through 2004 (CDC, 2003).

Violence and homicide continue to be the most serious health concerns for young African American men. According to our participants, the reasons for gun violence are multifactorial. A problem of such complexity will require a multilevel solution, one that targets the individual, the family, and public policy. As Wiiliams and Jackson point out, for the age group that has been the focus of this chapter, homicide is strongly patterned by educational attainment (Williams & Jackson, 2005). There is an inverse correlation between education and homicide rate, as African American men with less than a high school education have a homicide rate five times higher than African American men with at least some college. Providers can serve as role models and mentors for young men at the individual level to provide them with alternatives to gun violence, tools for conflict resolution, and social support, while also advocating for policy-level change.

Our study provides an inside view of young African American men's health. With this patient-centered perspective, the formative data from our study led to the development of Project Brotherhood, a Black Men's Clinic (http://www.project brotherhood.net/). Project Brotherhood, which opened its doors 2 years after our study was completed, focuses on the all dimensions of well-being rather than primarily disease, the traditional focus of medical centers. This clinic model is based on the WHO definition of health similar to the definitions developed by the young African American male participants. Project Brotherhood was designed to meet the health-care needs as well as the social needs of African American men. The clinic successfully accomplishes its mission with African American physicians, social workers, and staff recruited from the surrounding community. Study participants whose input helped to shape the clinic are now employed by Project Brotherhood. Services provided by the clinic are related to the study findings and include job-readiness training, housing programs, fatherhood training, ex-offender transition programs, and life skills for young men. The clinic also utilizes novel strategies to overcome the reticence of young men to come into the clinic to seek health care: free haircuts and food are provided during clinic hours. This aspect of the clinic proceedings effectively transforms the stigmatized and sterile traditional medical setting into a relaxed, nonmedical community forum for self-empowerment and improvement. Models such as Project Brotherhood may hold the key to improving the health of African American men, as it not only facilitates access to the low-cost, high-quality medical care they need but also the social and community services they want.

REFERENCES

Aday, L. A. & Andersen, R. (1974). A framework for the study of access to medical care. *Health Services Research, 9*(3), 208–220.

Allegrante, J. P. & Sleet, D. (Eds.). (2006). *Derryberry's Educating for Health: A foundation for contemporary health education practice* (1st ed.). New York: Jossey-Bass.

ALLHAT Collaborative Research Group. (2000). Major cardiovascular events in hypertensive patients randomized to doxazosin vs. chlorthalidone: The antihypertensive and lipid-lowering treatment to prevent heart attack trial (ALLHAT). *Journal of the American Medical Association, 283*(15), 1967–1975.

Andersen, R. M. (1995). Revisiting the behavioral model and access to medical care: Does it matter? *Journal of Health and Social Behavior, 36*(1), 1–10.

Appel, L. J., Brands, M. W., Daniels, S. R., Karanja, N., Elmer, P. J., & Sacks, F. M. (2006). Dietary approaches to prevent and treat hypertension: A scientific statement from the American Heart Association. *Hypertension, 47*(2), 296–308.

Barnett, E., Casper, M. L., Halverson, J. A., (2001). Men and heart disease: An atlas of racial and ethnic disparities in mortality. Atlanta, GA: Centers for Disease Control and Prevention.

Bliss, E. B., Meyers, D. S., Phillips, R. L. Jr., Fryer, G. E., Dovey, S. M., & Green, L. A. (2004). Variation in participation in health care settings associated with race and ethnicity. *Journal of General Internal Medicine, 19*(9), 931–936.

Brown, E., Ojeda, V., Wyn, R., & Levan, R. (2000). *Racial and ethnic disparities in access to health insurance and health care*. Los Angeles: UCLA Center for Health Policy Research and The Henry J. Kaiser Family Foundation.

Cargill, V. A. & Stone, V. E. (2005). HIV/AIDS: A minority health issue. *Medical Clinics of North America, 89*(4), 895–912.

Centers for Disease Control. (2001). Influence of homicide on racial disparity in life expectancy—United States, 1998. *Morbidity and Mortality Weekly Report, 50*, 780–783.

Centers for Disease Control and Prevention. (2003). Advancing HIV prevention: New strategies for a changing epidemic—United States, 2003. *Morbidity and Mortality Weekly Report, 52*(15), 329–332.

Chicago Department of Health. Health. 2004.

Chobanian, A. V., Bakris, G. L., Black, H. R., Cushman, W. L., Green, L. A., Izzo, J. L., et al. (2003). The seventh report of the Joint National Committee on Prevention, Detection, Evaluation, and Treatment of High Blood Pressure: The JNC 7 report. *Journal of the American Medical Association, 289*(19), 2560–2572.

Dunlop, D. D., Manheim, L. M., Song, J., & Chang, R. W. (2002). Gender and ethnic/racial disparities in health care utilization among older adults. *Journal of Gerontology Series B: Psychological Sciences and Social Sciences, 57*(4), S221–S233.

Karasek, R. & Theorell, T. (1990). *Healthy work.* New York: Basic Books.

Krueger, R. (1994). *Focus groups: A practical guide for applied research* (2nd ed.). Thousand Oaks, CA: Sage.

McCaig, L. F. & Burt, C. W. (2004). National hospital ambulatory medical care survey: 2002 emergency department summary. *Advance Data, 340,* 1–34.

McCord, C. & Freeman, H. P. (1990). Excess mortality in Harlem. *New England Journal of Medicine, 322*(3), 173–177.

National Center for Health Statistics, Centers for Disease Control and Prevention. (2005). *Health, United States, 2005 with chartbook on trends in the health of Americans.* Atlanta, GA: Author.

National Center for Health Statistics, Centers for Disease Control and Prevention. (2006). *LCWK2: Deaths, percent of total deaths, and death rates for the 15 leading causes of death in 10-year age groups, by race and sex: United States, 2003.* Atlanta, GA: Author.

Phillips, K. A., Morrison, K. R., Andersen, R., & Aday, L. A. (1998). Understanding the context of healthcare utilization: Assessing environmental and provider-related variables in the behavioral model of utilization. *Health Services Research, 33*(3 Pt 1), 571–596.

Rangel, M. C., Gavin, L., Reed, C., Fowler, M. G., & Lee, L. M. (2006). Epidemiology of HIV and AIDS among adolescents and young adults in the United States. *Journal of Adolescent Health, 39*(2), 156–163.

Rich, J. A. (2000). The health of African American men. *The Annals of the American Academy of Political and Social Science, 569* (May), 149–159.

Rich, J. & Ro, M., (2002/2006) *A poor man's plight: Uncovering the disparity in men's health.* Battle Creek, MI: W.K. Kellogg Foundation.

Sacks, F. M., Svetkey, L. P., Vollmer, W. M., et al. (2001). Effects on blood pressure of reduced dietary sodium and the dietary approaches to stop hypertension (DASH) diet. DASH-Sodium Collaborative Research Group. *New England Journal of Medicine, 344*(1), 3–10.

Satcher, D. (2003). Overlooked and underserved: Improving the health of men of color. *American Journal of Public Health, 93*(5), 707–709.

Saylor, C. (2004). The circle of health: A health definition model. *Journal of Holistic Nursing, 22*(2), 97–115.

Schneider, E. C., Cleary, P. D., Zaslavsky, A. M., & Epstein, A. M. (2001). Racial disparity in influenza vaccination: Does managed care narrow the gap between African Americans and Whites? *Journal of the American Medical Association, 286*(12), 1455–1460.

Schneider, E. C., Zaslavsky, A. M., Landon, B. E., Lied, T. R., Sheingold, S., & Cleary, P. D. (2001). National quality monitoring of Medicare health plans: The relationship between enrollees' reports and the quality of clinical care. *Medical Care, 39*(12), 1313–1325.

Sikora, A. G. & Mulvihill, M. (2002). Trends in mortality due to legal intervention in the United States, 1979 through 1997. *American Journal of Public Health, 92*(5), 841–843.

Vaughn, S., Schumm, J., & Sinagub, J. (1996). *Focus group interviews in education and psychology*. Thousand Oaks, CA: Sage.

Williams, D. R. (2003). The health of men: Structured inequalities and opportunities. *American Journal of Public Health, 93*(5), 724–731.

Williams, D. R. & Jackson, P. B. (2005). Social sources of racial disparities in health. *Health Affairs, 24*(2), 325–334.

Williams, D. R., Neighbors, H. W., & Jackson, J. S. (2003). Racial/ethnic discrimination and health: Findings from community studies. *American Journal of Public Health, 93*(2), 200–208.

World Health Organization. (1946). Preamble to the Constitution of the World Health Organization as adopted by the International Health Conference, New York, June 19–22, 1946; signed on July 22, 1946 by the representatives of 61 states (Official Records of the World Health Organization, no. 2, p. 100) and entered into force on April 7, 1948.

12

Health and Health-Care Service Use Among Middle-Class Black Men

SHERRILL L. SELLERS, VENCE L. BONHAM,
HAROLD W. NEIGHBORS, AND SHUNTAY MCCOY

Although research into physical health and use of health care systems has produced a plethora of scholarly works, very few studies have focused on non-poor black men. An examination of the existing literature revealed that there was no work, at least that we could locate in the published literature, that empirically investigated health and access/usage of health care systems among middle-class African American men.

As our data are comprised of only middle-class Black men, our analysis does not explicitly compare across race or gender groups. However, race and gender comparative data provide the context in which the study is embedded. Specifically, the poor health status of Black men, relative to other race and gender groups prompted this investigation. Black men have the highest age adjusted death rate of any group, experience higher rates of preventable illness, and suffer an increased incidence of preventable deaths (Centers for Disease Control and Prevention CDC, 2004, 2005; Rich, 2000). Compared to White men, Black men have lower 5-year cancer survival rates for lung and pancreatic cancer and were 2.4 times as likely to die from prostate cancer. Black men are 2.3 times as likely to start treatment for end-stage renal disease related to diabetes, are 20% more likely to die from heart disease and 1.5 times as likely as White men to have high blood pressure. Black men are less likely than White men to see a doctor, even when they are in poor health. Black men are more likely to be uninsured than are White men, largely reflecting lower rates of employer-based coverage. Regardless of insurance status, Black men are less likely to receive timely preventive services, and they are more likely to suffer the consequences of delayed attention, such as limb amputations (Brown, Ojeda. Wyn, & Levan, 2000).

Several factors have been examined to explain these health disparities, including racial discrimination, income inequalities, lack of insurance, poor health behaviors, difficulty in obtaining care and mistrust of health care providers (Andersen, 1995; Dressler, Oths & Gravlee, 2005; Penn, et al., 2000; Rich, 2000; Shavers, Shankar & Alberg, 2002; Williams, 2003a). Recent research has focused on four areas—socioeconomic factors, experiences of discrimination or unfair treatment, health behaviors, and patient-provider interactions. Socioeconomic disadvantage accounts for much of the racial disparities in health (Krieger, Williams, & Moss, 1997; Plowden 2003). Some researchers suggest that the solution to disparities in health for Black men lies in the complete redistribution of income (Marmot, 2002; Nazroo, 2003).

Experiences of racial discrimination and discriminatory policies that disadvantage Black men have been associated with poor health (Paradies, 2006; Williams & Mohammed, 2009). In a recent review, Paradies noted that studies generally found that after adjusting for a range of confunders, studies generally found that discrimination was inversely related to health, with associations for mental health stronger than those for physical health.

Within this emerging area of research, a few scholars are beginning to examine both implicit and explicit dimensions of discrimination (Krieger, Carney et al. 2009). Researchers who propose that race has an important influence of health care disparities among Black men (Meyer, 2003; Rich, 2000; Satcher, 2003; Williams, 2003a, 2003b) suggest that the services of health care providers could inadvertently be influenced by racial stereotypes. Satcher states, "Providers need to be conscious of these biases and the potentially negative impact they can have on treatment and the delivery of services" (2003, p. 2). Williams (2003) and others (Allen, Kennedy, Wilson-Glover, & Gilligan, 2007; Sellers, Bonham, Neighbors, & Amell, 2009) suggest that bias among providers may be one factor, but that there may also be a cumulative affect of discrimination that adversely effects Black men's health directly via mistrust of physicians and indirectly through not seeking care. It is possible that Black men, despite health insurance and adequate income, still may not have access to culturally competent health care providers (Rich, 2000).

In addition to examining economic and racial influences on health care, a growing body of literature has begun to explore the relationship of positive and negative health behaviors on the health outcomes of black men. These studies take an ecological perspective that considers the impact of individual characteristics, social relationships, and aspects of the health care system to understand health behaviors of Black men. Research has found that refraining from behaviors that place one's health at risk, such as smoking and excess alcohol consumption, positively affect physical and psychological health (Gallant & Dorn, 2001; Kobau, Safran, Zack, Moriarty, & Chapman, 2004). Further, there appears to be a relationship between health behaviors and health service use. Plowden (2003), for example, found that removing barriers to health services increased engagement in positive health behaviors of Black men across socioeconomic backgrounds. Despite these promising findings, research on health-promoting behaviors of Black men is sparce (Sellers, Bonham, Neighbors. & Amell, 2009).

This brief review suggests that race, gender and socioeconomic status all may influence physical health and health service use. Prior research has often considered each of the categories separately or two in combination, but seldom have these three categories been examined simultaneously (Brown & Keith, 2003; Carter, Sellers & Squires, 2002). In addition to presenting a window into the health status and health service use of middle class Black men, this study aims to further the development of a model of black men's health that accounts for micro and macro level factors. Specifically, this study used a strengths based-ecological approach to framing Black men's health. We argue that researchers must move beyond models that portray African American men negatively and consider models that focus on the strengths Black men employ in making decisions about their health and use of health care services.

Methods

Sample

Data were drawn from Project UPLIFT (Uncovering and Promoting Life-Saving Information for Tomorrow), a joint research project between Michigan State University and a community-based service organization. The cross-sectional survey was conducted through a series of computer assisted telephone interviews (CATI) by Michigan State University's Institute for Public Policy and Social Research, Office of Survey Research. Interviews were conducted by African American men to minimize differences between interviewers and respondents (Bonham, Sellers, Neighbors, 2004).

The sample population consisted of African American men who were members of a historically Black national fraternal organization. The international Black fraternity has over 130,000 members and over 550 chapters in 44 states, the District of Columbia, and abroad. Only those members (5,687) residing in Illinois, Indiana, Michigan, Minnesota, and Wisconsin that had reported a telephone number to the fraternal organization (about 35%) were included in the sample population for this study.

A total of 399 interviews were completed. The interview took between 30 to 35 minutes to conduct. Based on the American Association for Public Opinion Research ([AAPOR], 1998) strategy for calculating response rates, the total response rate for the survey was 78.7%. We speculate that this high response rate suggests the importance of the study for respondents.

Measures

OUTCOME VARIABLES   Physical health was measured using the physical health components of the SF-12 and a measure of self-reported health. The SF-12 is a multiple-purpose general measure of mental and physical health status commonly used as a health status survey instrument. Both the mental and physical health components of the SF-12 have a normed mean of 50 and a standard deviation of 10 in the general U.S. population (Ware, Kosinksi, & Keller, 1998). Higher scores are associated with increased levels of health. For self-reported health, respondents were asked, "In general, would you say that your health is . . ." Responses ranged from excellent (5) to poor (1).

To assess participation in the health care system, respondents were asked, "During the past 12 months, about how many times did you see or talk to a medical doctor or assistant for your health care (not counting doctors seen while overnight in a hospital)?" The responses ranged from 1 to 50 and were highly skewed. To adjust for this pattern, we examined the median split to include respondents who saw a medical provider three or more times during the past year (1 = yes, 0 = no). We further examined assessment of health provider with the question, "Overall, how satisfied or dissatisfied are you with your regular health care provider?" Responses ranged from very satisfied (4) to very dissatisfied (1).

PREDICTOR VARIABLES Demographic control variables included age, income, education and marital status. Age was measured by asking respondents for their date of birth. Income was a continuous measure based on self-report of annual income from all sources. In cases where respondents did not report an annual income, the mean income for the entire sample was imputed. Dichotomous measures of education (1 = graduate degree, 0 = else) and marital status (1 = married, 0 = not married) were also used in the analysis.

Respondents were asked, "Do you have any kind of health coverage, including health insurance, prepaid plans such as HMO's or government plans such as Medicare?" Responses were coded (1 = yes, 0 = no). A positive health behaviors index included three items: exercising, refraining from smoking and abstaining from drinking. Smoking was assessed by asking respondents, "Do you now smoke cigarettes everyday, some days, or not at all?" Responses were then coded as 1 = don't smoke, 0 = smoke. Drinking was assessed by asking respondents, "During the past month, how many days did you drink any alcoholic beverages?" These responses were coded as 1 = do not drink, 0 = drink. Exercise was assessed by asking men, "During the past month, did you participate in any physical activities or exercises such as running, calisthenics, golf, gardening or walking for exercise?" Responses were coded as 1 = yes, 0 = no. A positive health behaviors index was subsequently created by summing these three re-coded items. Responses ranged from 0 to 3, with 3 indicating higher levels of positive health behaviors.

For analysis of health service use, four additional variables were used. Provider demographics characteristics, race (1 = Black; 0 = else) and gender (1 = male; 0 = female), were used, as well as items on feeling welcomed and overall trust of provider. Respondents were asked "Overall, how welcomed does your health-care provider make you feel?" Responses ranged from very welcome (3) to not welcome at all (1). The final question assessed overall trust. Respondents were asked "In general, would you say you trust doctors and other health care providers to be able to help you with your medical problems." Responses ranged from very much (4) to not at all (1).

Analysis

Because the men in this study offer a unique window into the physical health status and health service use of middle-class Black men, we present a number of descriptive tables. Next, regression analysis was used to examine relationships among socio-demographic characteristics and physical health and health services utilization.

Results

Tables 12.1–12.6 present descriptive statistics about the respondents. Tables 12.7–12.9 reflect the correlation of demographic data, health routines and the feelings of respondents on their overall health and health behaviors. The men who were a part of this study reported earning a mean income of $87,653 a year. These men were highly educated with 56% holding a graduate degree (MA or PhD). Slightly over 69% of the respondents were married, and the mean age of the respondents was 47.6 years of age.

Table 12.2 indicates that less than 3% of the respondents did not have health care coverage. This percentage is well above the national average and reflects the strong occupational position for Black middle-class men where employment based coverage is an important benefit. We note that, in general, Black Americans have lower rates of employment-based coverage than their White counterparts. Furthermore, the disproportionate rates are consistent across all employment sectors. For instance, in professional services and other high coverage sectors such as manufacturing, 72% of African Americans are covered, compared to 86% of

Table 12.1 Demographic Characteristics

	%Yes	*N*
Age	47.6*	396
Income	87652.77*	359
Marriage	69.2	396
Employment	71.6	395
Education	55.9	395

*Scores reported in mean totals.

Table 12.2 Health Care

	%Yes	N
Health coverage	97.2	394
Different coverage to choose from	78.4	379
Saw medical provider	83.8	394
Particular medical facility	89.9	397
Times saw/talked to health provider	3.63 (mean)	394

Table 12.3 Health Status

	%Yes	N
Cancer	4.8	394
Diabetes	9.1	396
Heart disease	4.5	397
Hypertension	33.5	397
Health status self-report	3.8417*	398
PCS 12	52.9158*	396

*Scores reported in mean totals.

Table 12.4 Health Procedures

	%Yes	N
Routine check-up	81.7	393
Prostate	89.2	249
Digital rectal	87.4	247
Blood stool test	43	249
Signoidoscopy/protoscopy	50.2	245
Pneumonia vaccination	26.5	396

Table 12.5 Health Behaviors

	Yes	N
Participate in exercise	91.7	397
Smoked at least 100 cigarettes in lifetime	34.8	396
Smoke currently*	80.3	137
Spoken with provider about quitting**	85.2	27
Drink	23.7	396

*Scores reported apply to the 34.8% of men who reported smoking at least 100 cigarettes in their lifetime.

Table 12.6 Physician Characteristics and Perceptions

	%Yes	N
Option to choose race of provider	76.8	353
Male health provider	85.7%	357
Black health provider	26.5%	350
Time seeing the same provider	3.1 (mean)	326
Welcomed by provider	2.8 (mean)	355
Trust medical provider	3.5 (mean)	394

Whites. In low- coverage sectors such as sales and domestic service, 45% of African Americans are insured, compared to 66% of Whites (Mills, 2002).

Out of the 97.2% of men with health care coverage, 78.4% reported they had the option to choose from a variety of health care options. Nearly 90% of respondents stated they frequented a particular medical facility. These respondents saw or spoke with their health care provider an average of 3.6 times a year.

Table 12.3 provides an overall view of respondents' health status. Nine percent of respondents reported having diabetes, a rate below national averages. In 2003, the age-adjusted prevalence of diagnosed diabetes per 100 in the population was 7.0 for Black men. By way of contrast, the rate for Black women was 7.6 and 5.1 for White men (CDC, 2005). Thirty-three percent of respondents stated they had received a diagnosis of hypertension, also slightly below the national average. According to the National Health and Nutrition Examination Survey 1999-2002 (NHANES), the age-adjusted percentage of persons 20 years of age and over who have high blood pressure was 40.5% for Black men, 43.5% for Black women and 27.5% for White men (CDC, 2004). The mean total of 3.8 for the self-reported health status indicated respondents felt they were in good health.

The preventative health procedures of respondents are reported in Table 12.4. Unlike reports from the general male population (Williams 2003a), a majority of respondents received a routine check-up. Double the national average, 26.5% of respondents received a pneumonia vaccination. Although not available by gender, in 2002 the age-adjusted percentage of adults aged 18 to 64 years who received the pneumonia shot in the past 12 months was 13% for Blacks and 16% for Whites (CDC, 2005). Forty-three percent of respondents had a blood stool test. Over half of the respondents reported having more invasive preventative procedures performed, such as a sigmoidoscopy or proctoscopy[1]. This is in contrast to the findings of Anderson and May (1995) who found that only 28% of African Americans reported having a proctoscopic examination within the past 5 years. Anderson and May add that although the rate of colorectal screening tests has improved, the percentage of African Americans being screened still remains low.

The men in our study were nearly two times as likely to have these procedures. Nearly 90% of respondents stated they have had a prostate exam, and 87.4% had a digital rectal exam. The men were well above average on these health procedures, which is particularly important as colon and rectum cancer is the third leading cause of cancer death among both African American men and women (Allen et al., 2007). Further, death rates for cancer of the colon and rectum among African Americans are about 30% higher than among Whites, and African Americans have the highest death rate from colon and rectum cancer of any racial or ethnic group in the United States (American Cancer Society, 2000).

Table 12.5 reports the health promotion behaviors of respondents. A total of 91.7% of respondents reported they participate in exercise. These data are well above the national averages (American Obesity Association, 2005). Almost thirty-five percent of respondents stated they smoked, which is slightly above the national averages. In general, Black women (22.7%) and White women (24.4%) smoke at a similar rate, while Black men (31.4%) smoke at a higher rate than White men (27.6%) (American Cancer Society,2000). The smoking rates for the sample are somewhat surprising because among African Americans, as with other U.S. popu-lations, the prevalence of smoking tends to decline as education increases. Smoking rates are usually higher among African Americans who had less than a high school education (34.8%) compared to those with a college education (16.7%) (U.S. Department of Health, 1998). However, since the question asks about smoking 100 cigarettes over the course of their lifetime, it does not necessarily mean respon-dents smoke now or smoke a lot. On the other hand, out of the 34.8% of respon-dents that smoke, 85.2% reported they have spoken with their health-care provider about quitting.

Over 76% of all participants stated that they do not drink. This finding is consistent with the literature that suggests somewhat of a paradox: although African American men tend to have more alcohol-related health and social prob-lems (Harper, 2001), they have lower alcohol use rates than White men (Rich, 2000). Caetano, Clark, & Tam, (1998) suggest that alcohol consumption patterns and alcohol-related problems, "result from a complex interplay of individual attributes, environmental characteristics, and historical and cultural factors that shape the life history of Blacks in the United States" (p. 235). They note that society seems to be more tolerant of whites' use of alcohol than its use by other racial-ethnic groups.

The perceptions held by respondents regarding their health care providers and their physician's characteristics are reported in Table 12.6. Among the respondents who have health- care coverage, 76.8% of the men had an option to choose the race of their provider. However, even with this option, only 26.6% of the African American men in this sample reported having a Black health-care provider. This may reflect the limited number of Black physicians from which to draw on. Alternatively, race of provider may be of less importance to the respondents than other factors such as specialization, bed-side manner and convenient location. Just 14.3% of the men have female health-care providers.

Table 12.7 Correlation Matrix

	1	2	3	4	5	6	7	8	9	10	11	12	13	14	15
1. Age	1														
2. Income	.076	1													
3. Married	.215**	.440**	1												
4. MA, PhD	.326**	.260**	.224**	1											
5. Insurance	.118*	.178**	.173**	.019	1										
6. Positive health behaviors	.311**	.002	.048	.018	.065	1									
7. Male provider	.100	.053	-.041	.114*	.008	.033	1								
8. Black provider	.059	-.046	-.060	.124*	-.169**	-.047	-.080	1							
9. Long with provider	.299**	.239**	.194**	.233**	.054	.116*	.207**	.071	1						
10. Welcomed by provider	.191**	.100	-.026	.050	.003	.083	.064	.132*	.193**	1					
11. Trust doctors	.158**	.070	.018	.017	.125*	.024	.062	.014	.112**	.191**	1				
12. Physical health status	-.305**	.178**	-.072	-.051	-.083	-.077	-.055	-.048	.027	.011	.026	1			
13. Self-report health status	-.298**	.128*	-.090	.030	-.060	-.024	-.071	-.073	-.047	.031	-.041	.561**	1		
14. Saw medical provider	.243**	.086	.069	.109*	.054	.036	.010	-.004	.034	.129*	-.016	-.209**	-.159**	1	
15. Satisfied provider	.190**	.085	.042	.070	-.039	.141**	.026	.105	.252**	.495**	.286**	.037	.054	-.017	1
N	355	321	355	354	353	356	356	349	325	354	353	354	355	353	356

**.01; *.05

Table 12.8

	Physical Health	Health Status Self-Report
Age	-.078	-.018***
	(.023)	(.348)
Income	.000***	.000***
	(.000)	(.000)
Marriage	-1.349+	-.286**
	(.744)	(.116)
Post Bachelor education	-.890	.214*
	(.667)	(.104)
Health coverage	-2.243	-.371
	(2.098)	(.326)
Racial discrimination stress	-.114	-.053+
	(.202)	(.031)
Positive health behavior	.197	.185*
	(.506)	(.079)
Saw medical provider	-1.733**	-.203*
	(.628)	(.097)
Constant	57.620	4.735***
	(2.243)	(.348)
R square	.139	.143
	(5.629)	(.874)
N	396	398

<.1+, <.05*, .01**, .001***

When asked if they felt welcomed by their doctors, respondents reported a mean total of 2.8, indicating that the majority of them felt very welcomed by their health-care providers. Respondents also indicated they trusted their medical providers very much (mean = 3.5).

Tables 12.7–12.9 present correlational analyses. Table 12.8 shows physical health was associated with age, income, marital status, education and positive health behaviors. There was a strong correlation between the income of respondents and both their physical health. There was negative association between age and self-reported health status, although no relationship for SF-12 physical health. Marriage had an inverse relationship on respondents' physical and self-reported health status. This is somewhat surprising as marriage generally tends to be health promoting for men. Education was positively related to self-reported health, although not related to SF-12 physical health. No relationships were found for health coverage, racial discrimination and health behaviors on SF-12 or self reported physical health. However, there was a trend in the data for self-reported health and racial discrimination, such that those experiencing racial discrimination reported lower levels of health. Positive health behaviors were positively associated with self-reported health. For both the SF-12 measure of physical health and self-reported

Table 12.9

	Saw a Medical Provider	Satisfaction With Medical Provider
Age	.029*	.002
	(.009)	(.002)
Income	.000	.000
	(.000)	(.000)
Marriage	−.272	.045
	(.319)	(.071)
Post Bachelor education	.283	−.047
	(.279)	(.064)
Health coverage	.377	−.045
	(1.076)	(.283)
Gender of physician (1 = male)	−.100	.007
	(.377)	(.086)
Race of provider (1 = Black)	−.190	.049
	(.290)	(.065)
Length of time assigned to provider	.097	.086**
	(.131)	(.030)
Welcomed by provider	.562	.701***
	(.382)	(.083)
Trusting of health care providers	−.222	.196***
	(.233)	(.053)
Constant	−1.838	.549
	(1.640)	(.393)
2 log like	373.118	—
R square	—	.334
	—	(.470)
N	394	356

$p <.1+, <.05^*, .01^{**}, .001^{***}$

health, a negative association was found between the respondents seeing a medical provider and their physical health. It is possible that in the face of a chronic health diagnosis, respondents went more regularly to see their provider. As the data are cross-sectional, we are unable to tease out the causal order.

The differences between SF-12 and self-reported health were minor. However, more factors were significant for self-reported health. We speculate that the SF-12 measure of physical health suppresses some variation that is captured in the self reports. In support of this speculation, Fleishman and Lawrence (2003) observed differential item functioning in SF-12 scores for age, gender, education and race. Hence, although SF-12 is a common measure of health status, our findings suggest that to capture a more complete picture of physical health among African American men it will be necessary to investigate a range of physical health measures, including self-reports, health-related quality of life, and specific diagnoses.

As shown in Table 12.9, age was the only significant association related to whether respondents saw a medical provider. This positive association is consistent with research that indicates a negative relationship between age and physical health, and thus a positive relationship between age and physician visits. The length of time respondents saw their provider was positively related to provider satisfaction. There is a strong association between satisfaction with their medical provider and the extent to which respondents felt welcomed and trusting of their health care providers.

Discussion

This study of middle class African American men helps fill an important gap in the literature on Black men. A disproportionate amount of attention is often paid to negative images of Black men, usually pictured as poor, unemployed, and involved in the criminal justice system. Such portrayals present a skewed picture of African American men. To further our understanding of men's health it is important to examine the complex social contexts in which men live out their everyday lives. We believe that an understanding of the heterogeneity within the Black population is an essential step to eliminating racial disparities in health.

We found that the men who participated in this study reported above average health and had consistently accessed health care services. Physical health was associated with age, income, marital status, education and positive health behaviors. Regression analysis also revealed that accessing health care services was associated with characteristics of the respondent but not of the health care provider. Somewhat counter to prior theorizing, satisfaction with one's health care provider was not associated with race or gender of the provider but was related to length of time with the provider and feelings of welcome and trust.

Some study limitations are important to note. For instance, the cross-sectional design of the study limited our ability to examine whether men modified their health behaviors as a result of a health diagnosis or the causal order of the association between feelings of trust and satisfaction with medical provider. The study used self-reported data; hence biases are possible. The men may have over-reported participation in health related activities or overestimated the quality of their health. Subsequent research could benefit by employing a longitudinal sample of men across racial and ethnic and socioeconomic groups to more fully assess the dynamic relationships between physical health, sociodemographic factors, provider characteristics and patient satisfaction. Also, the sample was unique. Fraternal organizations are by their nature selective, and therefore they may not fully represent the population of middle class Black males. Nonetheless, our investigation lays the ground-work for future research and begins to identify important areas for intervention and public policy practice.

Research & Practice Implications

The examination of middle-class Black men provides insights that may guide the development of more precise health interventions. Our study only modestly reflects the claim that race-related factors are a primary influence on physical health and health service use of Black men. In fact, less than 30% of the men interviewed, who had an option to choose the race of their health-care provider, chose to receive services from an African American doctor. The men in our study expressed an overall trust in and very welcomed by their health-care provider. However, this does not mean that the race of the provider does not influence Black men's health at all. Instead, it implies that the extent to which racial factors, including provider characteristics, environmental circumstances, and social interactions, influence the health of Black American men is multidimensional.

Providers must view Black men as having the potential for positive health outcomes, and Black men must view themselves as active participants in promotion of their well-being (Airhihenbuwa, Kumanyika, TenHave, & Morssink, 2000). Researchers have the opportunity to aid in this process by examining the strengths Black men utilize in making decisions about health-care and participating in health-promoting behaviors. Middle-class African American men enjoy a socio-economic status that engenders a climate conducive to health-promoting behaviors. The culture is one of caring for oneself through the ability to take better care of one's health because of the availability of health insurance; the ability to take the time to care for health without risk of loss of income or undue interference from employers; the knowledge of the importance of health; and the lack of a paralyzing fear that one will be informed of a health problem without resources to address the concern.

Our study suggests three areas of importance if we are to improve the health of African American men: (1) more comprehensive research, (2) increased social resources, and (3) establish additional partnerships and enhanced practice relationships.

First, research related to African American men's health must be culturally based with a comprehensive focus on resources and risks (Sellers, et al. 2009). An ecological, strengths based approach provides a useful framework in which to examine the impact of individual characteristics, social relationships, and aspects of the health care system on health and health behaviors. Additional research is necessary to inform ways in which practitioners, policy makers and researchers can best address the overall health and use of health care services among African American men. A small, but growing body of qualitative research on the health and wellbeing of Black men has developed over the last few years (Allen et al., 2007; Plowden, John, Vasquez & Kimani, 2006; Ravenell, Johnson, Whitaker, 2006). Additional qualitative and large scale longitudinal quantitative studies are also needed.

Second, the data in this study supports other research that indicates increased household wealth would alleviate some of the health disparities that currently exist among Black male populations. Race is a factor; however, education, earning potential, and overall socioeconomic status tend to be significantly influential in determining which Black men will have poorer or better health and which Black men will utilize or not utilize health care services in the United States. Thus promoting access to high quality education, jobs with good insurance, and a livable wage become sound health, as well as public policy.

Third, the findings of this study offer health care providers a starting place to better serve the health needs of African American men. Although lower socioeconomic status African American men may not have access to the privileges their middle-class counterparts have (Isaacs & Schroeder, 2004), fostering a culture of self-care is a universal message that will benefit the health of Black men across socioeconomic status groups.

As mentioned, overall the men in our study trusted and felt welcomed by their physicians. However, the disparities in service that still remain among other populations suggest that a one-size-fits all approach to health service utilization will be only modestly effective. Rather than a singular focus on individual-level risks and resources, we suggest an intervention strategy that is multi-leveled, involving the individual, family and community. This strategy must encourage a culture of self-care that builds on individual (e.g., religiosity, self-esteem) and community (e.g., Black churches, schools) resources while making efforts to ameliorate social processes that impact the physical health of Black men. Or as Rich (2000) concludes, "The future health of African American men will depend upon improving their access to health care that address[es] health behaviors in their social context . . . (p. 158)." While research examining the extent to which race influences the health of Black men is needed, practitioners can begin to allow their clients to set the standard for service. Focusing on ensuring African American men feel welcomed and trust their providers while empowering them to take charge of their health sets the groundwork for alleviating disparities, not only for middle-class Black men, but perhaps for Black men across the socioeconomic spectrum.

Providers who partner with their clients will become a true resource that will enhance the therapeutic relationship and have a positive impact on clients' overall health. In tandem with the efforts of practitioners, Black men must become successful advocates for their own proper health care. The individual voices of Black men requesting clarification on their health status is essential during the time of their office visit. Assisting providers in understanding their needs is vital for African American men to improve the quality of service they receive.

Finally, it is vital that all health care providers are culturally competent to deliver quality services to African American men. While some physicians have a high level of cultural competence by virtue of their life and educational experiences, others are not culturally competent. Collaborating with national medical boards to ensure physicians and other health care providers have the ability to deliver culturally relevant services would greatly increase the quality of services given to African American men.

It is the combination of research, increased resources, enhanced practice and established partnerships between health care providers and African American men that will reduce and ultimately alleviate most disparities in health and health care service utilization among African American men.

NOTE

1. Sigmoidoscopy or protoscopy is a procedure in which a tube inserted in the rectum to view the bowel for any signs of cancer or other health problems.

REFERENCES

Airhihenbuwa, C., Kumanyika, S., TenHave, T & Morssink, C. (2000). Cultural identity and health lifestyles among African Americans: A new direction for health intervention research? *Ethnicity and Disease*, 10, 148–164.

Allen, J., Kennedy, M., Wilson-Glover, A., Gilligan, T., (2007). African-American men's perceptions about prostate cancer: Implications for designing educational interventions. *Social Science & Medicine*, 64, 2189–2200.

American Association for Public Opinion Research (AAPOR). (1998). *Standard Definitions: Final Dispositions of Case Codes and Outcome Rates for RDD Telephone Surveys and In- Person Household Surveys*. Ann Arbor, Michigan: AAPOR.

American Cancer Society. (2000). *Cancer facts and figures for African Americans 2000–2001*. Atlanta, GA: American Cancer Society.

American Obesity Association. (2005). Retrieved on May 26, 2006., from http://www. obesity.org/subs/fastfacts/Obesity_Minority_Pop.shtml.

Anderson L. and May D. (1995). Has the use of cervical, breast, and colorectal cancer screening increased in the United States? *American Journal of Public Health*, 85(6), 840–2.

Brown, E., Ojeda, V., Wyn, R. & Levan, R. (2000). *Racial and Ethnic Disparities in Access to Health Insurance and Health Care 2000*; Los Angeles CA: UCLA Center for Health Policy Research and the Henry J. Kaiser Family Foundation.

Brown, D. & Keith, V. (2003). *In and Out of Our Right Minds: the mental health of African American Women*. NY: Columbia University.

Bonham,VL, Sellers SL, Neighbors HW. (2004). John Henryism, and self reported physical health among high SES African American men. *American Journal of Public Health*, 94(5), 737–738.

Caetano, R. Clark, C. & Tam, T. (1998). Alcohol consumption among racial/ethnic minorities: Theory and Research. *Alcohol and Health Research World*, 22(4), 233–241.

Carter, P., Sellers, S., & Squire, C. (2002). Reflections on race/ethnicity, class, and gender inclusive research. *African American Research Perspectives*, 8(1), 111–124.

Centers for Disease Control and Prevention. (2004). *Heath, United States 2004*. Retrieved on May 26, 2006, from http://www.cdc.gov/nchs/data/hus/hus04trend.pdf#topic

Centers for Disease Control and Prevention (2005). *Healthy People 2010 Data Warehouse*. Retrieved on May 26, 2006, from http://wonder.cdc.gov/scripts/broker.exe

Dressler, W., Oths, K. & Gravlee, C. (2005). Race and ethnicity in public health research: Models to explain health disparities. *Annual Review of Anthropology*, 34, 231–252.

Fleishman, J. & Lawrence, W. (2003). Demographic variation in SF-12 scores: True differences or differential item functioning? *Medical Care*, 41, 11175–11186.

Gallant, M. & Dorn, G. (2001). Gender and race differences in the predictors of daily health practices among older adults. *Health Education Research, 16*(1), 21–31.

Harper, F.D. (2001). Alcohol use and misuse. In R.L. Braithwaite & S. E. Taylor.(Eds.), *Health issues in the African-American community* (pp. 403-418). San Francisco: Jossey-Bass Publishers.

Isaacs, S. & Schroeder, S. (2004). Class–The ignored determinant of the nation's health. *New England Journal of Medicine, 351*(11), 1137–1142.

Kobau, R. Safran, M. Zack, M., Moriarty, D., & Chapman, D. (2004). *Sad, blue, or depressed System, 1995-2000. Health and Quality of Life Outcomes.* 2:40. Retrieved May 5, 2006, from http://www.pubmedcentral.nih.gov/articlerender.fcgi?artid=514530 &tools=bot#B39

Krieger, N., Carney, D., Lancaster, K., Wateman, P., Kosheleva, A., & Banaji, M. (2009). Combining Explicit and Implicit Measures of Racial Discrimination in Health Research *American Journal of Public Health.* published online ahead of print Nov 17, 2009.

Krieger, N., Williams, D. & Moss, N. (1997). Measuring social class in US public health research: Concepts, methodologies, and guidelines. *Annual Review of Public Health, 18*, 341–378.

Marmot, M. (2002). The influence of income on health: Views of an epidemiologist. *Health Affairs, 21*(2), 31–46.

Meyer, J. (2003). Improving men's health: Developing a long-term strategy. *American Journal of Public Health, 93*(5), 709–711.

Mills, R., (2002). *Health insurance coverage: 2001.* Washington, DC: U.S. Census Bureau.

Nazroo, J. (2003). The structuring of ethic inequalities in health: Economic position, racial discrimination, and racism. *American Journal of Public Health*, 93, (2), 277–284.

Paradies Y. (2006). A systematic review of empirical research on self-reported racism and health. *International Journal of Epidemiology*, 35, 888–901.

Penn, N., Kramer, J., Skinner, J., Velasquez, R., Yee, B., Arellano, L. & Williams, J. (2000). Health practices and health care systems among cultural groups. In R.M. Eisler & M. Hersen (Eds.), *Handbook of gender, culture, and health* (pp. 105–137). Mahwah, NJ: Erlbaum.

Plowden, K., John, W., Vasquez, E., & Kimani, J. (2003). A theoretical approach to understanding Black men's health-seeking behavior. *The Journal of Theory Construction and Testing, 7*(1), 27–31.

Plowden, K. (2006). Reaching African American men: A qualitative analysis. *Journal of Community Health Nursing,* 23(3), 147–158.

Ravenell, J. Johnson, W., Whitaker, E. (2006). African-American men's perceptions of health: A focus group study. *Journal of the National Medical Association,* 98(4), 544–550.

Rich, J. (2000). The health of African American men. *The Annals of the American Academy of Political and Social Science,* 569(1), 149–159.

Satcher, D. (2003). Overlooked and underserved: Improving the health of men of color. *American Journal of Public Health,* 93(5), 707–709.

Sellers, S. L., Bonham, V., Neighbors, H. & Amell, J. (2009). Effects of racial discrimination and health promoting behaviors on mental and physical health of middle-class African American men. *Health Education and Behavior,* 36(1), 33–44.

Shavers, V., Shankar, S. & Alberg, A.J. (2002). Perceived access to health care and its influence on the prevalence of behavioral risks among urban African Americans. *Journal of the National Medical Association,* 94 (11), 952–962.

U.S. Department of Health and Human Services. (1998). Tobacco Use Among U.S.
Racial/Ethnic Groups – *African Americans, American Indian and Alaska Natives, Asian
Americans and Pacific Islanders, and Hispanics: A Report of the Surgeon General.*
Atlanta: U.S. Department of Health and Human Services, Centers for Disease Control
and Prevention.

Ware, J., Kosinski, M., & Keller, S. (1998). *SF-12: How to score the SF-12 physical and mental
health summary scales.* Lincoln: Quality Metric Incorporated.

Williams, D. (2003a). The health of men: structured inequalities and opportunities.
American Journal of Public Health, 93 (5), 724–731.

Williams, D. (2003b). Race, health and health care. *Saint Louis University Law Journal,
48* (13), 13–35.

Williams D. & Mohammed, S. (2009). Discrimination and racial disparities in health:
evidence and needed research. *J Behavior Medicine,* 32, 20–47.

13

At the Intersection of HIV/AIDS Disparities

Young African American Men Who Have Sex With Men

BRIAN MUSTANSKI, AMY JOHNSON, AND
ROBERT GAROFALO

Acquired immune deficiency syndrome (AIDS) is now the leading cause of death among African American women aged 25–34. It is among the top three leading causes of death among African American men aged 25–54 (National Center for Health Statistics, 2006). The fight against human immunodeficiency virus (HIV) and AIDS should be framed as a civil rights and social justice campaign, with the focus on the many inequalities that advance transmission in certain populations. Although the United States has seen many advances in HIV/AIDS prevention and care in the last 25 years, not all communities have benefited equally. Racial disparities continue to deepen, and the risk of transmission is compounded by being a member of multiple minority groups (National Prevention Information Network, 2006). Specifically, the epidemic is affecting subgroups of African Americans at alarming rates: youth, women, and men who have sex with men (MSM) are particularly affected (The Kaiser Family Foundation, 2005).[1] This multiple-minority status compounds risk, with young African American MSM showing disturbingly high HIV prevalence rates. Advocates, researchers, policy makers, and community members must look to the multilevel factors that facilitate HIV transmission as well as factors that impede intervention and prevention efforts in these hard-hit communities. Commitment to developing and implementing long-term sustainable solutions must begin with focused research, funding, and inclusive policies.

This chapter reviews the HIV/AIDS epidemiology of young African American MSM and the characteristics that affect prevention efforts within the African American MSM community. The chapter also reviews the racial disparities in the Centers for Disease Control and Prevention (CDC)'s Young Men's

Survey, as well as findings from another study of young MSM conducted in Chicago (Project Q) that examines the psychosocial and sociodemographic characteristics that underlie racial disparities. Finally, it offers practical policy solutions and implications for social work practice and suggests areas for future research and advocacy.

Theoretical Framework

Ecodevelopmental theory focuses on the multiple, interrelated contexts (macrosystems, exosystems, mesosystems, and microsystems) that affect development (Bronfenbrenner, 1986; Pantin, Schwartz, Sullivan, Prado, & Szapocznik, 2004). According to this theory, positive social support within and between systems can facilitate positive social outcomes. Likewise, conflict within and between systems can lead to negative or problematic outcomes. Microsystems for young African American MSM are the contexts in which they directly participate, such as family, school, and peers. Their macrosystems include the broad social contexts such as cultural values, policy, language, and societal values.

Currently, most HIV prevention efforts occur at the microsystem of individual behavior (CDC, 2003a). However, structural or macrosystem factors also interact and fuel inequities in HIV transmission. For example, stigma and discrimination affect many levels of social development. To be effective, therefore, interventions must include efforts to combat structural factors that facilitate transmission. For instance, a macro intervention could focus on creating living-wage jobs, improving public education, or increasing the nation's stock of affordable and safe housing. Through structural-level changes, disenfranchised groups can gain equal access to society's benefits. Coupled with individual-level interventions, these macro interventions can help curtail the spread of HIV.

Epidemiology

Youth, African Americans, and MSM are disproportionately affected by HIV. African Americans represent 13% of the U.S. population, yet they account for approximately one-half (49%) of the new cases diagnosed in 2004 and 40% of all AIDS cases diagnosed since 1981 (The Kaiser Family Foundation, 2005). As noted in the introduction, AIDS is a leading cause of death for African Americans in young adulthood (National Center for Health Statistics, 2006). Of the estimated 1 million people living with HIV in the United States, 42% are African American (The Kaiser Family Foundation, 2005). Although the rate of HIV and AIDS diagnoses decreased from 2001 through 2004, African Americans continue to have the highest rate for all racial and ethnic groups, currently 10 times that for Whites (The Kaiser Family Foundation, 2005).

Adolescents aged 13 to 19 are among the age groups witnessing the most dramatic increases in new HIV cases (CDC, 2006c). In 2004, an estimated 13% of

HIV diagnoses were among youth aged 13–24 (CDC, 2006c). In the same year, 7761 youth were living with AIDS, a 42% increase since 2000 (CDC, 2006c). Unfortunately, these rates are even more alarming for African American youth. Only 15% of the adolescent population (13–19) is African American, yet they accounted for 66% of new AIDS cases among youth in 2003 (The Kaiser Family Foundation, 2005).

HIV/AIDS has had a devastating impact on MSM since the beginning of the epidemic. Currently, MSM account for 70% of all HIV infections among male adults and adolescents, even though only 5%–7% of U.S. males self-identify as MSM (CDC, 2006b). At the end of 2004, MSM accounted for 51% of all people living with AIDS, and since the beginning of the epidemic, MSM have accounted for 54% of all AIDS diagnoses (CDC, 2006b). Tragically, almost 300,000 MSM have died of AIDS in the United States since the epidemic began in the early 1980s. Even within the category of MSM, racial disparities exist. In a five-city CDC study of adult MSM, 46% of participating African Americans were HIV positive compared with 21% of White participants (CDC, 2006a). In addition, 64% of the African American men were unaware of their diagnosis compared with 11% of the HIV-positive White men.

As shown in Figure 13.1, young African American MSM are particularly affected by HIV and AIDS given that they are members of three of the highest-risk groups. The largest epidemiological study to date reports that 14% of young African American MSM are infected with HIV (CDC, 2006c).

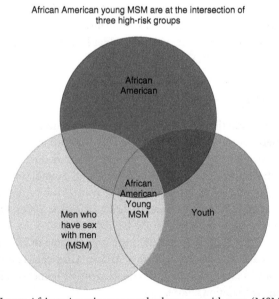

Figure 13.1 Young African American men who have sex with men (MSM) are at the intersection of three high-risk groups.

Factors That Affect Prevention and Intervention

As alarming as these epidemiological data are, even more disturbing is the lack of preparedness to address HIV risk and prevention among young African American MSM. The vast majority of school-based sex education programs do not address the concerns and questions of many young MSM (Santelli et al., 2006), and data suggest that young MSM are less likely to receive school-based sex education at all (Goodenow, Netherland, & Szalacha, 2002), despite their desire for it (Seal et al., 2000). Currently, federal mandates require abstinence-only curricula in exchange for federal funding for sexual education. The information presented in abstinence-only curriculum is as disturbing as the total lack of educational programs for young MSM. In a 2004 congressional review of 13 federally funded abstinence-only programs, 11 contained false, misleading, or partial information (U.S. House of Representatives Committee on Government Reform- Minority Staff, 2004). These programs either ignore gay youth or show a clear bias against homosexuality (Sexuality Information and Education Counsel of the United States [SIECUS]). Attempts to include topics on same-sex relationships in sex education classes have been met with resistance. Opponents claim that teaching topics related to same-sex relationships forces ideology on students (Llana, 2006). However, proponents argue that bringing these topics to the forefront of education teaches respect for diversity and creates a safer environment for youth of all sexual orientations (Llana, 2006).

The lack of HIV prevention efforts for highly vulnerable young MSM extends beyond the classroom. Of the five HIV-specific interventions the CDC considers effective for MSM, none are youth specific or culturally specific (CDC, 2001). Although several interventions are effective in reducing HIV risk among adult MSM (Johnson, Hedges, & Diaz, 2003) and ethnically diverse heterosexual youth (Pedlow & Carey, 2003), no empirically supported behavioral intervention exists to prevent HIV among young MSM. Adult-oriented interventions may not be applicable to young MSM because the interventions fail to attend to developmental factors (Pedlow & Carey, 2004), and interventions designed for heterosexual youth ignore the unique risks specific to sexual minority adolescents. Yet the only way to combat the growing HIV epidemic among young MSM is to develop, implement, test, and disseminate interventions tailored to this group.

Researchers and advocates face many challenges in intervening against the HIV/AIDS crisis among young African American MSM. Some of the challenges include stigma, homophobia, misconceptions, poverty, and the criminal justice system. These characteristics are manifested in various ways throughout the community, from environmental factors to reinforced societal norms. Despite these challenges, each community offers many factors that protect against the transmission of HIV/AIDS. For example, African American youth are less likely to report use of alcohol and other drugs than their White counterparts—a difference widely attributed to religious and cultural factors (Bachman et al., 1991; Johnston, O'Malley, & Bachman, 1993; Maddahian, Newcomb, & Bentler, 1988;

Wallace et al., 2003). For interventions to succeed, these population-specific risk and protective factors must be identified and used to refine existing interventions or to develop new ones.

Stigma concerning sexual orientation or same-sex relationships is apparent in many arenas, including churches and schools (Cohen, Bell, & Ifatunji, 2005). Many young African American MSM do not see where their sexuality fits in with their community's cultural values. In addition, young African American MSM are "double minorities." They may feel they have to choose between their sexual identity and their cultural identity, or risk fitting into neither community (Harper, Jernewall, & Zea, 2004). One study found that one-half of young African American MSM agreed with the statement "Most people of my ethnicity disapprove of gays" compared with only 34% of White young MSM (CDC, 2003b). Homophobia and heterosexism create an unhealthy environment for young MSM (Cohen et al., 2005). The insecure position this imposes on young men may make it difficult to learn and practice safer sex methods. In fact, the internalization of heterosexism (that is, internalized homophobia) has been associated with reduced participation in HIV prevention activities (Huebner, Davis, Nemeroff, & Aiken, 2002). Prevention programs that do not address the culturally related stigma associated with being African American and MSM risk not only being outdated but also irresponsible.

Although their dual-minority status may magnify the stigma experienced by African American MSM, some scholars have suggested unique opportunities for resiliency to emerge. For example, one study found similarities among the strategies used to cope with heterosexism and the strategies that theorists have identified for coping with racism (Della, Wilson, & Miller, 2002). This suggests the possibility that if parents teach African American youth strategies for coping with racial discrimination, these strategies can be co-opted by young African American MSM to cope with outside adversity due to their sexual orientation. Little research has focused on the positive development of young MSM (Fergus & Zimmerman, 2005), and more is sorely needed to successfully capitalize on the unique factors that promote resiliency among young African American MSM.

Misconceptions concerning HIV and AIDS also present a challenge to prevention efforts. Many people believe that AIDS is a White, gay male disease. However, the paradigm must be shifted to include the intersection of the MSM and African American communities. Public service announcements (PSAs) concerning the impact of HIV and AIDS on the African American community have begun to air in media geared toward African American audiences (Cohen et al., 2005), which is one step in the right direction.

Also facilitating the transmission are misconceptions and conspiracy theories about HIV and AIDS, which may stem from the lack of accurate, reliable, accessible, and culturally specific information. Studies that have examined the relationship between HIV and AIDS conspiracy theories and consistent condom use have found that African American men hold stronger conspiracy beliefs (about individual, government, and treatment-related issues) than African American women, and their beliefs are associated with negative attitudes toward condom use and less consistent condom use (Bogart & Thorburn, 2005). The results of these studies suggest that addressing conspiracy theories within the curriculum of culturally sensitive prevention programs may increase the receptivity to information and increase the chance of making positive changes.

Some have suggested that the behavior of men "on the down low" may account, in part, for the racial disparities in HIV rates (King, 2004). Others have argued that the recent focus on African American men on the down low has shifted attention away from comprehensive prevention approaches for the African American community (Boykin, 2005; Wright, 2006). Men on the down low are characterized by their secret bisexual lifestyle, in which they have sex with men and do not disclose this with the women with whom they also have sex. Although there are men on the down low whose actions do contribute to the epidemic, they have not single-handedly caused the HIV/AIDS crisis in the African American community. The scope of the epidemic is much greater.

Poverty is another factor that affects the transmission of HIV and AIDS. A greater percentage of African American experience poverty than Whites (DeNavas-Walt, Proctor, & Lee, 2006). Nearly one in four African Americans were living below the poverty line in 1999 (CDC, 2006a). The link between poverty and HIV/AIDS transmission has been repeatedly demonstrated (Gilles, Tolley, & Woletenholme, 1996), as has the link between poverty and higher rates of untreated sexually transmitted diseases (STDs) (e.g., Cohen et al., 2000), which can also facilitate the transmission of HIV. In a meta-analysis of the role of STDs in sexual transmission of HIV, researchers found that both ulcerative and nonulcerative STDs increase the risk, primarily for the receptive partner, of contracting HIV (Fleming & Wasserheit, 1999). According to the CDC, in 2003 African Americans were 19 times as likely as Whites to be diagnosed with gonorrhea and 6 times as likely to be diagnosed with syphilis (CDC, 2006a). These findings highlight the importance of offering STD testing and treatment in conjunction with HIV testing, given the strong evidence that early detection and treatment of STDs can help prevent HIV (Fleming & Wasserheit, 1999).

The United States has the highest prison population per capita in the world (Walmsley, 2003). There is also an extreme racial disparity in the justice and juvenile justice systems. In 1997–1998, although African American youth represented 15% of the total youth population, they represented 26% of youth arrested and 44% of youth detained (Hoytt, Schiraldi, Smith, & Ziedenberg, 2002). In a report prepared for the U.S. Commission on Human Rights, Marc Mauer stated that an African American male born in 1991 has a 29% chance of spending time in prison, while a White male born in the same year has a 4% chance (Mauer, 1999). Considered another way, the number of African American youth who are incarcerated exceeds the number enrolled in undergraduate colleges and universities (Braithwaite & Arriola, 2003). Rates of HIV/AIDS in prisons are 3 to 8 times higher than in nonincarcerated populations (Braithwaite & Arriola, 2003). HIV risk behaviors are known to occur in prisons (Wohl et al., 2000), yet in the vast majority of U.S. prisons and jails, condoms and needles are considered contraband (May & Williams, 2002).

Give the noted factors and characteristics that affect prevention, it is essential to expand the scope of current prevention efforts to include structural changes, such as increased access to quality education, comprehensive universal health care, and reform of juvenile justice policies. It is also imperative to include community members in all phases of prevention efforts, as they can provide insight and knowledge that are unique to the community. Social workers and other social justice advocates can start by creating relationships with key community members, conducting needs assessments, and establishing multidisciplinary teams of prevention workers. To be effective in the fight against HIV and AIDS, advocates must become agents of change.

Young Men's Survey

The Young Men's Survey (YMS) is by far the largest study of HIV risk behaviors and seroprevalence among young MSM ever conducted. The YMS is a two-phase cross-sectional survey of MSM conducted in seven U.S. metropolitan areas: Baltimore, Dallas, Los Angeles, Miami, New York, San Francisco, and Seattle. The first phase surveyed MSM aged 15 to 22 in 1994 through 1998. Phase two was conducted in 1998 through 2000 with MSM aged 23 to 29. Participants completed a standard questionnaire, had blood drawn for HIV testing, and were provided with HIV and STD counseling.

Of the 4000 MSM aged 15–22 in the seven cities, 7.2% were HIV infected, 82% were unaware they were infected, and only 15% were receiving treatment (Valleroy, MacKellar, et al., 2000). Relative to prevalence rates in a comparable sample of heterosexual youth, these rates are particularly alarming. For example, 0.2% of the 16–21-year-old male applicants for the Federal Job Corps program tested HIV positive (Valleroy, MacKellar, Karon, Janssen, & Hayman, 1998). In other words, young MSM were 36 times as likely to be HIV positive as a set of disadvantaged, out-of-school male youth who applied for the Job Corps program.

The survey found significant racial differences in HIV rates in phase one. Sixteen percent of African Americans aged 15–22 were HIV positive compared with 3.3% of Whites (Harawa et al., 2004). Paradoxically, White youth more frequently reported sex and drug-use behaviors that increase HIV risk. A detailed analysis of a subsample of these youth from Baltimore and New York City found different risk factors depending on one's race/ethnicity. Among young African American MSM, history of a sexually transmitted infection (STI) and not being in school were risk factors (Celentano et al., 2005).

There were also racial differences in the proportions of youth who accurately knew their HIV serostatus. Overall, two-thirds of all participants reported being recently tested for HIV, yet only 18% of young MSM who tested positive knew they were currently infected, suggesting that many of the participants had become infected since their most recent test (Valleroy, Duncan, et al., 2000). MSM who were unaware of their infection were more likely to be African American, less educated, and out of school; 91% of African American HIV-infected MSM were unaware of their infection compared with 60% of Whites. Using only data for MSM (ages 15–22), African Americans were nearly seven times more likely to have an unrecognized HIV infection than were young White MSM (MacKellar et al., 2005).

Factors protective against HIV infection among young MSM included being currently employed, being in school, and being at or above the expected grade level (Harawa et al., 2004). In a race-specific analysis, Celentano and colleagues (2005) found different risk factors by race; for young African American MSM history of a STD and not being in school were particularly predictive of HIV-positive status. To increase the protective characteristics in young African American MSM, it is essential to establish and implement public school reform, increase access to employment, and promote and provide access to comprehensive sexual health care. Such structural changes will help create communities that support and promote resiliency in African American youth.

Project Q

Although the YMS was significant and innovative because of its large sample of ethnically diverse young MSM and assessment of HIV serostatus, it was limited in its assessment of process variables that may underlie racial disparities. Our own study of gay youth in Chicago was more limited in terms of sample size but had more detailed assessment of psychosocial and sociodemographic factors. Project Q was a community-based sample that included 310 ethnically diverse, 16–24-year-old, self-identified MSM in Chicago. As we have described elsewhere (Garofalo, Herrick, Mustanski, & Donenberg, 2005), the study recruited youth over 12 months in 2004–2005 from multiple sources, including flyers posted in retail locations frequented by lesbian, gay, bisexual and transgender (LGBT) individuals, flyers posted in LGBT youth-serving agencies, e-mail advertisements posted on high school and college list-serves, palm cards distributed in LGBT-identified neighborhoods, and snowball sampling. We did not recruit in traditional high-risk social venues such as bars, dance clubs, sex clubs, or bathhouses. Surveys were administered in a private room at a community-based health center providing primary care, STI and HIV specialty care, and social services to the LGBT community. Using a computer-assisted self-interview (CASI), youth completed a 90-minute survey assessing demographics, psychosocial health variables, and sexual risk behaviors.

The sample was racially diverse. Among those surveyed, 30.3% identified as White, 32.9% as Black, 25.8% as Latino, 3.2% as Asian, and 7.7% as other or multiracial. The majority of participants identified their socioeconomic status as middle class (70%), yet nearly one-third of both African American and White participants noted having trouble accessing health care. Although Project Q did not conduct HIV testing, 13.8% of White youth and 18.6% of African American youth responded that they had been told by a medical professional that they were HIV positive.

However, as previously stated, many in the MSM population do not know they are affected; thus, the percentage of youth participating in Project Q who are HIV positive is potentially much higher. We found no significant differences between races/ethnicities concerning STD history, a factor that increases susceptibility to HIV. See Table 13.1 for demographic details.

We focused preliminary analyses on assessing the level of risk behavior of participants to determine whether significant differences could be identified on the basis of race or ethnicity. As illustrated in Figure 13.2, African Americans reported less risky sexual behaviors, although the differences were not statistically significant. African American youth were significantly less likely to report using any street drugs such as cocaine, ecstasy, and so on (odds ratio (OR) =.27, 95% CI =.13–.56); using the Internet to meet sexual partners (OR =.14, 95% CI =.07–.28); or weekly binge drinking, defined as five or more drinks (OR =.26, 95% CI =.12–.54). These results suggest that factors beyond individual behavior drive racial disparities in HIV/AIDS. These data are consistent with those reported by the YMS, where African American MSM were engaging in HIV/AIDS risk behavior (such as unprotected anal sex, anal sex with a partner with unknown status, and injection drug use) at an equal or lesser extent than their White age mates (Valleroy, MacKellar, et al., 2000). Thus, in addition to behavior modification, HIV and AIDS

Table 13.1 Demographics of Project Q Participants

	N	%
Age		
16–20	167	53.9
21–24	143	46.1
Race/ethnicity		
White	94	30.3
Black	102	32.9
Hispanic/Latino	80	25.8
Asian/Pacific Islander	10	3.2
Other/multiracial	24	7.7
Socioeconomic status		
Lower	57	18.4
Middle	217	70.2
Upper	35	11.3
Sexual orientation		
Gay	254	81.9
Bisexual	49	15.8
Other/questioning	7	2.2

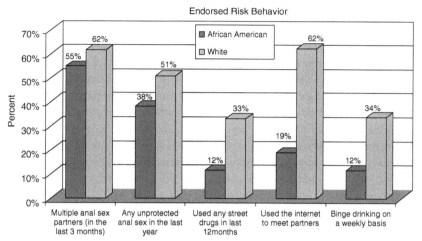

Figure 13.2   Endorsed risk behavior, by race.

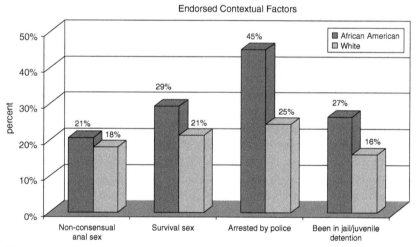

Figure 13.3   Endorsed contextual factors, by race.

prevention and intervention for young African American MSM must consider additional factors that facilitate the disparity.

Our next analyses focused on contextual factors, such as forced sex, survival sex, or incarceration histories, as shown in Figure 13.3. We selected these contextual variables, because as we reviewed above, involvement in the criminal justice system is a risk factor for HIV. Similarly, forced sex and survival sex directly place individuals at risk for HIV infection. White participants were less likely to have experienced all the contextual factors. However, the only statistically significant differences between White and African American MSM was in rates of arrest (OR = 2.54, 95% CI = 1.38– 4.67). African Americans had more than twice the odds of being arrested, which is consistent with the racial disparity in the criminal justice system. Although there were no statistically significant differences in rates of nonconsensual sex, we found dramatic differences in the age at which the experience first occurred (mean age for African Americans was 14, mean age for Whites was 17, $t = 2.22$, $df = 36$, $p <.05$).

Project Q data allow us to analyze both behavioral and contextual factors, which is essential in gaining a comprehensive picture of the impact that HIV and AIDS is having on young MSM. We are currently conducting further analyses exploring the role of behavioral, psychological, and contextual factors related to HIV across multiple ethnic groups. We are also launching a longitudinal study of ethnically diverse young MSM to explore these effects across developmental time. Finally, we are increasing our focus on transgender youth, who face substantial challenges related to HIV and many other aspects of their lives (Garofalo, Deleon, Osmer, Doll, & Harper, 2006).

Policy Solutions

In 2003, the CDC launched its new initiative, "Advancing HIV Prevention: New Strategies for a Changing Epidemic," which focuses on reducing barriers to early diagnosis and increasing access to care, treatment, and prevention services (CDC, 2003a). The initiative has four main strategies: make HIV testing a routine part of medical care, use new models of testing/diagnosing HIV, work with HIV-positive people and their partners, and decrease perinatal HIV transmission. The initiative, however, does not fully address the impact of HIV and AIDS on the most at-risk populations. Increasing rates of HIV testing may reduce stigma associated with HIV testing by normalizing the test, but directly targeting this stigma may also be required (e.g., with social marketing). Testing must be introduced into communities in various settings, and it must also be carried out in conjunction with STD testing and treatment. Although the CDC's initiatives do have potential for affecting individual behavior, disparities are likely in the reach of these programs in disadvantaged minority populations. Prevention policies must recognize the unequal transmission and effects on populations of color, sexual minorities, and youth and formally build in resources to address these disparities. The Minority HIV/AIDS Initiatives (MHAI) in the U.S. Department of Health and Human Services (DHHS) is enhancing HIV/AIDS efforts directed at racial and ethnic minority groups, including providing technical support and increasing access to prevention and care. The MHAI is a step in the right direction. However, the initiative does not address sexual minorities. It is critical to focus efforts on all disenfranchised groups.

Studies have demonstrated that HIV prevention efforts can be cost-effective compared with providing lifetime care (Holtgrave & Pinkerton, 2003; Holtgrave, Pinkerton, & Merson, 2002). The average cost of lifetime treatment for HIV is $210,000. At the current rate of about 40,000 new infections yearly, the cost to society for their care is estimated to be as high as $8.4 billion (CDC, 2003a).

Only 3430 infections a year must be prevented to result in cost savings (CDC, 2003a). Therefore, it is fiscally prudent as well as vitally important to increase the scope of HIV prevention efforts.

Although federal funding for global AIDS initiatives has increased dramatically over the course of the epidemic, it still represents less than 1% of the total U.S. federal budget (The Kaiser Family Foundation, 2006). More than one-half (58%) of the fiscal year 2007 budget request is for domestic care activities, only 4% is for domestic HIV prevention, and 12% for research (The Kaiser Family Foundation, 2006). This represents $956 million federal dollars spent on prevention efforts, which is a slight increase from fiscal year 2006, owing to increased rapid testing and testing in nonmedical settings (The Kaiser Family Foundation, 2006). Also included in the DHHS 2007 budget request is $250 million for healthy marriages initiatives and $204 million for abstinence-only education. Both of these initiatives ignore same-sex relationships and promote a heterosexist agenda. Federally funded policies should be inclusive, especially as the HIV and AIDS epidemic is affecting sexual minority groups at heightened rates.

Implications for Social Work Practice

Structural-level interventions must incorporate experts in various fields, such as social work, psychology, public health, policy, and law (Sumartojo, 2000). This multidisciplinary approach can strengthen efforts by combining expertise and professional networks. Social workers can empower and mobilize the young African American MSM community, using proven community development models, to increase their capacity to change structural barriers that facilitate the HIV/AIDS epidemic. Methodologists and community researchers will be needed for planning and implementing efforts that have measurable outcome goals.

Social workers must advocate for structural changes, particularly at state and local levels. Advocates can develop, implement, and monitor political campaigns and legislation concerning structural-level changes, such as increased access to living wages and universal health care. Involving trained community leaders in advocating for increased prevention efforts is essential to an effective campaign. On the individual level, social workers can encourage clients to live healthy and risk-free lives by making decisions that will ensure their safety, such as getting tested regularly and restricting risky behavior. Social workers can also develop resource lists of STD and HIV testing and counseling sites within their communities to distribute to clients. Social workers are in a unique position to coordinate prevention and care services for youth in a variety of settings, from medical, to social service, to schools.

In addition to incorporating prevention efforts into existing social work practice, we must also train future social workers to be competent and effective in the fight against HIV and AIDS. Curriculum reflecting the racial, sexual minority, and socioeconomic factors that stratify the impact of the HIV/AIDS epidemic must be integrated into social work standards and adopted by the Council on Social Work Education.

Suggestions for Future Research and Advocacy

Structural factors, such as poverty, racism, mental illness, homophobia, lack of access to health care, and stigma are barriers that contribute to the disparity young African American MSM face. However, it is difficult, costly, and controversial to create HIV and AIDS prevention programming at the structural level. Macro-level interventions are hard to evaluate, as the impact may not be immediately apparent and may be sustained in various immeasurable ways. Without concrete empirical evidence, it is nearly impossible to receive funding or support. Therefore, it is necessary to implement programming with evaluation components, develop new ways of analyzing structural data, and shift prevention efforts to include macro-level approaches.

Increased research with LGBT racial-ethnic minority populations must be conducted. Current research is lacking in studies of LGBT people of color. In a review of the 1674 empirical articles in five journals that focus on HIV/AIDS, only 18% contained gay or bisexual samples, and of those, only 3% sampled gay or bisexuals of color (Harper et al., 2004). This is particularly alarming as African American and Hispanic MSM are consistently overrepresented in the HIV/AIDS crisis. Furthermore, the vast majority of this research has been cross-sectional and has relied on community samples. Methodological advancements that increase our ability to characterize causal processes and generalize effects to the larger population of young MSM must be undertaken.

Racial-ethnic and sexual minority professionals should be at the forefront of innovative prevention efforts. As social justice advocates, we must consider the battle against HIV and AIDS a civil rights and social justice campaign, in which economic, racial-ethnic, and sexual orientation stratify who is affected. We must unite our efforts to include macro-level interventions and prevention that compliments micro-level programming, for this fight is not a singular fight. If we want to eradicate the devastating impact of HIV/AIDS on vulnerable populations, we must all do our part.

NOTE

1. "African American" in this chapter also includes Black males (e.g., of Caribbean descent). The term "MSM" reflects the inclusion of men who engage in sexual behavior with other men but who may not self-identify as gay or bisexual.

REFERENCES

Bachman, J. G., Wallace, J. M., Jr., O'Malley, P. M., Johnston, L. D., Kurth, C. L., & Neighbors, H. W. (1991). Racial/ethnic differences in smoking, drinking, and illicit drug use among American high school seniors, 1976–89. *American Journal of Public Health, 81*(3), 372–377.

Bogart, L. M. & Thorburn, S. (2005). Are HIV/AIDS conspiracy beliefs a barrier to HIV prevention among African Americans? *Journal of Acquired Immunodeficiency Syndrome, 38*(2), 213–218.

Boykin, K. (2005). *Beyond the down low: Sex, lies, and denial in black America.* New York: Carroll & Graf Publishers.

Braithwaite, R. L. & Arriola, K. R. (2003). Male prisoners and HIV prevention: A call for action ignored. *American Journal of Public Health, 93*(5), 759–763.

Bronfenbrenner, U. (1986). Ecology of the family as a context for human development: Research perspectives. *Developmental Psychology, 22*(6), 723–742.

Celentano, D. D., Sifakis, F., Hylton, J., Torian, L. V., Guillin, V., & Koblin, B. A. (2005). Race/ethnic differences in HIV prevalence and risks among adolescent and young adult men who have sex with men. *Journal of Urban Health, 82*(4), 610–621.

Centers for Disease Control and Prevention. (2001). *Compendium of HIV prevention interventions with evidence of effectiveness.* Retrieved September 15, 2006, from http://www.cdc.gov/hiv/pubs/hivcompendium/HIVcompendium.hm

Centers for Disease Control and Prevention. (2003a). Advancing HIV prevention: New Strategies for a changing epidemic. *Morbidity and Mortality Weekly Report, 52,* 329–332.

Centers for Disease Control and Prevention. (2003b). HIV/STD risks in young men who have sex with men who do not disclose their sexual orientation—Six U.S. cities, 1994–2000. *Morbidity and Mortality Weekly Report, 52,* 81–85.

Centers for Disease Control and Prevention. (2006a). *HIV/AIDS among African Americans.* Atlanta, GA: U.S. Department of Health and Human Services.

Centers for Disease Control and Prevention. (2006b). *HIV/AIDS among men who have sex with men.* Atlanta, GA: U.S. Department of Health and Human Services.

Centers for Disease Control and Prevention. (2006c). *HIV/AIDS among youth.* Atlanta, GA: U.S. Department of Health and Human Services.

Cohen, C. J., Bell, A., & Ifatunji, M. (2005). *Reclaiming our future: The state of AIDS among Black youth in America.* Los Angeles, CA: Black AIDS Institute.

Cohen, D., Spear, S., Scribner, R., Kissinger, P., Mason, K., & Wildgen, J. (2000). "Broken windows" and the risk of gonorrhea. *American Journal of Public Health, 90*(2), 230–236.

Della, B., Wilson, M., & Miller, R. L. (2002). Strategies for managing heterosexism used among African American gay and bisexual men. *Journal of Black Psychology, 28*(4), 371–391.

DeNavas-Walt, C., Proctor, B. D., & Lee, C. H. (2006). *Income, poverty, and health insurance coverage in the United States: 2005.* Washington, DC: U.S. Census Bureau.

Fergus, S. & Zimmerman, M. A. (2005). Adolescent resilience: A framework for understanding healthy development in the face of risk. *Annual Review of Public Health, 26*(1), 399–419.

Fleming, D. T. & Wasserheit, J. N. (1999). From epidemiological synergy to public health policy and practice: The contribution of other sexually transmitted diseases to sexual transmission of HIV infection. *Sexually Transmitted Infections, 75,* 3–17.

Garofalo, R., Deleon, J., Osmer, E., Doll, M., & Harper, G. W. (2006). Overlooked, misunderstood and at-risk: exploring the lives and HIV risk of ethnic minority male-to-female transgender youth. *Journal of Adolescent Health, 38*(3), 230–236.

Garofalo, R., Herrick, A., Mustanski, B., & Donenberg, G. R. (2005). Tip of the iceberg: Young men who have sex with men, the internet, and HIV risk. *American Journal of Public Health, 97* (6), 1113-1117.

Gilles, P., Tolley, K., & Woletenholme, J. (1996). Is AIDS a disease of poverty? *AIDS Care*, *8*(3), 351–364.

Goodenow, C., Netherland, J., & Szalacha, L. (2002). AIDS-related risk among adolescent males who have sex with males, females, or both: Evidence from a statewide survey. *American Journal of Public Health*, *92*(2), 203–210.

Harawa, N. T., Greenland, S., Bingham, T. A., Johnson, D. F., Cochran, S. D., Cunningham, W. E., et al. (2004). Associations of race/ethnicity with HIV prevalence and HIV-related behaviors among young men who have sex with men in 7 urban centers in the United States. *Journal of Acquired Immune Deficiency Syndromes*, *35*(5), 526–536.

Harper, G. W., Jernewall, N., & Zea, M. C. (2004). Giving voice to emerging science and theory for lesbian, gay and bisexual people of color. *Cultural Diversity and Ethnic Minority Psychology*, *10*, 187–199.

Holtgrave, D. R. & Pinkerton, S. D. (2003). Brief report: Economic implications of failure to reduce incident HIV infections by 50% by 2005 in the United States. *Journal of Acquired Immunodeficiency Syndrome*, *33*, 171–174.

Holtgrave, D. R., Pinkerton, S. D., & Merson, M. (2002). Estimating the cost of unmet HIV-prevention needs in the United States. *American Journal of Preventive Medicine*, *23*(1), 7–12.

Hoytt, E. H., Schiraldi, V., Smith, B. V., & Ziedenberg, J. (2002). *Reducing racial disparities in juvenile detention*. Washington, DC: Justice Policy Institute.

Huebner, D. M., Davis, M. C., Nemeroff, C. J., & Aiken, L. S. (2002). The impact of internalized homophobia on HIV preventive interventions. *American Journal of Community Psychology*, *30*(3), 327–348.

Johnson, W. D., Hedges, L. V., & Diaz, R. M. (2003). Interventions to modify sexual risk behaviors for preventing HIV infection in men who have sex with men. *Cochrane Database of Systematic Reviews*, *1*, Art No.: CD001230.

Johnston, L., O'Malley, P. M., & Bachman, J. G. (1993). *National survey results on drug use from Monitoring the Future Study (No. NIDA publication number 93-3597)*. Washington, DC: U.S. Government Printing Office.

The Kaiser Family Foundation. (2005). *HIV/AIDS policy fact sheet: African Americans and HIV/AIDS*. Retrieved on August 31, 2006, from http://www.kff.org/hivaids/upload/ Fact-Sheet-African-Americans-and-HIV-AIDS-UPDATE.pdf

The Kaiser Family Foundation. (2006). *US federal funding for HIV/AIDS: The FY07 budget request*. Retrieved on September 2, 2006, from http://www.kff.org/hivaids/ upload/7029-03.pdf

King, J. L. (2004). *On the down low: A journey into the lives of "straight" black men who sleep with men*. New York: Broadway Books.

Llana, S. M. (2006). New flash point in sex ed: Gay issues. *The Christian Science Monitor*. Retrieved on August 31, 2006, from www.csmonitor.com/2006/0215/p02s01-ussc.html

MacKellar, D. A., Valleroy, L. A., Secura, G. M., Behel, S., Bingham, T., Celentano, D. D., et al. (2005). Unrecognized HIV infection, risk behaviors, and perceptions of risk among young men who have sex with men: Opportunities for advancing HIV prevention in the third decade of HIV/AIDS. *Journal of Acquired Immunodeficiency Syndrome*, *38*(5), 603–614.

Maddahian, E., Newcomb, M. D., & Bentler, P. M. (1988). Adolescent drug use and intention to use drugs: Concurrent and longitudinal analyses of four ethnic groups. *Addiction Behaviors*, *13*(2), 191–195.

Mauer, M. (1999). The crisis of the young African American male and the criminal justice system. Prepared for the U.S. Commission on Civil Rights. Retrieved on September 2, 2006, from http://www.sentencingproject.org/pdfs/5022.pdf

May, J. P. & Williams, E. L., Jr. (2002). Acceptability of condom availability in a U.S. jail. *AIDS Education and Prevention, 14*(5, Suppl. B), 85–91.

National Center for Health Statistics. (2006). Health data for all ages: Mortality. Retrieved on September 12, 2006, from http://www.cdc.gov/nchs/FASTATS

National Prevention Information Network. (2006). Who is affected? The changing face of HIV/AIDS. Retrieved on September 14, 2006, from http://www.cdcnpin.org/scripts/hiv/hiv.asp

Pantin, H., Schwartz, S. J., Sullivan, S., Prado, G., & Szapocznik, J. (2004). Ecodevelopmental HIV prevention programs for Hispanic adolescents. *American Journal of Orthopsychiatry, 74*(4), 545–558.

Pedlow, C. T. & Carey, M. P. (2003). HIV sexual risk-reduction interventions for youth: a review and methodological critique of randomized controlled trials. *Behavior Modification, 27*(2), 135–190.

Pedlow, C. T. & Carey, M. P. (2004). Developmentally appropriate sexual risk reduction interventions for adolescents: Rationale, review of interventions, and recommendations for research and practice. *Annals of Behavioral Medicine, 27*(3), 172–184.

Santelli, J., Ott, M. A., Lyon, M., Rogers, J., Summers, D., & Schleifer, R. (2006). Abstinence and abstinence-only education: A review of U.S. policies and programs. *Journal of Adolescent Health, 38*(1), 72–81.

Seal, D. W., Kelly, J. A., Bloom, F. R., Stevenson, L. Y., Coley, B. I., & Broyles, L. A. (2000). HIV prevention with young men who have sex with men: What young men themselves say is needed. Medical College of Wisconsin CITY Project Research Team. *AIDS Care, 12*(1), 5–26.

Sexuality Information and Education Counsel of the United States (SIECUS). (n.d.) How are LGBTQ youth affected by abstinence-only-until marriage programs? Retrieved on September 5, 2006, from http://www.siecus.org/policy/LGBTQ_FS.pdf

Sumartojo, E. (2000). Structural factors in HIV prevention: Concepts, examples, and implications for research. *AIDS, 14*(Suppl. 1), S3–10.

U.S. House of Representatives Committee on Government Reform-Minority Staff. (2004). *The content of federally funded abstinence-only education programs.* Washington, DC:

Valleroy, L. A., Duncan, A. M., Karon, J. M., Rosen, D. H., McFarland, W., Shehan, D. A., et al. (2000). HIV prevelance and associated risks in young men who have sex with men. *Journal of the American Medical Association, 284*(2), 198-204.

Valleroy, L. A., MacKellar, D. A., Karon, J. M., Janssen, R. S., & Hayman, C. R. (1998). HIV infection in disadvantaged out-of-school youth: prevalence for U.S. Job Corps entrants, 1990 through 1996. *Journal of Acquired Immune Deficiency Syndromes and Human Retrovirology, 19*(1), 67–73.

Valleroy, L. A., MacKellar, D. A., Karon, J. M., Rosen, D. H., McFarland, W., Shehan, D. A., et al. (2000). HIV prevalence and associated risks in young men who have sex with men. Young Men's Survey Study Group. *Journal of the American Medical Association, 284*(2), 198–204.

Wallace, J. M., Jr., Bachman, J. G., O'Malley, P. M., Schulenberg, J. E., Cooper, S. M., & Johnston, L. D. (2003). Gender and ethnic differences in smoking, drinking and illicit drug use among American 8th, 10th and 12th grade students, 1976–2000. *Addiction, 98*(2), 225–234.

Walmsley, R. (2003). *World prison population list* (4th ed.). London: The Research, Development and Statistics Directorate.

Wohl, A. R., Johnson, D., Jordan, W., Lu, S., Beall, G., Currier, J., et al. (2000). High-risk behaviors during incarceration in African-American men treated for HIV at three Los Angeles public medical centers. *Journal of Acquired Immune Deficiency Syndromes, 24*(4), 386–392.

Wright, K. (2006). *The way forward: The state of AIDS in Black America.* Los Angeles, CA: Black AIDS Institute.

14

Suicide Among African Americans

A Male's Burden

SEAN JOE

Suicide is becoming a significant health risk for many African Americans (Centers for Disease Control and Prevention [CDC], 1998), especially for males, who are at a higher risk for suicide completion (Fernquist, 2004). Uncommon in the past, suicide among African American adolescents and young adults has also increased sharply (CDC, 1998; Joe & Kaplan, 2001), especially since 1985, and is now the third leading cause of death among 15- to 24-year-old African Americans (Hoyert, Heron, Murphy, & Kung, 2006).[1] As seen in Figure 14.1, the suicide rate for 15- to 24-year-old African American men increased markedly from a rate of 14 suicides per 100,000 people to a high of nearly 20 suicides per 100,000 people in 1994. This disproportionate increase in the suicide rate among young African American males closed a significant amount of the gap in suicide rates between African American and White males, with African American males' suicide rates increasing by nearly 6 suicides per 100,000 people, while White males' suicide rate increased by 3 suicides per 100,000 people during the same time period. Since 1994, however, suicide rates have seen a significant decrease, with the rate for both groups falling below their 1979 rates in 2002. Yet little is known about why the trend reversed after 1994. In fact, the rates of suicide have been on a declining trend for all race, age, and ethnic groups (Kessler, Berglund, Borges, Nock, & Wang, 2005). Nonetheless, the reduced racial disparities between African American and White males persist. Furthermore, as we witnessed decline in suicide, the rate on nonfatal attempts for African American males increased 140% (3.3% to 7.7%), exhibiting an ominous upward trend (Joe, 2006b).

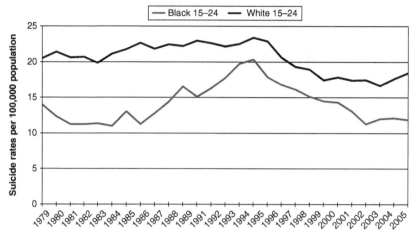

Figure 14.1   Suicide Rates for Black and White Males Aged 15–24 between 1979–2005.
Source: Centers for Disease Control, National Center for Health Statistics, Compressed Mortality Files, 1979–1980; and Centers for Disease Control, Web-based Injury Statistics Query and Reporting System, 1981–2005.

Overall recent research has confirmed that younger generations of African American males are at a higher risk of suicide. For instance, several studies have shown that African American males are more likely to commit suicide before age 35 (Garlow, Purselle, & Heninger, 2005; Joe, 2006a; Willis, Coombs, Drentea, & Cockerham, 2003). These rates may, however, be underreported, given the probability that suicide deaths may be misclassified as homicides or accidents (Kaslow et al., 2004). Joe and Kaplan (2002) attribute this increase in suicide among African American males to a growing use of firearms among adolescent males aged 15 to 19, who experienced 132% rise in firearm suicides.

African American females, in contrast, are more likely to attempt suicide but not complete it than are African American males. Women, in general, make three times as many suicide attempts as men (Canetto & Lester, 1995; Kaslow et al., 2000). Similarly, adolescent females attempt suicide more than adolescent males (CDC, 2006). Figures 14.2 and 14.3 present data that reveal the stark gender differences in the suicidal method and in the proportion of suicides among African Americans. Figure 14.2 provides evidence of important gender differences in the rates of suicide, and it clearly illustrates that suicide among African Americans disproportionately burdens males, with males composing over 60% of all African American suicides in each of the age groups. As illustrated, the ratio of African American male to female suicide death ranges from as low as 2 to 1 to as high as 7 to 1 among the age groups in 2005. Figure 14.3 illustrates vividly that males are more likely to use a firearm to complete suicide than females. As mentioned above, despite significant declines in the firearm suicide rate in recent years, on average firearm use accounts for more than half of the suicides nationally among all African

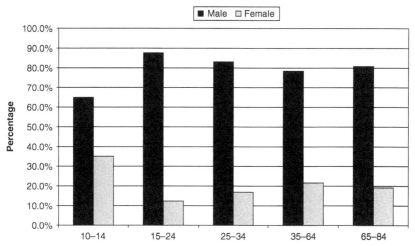

Figure 14.2   Suicide among Blacks by Age Groups and Gender, 2005.
Source: Centers for Disease Control, Web-based Injury Statistics Query and Reporting
System, 2005, ICD-10 X60-X84, Y87.0, *U03

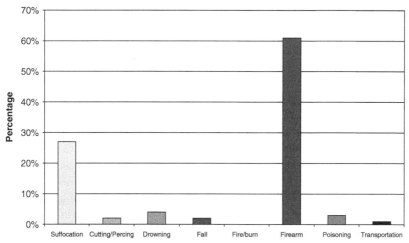

Figure 14.3   Suicide Rates in African American Males by Method for Age Group
15–24: 2005.
Source: Centers for Disease Control, Web-based Injury Statistics Query and Reporting
System, 2005.

Americans, especially African American youth. As seen in Figure 14.3, in 2002,
more than half of male suicides involved a firearm, in contrast to about a third
among female suicides.

Despite these alarming statistics and increased attention from the public health
community, very little is known about what has caused this rise in suicidal behavior
among young African American males or the reasons for the gender disparities in
suicide. This chapter is an initial step in filling in the gaps in our understanding of
suicide in the African American community. This study uses data from the 1993

National Mortality Followback Survey (NMFS), the most recent and largest nationally representative psychological autopsy survey of decedents' next of kin. The NMFS contains a wide range of sociodemographic, social, behavioral, and clinical factors associated with suicide completion. The 1993 NMFS provides a unique opportunity to empirically examine both proximal and distal suicide risk factors and their interactions, with a national cross-section of African Americans, which is the focus of this chapter. The chapter explores the factors associated with gender differences in suicide among this population to gain a deeper understanding of gender-specific suicide predictors—an understanding that is essential for developing and implementing culturally appropriate suicide prevention interventions (Goldsmith, Pellmar, Kleinman, & Bunny, 2002).

Gender Differences in the Risk Factor of African American Suicide

African American Male Suicide

There are several reasons that might explain the phenomenon of why African American men are more likely to complete suicide than African American women. Men complete suicide in numbers far greater than women (Goldsmith et al., 2002); therefore, much of what is discussed in this section is also true for the general population and not unique to African American males. First is the method of suicide: African American men are more likely to use lethal methods such as firearms than African American women (Joe & Kaplan, 2001). Substance use and abuse may also play a role in suicide among African American males by decreasing cultural inhibitions, thereby making the suicidal act easier (Castle, Duberstein, Meldrum, Conner, & Conwell, 2004; Willis et al., 2003). Another reason may be that African American men feel more alienated from both jobs and family. Although African American males have gained a culturally legitimate means to financial success through education and occupational attainment, they may be dissatisfied with financial compensation because the success they have gained is not converting to increased income; however, it has not been significantly determined such dissatisfaction could encourage abnormal behavior (Fernquist, 2004). Third, African American men may feel alienated from authority in the home and on the job because of the high frequency of single African American female-headed homes and because of the lack of stable jobs. When these feelings are combined with the irritation of harassment from the police, African American men may be more prone to committing self-harm (suicide) rather than inflicting harm on someone else (homicide) (Breed, 1970; Wasserman, 1999). Therefore, African American men may have higher rates of suicide completion than African American women because of their use of more lethal means while abusing substances, because financial compensation across race and gender is unequal, and because of feelings of alienation.

Among African American adolescent males, there are several explanations for the increase in suicide. Durkheim's work (1951) on status integration is among the most prominent explanation for changes in the rates of suicide completion among African Americans (Gibbs, 1988; Henry & Short, 1954; Maris, 1969; Prudhomme, 1938), although the evidence supporting Durkheim's hypothesis as applied to young African Americans' suicidal behavior is moderate and inconclusive (Burr, Hartman, & Matteson, 1999; Gould Fisher, Parides, Flory, & Shaffer, 1996; Joe, Romer, & Jamieson, 2005; Watt & Sharp, 2002). The status integration perspective contends that as African Americans assimilate into the broader majority culture, they migrate out of traditional African American communities to communities with less social support. The result of this migration is that African Americans have less access to traditional coping mechanisms, which results in higher rates of suicide completion (Joe, 2003; Prudhomme, 1938). Therefore, African American males living in middle-class families with the resources to move out of traditional African American neighborhoods may not have the social support that was afforded to previous generations. However, evidence is mixed on whether suicide rates are higher among middle-class African Americans, but some research has shown evidence that African Americans are less likely than Whites to respond to status strains (Watt & Sharp, 2002). Furthermore, these African American males have less access to the role models in the church and other traditional community institutions (Early, 1992), and this lack of social support places them at risk for unresolved psychological distress. Due to this migration out of traditional African American communities, many young African American males are left without suitable role models whose positive coping mechanisms they could replicate. The lack of African American male role models from which to draw social support and to learn positive coping mechanisms may be an important precipitant of African American adolescent and young adult male suicide.

Understanding attributional orientation and changes in attributional orientation of African American men may also be key in explaining the increase in the suicide rate of African American men and why they are more likely to become suicide completers than African American women. At one time, an external attributional orientation, such as system blaming, among African Americans buffered this group from internalizing limited personal success; however, this orientation has been exchanged with a more internal orientation, such as self-blaming. Traditionally African Americans were able to maintain a healthy psychological outlook by viewing personal setbacks in the context of societal discrimination and racism. This external attributional orientation helped them cope with personal disappointments and protected them from the negative consequences of exposure to various types of discrimination (LaVeist, Sellers, & Neighbors, 2001; Sellers & Shelton, 2003). The shift to a more internal attributional orientation offers no such protection; thus, increasing psychological distress of personal disappointments, which in turn may increase depression, and ultimately increase the possibility that African Americans will engage in self-harm. This shift from an external to an internal attributional style may affect African American men more than women because societal stereotypes of African Americans focus on men primarily, and therefore men may be more likely to experience racial discrimination (Sellers & Shelton, 2003). Additionally, African

American women may maintain a more external attributional orientation by ascribing discrimination based on gender as a component in personal disappointments and limited success. Therefore, African American women's ability to maintain a more external attributional style protects them from suicidal forces, which African American men are less protected from.

African American Female Suicide

Turning to the question of why African American females are less likely to complete suicide and are more likely to engage in suicidal behavior than African American males, Chaudran and Remington (1999) offer a few explanations that may help us understand the differences. First, mental disorders among females are generally detected and treated more readily, particularly depression, than among males. The danger of suicide rises if psychiatric disorders go untreated or are inadequately treated (Klerman, 1987). Second, females use outpatient health care and mental health-care services more than males, increasing the likelihood of detection of depression. However, although African American females use health-care services more often than males, they still may have inadequate access to health care and therefore may not be treated at all (Chaudran & Remington, 1999). Research has yet to explain why women engage in more suicidal behavior yet complete suicide less than men. African American females may be more likely than males to engage in suicidal behavior because they conceptualize suicide as a way to avoid painful life situations, which is accomplished through dissociation, substance abuse, or low lethal attempts (Anderson, Tiro, Price, Bender, & Kaslow, 2002; Thompson, Kaslow, Short, & Wyckoff, 2002). In contrast, men are encouraged to weather difficult situations and not engage in behaviors that would signal a cry for help. This avoidant behavior may be a desperate response to inadequate social support in difficult situations (Anderson et al., 2002). Therefore, higher rates of unsuccessful suicide among African American females may be due to their significantly higher levels of access to health-care services, social support, and an increased likelihood of engaging in avoidant and low-lethality self-destructive behaviors.

Protective Factors

Information on the risk factors and correlates of African American suicidal behavior reveals several factors that reduce suicide risk among African Americans. Early (1992), for instance, found that religious beliefs buffered many African Americans against the adverse effects associated with suicidal behavior. Other studies found that African Americans who lived in the South (Prudhomme, 1938; Shaffer, Gould, & Hicks, 1994; Willis et al., 2003), who are elderly (Meehan, Lamb, Saltzman, & O'Carroll, 1992), and who have social supports (Dunston, 1990; Gibbs & Martin, 1964; Nisbet, 1996) are less likely to ever attempt or complete suicide. While no one has examined the role of cultural identity in preventing suicidal behaviors in African Americans, several studies have found that adolescents with positive ethnic identity are less prone to have dysphoric affect (Charlot-Swilley, 1998) and poor mental health (Sellers, Caldwell, Schmeelk-Cone, & Zimmerman, 2003), which are associated with suicidal behavior.

Acceptance of suicide is thought to play an important role in regulating individuals' consideration of suicide as a solution to life problems. It has been presumed that more religious involvement among African Americans and other ethnic minorities has resulted in a less accepting attitude toward suicide that might be protective against suicidal behavior (Joe, 2003; Neeleman, Wessely, & Lewis, 1998; Prudhomme, 1938). This explanation assumes that suicide acceptance plays an important role in regulating people's consideration of suicide as a solution to life problems (Goldsmith et al., 2002). Joe (2003) suggests that research is needed to understand whether gender differences in the risk for suicide are related to attitudes toward suicide. An analysis of long-term trends in suicide acceptability indicates that younger African Americans have exhibited increasing acceptance of such anomic reasons for suicide (Joe et al., 2005). In addition, Joe and colleagues (2007) found that adolescents who most strongly believe that it is acceptable to end one's life were more than seven times more likely to make a plan to kill themselves than those who do not have such beliefs ($p < .001$). More religious involvement among African Americans and other ethnic minorities has been shown to result in a less accepting attitude toward suicide, which might be protective against suicidal behavior (Joe, 2003; Neeleman et al., 1998; Prudhomme, 1938). In order to reduce the incidence of suicide in the African American community, it is equally important to focus on those factors that serve as buffers against suicide, and not just on the risk factors. Future research will have to address many of the gaps in the research literature that might explain the higher incidence of suicide among African American males than females.

Method

Sample

The 1993 NMFS (released for public use in 1997) includes extensive data on a sample of 22,958 death certificates (10% of all U.S. deaths) from the 1993 Current Mortality Sample (CMS) for decedents 15 years of age or older in the United States (excluding South Dakota). The 1993 NMFS was conducted by the National Center for Health Statistics, Center for Disease Control and Prevention (CDC, 2005). African American suicide decedents and decedents under age 35 were oversampled. NMFS data are derived from the death certificate, informant questionnaires (obtained from interviews with next of kin), and medical examiner/coroner records. The data set includes extensive information regarding cause of death, demographic factors, health status, lifestyle, problem behaviors, health and mental health-care utilization, and other factors prior to death that may affect when and how death occurred, including information on the decedents' ownership and access to firearms (National Center for Health Statistics, 1998). The sample used for our analyses included all cases for which suicide (International Classification of Disease [ICD] codes E950.0–E958.9) was listed as the cause of death. Analyses compared suicides to non-suicide-related death for African Americans.

Predictor Variables

Sociodemographic and clinical risk factor variables were constructed based on previous findings in the literature. Age, race, gender, and geographic region were obtained from death certificate data. The variable and *region* (Northeast, Midwest, South, West) were created to assess the decedent's geographic status. The next-of-kin interview data were used to derive the other predictors used in the analyses. Dichotomous variables were constructed to assess *educational status* (education beyond high school vs. high school or less) and the presence of mental disorders or symptoms. To assess *mental health-care utilization*, the respondents were asked whether the deceased had visited a mental health professional about any problems during the last year of life. To assess use of *antidepressant medication*, respondents were asked if the decedent used antidepressants at any time during the last year of life. *Religiosity/church attendance* was collapsed into two categories: those who never participated in church activities and those who participated once a month or more during the past year. To assess *firearm ownership/access*, proxy respondents were asked if there had been any firearms kept in or around the decedent's home during the last year of life.

Data Analytic Approach

Chi-square analysis was first used to compare the distribution of the sociodemographic and clinical factors for those with a suicide versus those whose death resulted from another cause. These comparisons were then repeated separately for males and females. Multiple logistic regression analyses were then used to examine the overall impact of the sociodemographic and clinical predictors (independent variables) on suicide (dependent variable). Separate models were then run among male and female African Americans.

All analyses were conducted using the SAS callable SUDAAN software package to accommodate stratification and sampling weights and to produce nationally representative estimates. All statistics are presented at the .05 significance level to be consistent with previous studies using the NMFS (Castle et al., 2004; Kung, Liu, & Juon, 1998, Kung, Pearson, & Liu, 2003; Willis et al., 2003); however, the results would be essentially unchanged if we tested at the more conservative .01 level to account for multiple comparisons. All numbers reported in the tables are actual numbers of study participants, whereas all reported percentages and odds ratios are weighted to provide nationally representative estimates. The multivariate models are moderately powered using the 10 events per parameter rule (Hosmer & Lemeshow, 2000), particularly given the impact of NMFS design weights to produce nationally representative estimates and error terms.

Findings

At the bivariate level, several factors were significantly associated with African Americans' suicidal behavior. As seen in Table 14.1, several characteristics

Table 14.1 Risk Characteristics by Manner of Death Among African American in the National Mortality Followback Survey, 1993

Variables	Unweighted N	Suicide Percent (%)	Non-Suicide Death Percent (%)
Age		\multicolumn{2}{c}{$(\chi^2 = 129.57, df = 3, p < .001)$}	
15–24	697	27.7	3.4
25–39	1634	42.3	10.6
40–59	1281	15.4	20.5
60+	2091	14.6	65.5
Sex		$(\chi^2 = 94.07, df = 1, p < .001)$	
Male	3707	87.9	54.0
Female	1996	12.1	46.0
Education		$(\chi^2 = 29.98, df = 1, p < .001)$	
< High school	2395	32.3	56.0
≥ High school	2722	67.7	44.0
Marriage		$(\chi^2 = 62.25, df = 2, p < .001)$	
Single/never married	2198	20.2	52.3
Married	1291	31.3	26.9
Widowed/divorce/separated	2065	48.5	20.8
Depressive symptoms		$(\chi^2 = 8.36, df = 1, p < .01)$	
No	5487	88.8	96.4
Yes	216	11.2	3.6
Use mental health services		$(\chi^2 = 15.38, df = 1, p < .001)$	
No	5297	82.0	94.3
Yes	406	18.0	5.7
Firearm in home		$(\chi^2 = 23.06, df = 1, p < .001)$	
No	4648	60.5	80.1
Yes	1055	39.5	19.9
Church attendance		$(\chi^2 = 3.42, df = 1, p < .06)$	
No	2255	44.9	37.5
Yes	3448	55.1	62.5
Geographic region		$(\chi^2 = 0.99, df = 1, p = .80)$	
Northeast	1027	15.6	18.7
Midwest	1061	18.8	18.3
South	3038	57.4	54.9
West	577	8.2	8.1

Note. Valid weighted column proportions are shown. Cases were missing data on one or more variables.

differentiated African American decedents who completed suicide from those who did not. African American suicide completers were more likely to be male (88%), to have higher levels of education (68%), to be from a failed marriage or widowed (49%), and to live in the South (57%). Even differences across region were not significant in the full sample model. There appears to be an inverse relationship between age and suicide among African Americans. Most African American decedents who completed suicide were in the younger age groups (15–24 and 25–39). According to the proxy respondents, African Americans who completed suicide were less likely to have been treated for depressive symptoms and use mental health services in their last year of life. Those who did not use mental health services or antidepressant medication accounted for a high proportion of suicides: 82% and 89%, respectively. Surprisingly, there was only a moderately significant association between religiosity and suicide, with those who attended church completing suicide more often than those who did not.

Table 14.2 shows the results from the multivariate logistic regression analyses overall and stratified by gender. In the overall model, after controlling for demographic, socioeconomic, and clinical variables, African American men were three times more likely than women to complete suicide. The result indicates that having a firearm at home (odds ratio = 3.5, 95% CI = 2.4–5.15) and being more educated (odds ratio = 1.9, 95% CI = 1.27–2.76) were predictive of suicide among decedents. Decedents with depressive symptoms or who used mental health services were about three and two times as likely to die by suicide, respectively. Finally, there was no significant relationship between church attendance, region, and completing suicide.

In the stratified multivariate models, males were more likely to complete suicide if they were of younger age, had more than a high school education, had a firearm in the home, and lived in the Midwest or South. Surprisingly, males who use mental health services were at higher risk for suicide. Males who attended church were less likely to complete suicide. Only two correlates, age and depressive symptoms, were statistically significant in the model for African American females. African Americans females with depressive symptom were about 10 times more likely to complete suicide than those without depressive symptoms. The results for African American females, although significant, must be interpreted with caution because of the small cell sizes.

In the stratified multivariate models, males were more likely to complete suicide if they were of younger age, had more than a high school education, had a firearm in the home, and lived in the Midwest or South. Surprisingly, males who use mental health services were at higher risk for suicide. Males who attended church were less likely to complete suicide. Only two correlates, age and depressive symptoms, were statistically significant in the model for African American females. African Americans females with depressive symptom were about 10 times more likely to complete suicide than those without depressive symptoms. The results for African American females, although significant, must be interpreted with caution because of the small cell sizes.

Table 14.2 Likelihood of Suicide for African Americans in the United States, 1993

Variables	Total (Unweighted n = 144) Odds Ratio (95% CI)	Males (Unweighted n = 126) Odds Ratio (95% CI)	Females (Unweighted n = 18)Odds Ratio (95% CI)
Age			
15–24	35.81 (18.45, 69.53)	47.0 (21.91, 103.47)	20.75 (3.20, 134.66)
25–39	14.01 (7.69, 25.55)	21.12 (10.55, 42.25)	3.72 (1.02, 13.52)
40–59	2.40 (1.25, 4.59)	3.21 (1.52, 6.76)	1.11 (0.28, 4.45)
60+	1.00	1.00	1.00
Sex			
Male	3.16 (1.93, 5.18)	—	—
Female	1.00	—	—
Education			
≥High school	1.00	1.00	1.00
<High school	1.87 (1.27, 2.76)	1.76 (1.16, 2.67)	2.31 (0.78, 6.86)
Marriage			
Single/never married	1.00	1.00	1.00
Married	1.12 (0.66, 1.91)	1.09 (0.61, 1.96)	3.25 (0.66, 15.91)
Widowed/divorce/ separated	1.27 (0.76, 2.14)	1.26 (0.72, 2.18)	1.66 (0.28, 9.92)
Depressive symptoms			
No	1.00	1.00	1.00
Yes	3.15 (1.50, 6.61)	2.13 (0.90, 5.05)	9.82 (1.87, 51.55)
Use mental health services			
No	1.00	1.00	1.00
Yes	2.31 (1.38, 3.87)	2.09 (1.24, 3.53)	3.60 (0.56, 23.14)
Firearm in home			
No	1.00	1.00	1.00
Yes	3.51 (2.40, 5.15)	3.70 (2.48, 5.52)	2.82 (0.67, 11.80)
Church attendance			
No	1.00	1.00	1.00
Yes	.72 (.50, 1.05)	0.67 (0.45, 0.99)	1.33 (0.41, 4.28)
Geographic region			
Northeast	1.00	1.00	1.00
Midwest	1.47 (.79, 2.71)	2.03 (1.04, 3.98)	0.35 (0.06, 2.08)
South	1.35 (0.77, 2.34)	1.92 (1.05, 3.50)	0.24 (0.04, 1.25)
West	0.81 (0.38, 1.72)	0.91 (.39, 2.10)	0.59 (0.10, 3.56)

Notes. Adjusted odds ratios presented have been statistically adjusted for the other variables listed in the table. Cases were missing data on one or more variables.
CI, confidence interval.

Discussion

Suicide is a major public health problem threatening many African American males. Although more is known about correlates of suicide in general, few studies have examined the important gender variations in the correlates of suicide (Juon & Ensminger, 1997; Kung et al., 2003). The findings of this study update and advance empirical research on gender differences in vulnerability factors associated with African American suicide using a large, nationally representative sample. The study results reveal in the total sample model that the odds for suicide were highest for African American males, even after controlling for numerous clinical, geographic, and sociodemographic vulnerability factors associated with suicide. This finding supports previous risk factor studies (Garlow et al., 2005; Willis et al., 2003) and epidemiological research that illustrated a rise in suicide among African Americans (CDC, 1998; Gibbs, 1997), particularly the younger age groups (Joe & Kaplan, 2002). Consistent with prior analysis of suicidal behavior (Garlow et al., 2005), the analyses reveal that African Americans are more likely to die at younger ages of suicide. The study also confirmed prior research showing that having a gun in the home substantially increases the risk for suicide (Beautrais, Joyce, & Mulder, 1996; Brent & Bridge, 2003; Brent et al., 1991; Wintemute, Parham, Beaumont, Wright, & Drake, 1999). This is particularly true for males, as illustrated by the almost four-fold increase in the risk for suicide when a gun is known to be in the home. Finally, the increased risk for suicide among African American males living in the south contradicts previous research that has consistently found that among blacks, southern residence confers some protective effects against suicide (Kaplan & Joe 2001). Future research should examine whether the protective effect of southern residence significantly advantages African American female only and what factors are the causal processes and mechanisms.

Mental health is considered one of the most important risk factors for suicide (Brent et al., 1993; Rich, Young, & Fowler, 1986). Kung and colleagues (1998) used a race-specific analysis of the risk factors associated with suicide and found that use of mental health services was the only factor associated with African Americans' suicide risk after controlling for age, gender, and education. Although previous studies have shown that suicide is related to depressive symptoms (Brent, Baugher, Bridge, Chen, & Chiappetta, 1999; Harris & Barraclough, 1997), this relationship is not supported by the male-specific model in our study. Depression research is said to be biased toward females, in that the diagnostic symptoms were developed from research using primarily female populations, which might explain why in the female model depressive symptoms increased the suicide risk 10-fold for African American females. Surprisingly, there was a positive relationship between mental health service use and suicide risk among African American males. This association may be explained by previous research highlighting that African American males are less likely to use mental health services (U. S. Public Health Service, 2001); therefore, males are more likely to arrive for treatment after significant delays and tend to be among severely high-risk clients. The relationships between the mental health variables and African American male suicide risk encourage speculation that males with psychiatric disorders, particularly those delaying treatment, might be at significant risk for engaging in lethal self-destructive behaviors.

There was some evidence to support the increasingly popular yet controversial explanation for the recent increase in African Americans' historically low suicidal behavior: the status-integration hypothesis. This hypothesis posits a positive relationship between socioeconomic status and suicide risk (Henry & Short, 1954; Lester, 1993; Maris, 1969; Prudhomme, 1938). The multivariate results found a relationship between socioeconomic status, measured by education, and suicide among African American males. Increasingly, researchers are giving more attention to the possibility that there are protective factors guarding against suicide that may be unique to specific groups. However, in contrast to previous assumptions and findings regarding religiosity and African American suicidality (Early & Akers, 1993; Joe, 2003; Willis et al., 2003), we found no evidence that church attendance was associated with suicide for this population, except among males. However, this might be due to limited sample size for the female-specific analysis. Also, this lack of evidence may result from the single measure of religiosity available in the NMFS. There currently is no single index or scale that is regarded as the gold standard and that adequately represents the construct of religiosity. Studies of a three-dimensional model of religious involvement among African American adults (Chatters, Levin, & Taylor, 1992; Levin, Chatters, & Taylor, 1995; Lincoln & Chatters, 2003) indicate that it provides a good fit to the data, is preferable to other alternative models, and is convergently valid.

Implications for Public Policy, Practice, and Research

The trend data and review of the research literature on African American suicide clearly refute conventional beliefs about negligible rates of suicidal behavior among this population. Prior to this study, relatively little was known about the gender-specific correlates of suicide, in particular for African Americans. The higher risk of suicide among African American males, young adults, and those who have a firearm in the home should be addressed in future research and considered by clinicians when screening, intervening, and treating African Americans. When designing suicide prevention interventions, clinicians, social workers, and public health professionals should give particular attention to the finding that African American males have the greatest likelihood to use a firearm to complete suicide (Joe, Marcus, et al., in press). Therefore, priority should be given to identifying African American males that are depressed and suicidal and developing strategies for limiting their access to firearms.

Social workers and other mental health professionals should be skilled in talking with African American clients, particularly younger males, about the risk for suicide, providing interventions for those at imminent risk for suicidal behavior, and referring clients for expert assessment and treatment. Future research with a larger sample size should also explore how African American suicidal behavior is associated with multiple measures of socioeconomic status and the use, timing, duration, and adequacy of treatment for mental disorders. Future research is needed with larger samples of African Americans that is grounded in robust theoretical frameworks. Though the failure to support the religion–suicide nexus might result from the model being underpowered, these nonsignificant findings are illustrative of the atheoretical nature of suicide research. While there is an abundance of empirical studies on suicidal behavior, suicidal behavior research is not adequately inspired by theory (Joiner, 2005). Suicide research is more often guided by hypotheses regarding risk or protective factors than by theoretical frameworks. These findings suggest that more theory development with regard to intersections of ethnicity/race and gender seem warranted. For instance, how might the values, norms, and roles of African American men contribute to risk of suicide in general and by firearms in particular? It may be that research looking at male role expectations rather than just "male" as a global gender category would yield significant results. However, future suicide science must be grounded in robust theoretical frameworks that provide testable hypotheses. This would provide a richer investigative context in which to parse the effects that gender, culture, ethnicity, and social class have on suicide risk. More important, it would provide a common framework for examining population-specific and potentially modifiable risk factors that could be targeted in suicide interventions for a diversity of populations.

Social workers, like physicians, have a significant role to play in the national strategy to prevent suicide. Many social workers have little incentive to take active steps to become skilled in suicide assessment or treatment, and very little is known about how suicide assessment and treatment is addressed in the research on graduate education for social work professionals. Moreover, social workers may also be unaware of the patterns of suicide among African American youth, so their practice may be based in the belief that African Americans do not commit suicide (Early, 1992), leading to misinterpretation of self-destructive behaviors among this population. For these reasons, social workers should be aware of the information presented in this chapter. Social workers can also impact public policy to advance the National Strategy for Suicide Prevention, which is mental health parity legislation that requires insurance companies to cover mental health treatment the same way they do physical health. They can also support national efforts to limit access to firearms in this country. To save more lives, we must also further invest in key protective factors, including social and emotional support, religiosity, reduction of mental health stigma, and the promotion of healthy marriages (Greening & Stoppelbein, 2002; Marion & Range, 2003; Nisbet, 1996; Poussaint & Alexander, 2000).

Study Limitations

The NMFS findings must be considered in the context of several important limitations. Although the NMFS oversampled African Americans and the data constitute the largest sample of its kind, the results reported here are limited by the fact the small sample still may bias the effect size or prevent us from identifying statistically significant findings. This bias is probably responsible for the failure of some of the relationships to attain conventional levels of statistical significance. The remaining limitations to the study have been discussed in previous studies using the National Mortality Followback data (Castle et al., 2004; Kung et al., 1998). In particular, a second limitation pertains to the measures used in the study, as we relied on next of kin reporting decedent habits and all other information except for what was on the death certificate. Proxy reporting may introduce retrospective bias, particularly for information about substance use, mental health problems, and firearm presence in the home. Based on data analysis, Kung and colleagues (2003) argue against the presence of a significant bias in this direction. Proxy response has been investigated and found to be reliable across diverse samples, despite the potential for bias (Kung et al., 1998).

Previous research has also demonstrated that compared to Whites, African American suicides were more likely to be underestimated in official mortality data because of greater misclassification (Phillips & Ruth, 1993). Finally, we did not have a control group as a comparison to study exposure variables. Although studies examining the impact on exposure history for deceased controls are rare (Kung et al., 2003), a case-control model would provide a more direct and appropriate unbiased risk estimation for firearm suicide. Despite these limitations, the psychological autopsy method of the NMFS (1993) has been used to study risk factors for completed suicide for more than three decades and has shown high compliance and consistency of results across a wide range of diverse and geographic samples (Brent et al., 1988; Castle et al., 2004; Kung et al., 1998; Willis et al., 2003). This study clearly highlights important similarities and differences in the factors related to firearm use in suicide completers that warrant further investigation with a larger sample of African American suicide decedents.

Conclusion

Suicide among African Americans is a significant public health problem that social work practice and professional education should address. Suicide disproportionately affects young African American males, but females are more likely to engage in nonfatal suicidal behavior. This chapter provides the most recent information on African American suicidal behavior, especially among males; it also provides the current state of research on gender differences in the risk and protective factors. The case is made that a failure to advance research on African American suicide may leave many social workers and other helping professionals inadequately prepared to respond to the needs and experiences of depressed and suicidal African Americans. Finally, given that the empirical literature on African American suicide and suicidal behaviors is not sufficient for designing treatment interventions, social work researchers have the opportunity to make considerable scholarly contributions to the study of suicide.

Future research examining the role of cultural identity in preventing suicidal behaviors in African Americans is needed, as well as research explaining the gender differences and the rapid rise from 1979 to 1994 in suicide rates among African American males. Research is also needed to examine the relationship between suicide attempts and suicide completion among African Americans and to identify the situational or contextual triggers and mental health risk factors that may be unique to this group. Information gained from such studies will further national efforts to develop suicide prevention policy and interventions for this high-risk group. Future investigations are also needed to enhance our understanding of potentially modifiable protective factors that can be targeted in any treatment service or preventative intervention.

NOTE

1. Data are from the National Center for Injury Control and Prevention, Centers for Disease Control and Prevention. The division collects mortality data from death certificates that are reported to the National Center for Health Statistics. Dr. Joe's time in preparing this chapter was supported by a grant (R01-MH82807) from the National Institute of Mental Health.

REFERENCES

Anderson, P. L., Tiro, J. A., Price, A. W., Bender, M. A., & Kaslow, N. J. (2002). Additive impact of childhood emotional, physical, and sexual abuse on suicide attempts among low income African American women. *Suicide & Life-Threatening Behavior, 32*(2), 131–138.

Beautrais, A., Joyce, P., & Mulder, R. (1996). Access to firearms and the risk of suicide: A case control study. *Australian and New Zealand Journal of Psychiatry, 30*, 741–748.

Breed, W. (1970). The Negro and fatalistic suicide. *Pacific Sociological Review, 13*, 156–162.

Brent, D. A., Baugher, M., Bridge, J., Chen, T., & Chiappetta, L. (1999). Age- and sex-related risk factors for adolescent suicide. *Journal of the American Academy of Child and Adolescent Psychiatry, 38*, 1497–1505.

Brent, D. A. & Bridge, J. (2003). Firearms availability and suicide. *American Behavioral Scientist, 46*(9), 1192–1210.

Brent, D. A., Perper, J. A., Allman, C. J., Mortiz, G. M., Wartella, M. E., & Zelenak, J. P. (1991). The presence and accessibility of firearms in the homes of adolescent suicide: A case-control study. *Journal of the American Medical Association, 266*(21), 2989–2995.

Brent, D. A., Perper J. A., Goldstein, C. E., Kolko, D. J., Allan, M. J., Allman, C. J., et al. (1988). Risk factors for adolescent suicide. *Achieves of General Psychiatry, 45*, 581–588.

Brent, D. A., Perper, J. A., Moritz, G., Allman, C., Friend, A., Roth, C., et al. (1993). Psychiatric risk factors for adolescent suicide: A case-control study. *Journal of the American Academy of Child and Adolescent Psychiatry, 32*, 521–529.

Burr, J. A., Hartman, J. T., & Matteson, D. W. (1999). Black suicide in U.S. metropolitan areas: An examination of the racial inequality and social integration-regulation hypotheses. *Social Forces, 77*, 1049–1081.

Canetto, S. S. & Lester, D. (1995). *Women and suicidal behavior*. New York:Springer Publishing Company.

Castle, K., Duberstein, P. R., Meldrum, S., Conner, K. R., & Conwell, Y. (2004). Risk factors for suicide in blacks and whites: An analysis of data from the 1993 National Mortality Followback Survey. *American Journal of Psychiatry, 161,* 452–458.

Centers for Disease Control and Prevention. (1998). Suicide among African-American youths–United States, 1980-1995. *Morbidity and Mortality Weekly Report, 47,* 193–196.

Centers for Disease Control and Prevention. (2005). National Mortality Followback Survey: Background information. Retrieved February 3, 2003, from http://www.cdc.gov/nchswww/about/major/nmfs/nmfs.htm

Centers for Disease Control and Prevention. (2006). *Youth risk behavior surveillance–United States, 2005 (55/SS05).* Atlanta, GA: Author.

Charlot-Swilley, D. (1998 July). *Improving the socio-emotional functioning of African American girls: An investigation based on culturally and gender specific intervention programs.* Paper presented at the Annual Conference of the Association of Black Psychologists, Atlanta, GA.

Chatters, L. M., Levin, J. S., & Taylor, R. J. (1992). Antecedents and dimensions of religious involvement among older Black adults. *Journal of Gerontology: Social Sciences, 47,* S269–S278.

Chaudran, L. H. & Remington, P. (1999). Age and gender differences in suicide trends, Wisconsin and the United States, 1980-1994. *Wisconsin Medical Journal, 6,* 35–38,98.

Dunston, P. J. (1990). Stress, coping, and social support: Their effects on black women. In D. S. Ruiz (Ed.), *Handbook of mental health and mental disorders among Black Americans* (pp. 133–147). New York: Greenwood Press.

Durkheim, E. (1951). *Suicide.* Glencoe, IL: Free Press.

Early, K. E. (1992). *Religion and suicide in the African-American community.* Westport, CT: Greenwood Press.

Early, K. E. & Akers, R. L. (1993). "It's a white thing": An explanation of beliefs about suicide in the African-American community. *Deviant Behavior, 14,* 227–296.

Fernquist, R. M. (2004). Educational attainment and the payoff of education: Black male suicide in the United States, 1947-1998. *Current Research in Social Psychology, 9*(13), 184–192.

Garlow, S. J., Purselle, D., & Heninger, M. (2005). Ethnic differences in patterns of suicide across the life cycle. *American Journal of Psychiatry, 162,* 319–323.

Gibbs, J. P. & Martin, W. T. (1964). *Status integration and suicide.* Eugene: University of Oregon Press.

Gibbs, J. T. (1988). Conceptual, methodological, and structural issues in black youth suicide: Implications of assessment and early intervention. *Suicide and Life-Threatening Behavior, 18,* 73–89.

Gibbs, J. T. (1997). African-American suicide: A cultural paradox. *Suicide and Life-Threatening Behavior, 27*(1), 68–79.

Goldsmith, S. K., Pellmar, T. C., Kleinman, A. M., & Bunney, W. E. (2002). *Reducing suicide: A national imperative.* Washington, DC: Institute of Medicine, National Academies Press.

Gould, M. S., Fisher, P., Parides, M., Flory, M., & Shaffer, D. (1996). Psychosocial risk factors of child and adolescent completed suicide. *Archives of General Psychiatry, 53,* 1155–1162.

Greening, L. & Stoppelbein, L. (2002). Religiosity, attributional style, and social support as psychosocial buffers for African American and White adolescents' perceived risk for suicide. *Suicide and Life-Threatening Behavior, 32*(4), 404–417.

Harris, E. C. & Barraclough, B. (1997). Suicide as an outcome for mental disorders: A meta-analysis. *British Journal of Psychiatry, 170*, 205–228.

Henry, A. F. & Short, J. F. (1954). *Suicide and homicide.* Glencoe, IL: Free Press.

Hosmer, D. W. & Lemeshow, S. (2000). *Applied survival analysis: Regression modeling of time to event data.* New York: John Wiley & Sons, Inc.

Hoyert, D. L., Heron, M., Murphy, S. L., & Kung, H. C. (2006). *Deaths: Final data for 2003. National vital statistics reports; Vol. 54* No. 13. Hyattsville, MD: National Center for Health Statistics.

Institute of Medicine. (2002). *Reducing suicide: A national imperative.* Washington: National Academy Press.

Joe, S. (2003). Implications of focusing on black youth self-destructive behaviors instead of suicide when designing preventative interventions. In D. Romer (Ed.), *Reducing adolescent risk: Toward an integrated approach* (pp. 325–332). Thousand Oaks, CA: Sage Publications.

Joe, S. (2006a). Explaining changes in the patterns of Black suicide in the United States from 1981-2002: An age, cohort, & period analysis. *Journal of Black Psychology, 32*(3), 262–284.

Joe, S. (2006b). Implications of national suicide trends for social work practice with Black youth. *Child and Adolescent Social Work Journal, 24*(2).

Joe, S. & Kaplan, M. S. (2001). Suicide among African American men. *Suicide and Life-Threatening Behavior, 31*(Suppl.), 106–121.

Joe, S. & Kaplan, M. S. (2002). Firearm-related suicide among young African-American males. *Psychiatric Services, 53*(3), 332–334.

Joe, S., Marcus, S. M., & Kaplan, M. S. (2007). Racial differences in the characteristics of firearm suicide decedents in the United States. *American Journal of Orthopsychiatry, 77*(1), 124–130.

Joe, S., Romer, D., & Jamieson, P. (2005). *Race and gender differences in U. S. trends in suicide acceptability.* Paper presented at the annual meeting of the American Association of Suicidology.

Joe, S., Romer, D., & Jamieson, P. (2005, April). Suicide acceptability and suicidal behavior among US adolescents. A paper presentation for the American Association of Suicidology, Boulden, Colorado.

Joe, S., Romer, D., & Jamieson, P. (2007) Suicide acceptability is related to suicidal behavior among US addescents. *Suicide and Life Threatning Behavior, 37*(2), 165–178.

Joiner, T. (2005). *Why people die by suicide* (pp. 16–46). Cambridge, MA: Harvard University Press.

Juon, H. S. & Ensminger, M. E. (1997). Childhood, adolescent, and young adult predictors of suicidal behaviors: A prospective study of African Americans. *Journal of Child Psychology and Psychiatry, 38*(5), 553–563.

Kaslow, N. J., Price, A. W., Wyckoff, S., Bender, G. M., Sherry, A., Young, S., et al. (2004). Person factors associated with suicidal behavior among African American women and men. *Cultural Diversity and Ethnic Minority Psychology, 10*(1), 5–22.

Kaslow, N. J., Thompson., M., Meadows, M. A., Chance, S., Puett, R., Hollings, L., et al. (2000). Risk factors for suicide attempts among African American women. *Depression and Anxiety, 12*, 13–20.

Kessler, R. C., Berglund, P., Borges, G., Nock, M., & Wang, P. S. (2005). Trends in suicide ideation, plans, gestures, and attempts in the United States, 1990–1992 to 2001-2003. *Journal of the American Medical Association, 293*(20), 2487–2495.

Klerman, G. (1987). Clinical epidemiology of suicide. *Journal of Clinical Psychiatry, 48*(Suppl. 12), 33–38.

Kung, H.-C., Liu, X., & Juon, H. S. (1998). Risk factors for suicide in Caucasians and in African-Americans: A matched case-control study. *Social Psychiatry and Psychiatric Epidemiology, 33*, 155–161.

Kung, H. C., Pearson, J. L., & Liu, X. (2003). Risk factors for male and female suicide decedents ages 15-64 in the United States: Results from the 1993 National Mortality Followback Survey. *Social Psychiatry and Psychiatric Epidemiology, 38*, 419–426.

LaVeist, T. A., Sellers, R., & Neighbors, H. W. (2001). Perceived racism and self and system blame attribution: Consequences for longevity. *Ethnicity and Disease, 11*, 711–721.

Lester, D. (1993). Economic status of African Americans and suicide rates. *Perceptual and Motor Skills, 77*, 1150.

Levin, J. S., Chatters, L. M., & Taylor, R. J. (1995). Religious effects on health status and life satisfaction among Black Americans. *Journal of Gerontology: Social Sciences, 50B*, S154–S163.

Lincoln, K. D. & Chatters, L. M. (2003). Keeping the faith: Religion, stress, and psychological well-being among African American women. In D. R. Brown & V. M. Keith (Eds.), *In and out of our right minds: The mental health of African American women.* New York: Columbia University Press.

Marion, M. S. & Range, L. M. (2003). African American college women's suicide buffers. *Suicide and Life-Threatening Behavior, 33*(1), 33–43.

Maris, R. W. (1969). *Social forces in urban suicide.* Homewood, IL: Dorsey.

Meehan, P. J., Lamb, J. A., Saltzman, L. E., & O'Carroll, P. W. (1992). Attempted suicide among young adults: Progress toward a meaningful estimate of prevalence. *American Journal of Psychiatry, 149*, 41–44.

National Center for Health Statistics. (1998). *National Mortality Followback Survey.* Retrieved August 7, 2004, 2004, from http://www.cdc.gov/nchs/about/major/nmfs/nmfs.htm

Neeleman, J., Wessely, S., & Lewis, G. (1998). Suicide acceptability in African- and White Americans: The role of religion. *Journal of Nervous and Mental Disease, 186*(1), 12–16.

Nisbet, P. A. (1996). Protective factors for suicidal black females. *Suicide and Life-Threatening Behavior, 26*, 325–341.

Phillips, D. P. & Ruth, T. E. (1993). Adequacy of official suicide statistics for scientific research and public policy. *Suicide and Life-Threatening Behavior, 23*, 307–319.

Poussaint, A. F. & Alexander, A. (2000). *Lay my burden down.* Boston: Beacon Press.

Prudhomme, C. (1938). The problem of suicide in the American Negro. *Psychoanalytic Review, 25*, 187–204, 372–391.

Rich, C. L., Young, D., & Fowler, R. C. (1986). San Diego suicide study: I. Young vs. old subjects. *Archive of General Psychiatry, 43*, 577–582.

Sellers, R. M., Caldwell, C. H., Schmeelk-Cone, K. H., & Zimmerman, M. A. (2003). Racial identity, racial discrimination, perceived stress, and psychological distress among African American young adults. *Journal of Health and Social Behavior, 43*, 302–317.

Sellers, R. M. & Shelton, J. N. (2003). The role of racial identity in perceived racial discrimination. *Journal of Personality and Social Psychology, 84*(5), 1079–1092.

Shaffer, D., Gould, M., & Hicks, R. C. (1994). Worsening suicide rate in black teenagers. *American Journal of Psychiatry, 151*, 1810–1812.

Thompson, M. P., Kaslow, N. J., Short, L. M., & Wyckoff, S. (2002). The mediating roles of perceived social support and resources in the self efficacy—suicide attempts relation among African American abused women. *Journal of Consulting and Clinical Psychology, 70*(4), 942–949.

U. S. Public Health Service. (2001). *Mental health: Culture, race, and ethnicity —A supplement to mental health: A report of the Surgeon General.* Rockville, MD: U.S. Department of Health and Human Services.

Wasserman, I. M. (1999, April). *African Americans and the criminal justice system: An explanation for changing patterns of black male suicide.* Paper presented at the meeting of the Midwest Sociological Society, Minneapolis, MN.

Watt, T. T. & Sharp, S. F. (2002). Race differences in strains associated with suicidal behavior among adolescents. *Youth and Society, 34*(2), 232–256.

Willis, L. A., Coombs, D. W., Drentea, P., & Cockerham, W. C. (2003). Uncovering the mystery: Factors of African American suicide. *Suicide and Life-Threatening Behavior, 33*(4), 412–429.

Wintemute, G. J., Parham, C. A., Beaumont, J. J., Wright, M., & Drake, C. (1999). Mortality among recent purchasers of handguns. *New England Journal of Medicine, 341*, 1583–1589.

PART IV

Life Chances: Violence and Incarceration Among African American Males

15

Cultural Interventions for Reducing Violence Among Young, African American Males

LANCE WILLIAMS

Violence is the second leading cause of death for those aged 18 to 24. For Black youth aged 15 to 24, it has been the leading cause of death since 1978 (Bellamy et al., 1997; Satcher, 1999). Clearly violence is a major public health and social problem in the United States (Bellamy et al., 1997; Cooper, Lutenbacher, & Faccia, 2000; Kachur et al., 1996). Blacks of any age in 2002 were six times more likely to be murdered than Whites (U.S. Bureau of Justice Statistics, 2002). For Black youth residing in the inner city, homicides accounted for 47% of deaths in 1992 (Komro, Flay, Zelli, Rashid, & Hu, 1996). Among inner-city Black youth, males were 2.6 times more likely to die from gunfire than White males (Illinois Council Against Handgun Violence [ICHV], 1996). Although violent crime among all adults has steadily declined during the past 25 years, it has increased among all youth and is at epidemic proportions for inner-city Black youth.

In 1995, one-fourth of all known juvenile victims and perpetrators of homicide occurred in five cities: Chicago, New York, Los Angeles, Detroit, and Houston, which made up 10% of America's population. In the same year, 84% of all counties in the United States reported no juvenile homicides, and 10% reported only one (Garbarino, 1999). These startling statistics indicated that youth homicide is not, in fact, an American problem per se, but a problem relegated to a relatively small population, even though that small population consisted of millions of people. Cook County, Illinois, the site for this study, encompasses the city of Chicago and was one of the 6% of counties that annually reported multiple juvenile homicides. Between 1995 and 1997, 82% (2370) of all homicides that occurred in Cook County happened in Chicago (Illinois Department of Public Health [IDPH], 2000). In 1998, Chicago police identified Black men as the offenders in 173 of the 207 murders of African American males (Loury, 2000). Although more recent data indicate that the homicide rate is declining in Chicago among young, African American males, it is still too high. Take homicide out of the equation, and the life expectancy of African American men would be almost 1.4 years higher than it is today (MacKellar & Yanagishita, 1995).

Given these disturbing statistics, interventions to stem the violence are imperative. One promising intervention, Connections, integrates adaptive cultural resources from both the dominant American Anglo culture and the African culture. This chapter reviews the Connections program underway in Englewood, one of the poorest communities in Chicago, and its approaches to stemming the violence that pervades the lives of residents.

Cultural Interventions

Several studies have shown that adaptive cultural resources, resources preserved from prior generations that help individuals cope with contemporary pressing imperatives, are instrumental in the healthy development of African American youth (Bowman & Sanders, 1998; Flay & Petraitis, 1994; Jagers, 1993; Nobles, 1990).

Culturally specific programming may, in fact, be the missing component of youth interventions (Gavazzi, Alford, & McKenney, 1996; Harvey, 2001; Jagers, 1993; Jagers & Mock, 1993). Although such programming is not typically found in youth violence prevention programs, there is some indication that a culture- and gender-specific approach might be effective for young African Americans (Hudley & Graham, 1995; Tolan & Guerra, 1994). Preventions guided by an African-centered perspective, which helps promote indigenous cultural strengths, such as spirituality, collective efficacy, community, and social responsibility, may be particularly effective for African American youth by empowering them to reverse maladaptive response patterns (Bowman, 1990; Daly, Jennings, Beckett, & Leashore, 1995; Hudley & Graham, 1995; Jagers, 1993).

Culture shapes how individuals perceive their world, their community, and their family. It provides them with a blueprint for living and for interpreting their environment (Ani, 1994). Culture is often defined as the traditions, norms, shared values, customs, arts, history, and institutions of a group of people. A person's cultural affiliation often determines his or her values and attitudes about health issues, responses to messages, and even violent behaviors and perceptions.

Bowman (1990) suggests that adaptive cultural resources may empower Black youth by providing a general sense of personal efficacy. He states that "personal empowerment, which is rooted in culture and prior success, may be the basic formula for at-risk black youth to beat the odds" (p. 90). The literature on the socialization of African American youth supported the adaptive value of unique patterns of an African-centered moral and ethical value system as well as subjective cultural resources such as identity, empathy, collective efficacy, social cohesion, and comradeship (Bowman, 1989; Jagers, 1993; Ward, 1995; Warfield-Coppock, 1992). Promoting these adaptive cultural resources among Black youth might reduce antisocial behavior and lead to an improved sense of self and an endorsement of beliefs that reduce violence, aggression, impulsivity, and inflexibility (Hudley et al., 1998; Jagers, Smith, Mock, & Dill, 1993; Mattaini, Lowery, & PEACE POWER!, 2000).

Cultural Tool Kits

Culture is not a static, one-dimensional system that guides action in a linear direction; rather, "it is more like a 'tool kit' or repertoire from which actors select differing pieces for constructing lines of action" (Swindler, 1986, p. 277). For instance, the spirit of competition and possessive individualism are both essential tools needed to be successful in mainstream American society. Others are growth, a sense of progress, and a belief in rationalism (science). Those who use alternative tools not commonly found in mainstream America's tool kit–the spirit of cooperation, altruism, or Black pride–tend to be less culturally competent, and their degree of success in society is minimized.

Swindler's (1986) paradigm of culture as a tool kit serves as the foundation for discussing the Connections intervention as it relates to violence. Although Swindler's tool kit paradigm provided a solid foundation for discussing culture in general, it must be expanded to capture the unique and diverse cultural orientations present among African Americans, particularly those who live in marginalized communities such as Englewood. Building on Swindler's tool kit paradigm, I added the Boykin and Toms' triple quandary framework to help bring clarity and deeper meaning to the cultural findings from an African-centered perspective. The triple quandary framework posits that African Americans simultaneously operate through three distinct cultural orientations: *(1)* the Anglo cultural orientation, also referred to as a Eurocentric perspective or mainstream American orientation; *(2)* the marginal, or minority orientation; and *(3)* the Afro cultural, or African-centered orientation (Jagers & Mock, 1993, p. 392). Most African Americans tend to be rooted in one particular orientation; however, it is common for African Americans to simultaneously use tools from each as an adaptive response to given social situations. Combining Swindler's tool kit paradigm with the triple quandary framework creates three distinct cultural tool kits: *(1)* the Anglo cultural tool kit, which contains cultural tools needed to be successful in the mainstream American society; *(2)* the marginal tool kit, containing cultural tools that are maladaptive responses to structural barriers; and *(3)* the Afro cultural tool kit, including adaptive emic resources, or cultural patterns from prior generations that have been transferred into etic, or new, adaptive resources to meet pressing imperatives responses to current social imperatives (Table 15.1).

Table 15.1 Cultural Tool Kits

	Anglo Cultural Tool Kit	*Marginal Tool Kit*	*Afro Cultural Tool Kit*
Contents	Mainstream values, attitudes, and beliefs necessary for success in American society	Adaptive coping responses to lack of structural opportunities	Adaptive cultural resources preserved from prior generations that help individuals cope with contemporary pressing imperatives
Tools	Machiavellianism, possessive individualism, competitive spirit, egalitarian-based conformity, person/object relations (materialism), personal responsibility	Machiavellianism, predatory individualism, illicit economic activities, gang membership, male dominance, emotional nonresponsiveness, hypermaterialism	Spirituality, communalism, affect, empathy, social interaction/involvement, social responsibility/duties, social interconnectedness, emotional expressiveness
Associated behavior	Conforming	Antisocial	Prosocial
Existing perspective	Mainstream and pathological perspectives of self and community Want out of their communities, never to return	Pathological perspective of self and community No future for themselves or their communities	Adaptive coping and oppression perspectives of self and community View community as theirs and feel obligated to it through community service

The Connections Program

The Connections intervention program is a culturally based youth development program for African American adolescents. It is an African-centered rites of passage program that uses transitional initiation rites to instill youth with an African cultural social ethos, thereby promoting a sense of purpose and meaning. Since 1991, the program has been based in Chicago's West Englewood, a community perceived as one of the most violent in the nation. Studying the program from its inception offered a unique opportunity to see how adolescents exposed to a culturally based program perceived violent behaviors. This study was conducted over an 18-month period.

Three ethnographic techniques were used to collect data: *(a)* participant observation, *(b)* in-depth interviews, and *(c)* focus groups. The goal of participant observation was to observe the daily activities of people, physical characteristics of the social situation, and what it feels like to be part of the scene in an unobtrusive way. From a pool of former and current staff members and youths who participated in the Connections intervention program between 1991 and 2001, 36 were recruited to participate in in-depth interviews and focus groups. All subjects were interviewed using in-depth interview or focus group guides.

The majority of the participants who joined the Connections intervention program joined with an Anglo cultural orientation, subscribing to such tools as possessive individualism, the spirit of competition, conformity, and effort optimism. It was not uncommon for the highest achieving students in the school to join Connections. Although these students lived in Englewood and were exposed to risks common to marginalized communities, they tended to be more amenable to the mainstream middle-class value system. They appeared to have more family support than most of their peers. They knew how to mobilize their resources to achieve their personal goals. These students used the Anglo cultural tool of personal responsibility to make the decision to join Connections: They felt that joining the program would enhance their chances to be successful in life. Many of the students also had frequently relied on the egalitarian conformity tool prior to joining the Connections intervention program, which is what kept them out of such troubles as gang activity, pregnancy, school-related problems, or drug involvement. These young people were *in* a risk-ridden environment but not *of* it, thanks to their adherence to the Anglo cultural value of conformity.

Other students, however, arrived with a pathological perspective on their community, their school, and the people in their communities. Their initial life goals included plans to use Anglo cultural tools to escape their communities, never to return to them. Still others arrived with a marginal, or minority, orientation. The marginal orientation is a result of maladaptive coping with the historical legacy of racial and economic oppression (Bowman, 1989; Jagers, 1993; Jagers & Mock, 1993; Warfield-Coppick, 1990, 1992; see also the unpublished paper by Jagers et al., 1993). The lack of structural opportunities, not the intrinsic pathologies of the people in these communities, is largely to blame for their marginalization. Although it is clear that people in marginalized communities share the values and aspirations of the middle class, the structural barriers to opportunities force many to develop behavior that is a defensive adaptation.

The predominant expressions in the marginal tool kit are a variety of self-deprecating antisocial behaviors such as predatory individualism and gang-related activities as well as aberrant achievement and survival strategies, such as rejection of formal schooling and consequent participation in street economy (Bowman, 1989; Jagers et al., 1993). Whereas only some of the students who joined the Connections program with an Anglo cultural orientation had a pathological perspective of their communities and the people in them, the majority of students with a marginal orientation believed that their communities and the people in them were pathological. This might explain why they adopted the marginal tool kit to cope. These more marginalized participants were referred to Connections primarily by school administrators or were identified by the Connections staff as being at greater risk for school failure.

Given the objective and subjective difficulties that both the Anglo cultural orientation and marginal orientation present to African American youth, an Afro cultural orientation is an alternative cultural orientation. The Afro cultural orientation suggests that African Americans have preserved and mobilized emic or old cultural patterns from prior generations. Subsequently, the emic cultural patterns have transformed into etic, or new adaptive resources to meet pressing imperatives. These adaptive resources function as an Afro cultural tool kit that provides Black people with expressions to help them cope with barriers that they may face in major life roles. As noted in Table 15.1, the tools in the Afro cultural tool kit include, but are not limited to, *spirituality*, the belief that all elements of reality contain a certain amount of life force; *communalism*, the awareness of the fundamental interdependence of people; and *affect*, the valuing of emotional experiences, the affective values of information, and sensitivity to the emotional cues of others.

Jagers and Mock (1993) found that African American youth who embraced more Afro cultural orientations than marginal orientation reported less delinquent behavior. Likewise, the more that African American youth reported embracing an Afro cultural as opposed to an Anglo cultural orientation, the less likely they were to have problematic attitudes and behaviors such as Machiavellianism, delinquency, and aggression. Thus, an Afro cultural orientation was consistent with more favorable social outcomes for African American youth.

Connections as a Cultural Retooling Agent

Given the potential detrimental effects that some elements of an Anglo cultural orientation and marginalization orientation have on African American youth, the Connections intervention program goal was to reorient participants to an Afro cultural perspective. My analysis of the Connections intervention program indicated that Connections attempted to purge the antisocial tools associated with the Anglo cultural and marginal tool kits and replace them with the following seven essential cultural tools from the Afro cultural tool kit:

1. Self-sufficiency, self-empowerment, and ethnic pride
2. Community building
3. Economic empowerment
4. Ritual as tools for preventing and solving interpersonal and intrapersonal conflict
5. The spirit of communalism
6. Empathy/affect
7. Spirituality/African centeredness

Cultural Tool 1: Self-Sufficiency, Self-Empowerment, and Ethnic Pride

The Connections intervention program worked hard to provide its participants with adaptive responses to institutional racism and oppression in America by cultivating the spirit of self-sufficiency, self-empowerment, leadership, economic independence, ethnic pride, and liberation through education. For instance, the Connections staff implored its participants to ferociously prepare for and pursue higher education, not just for the sake of getting a good job for personal wealth and status, but to acquire the necessary skills to create jobs for themselves and their community.

Connections used cultural awareness as a vehicle for self-awareness: Once the participants became more culturally aware, they became more open to self-exploration. This inward perspective provided each participant with the opportunity to take a self-inventory. Akil (all names have been changed) credited Connections with helping him to take an inward perspective as a means of self-empowerment:

> [Connections] helped me learn how to take a different approach and a different perspective on life. When things happen in my everyday life, instead of looking at what's going on around me, I kinda look inside myself and say, How can I deal with this situation better? Or, What is it that I want to come out of this situation? It's kinda like a constant reflection of what is going on internally in me, . . . It helps me to kinda have control over every situation, because I can control what's going on in me.

The ability to take control is a form of self-efficacy that can empower a person to cope with life stress in an adaptive, prosocial way.

The Connections intervention program cultivated the tools of self-sufficiency, self-empowerment, and ethnic pride among the participants by facilitating activities that simulated major events of oppression of African people, such as the transatlantic slave trade, the middle passage, the dehumanizing process of African people being sold as chattel, Jim Crow segregation, and police brutality. They offered these activities to educate the program participants on the atrocities committed against their ancestors so that the participants could better appreciate the strength of their people, who endured such human suffering, hoping that this knowledge would increase ethnic pride, self-empowerment, and self-sufficiency. For instance, Akil stated,

> It helped me to learn more about African American history. It's helped me to identify more with my culture. My family's from South America, and even being in America is a completely different experience. And an African American experience is completely different from my parents' immigrant experience, but it helped me to connect with that.

Cultural awareness helped Akil to form a stronger bond with his parents, which is particularly promising, given the link between strong parent–child bonding and reduced youth violence.

Simultaneously, Connections introduced resistance to institutional racism and oppression by exposing the youth to maroon life and revolutionary political activism. Ultimately, however, the program served as a natural intervention stemming antisocial behavior by fostering tools for self-sufficiency, self-empowerment, and ethnic pride, each a form of self-efficacy. Each then became a protective factor against violent behaviors.

Cultural Tool 2: Community Building

The Connections intervention program staff and participants clearly understood the community-level influences that contributed to role strain among inner-city African American youth. The data I collected consistently showed that the staff identified historical factors that contributed to the demographic changes in inner-city African American communities, which ultimately led to role strain among Black youth. The most fundamental of these changes has been the loss of traditional values and resources that fostered healthy roles. Staff and participants perceived that many of the norms and values that were once instrumental to adaptive coping had begun to break down. The breakdown of these traditional values had also frayed the strong bonds that existed between institutions within the Black community. Families and religious, educational, and social institutions, along with other social support networks, have lost their influence on many African Americans. Ultimately, the alienation of inner-city African American youth becomes so great that they suffer extreme forms of role strain that lead to severe maladaptive coping.

In an attempt to re-establish strong bonds between its participants and their community, Connections staff engaged students in leadership training and community service projects. Kwame, a Connections participant, elaborated on the positive impact that community service had on the lives of students:

> The community service component, I think it was very beneficial because we, I don't know, we got to feel like, what it meant to be needed and wanted rather than needy and wanting. You know what I mean? So it helped to boost, I think, our egos . . . . our confidence . . . . We received a lot of praise from adults, particularly when we did well, when we were there, you know, the benefits of being good, of service . . . . I think that helped to develop us as individuals.

Participants engaged in community service in their communities, but they were also intricately involved in community service projects in Africa, from which they gained a sense of connection to the global community. In 1996, Connections took its first of what would become annual trips to Africa, in this case an 8-day trip to Senegal. These trips have served to broaden the participants' perspectives of the global community and of human relations and service. In addition, the trip served as a culmination of the students' rites of passage.

Baba, a founding member of Connections, perceived the community service that he did in Africa as miraculous:

> I think that in Africa we were able to do some miracles. We did community building. We worked with a health care facility. We raised money to bring in generators, and we actually rolled our sleeves up and began to dig, we started to dig a library foundation. We always try to raise money over and above the cost of the trip so we can be able to impact the village.

As youth begin to become more active in working for social change in their community and to perceive themselves as community builders, they are less likely to be involved in behaviors such as violence that destroy the community (Moody, Childs, & Sepples, 2003; Scott, Tepas, Frykberg, Taylor, & Plotkin, 2002). Conversely, Ingoibi provided a powerful assessment of the tragic implications of the lack of a service ethic in his community:

> Because most times we see brothers and sisters when they go to college and they graduate and get their degrees, they move out the 'hood. They don't come back. Community service? What the hell is that? And that's another reason why the community dies–because the brothers and sisters with the knowledge, they leave.

Effective components of youth violence interventions include community service as a protective factor against violence (Center for the Study and Prevention of Violence, 1998; Kellermann, Fuqua-Whitley, Rivara, & Mercy, 1998). The specifics, however, of why youth who participate in community service are less inclined to engage in violence than those who do not has yet to be determined. Preliminary evidence indicates that youth involvement in community service increases their feeling of self-worth, which reduces violent behavior.

Cultural Tool 3: Economic Empowerment

Historically, Blacks have always experienced serious inequalities in the job market, with a persistently negative impact on Black families and their children. African American teenagers have consistently had the highest rate of unemployment in the United States, and there is no indication that this trend will change (Bowman, 1990). According to the U.S. Department of Labor, the 2004 unemployment rate among the Black civilian labor force aged 16 to 19 was more than twice as high at 31.7% than for White youth in the same age bracket (15.0%). Although both young African American males and females experience high unemployment, males may be at higher risk for chronic joblessness due to poorer educational preparation and problems with the school-to-work transition (Bowman, 1990; Mincy, 2006). In addition, with the U.S. labor market's rapid move away from unskilled industrial jobs, many young African American youth find themselves ill-prepared for the new jobs in the technology and service industries, and this creates job role strain.

In no place has job displacement been felt more strongly than in inner-city African American communities. In what appears to be a natural and planned response to the economic dilemma in the Connections community, the program's leadership attempted to foster the spirit of entrepreneurship among its participants, both to reduce the job role strain and to prepare participants to overcome the economic devastation that existed in their communities. For example, several respondents, including one of the Connections directors, indicated that the process of raising money to go to Africa instilled in the participants the spirit of entrepreneurialism. As one participant said of raising the money, "It was really a powerful thing."

Although the fundraising proved to be an ongoing challenge for Connections and its participants, Kwame, the young male . . . felt that it also had some benefits to the students:

I think it helped us realize what we could do if we put our energies together and our skills together. We were able to raise up to $50,000 at one time. I thought that was really a crucial component. Just seeing how we could generate money, knowing being poor individuals didn't necessarily mean that they couldn't raise money and so forth.

Cultural Tool 4: Ritual as a Tool for Preventing and Solving Interpersonal and Intrapersonal Conflict

African American youth most commonly are murdered by or murder other African American youth who are their friends, relatives, or acquaintances. From 1976 to 1982, 46% of African American youth homicide victims were killed by acquaintances, 20% by strangers, and 8% by family members (Gibbs, 1988). The rates of acquaintance and family violence have remained stable since the 1970s, but the rate of stranger violence has increased by one-third (Gibbs, 1988). The characteristics of young African American homicide offenders and their victims are very similar. They are both generally young (15–24 years old), both African American, both from lower socioeconomic backgrounds, and both live in large metropolitan areas and have previous arrest records for aggravated assault or other felonies (Gibbs, 1988).

According to Gibbs (1988), many Blacks in the inner cities no longer seem to feel connected to each other, responsible to each other, or concerned about each other. Rather than a sense of shared community and a common purpose, which once characterized Black neighborhoods, inner cities now reflect a sense of hopelessness, alienation, and frustration (p. 19). People attribute the conditions that exist in lower socioeconomic communities such as Englewood to institutionalized racism. When asked, "In what ways are young Black males that you know dealing with violence?" Afya said:

> From every arena . . . perpetrated by other men. Perpetrated on each other. Other cultures being violent to Black men, you know, just because they're Black men. Out of racism and out of their intimidation for us because of our power. So Black men get it from all areas.

The frustration caused by systemic racism manifests itself in many forms, such as violent and antisocial behavior, crime, and self-destructive behavior (Bell, 1997; Jagers, 1993). It simultaneously creates an environment of stress, which also contributes to violence. Kwame said that most of the young Black males whom he knew sought to avoid violence but braced themselves for the inevitable:

> I think a lot of young Black men, they know that they gon' have to deal with it, you know, eventually, particularly in the neighborhood. So, everybody is kinda on edge a little bit, a little uptight.

The effects of slavery, racism, and discrimination have led to an increased sense of frustration and anger among African Americans males. Particularly affected have been African American males who had been psychologically emasculated by White society. Ultimately, this rage is expressed in antisocial behavior. Although there is no known direct evidence of a link between subcultural values and antisocial behavior, this is an extremely challenging area to research, given that culture is such a pervasive phenomenon and that its influences are quite subtle and difficult to identify.

The Connections intervention program used a variety of approaches to help its male participants cope with stress, frustration, and rage within the context of the rites of passage training that is the centerpiece of the program. As the young participants enter into formal training in the program, they are immersed in an inward journey. The inward journey uses traditional African group psychotherapeutic techniques to enhance the emotional functioning of its participants. This process, referred to as *clearing*, facilitated the participants' move inward to confront past emotionally traumatic experiences that function as a current barrier to healthy emotional functioning.

THE STICK-ACTION RITUAL   The African-centered approach to youth violence prevention is that it provides interventionists with a structure that draws from time-tested cultural models that have proven to be efficacious for solving certain social problems. Connections used etic rituals, new cultural practices that were modified versions of older or emic cultural practices designed to meet pressing social imperatives. Stick action was one etic ritual that used traditional African core cultural patterns to help young people resolve conflict in a prosocial manner. Makini described how stick action is used among program participants and staff:

> If I had a conflict with another group member, I would probably go to Z, or Mr. Wright, or one of the elders, which is somethin' people always do . . . So, they'll [the elders] get the stick and put it in the center of the room. Everyone would gather in a circle around, you know, just as support. I would be on one side of the stick and the other person . . . [would be on the other side]. Yeah, I would call the person that I was having the conflict with [to the center of the circle]. I would say to the person, "You have to come up to the stick." I would ask the person, "Can you do this?"

> And the person would say, "Yeah, I'll do it," or "Yeah, it's cool."

> I'd put my hand on the stick. My hand would be on the top of the stick and the other person's hand is on the bottom. So then I tell them what happened, you know . . .

> I would just basically clear my stuff off with the person in the presence of the group and the elders. But the stick is not goin' directly at the person, all this negative feelings is goin' in the ground. The whole piece I'm doin' is to clear my feelin's about the person. The person is just there . . . basically the person is just a mirror for me. It's not really about the person, it's about me.

> When I'm thinkin' about people that's talkin' about me, I probably didn't say anything to them. I probably walked around with anger. But because I love the person, I wanna let them know that they may not be conscious of their behavior, or when they're playin', how it truly affects me. And if they love me they'll think about doin' it in a different way. Then usually what happens is the people will hug, or I may get to the point where I'm emotional, and we'll all connect. I'll tell them some good things that I see in them.

Makini's reference to the elders' involvement with helping to resolve conflict was an example of an older cultural practice. In most African cultures, key eldership roles involved a significant involvement in resolving conflict in society. Therefore, the stick-action ritual as practiced by Connections reflected a new cultural practice that modified versions of older cultural paradigms designed to meet pressing social imperatives.

THE P.I.E.S RITUAL   Many of the youth with a marginal orientation who joined the Connections intervention were emotionally unexpressive, as is common in youth who have suffered personal trauma from living in a high-risk environment, particularly young African American males. Through rituals involving clearing and *checking in physically, intellectually, emotionally, and spiritually* (P.I.E.S.), the program provided the participants with the tool of emotional expressiveness.

After ritual space was opened up and the realm of the sacred had been appropriately addressed, the participants began to engage in what Connections called "work." The first phase of this work, or inward journey, involved all participants checking in. Checking in required all of the participants to sit in a circle in silence while each participant told the group how they felt physically, intellectually, emotionally, and spiritually. Makini revealed the nature of P.I.E.S.:

> P.I.E.S. It's to get us to be honest about what we really feel. So, P.I.E.S. is how I feel physically—so our motto is (*P*) physically I feel good; intellectually, which is the *I*, I feel smart; *E*, which is emotionally, I feel peaceful; and *S*, which is spirituality– spirituality I feel, you know, I feel like I'm still searchin'. And after we check in, we would respond with sayin', 'I'm in.' And the group would respond back with *Ashe* [an Akan word of West Africa], which means, you know, "I hear you."

> That's real powerful'cuz a lot of times when we did check in, and Z [the Director] got us in a space when someone checked in sad, or angry, or even if we were still searchin', we would always address each others' check-in so that if you were sad, or angry, you know, we didn't just keep on going; we addressed it.

The stick-action and P.I.E.S. rituals were particularly powerful tools for young African American males exhibiting the maladaptive tool of emotional stoicism, which can lead to violence. Connections staff believed that providing members with tools for becoming more emotionally literate in a healthy way and in a way that was supported by the community reduced antisocial approaches to intrapersonal conflicts among the participants.

Cultural Tool 5: The Spirit of Communalism

Connections required all participants to do 75 hours of community service work in their respective communities each year. Organizing and participating in community service projects taught participants about civic issues and helped them develop important decision-making and communication skills while underscoring the importance of taking the initiative to solve problems in their communities. Alumni are expected to return to their communities and collaborate with other community service projects, which include tutoring high school and elementary school students; assisting with neighborhood beautification projects; tutoring and mentoring children in homeless shelters; facilitating preventive workshops on topics such as gangs, drugs, teenage pregnancy, and dropping out of school; and serving as big brothers/big sisters to elementary school students in the community.

Community service benefited Connections participants as much as did the community. Afya elaborated on how his community involvement led to a college scholarship:

> One reason why I was able to go to college, I actually got a scholarship. I think it was a $2000 scholarship because of my community service efforts. . . . I wasn't doing these things to get anything. I didn't even know I could get anything for doing it except for fulfillment,'cuz I enjoyed doing it. I was a part of student council. This is something that we said we would do for community service. I did it. It was very rewarding and because of my, you know, my obedience and love for doing the work, I was rewarded.

Malik talked about how assisting with a neighborhood beautification project inspired other neighborhood residents to come out and join in the project:

> You know, just 15 youths coming out cleaning up the block, you know, "What's going on?" . . . "Why you doin' this, why you doing that?" 'Cuz you know, don't you want your block to look, you know, look decent? So people started to come out and help and, you know, that made me realize that everyone isn't bad. Everyone doesn't want to have a nasty block, a nasty neighborhood, but it just takes some initiative, or it takes people to just take that initiative and start to do things on their own.

Community service activities in Africa proved to be some of the most inspirational and memorable aspects of the students' trips. Makini talked about how meaningful Connections' community service in Africa was for him:

> One of them, I would say, is the community service we did in Africa, buildin' the school. . . . Just buildin' the school, workin' in the village, buildin' the desks and the chairs, you know, just those smiles on the faces of those little kids you know, just touchin' my heart, you know. And then we donated to [pause] hospitals. I cried every time I left. It was like a home away from home for me. You know, the way those people made me feel. . . . They really wanted to know how I felt, what my sisters were doin', how I was treated, how I felt about bein' treated a certain way.

They really wanted to know, and, honestly, these were people who didn't have nothin'. Just how they felt good about us comin' there to make a difference and really bein' able, really bein' in a space where we didn't want anything for our service in return. We just wanted to do this. This is a part of our mission. My mission. I think those two huge things, you know, stand out. I mean, we did other small community service projects, but that's the one that will always stick with me forever.

The fact that the participants found community service to be rewarding and beneficial is extremely promising, given that preliminary empirical evidence suggests that increased collective efficacy as demonstrated by community service reduces the level of violence in a community (Bowman, 1989; Jagers, 1993; Sampson, Raudenbush, & Earls, 1997; Ward, 1995; Warfield-Coppock, 1992). Furthermore, the bonding and comradeship that occurs within prosocial peer groups, such as those involved in community service, can be highly influential in reducing antisocial behavior. Kweli described the trust that grew between participants:

The social atmosphere is a big strength. The trust, cuz, to still this day, everybody in there, if I ever see them on the street, I can trust'em. Cuz you've been exposed to that. They've been open with you and you've been open with them.

Cultural Tool 6: Empathy/Affect

Empathy, sensitivity to another's feelings or ideas, is critical to positive growth and development. It suggests a very close relationship between persons, especially one resulting in mutual understanding or affection. Conversely, Machiavellianism is a steadfast focus on personal achievement, a willingness to exploit others to achieve one's desired goals. Street culture is Machiavellian. "Only the strong survive" or "I gotta get mine, you gotta get yours" self-centeredness is prevalent among young African American males who belong to street culture (Jagers, 1993). At the time of this study, the most popular manifestation of this phenomenon was "thug life." Many Connections respondents said young African Americans who identified with thug life glamorized exploitative and opportunistic behavior and were willing to use deception or criminal activity to fulfill needs, wants, and desires—all typically Machiavellian. Gansta rap also increased role strain among African American youth.

Where thug life and street culture fostered increased role strain, there were several components of the Connections intervention program that fostered the Afro cultural tool of empathy among the participants. For example, the process of clearing allowed all group members to experience the most personal and private life experiences of other participants. In a focus group discussion, one member gave an account of a clearing ritual that was designed to allow students to purge themselves of problems that were troubling them:

This girl started crying. Nothing touched me more when I seen the sister crying and other people crying. I'm wondering, why are they crying so much?

Man, I want to know, you know what I'm saying? You get this feeling and you want to purge yourself, too. Man, maybe my life ain't as bad, you know what I'm saying?

These activities allowed the students to experience the misfortunes of others, which made them more empathetic. Being privy to their fellow participants' life traumas brought them closer together, also increasing the empathy.

Many of the Connections participants noted their trip to Africa and community service experiences made them appreciate their own family situations and communities more and feel empathy for the children in the shelters and for their African ancestors. The most moving and memorable aspect of the trips to Africa, according to the students, was their visit to the dungeons where captured Africans were held prior to being shipped off to become slaves. Visiting the dungeons was part of completing the Connections rites of passage. Mwazaji gave a firsthand account of what it was like to experience the dungeons:

> I have walked through the "door of no return" [the narrow exit passage from the dungeon to the boats that carried the enslaved to the ship] and come back. I visited the Cape Coast Slave Castle where my ancestors were held. I touched the wall. I walked on the floor. I saw the blood that was left on the wall untouched. I saw the fingerprints on the walls, little love symbols. Just to stand and know made me cry.

Cultural Tool 7: Spirituality/African Centeredness

The Afro cultural orientation involves spirituality. Spirituality is the enacted belief that all elements of reality contain a certain amount of life force. Spirituality is central in African-centered ontology, cosmology, and axiology; in its ideology, ethos, and worldview; and in adherents' behavior, values, and attitudes. Therefore, where there is African culture in any form, there is spirituality. The two are interlocked.

The principle of *Sankofa* is a mainstay in the Connections program. *Sankofa* is a principle from the Akan people of West Africa, and its translation means "return to fetch it" or "return to your source." Connections uses this principle to help its participants confront the challenges of life transitions and other stressful events, which appear to be central to young Blacks' identity crises that lead to violence. When participants are challenged with making difficult decisions about their life's purpose, they are challenged by the staff to do a personal *Sankofa*. Afya explains how the concept might help young people who are challenged by risky behavior that leads to violence:

> Going back, being able to find out how we once lived our lives. I believe that the youth and other people in general would be able to see that being violent is not a part of our culture. And it has nothing to do with how we live. And oftentimes, unfortunately, the media portrays it. . . . They project those things on to us and that make me very angry considering the fact that one reason why I believe we are

using these substances [drugs] is because we seem to think we have to do things the way they do things. This is how they solve their problems. "They" being Europeans.

Central to the Connections intervention program mission was the process of cultivating spirituality among the participants. The rituals of libation and smudging, among others, were obligatory at every Connections gathering. Libation is a traditional African ritual that symbolizes the calling forth of one's ancestors to participate in the event. This ritual also was used to invoke the spirits of the ancestors who were perceived to be helpers of their earthly relatives. Smudging symbolized the process of spiritual cleansing of a sacred ritual space.

Spirituality was an Afro cultural tool of particular interest in this study because preliminary empirical data indicated that spirituality, as it is practiced in Afro cultural rites, seemed to function as a protective factor against violence-related behaviors (Bowman, 1989; Hudley et al., 1998; Jagers, 1993; Jagers et al., 1993; Mattaini & Lowery, 2000; Ward, 1995; Warfield-Coppock, 1992).

Personal emic cultural resources are traditional core cultural patterns from prior generations mobilized in personal affairs. A key tradition in African spirituality included in Connections was the deification of African ancestors as the helpers of their descendants in the material world. These young people perceived themselves as being protected by their ancestors, which made carrying weapons and engaging in other risky behaviors unnecessary. Commenting on how young people might behave differently if they thought they had the protection of ancestors, Afya said,

> They wouldn't have to worry about carrying a gun. They wouldn't even think about doing anything to anybody else or bodily harm. It wouldn't be like waking up everyday, "Oh, man it's a struggle and I gotta look out for myself and I need to be a part of this organization [street gang] cuz they got my back." They gotta protect me cuz they have no power without what? The source, the omnipotent, without all those other positive, you know, entities there to protect him or her. That's why I say I don't need no gun. I know I don't need a gun. I know this now. I think that even my family believes it because growing up, we had a gun in the house. My father had a gun, and if somebody came to the door, boom, boom, boom at night, he'd be like "Who the hell is it?" He would have his gun in his hand. I remember that. And that gun is probably still in the house, but it's so old it probably doesn't work anymore. We don't have bullets in the house. We don't need a gun because we understand who we are now. We've grown as a family. That's why I'm like whatever, ain't no bullet gon' hit me, you know.

Another core component of Connections is to help its participants address life difficulties in a way that is solution focused. The following praise by Makini is an example of how the director of the program, nicknamed Z by the participants, empowered him with an alternative to physical fighting:

> Z would talk about, we would have heated discussions about not fightin' with your fist but with your mind, fightin' with your spirit. And just how he broke it down,

that was cold [impressively clever] to me, to be able to fight you with my words and my mind. And even without sayin' anything. So learnin' the power that I hold, the weapon, my mind is a weapon. So I always carry a weapon.

Instilling an Afro Cultural Social Ethos and Spirituality

The youth violence literature has called for interventions that are gender specific and culturally based for African American youth in general and young African American males specifically (Bowman, 1990; Gibbs, 1988; Jagers, 1993; Ward, 1995). To answer this call, the Connections intervention program went beyond simply reconnecting youth with family, community, and racial group. Work by Jagers et al. (1993) reported on a large effort to reestablish a communal base and introduce spiritual and affective issues. This transitional process facilitates the cultural transmission that Bowman (1990) and others have consistently called for. The Connections program sought to instill an Afro cultural social ethos and spirituality by focusing on four areas. First, the program made a considerable effort to introduce traditional African and African American values, morals, and ethics. The traditional societal African values of "we," "cooperation," and "the internal" opposed the Euro-American societal values of "I," "competition," and "the external" (Kunjufu, 1986). The principles of the *Nguzo Saba*, the Theory of Kawaida, were central to these values (Karenga, 2003). Second, the program promoted a Black value system (as set forth by Jordan, 1981) that stressed the importance of commitment to God, the Black community, the Black family, self-discipline, and self-respect. Third, the program attempted to promote dedication to the pursuit of excellence and education and the disavowal of the pursuit of middle-class status, or the Anglo cultural value system. Fourth, the participants were encouraged to adhere to an Afro cultural value system (Kunjufu, 1986).

The program also instilled a sense of empathy and compassion for others. Connections participants had the opportunity to develop a sense of community and a perspective of the community as a village. By learning collective efficacy, the participants understood the importance of interdependence and increased communal values, which can help to decrease delinquent behavior (Sampson et al., 1997). Finally, social cohesion among the participants grew from working to lessen the degree of violence in the community (Sampson et al., 1997). According to Bell (1997), interpersonal conflict leads to the greatest degree of fatal social deterioration among young African Americans. To solve these problems, the staff was trained in intensive conflict resolution and anger management skills.

Suggestions for Future Research

The literature proves that more rigorous evaluation, both quantitative and qualitative, of promising programs for youth violence prevention is warranted

(Cooper et al., 2000; Prothrow-Stith, 1987; Tolan & Guerra, 1994). Recent research on the likelihood and pattern of violent acts and victimization by ethnic group suggests a need to understand violence within a cultural context. Evaluations of violence prevention programs that alter behavior in Black youth, that are culturally specific, that are developmentally appropriate, and that are conducted by African American adults are badly needed. Much of the prevention directed at this group has been ineffective.

Identity and social development programs designed to counter violence by providing African-centered moral education and fellowship and leadership training have become increasingly popular. However, evaluation research on rites-of-passage programs has been minimal, and evaluations of culturally specific rites-of-passage programs are almost nonexistent (McKenry, Kim, Bedell, Alford, & Gavazzi, 1997).

Research on the historical and nonnormative influences on antisocial behavior development is shallow. For example, there are virtually no data on the effects of cultural disconnection and patterns of antisocial behavior among African American youth. The impact and spectrum of nonnormative influences on antisocial behavior at various stages in the life cycle and how these differences vary across and within cultures and subcultures are topics of obvious importance.

We need to know more about the age-related changes in African American youths' motives and behaviors and whether various antisocial behaviors differ in the degree to which they are due to ontogenetic or nonnormative factors. Although too few studies have been done to be able to make any definitive statements concerning an Afro cultural orientation, preliminary indications are that an Afro cultural ethos may be associated with increased empathy and reduced aggressive and deviant behavior among young, African American males (Bowman, 1990; Hudley & Graham, 1995; Jagers, 1993; Ward, 1995).

The Connections intervention program appears, on the basis of preliminary evidence (Hudley et al., 1998; Jagers et al., 1993; Mattaini & Lowery, 2000) to be successful in keeping adolescents safe, in reducing their levels of risk behavior, and in providing them with ways of diffusing or avoiding potentially dangerous situations despite their continued residence in inner-city communities known for high levels of violence, crime, poverty, and drug use.

Connections staff attempted to make at-risk youth more aware of their adverse responses to environmental and social disorder and to help them to feel more committed to, and responsible for, their community, and as a result perhaps reducing their inclination or desire to bring harm to the people there. The program appears to equip students with life skills that will help them to make healthy decisions and become educated community leaders.

REFERENCES

Ajzen, I. (1985). From intentions to actions: A theory of planned behavior. In J. Kuhl & J. Beckman (Eds.), *Action control: From cognition to behavior* (pp. 11–39). New York: Springer.

Alexander, J., Pugh, C., & Parsons, B. (1998). *Functional family therapy* (Blueprints for Violence Prevention, Book Three). Boulder: Center for the Study and Prevention of Violence, Institute of Behavioral Science, University of Colorado at Boulder.

Allen, G. E. (1993). Modern biological determinism: The violence initiative, the Human Genome Project, and the new eugenics. In M. Fortune & E. Mendelsohn (Eds.), *The practice of human genetics* (pp. 1–23). Dordrecht, The Netherlands: Kluwer.

American Psychological Association, Commission on Violence and Youth. (1993). *Violence & youth: Psychology's response.* Washington, DC: Author.

Ani, M. (1994). *Yurugu: An African-centered critique of European cultural thought and behavior.* Trenton, NJ: Africa World Press.

Asante, M. K. (1987). *The Afrocentric idea.* Philadephia: Temple University Press.

Baltes, P. B. (1987). Theoretical propositions of life-span developmental psychology: On the dynamics between growth and decline. *Developmental Psychology, 23,* 611–626.

Bandura, A. (1977). Self-efficacy: Toward a unifying theory of behavioral change. *Psychological Review, 84,* 191–215.

Battistich, V. & Hom, A. (1997). The relationship between students' sense of their school as a community and their involvement in problem behavior. *American Journal of Public Health, 87,* 1997–2001.

Bell, C. C. (1997). Community violence: Causes, prevention, and intervention. *Journal of the National Medical Association, 89,* 657–662.

Bellamy, N. D., Hayes, J. G., Sorenson, S. L., Delorey, M., Chow, D., & Walsh, E. M. (1997). *Youth violence prevention: A resource manual for preventing violence in public housing and community settings.* U.S. Department of Housing and Urban Development, Office of Crime Prevention and Security, in collaboration with the Centers for Disease Control. Bethesda, MD: SPARTA Consulting Corporation.

Bernard, H. R. (1988). *Research methods in cultural anthropology.* Newbury Park, CA: Sage.

Black, M. M. & Ricardo, I. B. (1994). Drug use, drug trafficking, and weapon carrying among low-income, African-American, early adolescent boys. *Pediatrics, 93*(6, Suppl. 2), 1065–1072.

Borduin, C. M. (1999). Multisystemic treatment of criminality and violence in adolescents. *Journal of the American Academy of Child and Adolescent Psychiatry, 38,* 242–249.

Borduin, C. M., Mann, B. J., Cone, L. T., Henggeler, S. W., Fucci, B. R., Blaske, D. M., et al. (1995). Multisystemic treatment of serious juvenile offenders: Long-term prevention of criminality and violence. *Journal of Consulting and Clinical Psychology, 63,* 569–578.

Botvin, G. J., Mihalic, S. J., & Grotpeter, J. K. (1998). *Life skills training* (Blueprints for Violence Prevention, Book Five). Boulder: Center for the Study and Prevention of Violence, Institute of Behavioral Science, University of Colorado at Boulder.

Bowman, P. J. (1988). Post-industrial displacement and family role strains: Challenges to the black family. In P. Voydanoff & L. C. Makja (Eds.), *Families and economic distress* (pp. 75–96). Beverly Hills, CA: Sage.

Bowman, P. J. (1989). Research perspectives on black men: Role strain and adaptation across the adult life cycle. In R. L. Jones (Ed.), *Black adult development and aging* (pp. 117–150). Berkeley, CA: Cobb and Henry.

Bowman, P. J. (1990). The adolescent-to-adult transition: Discouragement among jobless black youth. In V. C. McLoyd & C. Flanagan (Eds.), *New directions for child development. No. 46. Economic stress: Effects on family life and child development* (pp. 87–105). San Francisco: Jossey-Bass.

Bowman, P. & Sanders, R. (1998). Unmarried African American fathers: A comparative life span analysis. *Journal of Comparative Family Studies, 29,* 39–56.

Brady Center to Prevent Gun Violence. (n.d.). *STOP2: Fact Sheets: Gun violence in the African American community.* Retrieved February 1, 2004, from http://www. bradycenter.org/stop2/facts/fs3.php

Braithwaite, R. L. & Taylor, S. E. (Eds.). (1992). *Health issues in the black community.* San Francisco: Jossey-Bass.

Brener, N. D., Simon, T. R., Krug, G., E., & Lowry, R. (1999). Recent trends in violence-related behaviors among high school students in the United States. *Journal of the American Medical Association, 282,* 440–446.

Bureau of Justice Assistance. (1998). *Addressing community gang problems: A practical guide.* Washington, DC: U.S. Department of Justice, Office of Justice Programs.

Center for the Study and Prevention of Violence. (1998). *Blueprints for violence prevention.* Boulder: Center for the Study and Prevention of Violence, Institute of Behavioral Science, University of Colorado at Boulder.

Chamberlain, P. & Mihalic, S. F. (1998). *Multidimensional treatment foster care* (Blueprints for Violence Prevention, Book Eight). Boulder: Center for the Study and Prevention of Violence, Institute of Behavioral Science, University of Colorado at Boulder.

Chavez, L., Hubbell, F. A., & Mishra, S. I. (1999). Ethnography and breast cancer control among Latinas and Anglo women in Southern California. In R. A. Hahn (Ed.), *Anthropology in public health: Bridging differences in culture and society* (pp. 117–141). New York: Oxford University Press.

Children's Defense Fund. (1985). *Black and white children in America: Key facts.* Washington, DC: Author.

Children's Defense Fund. (1986). *A children's defense budget: An analysis of the president's FY 1986 budget and children.* Washington, DC: Author.

Christie, R. & Geis, F. L. (1970). *Studies in Machiavellianism.* New York: Academic Press.

Cole, T. B. (1999). Ebbing epidemic: Youth homicide rate at a 14-year low. *Journal of the American Medical Association, 281,* 25–26.

Cooper, W. O., Lutenbacher, M., & Faccia, K. (2000). Components of effective youth violence prevention programs for 7- to 14-year-olds. *Archives of Pediatrics and Adolescent Medicine, 154,* 1134–1139.

Daly, A., Jennings, J., Beckett, J. O., & Leashore, B. R. (1995). Effective coping strategies of African Americans. *Social Work, 40,* 240–248.

Dembo, R. (1988). Delinquency among black male youth. In J. T. Gibbs (Ed.), *Young, black and male in America: An endangered species* (pp. 129–165). Dover, MA: Auburn House.

Demo, D. H. & Cox, M. J. (2000). Families with young children: A review of research in the 1990s. *Journal of Marriage and the Family, 62,* 876–895.

DeWalt, K. M., DeWalt, B. R. & Wayland, C. B. (1998). Participant observation. In H. R. Bernard (Ed.), *Handbook of methods in cultural anthropology* (pp. 259–300). Walnut Creek, CA: Altamira Press.

DiIulio, J. J., Jr. (1994). The question of black crime. *The Public Interest, 117*(Fall), 3–32.

Dodge, K. A. (1993). Social cognitive mechanisms in the development of conduct disorder and depression. *Annual Review of Psychology, 44,* 559–584.

Edmonson, H. & Bullock, L. (1998). Youth with aggressive and violent behaviors: Pieces of a puzzle. *Preventing School Failure, 42,* 135–141.

Eisenberg, N. & Fabes, R.A. (1988). The development of prosocial behavior from a life-span perspective. *Life-Span Development and Behavior, 9,* 173–203.

Eliade, M. (1965). *Rites and symbols of initiation: The mysteries of birth and rebirth* (W. R. Trask, Trans.). New York: Harper & Row.

Elkins, I. J., Iacono, W. G., Doyle, A. E., & McGue, M. (1997). Characteristics associated with the persistence of antisocial behavior: Results from recent longitudinal research. *Aggression and Violent Behavior, 2,* 101–124.

Emerson, R. M., Fretz, R. I., & Shaw, L. L. (1995). *Writing ethnographic fieldnotes.* Chicago: University of Chicago Press.

Environmental Protection Agency. (1998, July 8–9). *Proceedings of the 1998 Children at Risk Conference: Environmental health issues in the Great Lakes region, Chicago.* Retrieved on November 4, 2009, from http://www.epa.gov/reg5rcra/wptdiv/children/carproc.pdf

Erchak, G. M. (1984). Cultural anthropology and spouse abuse. *Current Anthropology, 25,* 331–332.

Featherman, D. (1983). Life-span perspectives in social science research. *Life-Span Development and Behavior, 5,* 1–57.

Federal Trade Commission. (2000). *Marketing violent entertainment to children: A review of self-regulation and industry practices in the motion picture, music recording & electronic game industries.* Washington, DC: Author.

Fishbein, M. (1979). A theory of reasoned action: Some applications and implications. In H. Howe & M. Page (Eds.), *Nebraska Symposium on Motivation: Vol. 27. Beliefs, attitudes, and values* (pp. 65–116). Lincoln: University of Nebraska Press.

Flay, B. R. & Petraitis, J. (1994). The theory of triadic influence: A new theory of health behavior with implications for preventive interventions. *Advances in Medical Sociology, 4,* 19–44.

Freire, P. (1997). *Pedagogy of the oppressed.* New York: Continuum.

Freudenberg, N., Eng, E., Flay, B., Parcel, G., Rogers, T., & Wallerstein, N. (1995). Strengthening individual and community capacity to prevent disease and promote health: In search of relevant theories and principles. *Health Education Quarterly, 22,* 290–306.

Furin, J. J. (1997). You have to be your own doctor: Sociocultural influences on alternative therapy use among gay men with AIDS in West Hollywood. *Medical Anthropology Quarterly, 11,* 489–504.

Garbarino, J. (1999). *Lost boys: Why our sons turn violent and how we can save them.* New York: The Free Press.

Garro, L. C. (2000). Cultural knowledge as resource in illness narratives: Remembering through accounts of illness. In C. Mattingly & L. C. Garro (Eds.), *Narrative and the cultural construction of illness and healing* (pp. 70–87). Berkeley: University of California Press.

Garro, L. C. & Mattingly, C. (2000). Narrative as construct and construction. In C. Mattingly & L. C. Garro (Eds.), *Narrative and the cultural construction of illness and healing* (pp. 1–49). Berkeley: University of California Press.

Gavazzi, S. M., Alford, K. A., & McKenney, P. C. (1996). Culturally specific programs for foster care youth: The sample case of an African-American rites of passage program. *Family Relations, 45,* 166–174.

Geis, F. L. (1978). Machiavellianism. In H. London & J. E. Exner (Eds.), *Dimensions of personality* (pp. 305–363). New York: Wiley.

Gennep, A. V. (1960). *The rites of passage* (M. B. Vizedom & G. L. Caffee, Trans.). Chicago: University of Chicago Press.

Gibbs, J. T. (Ed.). (1988). *Young, black, and male in America: An endangered species*. Dover, MA: Auburn House.

Glaser, B. G. & Strauss, A. L. (1967). *The discovery of grounded theory: Strategies for qualitative research*. Chicago: Aldine.

Graham, S., Hudley, C., & Williams, E. (1992). Attributional and emotional determinants of aggression among African American and Latino young adolescents. *Developmental Psychology, 28*, 731–740.

Greenbaum Ucko, L. (1994). Culture and violence: The interaction of Africa and America. *Sex Roles, 31*, 185–204.

Greenberg, M. T. & Kusche, C. (1998). *Promoting Alternative Thinking Strategies (PATHS)* (Blueprints for Violence Prevention, Book Ten). Boulder: Center for the Study and Prevention of Violence, Institute of Behavioral Science, University of Colorado at Boulder.

Greene, M. B. (1998). Youth violence in the city: The role of educational interventions. *Health Education and Behavior, 25*, 175–193.

Grund, J. P., Kaplan, C. D., & Adriaans, N. F. (1991). Needle sharing in the Netherlands: An ethnographic analysis. *American Journal of Public Health, 81*, 1602–1607.

Guerra, N. G. & Slaby, R. G. (1990). Cognitive mediators of aggression in adolescent offenders: 2. Intervention. *Developmental Psychology, 26*, 269–277.

Hagedorn, J. M. (1998). *The business of drug dealing in Milwaukee* (Wisconsin Policy Research Institute Report, Vol. 11, No. 5). Thiensville: Wisconsin Policy Research Institute.

Hahn, R. A. & Harris, K. W. (Eds.), (1999). *Anthropology in public health: Bridging differences in culture and society*. New York: Oxford University Press.

Hare, N. & Hare, J. (1985). *Bringing the black boy to manhood: The passage*. San Francisco: Black Think Tank.

Harris, A. R. & Lewis, M. (August, 1974). *Race and criminal deviance: A study of youthful offenders*. Paper presented at the Annual meeting of the American Sociological Association.

Harvey, D. (2001). Youth violence prevention through cultural change. *Social Work, 1*(1), 9–12.

Hazler, R. J. (1998). Promoting personal investment in systemic approaches to school violence. *Education, 119*, 222–231.

Henggler, S.W., Michalic, S.F., Rone, L., Thomas, C., & Timmons-Mitchell, J. (1998). *Multisystemic therapy* (Blueprints for Violence Prevention, Book Six). Boulder: Center for the Study and Prevention of Violence, Institute of Behavioral Science, University of Colorado at Boulder.

Hill, P. (1991). *Sankofa-1: A historical perspective of the rites of passage for the African American Youth*. Cleveland, OH: The Rites of Passage Institute & East End Neighborhood House.

Hill, R. B. (1997). *The strengths of African-American families: Twenty-five years later* (2nd ed.). Washington, DC: R&B.

Hoffman, M. L. (1984). Interaction of affect and cognition in empathy. In C. E. Izard, J. Kagan, & R. B. Zajonc (Eds.), *Emotions, cognition and behavior* (pp. 103–131). Cambridge, England: Cambridge University Press.

Holzer, H., Edelman, P., & Offner, P. (2006). *Reconnecting disadvantaged young men*. Washington, DC: Urban Institute Press.

Hudley, C. (1993). Comparing teacher and peer perceptions of aggression: An ecological approach. *Journal of Educational Psychology, 85,* 377–384.

Hudley, C., Britsch, B., Wakefield, W., Smith, T., Demorat, M., & Cho, S-J. (1998). An attribution retraining program to reduce aggression in elementary school students. *Psychology in the Schools, 35,* 271–282.

Hudley, C. & Graham, S. (1995). School based interventions for aggressive African American boys. *Applied & Preventive Psychology, 4,* 185–195.

Huizinga, D., Loeber, R., & Thornberry, T. P. (1994). *Urban delinquency and substance abuse: Initial findings.* Washington, DC: U.S. Department of Justice, Office of Juvenile Justice and Delinquency Prevention.

Hutson, H. R., Anglin, D., Kyriacou, D. N., Hart, J., & Spears, K. (1995). The epidemic of gang-related homicides in Los Angeles County from 1979 through 1994. *Journal of the American Medical Association, 274,* 1031–1036.

Illinois Council Against Handgun Violence. (1996). *Recent firearm statistics.* Chicago: Author.

Illinois Department of Public Health. (2000). *Selected vital statistics.* Springfield, IL: Author.

Israel, B. A., Checkoway, B., Schulz, A., & Zimmerman, M. (1994). Health education and community empowerment: Conceptualizing and measuring perceptions of individual, organizational, and community control. *Health Education Quarterly, 21,* 149–170.

Jagers, R. J. (1993). Culture and problem behaviors among inner-city African-American youth: Further explorations. *Journal of Adolescence, 19,* 371–381.

Jagers, R. J. & Mock, L. O. (1993). Culture and social outcomes among African American children: An Afrographic exploration. *Journal of Black Psychology, 19,* 391–405.

Jagers, R. J., Smith, ?., Mock, L.O., & Dill, (1993). *An Afro cultural social ethos: Orientations, enculturation and social correlates among inner-city youth.* [Unpublished paper]. Chicago: University of Illinois at Chicago.

Janz, N. K. & Becker, M. H. (1984). The health belief model: A decade later. *Health Education Quarterly, 11,* 1–47.

Johnson, J. C. (1990). *Selecting ethnographic informants.* Newbury, CA: Sage.

Jordan, V. (1981). *The Black value system.* Chicago: Trinity United Church of Christ.

Judd, C. M., Smith, E. R., & Kidder, L. H. (1991). *Research methods in social relations* (6th ed.). Fort Worth, TX: Holt, Rinehart, and Winston.

Kachur, S. P., Stennies, G. M., Powell, K. E., Modzeleski, W., Stephens, R., Murphy, et al. (1996). School-associated violent deaths in the United States, 1992 to 1994. *Journal of the American Medical Association, 275,* 1729–1733.

Kaljee, L. M., Stanton, B., Ricardo, I., & Whitehead, T. L. (1995). Urban African American adolescents and their parents: Perceptions of violence within and against their communities. *Human Organization, 54,* 373–382.

Karenga, M. (2003). *Kawaida theory: An African communitarian philosophy.* Los Angeles: University of Sankore Press.

Kawachi, I., Kennedy, B. P., & Glass, R. (1999). Social capital and self-rated health: A contextual analysis. *American Journal of Public Health, 89,* 1187–1193.

Kazdin, A. E., Bass, D., Siegel, T., & Thomas, C. (1989). Cognitive-behavioral therapy and relationship therapy in the treatment of children referred for antisocial behavior. *Journal of Consulting and Clinical Psychology, 57,* 522–535.

Kelle, U. (1997). Theory building in qualitative research and computer programs for the management of textual data. *Sociological Research Online, 2(2).* Retrieved from http://www.socresonline.org.uk/2/2/1.html

Kellermann, A. L., Fuqua-Whitley, D. S., Rivara, F. P., & Mercy, J. (1998). Preventing youth violence: What works? *Annual Review of Public Health, 19,* 271–292.

Kennedy, B. P., Kawachi, I., Prothrow-Stith, D., Lochner, K., & Gupta, V. (1998). Social capital, income inequality, and firearm violent crime. *Social Science and Medicine, 47,* 7–17.

Kenyatta, J. (1979). *Facing Mount Kenya: The traditional life of the Gikuyu.* London: Heinemann Educational Books. (Originally work published in 1938)

Khan, M. E. & Manderson, L. (1992). Focus groups in tropical disease research: Some methodological issues. *Health Policy and Planning, 7,* 56–66.

Khanna, S. K. (1997). Traditions and reproductive technology in an urbanizing north Indian village. *Social Science & Medicine, 44,* 171–180.

Komro, K., Flay, B., Zelli, A., Rashid, J., & Hu, F. (1996). *Where and how young adolescents living in disadvantaged neighborhoods in Chicago obtain tobacco, alcohol, marijuana, knives and guns.* Paper presented at the Annual Meeting for the American Public Health Association, Chicago.

Kotulak, R. (1993, December 12). Unlocking the mind: Roots of violence. *Chicago Tribune,* p. 1.

Kratz, C. A. (1993). *Affecting performance: Meaning, movement, and experience in Okiek women's Initiation.* Washington, DC: Smithsonian Institution Press.

Kunjufu, J. (1986). *Countering the conspiracy to destroy black boys* (Vol. 1, Rev. ed.). Chicago: African American Images.

Lattimore, C. B., Mihalic, S. F., Grotpeter, J. K., & Taggart, R. (1998). *The Quantum Opportunities Program* (Blueprints for Violence Prevention, Book Four). Boulder: Center for the Study and Prevention of Violence, Institute of Behavioral Science, University of Colorado at Boulder.

Lefkowitz, M. M., Eron, L. D., Walder, L. O., & Huesmann, L. R. (1977). *Growing up to be violent: A longitudinal study of the development of aggression.* New York: Pergamon Press.

Loeber, R. & Farrington, D. P. (Eds.). (1998). *Serious & violent juvenile offenders: Risk factors and successful interventions.* Thousand Oaks, CA: Sage Publications.

Loury, A. K. (2000, April). Fighting the odds: African American men are in crisis. Our reporter confronts the numbers—and himself. *The Chicago Reporter, 29,* 4–16.

MacKellar, L. & Yanagishita, M. (1995, July/August). Homicide rates in the U.S. rise. *The Futurist, 29,* 54–55.

Mattaini, M., Lowery, C. & The PEACE POWER! Working Group. (2000). Constructing cultures of non-violence: The PEACE POWER! toolkit. In D. S. Sandhu & C. B. Aspy (Eds.), *Violence in American schools: A practical guide for counselors* (pp. 123–138). Alexandria, VA: American Counseling Association.

Mauer, M. (1990). *Young black men and the criminal justice system: A growing national problem.* Washington, DC: The Sentencing Project.

Mauer, M. & Huling, T. (1995). *Young black Americans and the criminal justice system: Five years later.* Washington, DC: The Sentencing Project.

Mayer, G. R. (1995). Preventing antisocial behavior in the schools. *Journal of Applied Behavior Analysis, 28,* 467–478.

McCord, J. & Tremblay, R. E. (Eds.). (1992). *Preventing antisocial behavior: Interventions from birth through adolescence.* New York: The Guilford Press.

McDermott, R. J. (1993). Qualitative evaluation models, methods, and designs. In P. D. Sarvela & R. J. McDermott (Eds.), *Health education evaluation and measurement: A practitioner's perspective.* Madison, WI: Brown & Benchmark.

McGill, D. E. (Ed.). (1997). *Big Brothers Big Sisters of America* (Blueprints for Violence Prevention, Book Two). Boulder: Center for the Study and Prevention of Violence, Institute of Behavioral Science, University of Colorado at Boulder.

McKenry, P. C., Kim, H. K., Bedell, T., Alford, K., & Gavazzi, S. M. (1997). An Africentric rites of passage program for adolescent males. *Journal of African American Men*, 3, 7–20.

McLeroy, K. R., Bibeau, D., Steckler, A., & Glanz, K. (1988). An ecological perspective on health promotion programs. *Health Education Quarterly*, 15, 351–377.

McLeroy, K. R., Clark, N. M., Simons-Morton, B. G., Forster, J., Connell, C. M., Altman, D., et al. (1995). Creating capacity: Establishing a health education research agenda for special populations. *Health Education Quarterly*, 22, 390–405.

McLeroy, K. R., Steckler, A., Simons-Morton, B., Goodman, R. M., Gottlieb, N., & Burdine, J. (1993). Social science theory in health education: Time for a new model? *Health Education Research*, 8, 305–312.

McMahon, E. T. & Taylor, P. A. (1990). *Citizens' action handbook on alcohol and tobacco billboard advertising.* Washington, DC: Center for Science in the Public Interest.

Mensah, A. (1990). *Preliminary materials for the rites of passage of our youth.* Milwaukee: University of Wisconsin-Extension Center for Urban Community Development.

Miles, M. B. & Huberman, A. M. (1994). *Qualitative data analysis: An expanded sourcebook* (2nd ed.). Thousand Oaks, CA: Sage.

Mincy, Ron. (2006). *Black males left behind.* Washington, DC: Urban Institute Press.

Mitchell, M. A. & Daniels, S. (1989). Black-on-black homicide: Kansas City's response. *Public Health Reports*, 104, 605–608.

Moody, K. A., Childs, J. C., & Sepples, S. B. (2003). Intervening with at-risk youth: Evaluation of the Youth Empowerment and Support Program. *Pediatric Nursing*, 29(4), 263–270.

Nadel, H., Spellman, M., Alvarez-Canino, T., Lausell-Bryant, L. L., & Landsberg, G. (1996). The cycle of violence and victimization: A study of the school-based intervention of a multidisciplinary youth violence-prevention program. *American Journal of Preventive Medicine*, 12(Suppl. 5), 109–119.

Nesselroade, J. R. & Baltes, P. B. (Eds.). (1979). *Longitudinal research in the study of behavior and development.* New York: Academic Press.

Nobles, W. (1985). *Africanity and the black family: The development of a theoretical model.* Oakland, CA: Black Family Institute Publications.

Nobles, W. (1990). *African centered educational praxis.* San Francisco: San Francisco State University, Center for Applied Cultural Studies and Educational Achievement.

Office of Violence Prevention. (2000). *Chicago violence prevention strategic plan.* Chicago: Chicago Department of Public Health.

Ogbu, J. U. & Wilson, J., Jr. (1990). *Mentoring minority youth: A framework.* New York: Institute for Urban and Minority Education, Teachers College, Columbia University.

Olds, D. L., Hill, P. L., Mihalic, S. F., & O'Brien, R. A. (1998). *Prenatal and infancy home visitation by nurses* (Blueprints for Violence Prevention, Book Seven). Boulder: Center for the Study and Prevention of Violence, Institute of Behavioral Science, University of Colorado at Boulder.

Onuh, C. O. (1992). *Christianity and the Igbo rites of passage: The prospects of inculturation.* New York: Peter Lang.

Ottenberg, S. (1989). *Boyhood rituals in an African society: An interpretation.* Seattle: University of Washington Press.

Oyserman, D., Sakamoto, I., & Lauffer, A. (1998). Cultural accommodation: Hybridity and the framing of social obligation. *Journal of Personality and Social Psychology, 74,* 1606–1618.

Patton, M. Q. (1980). *Qualitative evaluation methods.* Beverly Hills, CA: Sage.

Pinnock, D. & Douglas-Hamilton, D. (1997). *Gangs, rituals and rites of passage.* Cape Town, South Africa: African Sun Press with the Institute of Criminology, University of Cape Town.

Powell, A. (1996). *Message'n a bottle: The 40 oz. scandal.* Chicago: Renaissance Press.

Prochaska, J. O., DiClemente, C. C., & Norcross, J. C. (1992). In search of how people change: Applications to addictive behaviors. *American Psychologist, 47*(9), 1102–1114.

Prothrow-Stith, D. (1987). *Violence prevention: Curriculum for adolescents.* Newton, MA: Education Development Center.

Prothrow-Stith, D. (1995). The epidemic of youth violence in America: Using public health prevention strategies to prevent violence. *Journal of Health Care for the Poor and Underserved, 6,* 95–101.

Prothrow-Stith, D. & Weissman, M. (1991). *Deadly consequences.* New York: Harper Collins.

Public Health Reports. (1991). Forum on youth violence in minority communities: Setting the agenda for prevention. A summary. *Journal of the U.S. Public Health Service, 106,* 225–269.

Rao, V. (1997). Wife beating in rural south India: A qualitative and econometric analysis. *Social Science and Medicine, 44*(8), 1169–1180.

Reppucci, N. D., Woolard, J. L., & Fried, C. S. (1999). Social, community, and preventive interventions. *Annual Review of Psychology, 50,* 387–418.

Rice, P. L. & Ezzy, D. (1999). *Qualitative research methods: A health focus.* New York: Oxford University Press.

Rogers, A. B. (1988). *The development and evaluation of a violence prevention program for secondary schools.* Unpublished doctoral dissertation, Georgia State University, Atlanta.

Rosenberg, M. L., Powell, K. E., & Hammond, R. (1997). Applying science to violence prevention. *Journal of the American Medical Association, 277,* 1641–1642.

Rosenstock, I. M., Strecher, V. J., & Becker, M. H. (1988). Social learning theory and the health belief model. *Health Education Quarterly, 15,* 175–183.

Rosenthal, T. T. (1989). Using ethnography to study nursing education. *Western Journal of Nursing Research, 11,* 115–127.

Sampson, R. J., Raudenbush, S. W., & Earls, F. (1997). Neighborhoods and violent crime: A multilevel study of collective efficacy. *Science, 277,* 918–924.

Satcher, D. (1999). Unlearning violence. *Public Health Reports, 114,* 478–479.

Satel, S. (1996, December 12). The politicization of public health. *Wall Street Journal,* p. A12.

Satel, S. L. (1997, February 17). Race for the cure. *New Republic,* pp. 12–14.

Schiele, J. H. (2000). *Human services and the Afrocentric paradigm.* Binghamton, NY: Haworth Press.

Scrimshaw, S. C. M. & Hurtado, E. (1987). *Rapid assessment procedures for nutrition and primary health care: Anthropological approaches to improving programme effectiveness.* Tokyo: United Nations University.

Scott, K. K., Tepas, J. J., III, Frykberg, E., Taylor, P. M., & Plotkin, A. J. (2002). Turning point: Rethinking violence-evaluation of program efficacy in reducing adolescent violent crime recidivism. *Journal of Trauma*-Injury *Infection and Critical Care, 53*(1), 21–27.

Smith, P., Flay, B. R., Bell, C. C., & Weissberg, R. P. (2001). The protective influence of parents and peers in violence avoidance among African American youth. *Maternal and Child Health Journal, 5,* 245–252.

Spradley, J. (1980). *Participant observation.* New York: Holt, Rinehart and Winston.

Steckler, A., McLeroy, K. R., Goodman, R. M., Bird, S. T., & McCormick, L. (1992). Integrating qualitative and quantitative methods. *Health Education Quarterly, 19,* 1–135.

Stewart, D. W. & Shamdasani, P. N. (1990). *Focus groups: Theory and practice.* Newbury Park, CA: Sage.

Stokols, D. (1992). Establishing and maintaining healthy environments: Toward a social ecology of health promotion. *American Psychologist, 47,* 6–22.

Swindler, A. (1986). Culture and action: Symbols and strategies. *American Sociological Review, 51,* 273–286.

Takahashi, K. (1990). Affective relationships and their lifelong development. *Life-Span Development and Behavior, 10,* 1–27.

Tierney, J. P. & Branch, A. Y. (1992). *College students as mentors for at-risk youth: A study of six Campus Partners in Learning programs.* Philadelphia: Public/Private Ventures.

Tolan, P. & Guerra, N. (1994). *What works in reducing adolescent violence: An empirical review of the field (F-888).* Boulder: Center for the Study and Prevention of Violence, Institute of Behavioral Science, University of Colorado at Boulder.

Tolan, P. H., Guerra, N. G., & Kendall, P. C. (1995). A developmental-ecological perspective on antisocial behavior in children and adolescents: Toward a unified risk and intervention framework. *Journal of Consulting and Clinical Psychology, 63,* 579–584.

Turner, V. (1987). Betwixt and between: The liminal period in rites of passage. In L. Mahdi, S. Foster, & M. Little (Eds.), *Betwixt & between: Patterns of masculine and feminine initiation* (pp. 3–19). LaSalle, IL: Open Court.

U.S. Bureau of Justice Statistics. 2002. *Homicide trends in the U.S.: Trends by race.* Washington, DC: U.S. Department of Justice, Office of Justice Programs.

U.S. Census Bureau. (2001). *Census 2000. Summary File 1.* Retrieved from http://www.nipc.cog.il.us/Y2K_SF1_prof_CA.pdf

Wallace, D. & Wallace, R. (1998). Scales of geography, time, and population: The study of violence as a public health problem. *American Journal of Public Health, 88,* 1853–1858.

Wallerstein, N. & Bernstein, E. (1994). Introduction to community empowerment, participatory education, and health. *Health Education Quarterly, 21,* 142–148.

Wallerstein, N. & Sanchez-Merki, V. (1994). Freirian praxis in health education: Research results from an adolescent prevention program. *Health Education Research, 9,* 105–118.

Ward, J. V. (1995). Cultivating a morality of care in African American adolescents: A culture-based model of violence prevention. *Harvard Educational Review, 65,* 175–188.

Warfield-Coppock, N. (1990). *Afrocentric theory and applications. Vol. I: Adolescent rites of passage.* Washington, DC: Baobab Associates.

Warfield-Coppock, N. (1992). The rites of passage movement: A resurgence of African-centered practices for socializing African American youth. *Journal of Negro Education*, *61*, 471–482.

Waterman, A. S. & Archer, S. L. (1990). A life-span perspective on identity formation: Developments in form, function, and process. *Life-Span Development and Behavior*, *10*, 29–57.

Waterson, A. (1997). Anthropological research and the politics of HIV prevention: Towards a critique of policy and priorities in the age of AIDS. *Social Science and Medicine*, *44*, 1381–1391.

Weitzman, M. (1998). Developmental effects of lead: Childhood lead poisoning: What's new, what's sadly not. *Proceedings of the 1998 Children at Risk Conference: Environmental health issues in the Great Lakes Region, July 8 and 9, 1998, Chicago.* (pp. 71–75). Retrieved November 4, 2009, from http://www.epa.gov/reg5rcra/wptdiv/children/carproc.pdf

Whitman, D. (1993, May 31). The untold story of what really happened in the L.A. riot. *U.S. News & World Report*, 34–57.

Wilson, A. N. (1990). *Black-on-black violence: The psychodynamics of black self-annihilation in service of white domination.* New York: Afrikan World Infosystems.

Wilson, A. N. (1992). *Understanding black adolescent male violence: Its remediation and prevention.* New York: Afrikan World Infosystems.

Wrightsman, L. S. (1992). *Assumptions about human nature: Implications for researchers and practitioners* (2nd ed.). Newbury Park, CA: Sage.

Yin, R. K. (1994). *Case study research: Design and methods* (2nd ed.). Thousand Oaks, CA: Sage.

Zeitlyn, S. & Rowshan, R. (1997). Privileged knowledge and mothers' "perceptions": The case of breast-feeding and insufficient milk in Bangladesh. *Medical Anthropology Quarterly*, *11*, 56–68.

16

Incarceration and Family Formation

CHARLES E. LEWIS, JR.

Conservatives have had a profound influence on social welfare policy during the course of the last three decades, beginning with the election of Ronald Reagan in 1980 and accelerating with the Republican takeover of the House of Representatives in 1994. The Republicans' prepared policy agenda—the Contract with America—ushered in an era of heightened personal responsibility. Jumpstarting an accountability of individuals was the transformation of welfare with the passage of the Personal Responsibility and Work Opportunity Reconciliation Act (PRWORA) in 1996. Work was now a requirement for assistance.

In addition, it was assumed by some that marriage, as well as work, was a tradition valued by responsible adults. One of the four goals of the PRWORA was to promote healthy marriages as a means to reduce poverty. In 2002, the Bush administration put teeth in that idea by proposing to spend $1.5 billion over 5 years on marriage promotion programs with an eye toward strengthening existing marriages while encouraging low-income couples to make the critical choice to get married. The Deficit Reduction Act of 2005 provided $150 million a year for five years for marriage promotion and responsible fatherhood programs.

Robert Rector (2005) of the Heritage Foundation is a prominent conservative who argues that the collapse of marriage is the primary cause of lingering poverty in the United States. Researchers Haskins and Sawhill (2003) echoed that sentiment by concluding that the U.S. poverty rate could be reduced by 71% through a combination of work and marriage. Ahituv and Lerman (2004) reached a similar conclusion that marriage enhances job stability and wage rates.

A significant body of research seems to support advocates of marriage promotion policies. A review of the literature by Lerman (2002) found substantial evidence that marriage has a positive association with economic and social outcomes for men, families, and children. The growth of single-mother families in the United States has been credited with a plethora of poor outcomes for children, from poverty to higher rates of school dropouts, substance use, teen pregnancy, and juvenile delinquency (Lang & Zagorsky, 2000; McLanahan & Sandefur, 1994).

The fact that children in single-mother households are more likely to be impoverished seems indisputable. Between 1968 and 2003, the percentage of all American children under age 18 living in single-mother households more than doubled, from 10.7% to 23% (U.S. Census Bureau 2004). The percentage of Black children under age 18 in these households rose from 29% in 1968 to 50.1% in 2003, compared with 18% among White children, up from 7% in 1968.

According to 2003 census data, more than two in five (41.7%) children[1] in female-headed households live below the poverty threshold, compared with fewer than one in ten (8.6%) living in married households. The numbers for Black children are abysmal, with nearly one-half living in poverty. Nearly twice as many (59.7%) Black children than White children (30.7%) younger than age 5 live below the poverty line. Black children living in married families fare much better, with just 11.2% under age 18 living below the poverty line. The late Senator Daniel Patrick Moynihan (1965) was among the first to raise the issue of problems caused by the growing number of single-mother families in the Black community in his groundbreaking report *The Negro Family: The Case for National Action*. Moynihan was pilloried for his characterization of Black families as "near total breakdown," although he attributed this erosion to the legacy of slavery.

Although the positive correlation between marriage and economic outcomes seems to be supported by ample research, other policy makers remain skeptical. They believe that unemployment, low wages, and poverty among males discourage marriage (Coontz & Folbre, 2002). Other policy makers caution that although some families and couples may benefit from marriage programs, there are a number of barriers to marriage that must be considered (Bendheim-Thomas Center, 2003). Sociologist William Julius Wilson (1987) broke ground with his theory that low marriage rates among African Americans were the result of the decreasing "marriageable pool" of Black men owing to their poor earnings and employment rates. Edin (2000) also suggested that women—particularly those on welfare or with low incomes—are averse to marrying men with poor economic viability, particularly those with a criminal history.

The evidence of the fragility of Black marital relationships goes back to the work of sociologist W. E. B. DuBois, whose 1899 study of Blacks in Philadelphia's seventh ward found low marriage rates attributable to the vestiges of slavery and the difficulties of supporting a family on insufficient wages. E. Franklin Frazier (1939) also found evidence of instability among Black families.

If significant barriers to marriage exist, such as unemployment, underemployment, poor education, and a history of incarceration, then conventional marriage-strengthening programs will fall short for a significant segment of low-income males. This is particularly true for African American males, who are overrepresented among the unemployed and underemployed and in the growing number of Americans who have been scarred by the criminal justice system. As resources for social welfare programs diminish, investment in marriage promotion strategies could mean balancing new program funding with cuts in traditional services that address these human capital deficits.

This chapter considers how incarceration of Black men, who are incarcerated at seven times the rate of White men, comes into play in a woman's decision to marry the father of her child. Incarceration has been shown to have significant negative effects on future earnings, and rates of re-arrest among men are high, both of which could make women hesitant to marry a man with a criminal past.

The Growth of Incarceration in the United States

According to the Bureau of Justice Statistics, the nation's prisons and jails held 2.1 million people in custody at midyear 2004 (Harrison & Beck, 2005). This is a tenfold increase since the early 1970s, when the prison population hovered around 200,000. By the year 2000, an astounding 6.3 million Americans were under supervision of federal and state criminal justice systems, representing 3.1% of the adult population in the United States, or 1 in every 32 adult residents (Beck & Karberg, 2000).

Although many point to the get-tough policies of the Reagan administration for this huge increase, the system expanded more during Bill Clinton's presidency, which saw 225,000 more prison and jail inmates added to the system than during the Reagan years. When Clinton took office, 1.4 million offenders were in the nation's prisons and jails; at his departure, more than 2 million people were behind bars and the country was spending more than $70 billion annually on criminal justice (Justice Policy Institute, 2001).

African American males continue to bear the brunt of these expansive prison policies. Although Black males are roughly 6% of the nation's population, they represent 40% of the nation's 2 million–plus prisoners. Black males are incarcerated at the rate of 4919 per 100,000, compared with 717 per 100,000 for White males. Almost 13% of all Black males between the ages of 20 and 29 years—critical years for family formation—were in prison and jail at midyear 2004, compared with 3.6% of Hispanics and 1.7% of Whites (Harrison & Beck, 2005).

Any barriers to family formation for the general population created by incarceration affect Black males significantly more because of their overrepresentation in the criminal justice system. If Edin (2000) and others are correct in their analysis of the reluctance of low-income women to marry men with incarceration histories, then efforts to promote marriage among low-income men and women will be severely hampered if the male has a prison or jail record.

Incarceration and Labor Market Outcomes

Before we discuss incarceration and family formation, it is important to review some of the literature on the association between incarceration and labor market outcomes, given that theory suggests that the links between marriage and incarceration are connected to poor labor market outcomes of males (Edin, 2000). Research in criminology and economics on the relationship between crime and the labor market has focused on the effects of economic disadvantage on criminal activity (e.g., Freeman, 1991; Hagan & Peterson, 1995). However, a few studies reverse the causal sequence to examine how involvement with the criminal justice system affects employment opportunities.

Using *Fragile Families* data, Lewis, Garfinkel, and Gao (2007) found that fathers who had been incarcerated worked and earned substantially less in the legitimate market than those who were never incarcerated. They found that fathers who had been incarcerated also worked and earned more in underground activities. Western (2002) used a nationally representative sample of young men, the National Longitudinal Survey of Youth (NLSY) and found that incarceration reduced wage rates by 16%.

An earlier study by Freeman (1991) found that incarceration reduced work probability by 25% to 30%. Waldfogel (1993) found that conviction of offenders who committed fraud or breached jobs that required trust reduced employment opportunities by 5% and depressed income by as much as 30%. Grogger (1995) found large incarceration effects on annual earnings, quarterly earnings, wage rates, and employment for both jail and prison experiences over time.

If fathers who had been incarcerated suffer significant labor market penalties, then one would expect lower marriage rates among incarcerated fathers. And the negative association with incarceration should be greater on marriage than on cohabitation, given that the former requires a legally binding and stronger economic tie between the couple.

Labor Market Outcomes and Family Formation

Becker (1981) first proposed a link between family formation and the labor market, suggesting that marriage and marital stability depended on couples having greater utility in marriage than as single persons. He linked the rise in divorce and decline in fertility to the increase in female labor market participation. There have been a number of studies since examining the confluence of greater female labor market participation and declines in marriage among the general population and particularly among African Americans.

A study by Schultz (1994) found men's market wages were significantly associated with more frequent marriage and higher fertility, and higher wage opportunities for women substantially reduced marriage and fertility. He found that Aid to Families with Dependent Children and Medicaid had modest effects on marriage and fertility.

Tzeng and Mare (1995) used a probability sample of 12,686 men and women in the NLSY for 1979–1987, the National Longitudinal Survey of Young Men, and the National Longitudinal Survey of Young Women to measure the effect of the labor market and socioeconomic factors on marital stability. They found that couples who were better educated and had stronger attachment to the workforce enjoyed more stable marriages. They attributed the lower socioeconomic status of Blacks to their high rates of marital dissolution.

Smock and Manning (1997) used data from the 1987–1988 National Survey of Families and Households and its follow-up survey in 1992–1994 to examine the effects of cohabiting partners' economic circumstances on their chance of marrying. They found significant effects only for men's economic circumstances. Men with higher earnings, greater education, and full-time employment had higher odds of marrying and lower odds of terminating the relationship. They found that women's economic circumstance had no effect on transitions out of cohabitation.

Using 1970, 1980, and 1990 U.S. census data, Blau, Kahn, and Waldfogel (2000) found that better labor markets for women and a less favorable ratio of marriageable men reduced marriage rates for young White women (16 to 24 years old) in all education groups. They found that better male market prospects raised rates among these women. They found similar effects among older White women (25 to 34 years old) and stronger effects for older Black women. Higher adult male unemployment rates and lower adult average wage rates lowered marriage rates.

A few studies support sociologist William Julius Wilson's thesis of the declining marriageable pool (see Darity & Myers, 1995; Lichter, McLaughlin, Kephart, & Landry, 1992; Testa & Krogh, 1995), arguing that the declining economic prospects of Black men were largely responsible for the worsening marriage rates among Black women. Mare and Winship (1991) attributed 20% of the decline in marriage among young Black men to declining job prospects, pointing out that marriage rates had declined among employed Black males as well.

Lerman (1989), however, disputed Wilson's theory, pointing out that marriage rates among marriageable men declined almost as much as they did for less marriageable men. He found that between 1973 and 1986, the percent married and living with their wives fell as much for college graduates and for less-educated groups suffering losses in earnings. Wood (1995), like Lerman, found that the dwindling marriageable pool of Black men accounted for only 3% to 4% of the falling marriage rates of young Black women during the 1970s.

Labor market theory suggests that poor economic prospects among unmarried men would render them less likely to marry or have stable unions. However, the evidence is inconclusive. Ellwood and Crane (1990) suggest that economic models have not been successful in explaining changes in Black or White families, which are the results of a "complex interaction of social, cultural, legal, and economic factors" that would be difficult to unweave (see also Dickson, 1993, p).

Incarceration and Family Formation

Few studies have focused specifically on how incarceration affects marital or cohabiting relationships. Although a substantial body of literature examines the impact of incarceration on families, few empirical studies have been published. Few, if any, studies have examined the effects of incarceration on family formation.

Although theory would suggest that incarceration has a negative effect on family formation, researchers caution that the marriage prospects of criminal offenders are poor even without incarceration (Western, Lopoo, & McLanahan, 2002). They warn that criminal offenders "may be egocentric, have little self-control, and have weak social connections to stable family and economic life" (p. 4).

A recent study conducted by Princeton University sociologist Bruce Western (2004) found that incarcerated men were only about half as likely to be married as noninstitutionalized men of the same age. Western cautions about the difficulty of studying the links between incarceration and marriage that—unlike economic factors—have tangled correlations among marriage, economic disadvantage, criminal behavior, and incarceration.

Western and McLanahan (2000) also used data from the *Fragile Families and Child Well-being Study* to examine the links between incarceration and cohabitation or marriage, using logistic regression analysis to determine the probability of a couple living together 1 year after the birth of their child. Based on the reports of mothers, they found that if the father had been incarcerated, he was 19% less likely to be cohabiting and 37% less likely to be married than fathers who were never incarcerated. They found that Black couples were half as likely to be living together as White couples and that Latinos had outcomes similar to Whites. The surprising finding here was that the effects using mother-reported data were stronger than those from fathers' reports.

Tracing the Link Between Incarceration and Marriage: Design of Current Study

The *Fragile Families and Child Well-being Study* tracks various outcomes of new parents who live in 20 large cities (with populations of 200,000 or more). The study contains rich criminal justice history data. The findings reported here are from the first wave of data collected in Austin, Texas, and Oakland, California. The Oakland and Austin cohorts consisted of 325 families each—250 unmarried couples and 75 married couples who served as a comparison group. Data were collected in Oakland at the Summit and Highland Hospitals from February 14, 1998 through June 15, 1998. Data were collected in all Austin birthing hospitals from April 9, 1999 through June 30, 1999.

All mothers who gave birth during the data collection period were approached in the hospital and asked to participate in the study. Approximately 93% of the mothers agreed to participate and provide locating information about the fathers, who were contacted at the hospital or shortly after the birth of the child. Approximately 90% of married fathers and 75% of unmarried fathers agreed to participate. The main advantage of *Fragile Families* data is that they contain not only self-reports of incarceration from the ex-offender but also reports from his child's mother, which may be more reliable than self-reports.

The sample includes 656 mothers and 524 fathers who were interviewed during the baseline phase. A follow-up was conducted 1 year after baseline data were collected. During the follow-up phase, 577 mothers and 441 fathers were interviewed again.

Because this sample excluded men who were not fathers, we could not detect the effects of incarceration on fertility. Because fathers are more likely to be in close relationships with the mothers of their children than men without children, it is reasonable to assume the effects would be greater among men without children.[2] We supplemented self-reported data on fathers, who were often difficult if not impossible to locate, with information obtained from the mothers, and in a few cases, fathers' reports on mothers. We used logistic regression analysis to examine the association between incarceration and the likelihood that the father would be married or cohabiting with his baby's mother at the time of birth.

The mean age of the fathers is 28 years old. About one-third of the sample is Black. Approximately 45% of the fathers are Latino, about 15% are White, and 4% are of another race. For the purposes of this study, if a respondent reported being Black and Latino, he was coded as Black. If he reported being Latino and White, he was coded Latino.

Based on mothers' reports, 28% of the fathers had been incarcerated, and 21% of the mothers reported incarceration when the father had not. Eighteen percent of the fathers interviewed reported having been incarcerated. The higher rate of incarceration reported by mothers provides evidence that fathers underreport their incarceration history. It is reasonable to believe that the mothers' reports are more accurate. They would know the father's incarceration history, and it is likely that some fathers would like to suppress these facts, particularly if they are trying to move beyond regrettable pasts.

Nearly 40% of the fathers in the sample did not complete high school, approximately 30% had a high school diploma or equivalent, less than one-quarter had attended college, and approximately 10% had graduated college or held a professional or postgraduate degree. More than one-quarter of the fathers (28%) reported that they had not been involved with their biological father.

About one-fifth (21%) reported that they had less than good health (fair or poor) or had an impairment that diminished their ability to work. Approximately 17% of the fathers had a problem with alcohol or drugs. One in ten fathers reported being depressed for 2 weeks or more after their child was born. About one-third of the fathers were married or cohabiting with the baby's mother at the time of birth.

The mean age of mothers in the sample was 25 years old. Slightly more than one-third (37%) were Black, 42% were Latino, 15% were White, and 5% were of another race. Nearly one-half of the mothers in the sample (45%) failed to complete high school. Slightly more than one-quarter (26%) earned a high school diploma or its equivalent, 20% attended some college, and 10% graduated college or held a professional or postgraduate degree.

Nearly one-third of the mothers (32%) had one other child in addition to the child reported in these data, and almost the same percentage (31%) had more than one child. Only 6% reported that they used alcohol or drugs during their pregnancy, and 16% said they smoked cigarettes. Almost all of the mothers (91%) reported their health during pregnancy as good or better.

Findings on Incarceration and Family Formation

Table 16.1 presents the results of cross-tabulations of incarceration and marriage and cohabitation. As expected, just 22% of the fathers who had been incarcerated were married to their baby's mother compared with 42% of the never-incarcerated fathers. The difference in cohabitation rates was not statistically significant; 47% of those who had been incarcerated were living with the mother compared with 45% of those never incarcerated. Nearly equal percentages of the never-incarcerated were married as were cohabiting.

Marriage was even less common among fathers whose past incarceration history was unknown. A mere 13% of the unknowns were married compared with 42% for those with no history of incarceration. The gaps are similar for cohabiting; only 20% were living with the child's mother. These statistics would lend further credence to the theory that some of these men did not report their incarceration histories. However, the fact that the mothers did not know whether the fathers had been incarcerated also suggests that they had weaker relationships with these fathers.

For the multivariate analysis, we use a multinomial logit model to measure the association between incarceration and the probability that a mother would choose to marry, cohabit, or do neither. A multinomial logit model allows several discrete alternatives to be considered simultaneously during the regression. The omitted category in this analysis is nonmarried and noncohabiting.

We use four models to examine the association between incarceration and family formation. Model 1 includes incarceration variables only. In model 2, we add control variables for mothers' age, ethnicity, education, and city of interview. In model 3, controls were added for mothers' substance use, whether or not the mother was raised in an intact family, the number of children she has, and fathers'

Table 16.1 Marriage and Cohabitation by Incarceration Status

	Never Incarcerated	Had Been Incarcerated	Unknown
Married	.42	***.22	***.13
	(.03)	(.02)	(.03)
		7.94	6.16
Cohabiting	.45	.47	***.20
	(.03)	(.04)	(.04)
		0.46	4.80

Note. Standard deviations are in parentheses; *t* scores are listed below them.
*$p \leq .05$, **$p \leq .01$, ***$p \leq .001$.

characteristics for age, education, and ethnicity. Finally, in model 4, we include controls for the fathers for alcohol use, marijuana use, depression, father absence, and poor health. A dummy variable is also included to correct for the 150 fathers who were not interviewed in the follow-up.

Table 16.2 presents the results of the multinomial logit models. The results are interpreted as the likelihood that the specified variable would be in the noncommitted group (marriage or cohabitation) relative to the omitted category of the specified variable. For example, in model 2, the likelihood that Black mothers would be married rather than in a nonmarital, noncohabiting relationship is 16% that of White mothers.

As expected, the association between incarceration and marriage and cohabitation diminishes across models as control variables are added. As more variables are added, they help to explain changes in marriage and cohabitation rates. Logistic regression models generate coefficients that are expressed as odds ratios and therefore are expressed as being as likely to occur as the omitted category.

In model 1, mothers whose partners had been incarcerated were 7% as likely to be married as those whose partners were never incarcerated. They were 32% as likely to be cohabiting as the mothers whose partners had never been incarcerated. Both findings are statistically significant (at the $p \leq .001$ level).

As controls are added, the effect diminishes but remains significant. In model 4, which includes all control variables, mothers whose partners had been incarcerated were still only 30% as likely to be married as mothers whose partners were never incarcerated, significant at the $p \leq .01$ level. They were slightly more than one-half as likely (53%) to be cohabiting as were mothers with never-incarcerated partners, significant at the .05 level. It is clear from these findings that mothers who do form households with incarcerated fathers are more likely to cohabit than to marry, compared with mothers who form households with never-incarcerated fathers.

The likelihood of marriage or cohabitation when the father's incarceration status is unknown is the least. Mothers are less likely to marry or cohabit with fathers whose incarceration history is unknown than with fathers whose incarceration history is known. Two factors could be at work: *(1)* these fathers are hiding their pasts, and *(2)* these relationships may be more tenuous, given that the mother is not privy to this important information.

These results are consistent with the findings of Western and McLanahan (2000), who found that couples in which the father was incarcerated were significantly less likely to be living together 1 year after the birth of their children. They also found, as we did, that Black couples are far less likely to be living together a year after their baby's birth.[3]

One interesting finding was that results based on mothers' reports had stronger effects than those based on fathers' reports. Based on the fathers' reports, couples with histories of incarceration were about 50% less likely to be living together, whereas based on mothers' reports, they were 70% less likely to live together. Obviously the fathers were more likely to describe themselves as living with a partner than was the mother. To test whether these findings were consistent, we ran

Table 16.2 Multinomial Logistic Regression for Marriage and Cohabitation

	Model 1		Model 2		Model 3		Model 4	
	Married	Cohabiting	Married	Cohabiting	Married	Cohabiting	Married	Cohabiting
Incarceration status (omitted = never)								
Incarcerated	***.07 (−8.18)	***.32 (−4.61)	***.14 (−5.73)	***.35 (−4.04)	***.21 (−4.22)	***.39 (−3.33)	**.30 (−2.77)	*.53(−1.98)
Incarceration unknown	***.06 (−8.50)	***.09 (−8.16)	***.08 (−6.79)	***.09 (−7.79)	***.09 (−6.07)	***.09 (−7.55)	*.24(−2.39)	***.21 (−3.71)
Mother's age			*** 1.09(3.58)	1.00(0.08)	* 1.08(2.11)	1.00(0.09)	* 1.09(2.24)	1.015(0.46)
Mother's race (omitted =White)								
Black			***.16(−3.95)	.60(−1.32)	.47(−0.98)	.81(−0.37)	.42(−1.04)	.80(−0.38)
Latino			.64(−1.01)	.90(−0.26)	.47(−1.25)	.66(−0.88)	.39(−1.39)	.67(−0.76)
Other race			.46(−1.15)	.57(−0.91)	.67(−0.42)	.88(−0.15)	.53(−0.60)	1.09(0.09)
Mother's education (omitted = high school graduate)								
Less than high school			1.01(0.02)	.89(−0.43)	.71(−0.83)	.80(−0.81)	.73(−0.69)	.71(−1.13)
Some college			1.59(1.18)	.79(−0.72)	1.32(0.65)	.71(−1.04)	1.58(0.96)	.81(−0.56)
College graduate			** 6.07(2.83)	1.26(0.36)	3.27(1.60)	1.25(0.32)	3.74(1.64)	1.12(0.14)
City of interview (Oakland = 1)			1.71(1.80)	.88(−0.54)	1.77(1.79)	.95(−0.20)	1.44(1.04)	.79(−0.88)

Mother's characteristics

With both parents at age 15	1.73(0.73)	1.33(1.20)	* 2.22(2.38)	2.58(1.23)
Health excellent (omitted = fair/poor)	.81(−0.34)	.60(−1.16)	.94(−0.09)	.58(−1.11)
Health very good	1.63(0.83)	.56(−1.37)	1.78(0.89)	.52(−1.39)
Health good	1.83(1.03)	.62(−1.11)	1.78(0.91)	.60(−1.10)
One other child	1.45(1.02)	1.30(0.95)	1.23(0.52)	1.19(0.56)
More than one other child	1.65(1.25)	1.26(0.73)	1.33(0.66)	1.19(0.49)
Used drugs/alcohol	1.49(0.59)	.48(−1.60)	1.51(0.55)	.70(−0.63)
Smoked cigarettes	**.20(−2.80)	1.23(0.66)	*.28(−2.14)	1.35(0.85)
Father's age	.99(−0.29)	.99(−0.43)	.98(−0.73)	.98(−0.64)
Father's race/ethnicity (omitted = White)				
Black	*.18(−2.24)	.64(−0.75)	*.17(−2.08)	.69(−0.56)
Latino	.56(−0.88)	1.10(0.18)	.77(−0.36)	1.63(0.83)
Other race	.39(−0.94)	.51(−0.77)	.53(−0.56)	.67(−0.42)
Father's education (omitted = high schoolgraduate)				
Less than high school graduate	** 2.78(2.59)	1.39(1.22)	**3.03(2.62)	1.68(1.72)
Some college	* 2.41(2.00)	1.53(1.36)	* 3.33(2.47)	1.68(1.48)
College graduate	* 4.07(1.99)	1.07(0.10)	4.22(1.84)	.88(−0.16)

Continued

Table 16.2 Multinomial Logistic Regression for Marriage and Cohabitation (*Continued*)

	Model 1		Model 2		Model 3		Model 4	
	Married	*Cohabiting*	*Married*	*Cohabiting*	*Married*	*Cohabiting*	*Married*	*Cohabiting*
Father's characteristics								
Had problems with alcohol or drugs							.83(−0.40)	* .46(−2.33)
No days of 5 or more drinks(*omitted = no drinks in past month*)							1.42(0.80)	** 2.52(2.50)
1–2 days of 5 or more drinks							.90(−020)	1.18(0.38)
3 or more days of 5 or more drinks							.57(−0.93)	1.76(1.22)
Smoked marijuana in past month							.25(−1.82)	.92(−0.19)
In poor health							** 3.30(2.67)	1.41(0.93)
Was depressed in last 2 weeks							.47(−1.43)	1.21(0.49)
With both parents at age 15							.81(−0.58)	.68(−1.39)
Not interviewed							.92(−0.13)	1.21(0.46)
Log likelihood	−545.753	−545.753	−500.448	−500.448	−470.605	−470.605	−420.61	−420.61
χ2	155.20	155.20	245.81	245.81	305.50	305.50	405.48	405.48
Pseudo R2	.125	.125	.197	.197	.245	.245	.325	.325
No. of cases	577	577	577	577	577	577	577	577

*p ≤ .05, **p ≤ .01, ***p ≤ .001.
z scores are in parentheses.

a regression separating the incarceration variable into mothers' and fathers' reports and found similar results.

In model 4, with all controls added and using the multinomial logit model with father-reported data, couples in which the father was incarcerated were 32% as likely to be married ($p \leq .05$) and 91% as likely to cohabit as couples in which the father was not incarcerated. The effects were more pronounced using mother-reported data. Couples in which the father was incarcerated were only 25% as likely to be married ($p \leq .01$) and 37% as likely to be cohabiting ($p \leq .01$) as couples in which the father was not incarcerated.

These findings are surprising because, as we expected, father-reported data resulted in stronger effects on earnings and employment, and the same was expected to be true with marriage and cohabitation. Our expectation was that these fathers would have poorer outcomes overall. One theory is that mothers who knew that the father was incarcerated were less likely to enter a formal union with him.

Discussion and Implications

The results of this study suggest that incarceration has an effect on the decisions a couple makes about their relationship after having a child. If the father had been incarcerated, then it was less likely that the couple would marry. There was no significant difference in likelihood of cohabitation between those who had been incarcerated and those who had not. Further research is needed to quantify incarceration's effects.

In this study, mothers who had children with someone who was incarcerated were significantly less likely to be married or cohabiting than mothers whose mate had never been jailed. They were less likely to be married than they were to be cohabiting. They were 30% as likely to be married as were mothers whose partners were never incarcerated and 53% as likely to cohabit after controlling for all characteristics.

When the incarceration history of the father was unknown, the creation of a formal or informal household was even less likely, leading to the conclusion that these fathers were less attached to the mothers than were other fathers. There is a strong possibility that these fathers did not report their incarceration experiences.

Although it is still unclear whether current prison policies are the most cost-effective means of reducing crime, this study presents evidence that family formation is hindered if the male has a prison record. If marriage is indeed a pathway to reduced poverty and better socioeconomic outcomes for children, particularly those of low-income couples, then efforts must be made to reduce the incidence of incarceration. Among the reforms we recommend are the following:

Repeal mandatory minimum sentences. This law is particularly egregious in respect to low-level nonviolent drug offenders. Policy makers should follow the lead of California voters who approved Proposition 30 in November 2000, which mandates treatment in lieu of incarceration. Get-tough-on-crime advocates like John DiIulio and James Q. Wilson have recently advocated more judicial discretion in sentencing and a rethinking of the mandatory minimum guidelines. Reducing the use of incarceration, particularly for nonviolent offenders, would free up billions of dollars that could support employment programs and drug treatment services that would increase the economic viability of low-income fathers.

Increase drug treatment in prisons and jails. Using the "carrot and stick" approach, drug treatment should be mandated for low-level nonviolent offenders. However, for those who refuse to receive treatment, incarceration can be an effective punishment if it includes treatment. In a 1997 report by the Justice Department, 57% of state prisoners and 45% of federal prisoners said they used drugs in the month before they had been incarcerated.

Thirty-three percent of state prisoners and 22% of federal prisoners said they committed their crime under the influence. Yet just 15% of state and federal prisoners received substance abuse treatment in 1997, down from 33% in 1991 (Mumola, 1997). Therapeutic treatment should not be limited, however, to substance abuse. In 1998, there were 283,800 mentally ill persons in state and federal prisons and local jails and another 547,800 on parole and probation (Ditton, 1999). These people should receive mental health treatment while they are incarcerated.

Support in-prison programs designed to assist inmates. Programs like FamilyWorks, created and operated in New York State prisons by Elizabeth Gaynes, executive director of the Osborne Society, work to maintain bonds between inmate fathers and their children during incarceration and upon release (Jeffries, Menghraj, & Hairston, 2001). More of these programs should be implemented in state and federal correction facilities.

Introduce clemency legislation for first-time nonviolent offenders. First-time nonviolent offenders who refrain from criminal activities for 5 years should be allowed to petition to have their records expunged. Criminal arrest and conviction records often follow released inmates for decades after they have paid their debt to society. Employers routinely deny jobs to individuals with criminal records, no matter how minor. Some states permanently deny ex-felons the right to vote. Thousands of people were denied—many unjustly—the right to vote in the 2000 presidential election in Florida because their names were on a list of people with past felony convictions.

Stop sending juveniles to adult prisons. Approximately 250,000 juveniles are sent to adult prisons each year; more than one-half are incarcerated for nonviolent and property crimes (Coalition for Juvenile Justice, 2005). These youth often have mental and emotional problems that are aggravated by being locked up with adults. They are often easy prey and susceptible to the criminogenic effects of prison.

Support alternatives to incarceration. A number of sanctions short of incarceration are available to prosecutors and judges, such as restitution and compensating victims, community service, mandated treatment for low-level drug offenders, day centers, and electronic monitoring.

Support youth development programs for at-risk youth. Ronald Mincy (1994) advocated for independent youth development programs serving young Black males as a means to help inner-city youth escape the snares of crime and incarceration. He saw these programs as among the most effective youth activities in the country. He pushed for a concerted effort on the part of health, labor, and criminal justice policy makers to reach Black males at younger ages. He believed that to be successful, the focus of programs aimed at young Black males must shift from deterrence to development, nurturing competencies that would lead to success.

Approximately 5.5 million young people between the ages of 16 and 24 years old are out of school and out of work (Sum, Khatiwada, Pond, & Trub'skyy, 2002). Yet 2006 budget proposals by the Bush administration would eliminate or reduce funds for many programs—Pell Grants, Youth Opportunity Grants, job training—geared to helping young people get a leg up in the job market. This is especially disturbing because teen employment has been declining despite an expanding labor market. Employment-to-population ratios for 16- to 19-year-olds declined from 36.8% in 2003 to 36.4% in 2004, the lowest in the 57 years for which Current Population Survey data are available (Sum, Khatiwada, McLaughlin, & Palma, 2005).

A Welcome Policy Move

This chapter ends on a positive note about recent youth policy developments in the nation's capital. In February 2005, Vincent Schiraldi, a long-time advocate of alternative programs for youth facing incarceration, left his executive director's post at the Justice Policy Institute to head the newly created Department of Youth Rehabilitation Services in Washington, D.C. Mayor Anthony Williams created the cabinet-level agency with an annual budget of $58 million to reduce the city's juvenile jail population.

Schiraldi has created a "continuum of care" system that involves court-mandated youth and their families in a variety of programs designed to capitalize on the strengths of these youth and their networks. Approaching this from a case management framework, the system provides youth with individualized and group treatments in small community facilities. These include Evening Reporting Centers, where court-mandated youth are transported from their schools to a nonresidential alternative to detention, where they receive 6 hours of supervision, tutoring, and counseling. They are fed and transported home at the end of the evening.

This is a welcome move from the increasingly punitive policies directed at the nation's youth during the last several decades. This hopeful policy initiative is occurring in the nation's capital even as Congress debates the Gang Deterrence and Community Protection Act of 2005 that would permit prosecutors to try 16- and 17-year-old defendants without any judicial review, paving the way for more juveniles to be placed in adult prisons.

Incarceration is punitive by nature, and its effects do much to harm individuals and families. Arguably, many (if not most) imprisoned individuals have made personal choices that landed them in prison. But as the industry grows and become more profitable, pressures evolve—through the lobbying efforts of correctional unions, private prison industries, and lawmakers whose districts depend on prisons—that undercut reforms that could deter people, particularly young Black males, from going into our nation's jails and prisons. If the plan is to rescue and strengthen families, society must resist the urge to put more people in prison.

Families begin with children, who are future husbands, wives, mothers, and fathers. Incarceration damages family structure by removing a parent from the home and limiting the amount of time that parents spend with their children (Currence & Johnson, 2003). The degree to which young people are allowed to develop human capital through education and on-the-job training without being scarred by the criminal justice system will affect their chances of forming stable families. To address poverty and unstable families through marriage promotion policies and programs without adequately addressing barriers to forming healthy families is short-sighted and wishful thinking.

NOTES

1.   Children in these statistics include those under age 18.
2.   It is reasonable to assume that incarceration would have a negative effect on fertility because the potential father would have less opportunity for procreation. Having children should increase the likelihood that the father would remain in a formal or close relationship with the mother. Therefore, the effects of incarceration in this study would be biased downward. It is likely that without children, the man and woman would be less likely to form a household. The effects of incarceration on marriage and cohabitation among men who are not fathers are likely to be greater than the effects on this cohort of fathers.
3.   It is important to note that our study examines incarceration's effects at baseline rather than at follow-up, which Western and McLanahan (2000) do in their study.

REFERENCES

Ahituv, A. & Lerman, R. (2004). *Job turnover, wage rates, and marital stability: How are they related?* Washington, DC: Urban Institute.

Beck, A. J. & Karberg, J. C. (2000). *Prison and jail inmates at midyear 2000.* Washington, DC: Bureau of Justice Statistics.

Becker, G. S. (1981). *A treatise on the family.* Cambridge, MA: Harvard University Press.

Bendheim-Thomas Center for Research on Child Wellbeing. (2003, May). *Barriers to marriage among fragile families.* (Research Brief No. 16). Princeton, NJ: Author.

Blau, F. D., Kahn, L. M., & Waldfogel, J. (2000). *Understanding young women's marriage decisions: The role of labor and marriage market conditions. National Bureau of Economic Research Working Paper 7510.* Cambridge, MA: National Bureau of Economic Research.

Coalition for Juvenile Justice. (2005, March). *Childhood on trial: The failure of trying and sentencing youth in adult criminal court.* Washington, DC: Author.

Coontz, S. & Folbre, N. (2002). *Marriage, poverty, and public policy. Discussion paper from the Council on Contemporary Families.* Retrieved June 10, 2005, from http://www.contemporaryfamilies.org/briefing.html.

Currence, P. L. J. & Johnson, W. E. (2003). *The negative implications of incarceration on black fathers.* Retrieved on November 4, 2009, from http://www.rcgd.isr.umich.edu/prba/perspectives/winter2003/currence.pdf.Darity, W. A., Jr. & Myers, S. L., Jr. (1995). Family structure and marginalization of black men: Policy implications.

In M. B. Tucker & C. Mitchell-Kernan (Eds.), *The decline in marriage among African Americans: Causes, consequences, and policy implications* (pp. 263–308). New York: Russell Sage Foundation.

Dickson, L. (1993). The future of marriage and family in black America. *Journal of Black Studies, 23*(4), 472–491.

Ditton, P. M. (1999). *Mental health and treatment of inmates and probationers.* Washington, DC: Bureau of Justice Statistics.

DuBois, W. E. B. (1899). *The Philadelphia Negro.* Philadelphia: University of Pennsylvania.

Edin, K. (2000). Few good men. *The American Prospect, 11*(4), Retrieved December 1, 2009 from http://www.prospect.org/cs/articles?article=few_good_men

Ellwood, D. T. & Crane, J. (1990). Family change among Black Americans: What do we know? *The Journal of Economic Perspectives, 4*(4), 65–84.

Frazier, E. F. (1939). *The Negro family in the United States.* Chicago: Chicago University Press.

Freeman, R. B. (1991). *Crime and the employment of disadvantaged youth. National Bureau of Economic Research Working Paper No. 3875.* Cambridge, MA: National Bureau of Economic Research.

Grogger, J. (1995). The effect of arrests on the employment and earnings of young men. *Quarterly Journal of Economics, 110*(1), 51–71.

Hagan, J. & Peterson, R. D. (Eds.). (1995). *Crime and inequality.* Stanford, CA: Stanford University Press.

Harrison, P. M. & Beck, A. J. (2005). *Prison and jail inmates at midyear 2004.* Washington, DC: Bureau of Justice Statistics.

Haskins, R. & Sawhill, I. (2003). *Work and marriage: The way to end poverty and welfare. Welfare Reform and Beyond, #28.* Washington, DC: The Brookings Institution.

Jeffries, J. M., Menghraj, S., & Hairston, C. F. (2001). *Serving incarcerated and ex-offender fathers and their families: A review of the field.* New York: Vera Institute of Justice.

Justice Policy Institute. (2001). *Too little too late: President Clinton's prison legacy.* Retrieved on December 1, 2009 from http://www.justicepolicy.org/images/upload/01-02_REP_TooLittleTooLate_AC.pdf

Lang, K. & Zagorsky, J. L. (2000). Does growing up with a parent absent really hurt? *Journal of Human Resources, 36*(2), 253–73.

Lerman, R. (1989). Employment opportunities of young men and family formation. *American Economic Review, 79*(2), 62–66.

Lerman, R. (2002). *Marriage and the economic well-being of families with children: A review of the literature.* Washington, DC: Urban Institute.

Lewis, C. E., Garfinkel, I. & Gao, Q. (2007). Incarceration and unwed fathers in fragile families. *Journal of Sociology and Social Welfare, 34*(3), 77–94.

Lichter, D. T., McLaughlin, D. K., Kephart, G., & Landry, D. J. (1992). Race and the retreat from marriage: A shortage of marriageable men? *American Sociological Review, 57*(6), 781–799.Mare, R. D. & Winship, C. (1991). Socioeconomic change and the decline of marriage for blacks and whites. In C. Jencks & P. E. Peterson (Eds.), *The urban underclass* (pp. 175–195). Washington, DC: The Brookings Institution.

McLanahan, S. & Sandefur, G. D. (1994). *Growing up with a single parent: What hurts, what helps.* Cambridge, MA: Harvard University Press.

Mincy, R. B. (1994). *Nurturing young black males: Challenges to agencies, programs, and social policy.* Washington, DC: Urban Institute.

Moynihan, D. P. (1965). *The Negro family: The case for national action.* Retrieved December 1, 2009 from http://www.dol.gov/oasam/programs/history/webid-meynihan.htm

Mumola, C. J. (1997). *Substance abuse and treatment, state and federal prisoners, 1997.* Washington, DC: Bureau of Justice Statistics.

Rector, R. (2005, February 10, 2005). *Welfare reform and the healthy marriage initiative.* Statement before the Subcommittee on Human Resources of the Committee on Ways and Means, U.S. House of Representatives. Washington, DC: Heritage Foundation. Retrieved December 1, 2009 from http://www.heritage.org/Research/welfare/tst021005a.cfm.

Schultz, T. P. (1994). Marital status and fertility in the United States: Welfare and labor market effects. *Journal of Human Resources, 29*(2), 636–669.

Smock, P. J. & Manning, W. D. (1997). Cohabiting partners' economic circumstances and marriage. *Demography, 34*(3), 331–341.

Sum, A., Khatiwada, I., McLaughlin, J., & Palma, S. (2005). *The paradox of rising teen joblessness in an expanding labor market: The absence of teen employment growth in the national jobs recovery of 2003–2004.* MA: Center for Labor Market Studies, Northeastern University.

Report prepared for Jobs for America's Graduates. Alexandria, VA:

Sum, A., Khatiwada, I., Pond, N., & Trub'skyy, M. (2002). *Left behind in the labor market: Labor market outcomes and the nation's out-of-school, young adult populations. Report prepared for Chicago Alternative Schools.* Retrieved December 1, 2009 from http://www.eric.ed.gov/ERICDocs/data/ericdocs2sql/content_storage_01/0000019b/80/1a/fb/d1.pdf. Retrieved on from http://www.nupr.neu.edu/2-03/left_behind.PDF

Testa, M. & Krogh, M. (1995). The effect of employment on marriage among black males in inner-city Chicago. In M. B. Tucker & C. Mitchell-Kernan (Eds.), *The decline in marriage among African Americans: Causes, consequences, and policy implications* (pp. 59-95)(pp. xx–xx) New York: Russell Sage Foundation.

Tzeng, J. M. & Mare, R. D. (1995). Labor market and socioeconomic effects on marital stability. *Social Science Research, 24*, 329–351.

U.S. Census Bureau. (2004). *Annual demographic survey, March supplement.* Retrieved on November 4, 2009, from http://pubdb3.census.gov/macro/032004/pov/new02_100.htm

Waldfogel, J. (1993). The effect of criminal conviction on income and the 'trust reposed in the workmen.' *Journal of Human Resources, 29*(1), 62–81.

Western, B. (2002). The impact of incarceration on wage mobility and inequality. *American Sociological Review, 67*, 526–546.

Western, B. (2004). *Incarceration, marriage, and family life.* Princeton, NJ: Russell Sage Foundation.

Western, B., Lopoo, L. M., & McLanahan. (2002). *Incarceration and the bands among parents in fragile families. Center for Researh on Child Wellbeing Working Paper #02-22-FF.* Princeton, NJ: Center for Research on Child Wellbeing.

Western, B. & McLanahan, S. (2000). *Fathers behing bars: The impact of incarceration on family formation. Center for Research on Child Wellbeing Working # 00-08.* Princeton, NJ: Center for Research on Child Wellbeing.

Wilson, W. J. (1987). *The truly disadvantaged: The inner city, the underclass, and public policy.* Chicago:University Press.

Wood, R. G. (1995). Marriage rates and marriageable men: A test of the Wilson hypothesis. *Journal of Human Resources, 30*(1), 163–193.

17

Understanding the Economic Costs of Incarceration for African American Males

MARK L. JOSEPH

This chapter explores the economic implications of the staggering incarceration rate in the United States for African American men, their families and communities, and society as a whole. There are well over 2 million individuals incarcerated in the United States and another 4 million on parole or probation under the supervision of the criminal justice system. For every 100,000 residents in the United States in 2003, 714 were incarcerated, an incarceration rate six times the rate in 1970 (Harrison & Beck, 2004).[1] Given current rates, it is estimated that, among men aged 16, 9% will be incarcerated in their lifetime (Bureau of Justice Statistics, 1997).

While the incarceration rates for the general U.S. population are shocking, the corresponding figures for American American men are almost beyond comprehension. Although only about 12% of the male population, African American men make up 44% of the male prison population (Harrison & Beck, 2004). While 415 White men are incarcerated for every 100,000 White male residents in the United States in 2003, the corresponding rate among African American men is 3405 per 100,000 (Harrison & Beck, 2004).[2] Almost 10% of all African American men are currently in prison or jail. The Bureau of Justice Statistics (1997) estimates that among the cohort of African American men currently aged 16, 30% will be incarcerated in their lifetime.

Given these rates of incarceration, prisoner re-entry and its ramifications have become major public policy challenges for the general population and are at crisis levels in the African American community. The average prison stay is 2.5 years, and each year over 600,000 individuals are released from prison or jail (Travis,

Solomon, & Waul, 2001). Unemployment has been estimated at between 25% and 40% among ex-offenders (Finn & Fontaine, 1985).[3] Many ex-offenders soon return to illegal activity; in one study of inmates released from prison in 15 states, 67.5% were rearrested within 3 years (Langan & Levin, 2002).

An emerging body of research on this topic has found evidence that past criminal involvement is negatively associated with labor market outcomes (Bushway, 1998; Freeman, 1992; Grogger, 1992, 1995; Kling, 1999, 2004; Lott, 1990; Nagin & Waldfogel, 1995, 1998; Needels, 1996; Pager, 2003; Waldfogel, 1993; Western, 2002; Western, Kling, & Weiman, 2001). Using the Panel Study of Income Dynamics, I have found empirical evidence to confirm the emerging consensus in the literature that incarceration has a negative impact in the range of a 10%–30% decrease in annual earnings for those men who have been incarcerated (Grogger, 1995; Kling, 1999; Western, 2002). I also found evidence to suggest that the earnings gap may be twice as high for African American ex-offenders. My analysis and that of others suggests that this earnings gap is sustained over time and does not necessarily diminish with time since release (Grogger, 1995).

In this chapter, I focus on the economic implications of this earnings gap for African American men. There are at least two levels of economic consequences of this sustained loss of earning power for those who have been incarcerated. On an individual level, rather than the "debt to society" being paid in full upon release from prison, ex-offenders are subject to a continued, perhaps lifelong, retribution that is exacted through the labor market. Perhaps more importantly from a public policy standpoint, the ex-offender earnings gap has economic costs at a societal level. The families of ex-offenders, the neighborhoods to which they return, and society as a whole incur economic losses from the lower earning power of those who have been incarcerated. As the U.S. incarceration rate increases, these ripple effects of the ex-offender earnings gap increase in size and scope (for other recent research on the ripple effects of incarceration, see also Pattillo, Weiman, & Western, 2004; Travis, 2005; Travis & Waul, 2003; Watts & Nightingale, 1996).

Despite the increased policy attention to the rate of incarceration, there has been inadequate consideration of the individual and societal costs of incarceration. First, it is not clear whether the full costs of incarceration to the individual ex-offender are intended or well-considered components of U.S. corrections policy. If we consider emerging evidence about the ex-offender earnings gap, does the punishment still fit the crime for most ex-offenders? Do those responsible for prosecution and sentencing consider the loss of earning power as a built-in component of an inmate's sentence?

Second, while the costs to society are likely not considered in sentencing, the economic costs of incarceration, including the ripple effects of the ex-con earnings gap, could outweigh the benefits. A frequently cited cost–benefit analysis of incarceration is by Levitt (1996), who concluded that the social benefit for each additional prisoner incarcerated is $53,900 annually. Comparing this benefit to DiIulio and Piehl's (1991) estimate of annual financial costs per prisoner of $25,000, he concluded that incarceration clearly seems cost-effective.[4] However, as Levitt notes, "The above estimates of prison costs fail to capture the true social costs of incarcerating the marginal prisoner in a number of ways. The estimates do not take into account . . . post-release decline in wages . . ." (Levitt, 1995, p. 347). And even Levitt failed to mention the potential ripple effects for families, neighborhoods, and society from the loss of earnings power by ex-offenders.

I contend that taking the cost of the earnings gap and its ripple effects into account calls into question the cost-effectiveness of current corrections policy. Clearly, a key factor in determining cost-effectiveness is the extent to which those criminals who represent the highest costs to society receive the longest sentences. To the extent that the recent increase in the U.S. incarceration rate has been driven by an increase in the proportion of incarcerated nonviolent drug offenders (Blumstein, 1995), then the cost-effectiveness of prison is even more in question.

The remainder of this chapter is organized as follows. First, I provide a theoretical framework for examining the relationship between incarceration and earnings. Next, I summarize the data and methodology used for my analysis of the earnings gap. Following that, I examine the size and causes of the earnings gap as suggested by my empirical analysis. I then consider my main concern in this chapter: the individual and societal economic costs of the earnings gap. The final section considers potential ways to reduce the earnings gap.

Theoretical Framework

There are several theoretical explanations for why a criminal background should lead to lower earnings. First, structural factors in the labor market, such as state laws banning ex-offenders from employment in certain professions and mandating background checks in others, constrain employment options for ex-offenders (Dale, 1976; Mukamal, 2000).

Second, the stigma of a criminal background is a signal to potential employers that the jobseeker is untrustworthy and may not be a productive employee. If employers have access to information about criminal background, it can serve as a key barrier to employment, what Pager (2003) calls "negative credentialling." Third, time spent engaged in criminal activity necessarily reduces time available for investment in human capital. Likewise, time spent incarcerated removes the individual from the conventional labor market and results in lost work experience. Finally, involvement in crime and time spent incarcerated increases the relationships that an individual has with other criminals and decreases opportunities to establish ties with individuals who might provide information and access to legitimate employment, thus weakening ex-offenders' social capital (Granovetter, 1995; Hagan, 1993; Sampson & Laub, 1993).

African American men are confronted with the additional barriers of structural and interpersonal racism, which have been demonstrated to have a negative effect on earnings through employer discrimination and less-productive human and social capital (see, for example, Darity & Mason, 1998; Kirshenman & Neckerman, 1991; Pager, 2003). Black men who have been incarcerated experience a confluence of these two factors, and we can theorize that their race and their ex-offender status combine to exacerbate the downward pressure on their earnings potential. Furthermore, research suggests that race serves as a signal of perceived criminality for some employers. Thus, African American males without a criminal background may experience employer discrimination as if they were ex-offenders (Holzer, Raphael, & Stoll, 2004).

Data and Methodology

My analysis was the first to examine data from the Panel Study of Income Dynamics (PSID), a rich source of longitudinal data on individual economic behavior (Hill, 1992), to explore this issue. The research questions that drove my analysis were as follows: *(1)* Is incarceration associated with a reduction in earnings? *(2)* What factors influence the size of any earnings gap between those who have been incarcerated and those who have not? The PSID was launched in 1968 with a representative sample of 4800 families, and the panel was surveyed every year, with biennial interviewing since 1997. By tracking family members who established their own families, the panel had grown to over 7000 families by 2001, with a total of almost 65,000 individuals. My analysis was focused on men of working age.

I used two analytical techniques to generate estimates of the relationship between incarceration and earnings. First, I ran a simple OLS model on a cross-section of the panel from 1993, attempting to control for as many possible factors that might be associated with both criminal activity and employment outcomes, including age, race, education, work experience, marital status, parental status, urban/rural residence, local labor market conditions, health, union status, and whether the individual works for the public sector. Second, I ran a fixed effects model on a panel of 10 years from 1983 to 1992.[5]

Estimating the Size of the Ex-Offender Earnings Gap

My analysis of the PSID suggests that if you take two men of the same age and physical ability to work, one of whom has been incarcerated and the other has not, there will be an approximately 50% earnings gap between them. Much of this earnings gap, about 30 percentage points, can be explained by differences between the two individuals such as race, human capital, and social attachment. After controlling for observable and unobservable factors, roughly 20 percentage points remain that can be attributed to incarceration.[6] For reference, as a percentage of U.S. median male income, this would be about $5600 a year. For African American men, my estimate of the incarceration earnings gap is 40%, which, as a percentage of median income among African American men, is about $8400.

The Individual and Societal Economic Costs of the Ex-Offender Earnings Gap

The aim of this paper is to calculate the costs that result from the gap in earnings that can be attributed to incarceration. There are both individual costs and societal costs associated with the gap. Given that the figures in this analysis are necessarily based on statistical estimates and demographic approximations, my goal here is not to derive precise estimates, but to demonstrate clearly the range of possible economic costs associated with incarceration, most of which are not considered in the current policy debate about incarceration. While the figures here are approximate, hopefully they make a compelling argument for considering more carefully the full costs of incarceration.

Individual Costs

As I will show in the following discussion, the individual costs include loss of annual earnings and, by extension, loss of lifetime earnings. Also, given lifetime probabilities of incarceration, we can estimate the cost to an entire generation of young African American men.

Lost Annual and Lifetime Earnings   I estimate that, on average, African American men who have been incarcerated face an earnings loss of about $8400 a year that can be attributed to their incarceration. Given that evidence suggests that this gap is sustained over the course of a lifetime, this accumulates to a significant loss of earnings power caused by having served time in prison. If an African American inmate who would have earned the median wage is released at age 35 and works until age 65, this estimate suggests that he would earn about $136,000 less over that 30-year period than another African American male who shared all his characteristics—education, work experience, and so on—but who had not been incarcerated.[7] For inmates released at age 25, the lifetime earnings loss is about $151,000.

Lost Aggregate Earnings   It is estimated that a Black man aged 16 has a 30% chance of spending some time in prison (Bureau of Justice Statistics, 1997). In 2000, using U.S. Census figures, we can estimate that there were about 270,000 young Black men aged 16 in the United States. Of those, about 90,000 are expected to spend some time in prison during their lifetime, which implies an annual earnings loss of over $747 million to that age cohort. If they were all released from their prison term at age 35, the collective wage loss just to African American men aged 16 in 2000 would be over $12 billion in lifetime earnings. The more current 16 year olds who are released before age 35, the greater the aggregate loss.

Societal Costs

Furthermore, besides lifetime costs to the individual ex-offender, there are costs to society that should be considered. As I will discuss below, societal economic costs include lost income to the families of ex-offenders and to the neighborhoods from which they leave and to which they often return. They also include costs to society as a whole, in the form of crime committed by ex-offenders who turn to crime due to their reduced earnings power and the increased prison costs from reincarcerated releasees.

FAMILY COSTS   About 1.5 million children in the United States have an incarcerated parent, including 7% of all African American children (Mumola, 2000). Obviously, there are numerous costs incurred by families of incarcerated individuals (for a discussion of the implications of incarceration for Black fathers, see Currence & Johnson, 2003). One of the more significant, lasting, economic costs, which is directly related to the earnings gap, is reduced child support payments. Given that only 3%–5% of marriages remain intact through the incarceration and subsequent release of a spouse and 75% of ex-offenders are fathers (Travis et al., 2001), most ex-offenders should be providing child support to the mothers of their children. Over 600,000 individuals are released from prison each year, of whom over 60% return within 3 years (Langan & Levin, 2002). Of the approximately 223,000 men released each year who do not return to prison, about 167,000 are fathers. Applying the incarceration rate for African American men, I can estimate that almost 74,000 of these releasees each year are African American fathers. Multiplying by the annual earnings gap of $8400, I estimate that these African American fathers who remain out of prison collectively lose well over $600 million in annual earnings.

What does that earnings loss imply for child support payments? Percentages of the father's income awarded by different states vary and in each case there is some discretion based on family circumstances. Based on information from the U.S. Department of Health and Human Services, a typical state might award in the range of 17% for one child, 25% for two children, 29% for three children, 31% for four children, and 34% for five or more children. For the sake of this analysis, I assume an average award of 25%. This would mean that over $154 million is lost in child support payments from African American fathers each year, due to their ex-offender status. Although many of these fathers may not have paid formal or even informal child support, this estimate provides an approximation of the amount that is potentially lost by the families of African American ex-offenders due to lost child support.

NEIGHBORHOOD COSTS   There is also an economic cost borne by the neighborhoods to which ex-offenders return. Lost earnings to individuals means less buying power that can be invested locally. In inner-city communities with particularly high concentrations of ex-offenders, this impact can be severe. In the North Lawndale neighborhood on the West Side of Chicago, for example, about 70% of the men between ages 18 and 45 are ex-offenders (Chicago Tribune, 2001). The population of North Lawndale in 2000 was about 42,000 and well over 90% of the residents are African American. Based on the available age demographics (47% are male, 30% are under age 18), I can estimate that there are roughly 10,000 men between ages 18 and 45, and thus about 7000 men with a criminal background. The median income in North Lawndale is $16,500, 40% (the Black ex-con earnings gap) of which is $6600. Multiplied by the number of ex-offenders, this yields $45.6 million in lost annual earnings in that community alone from men aged 18 to 45.

THE SOCIAL COST OF INCREASED CRIME   Given the earnings gap they face in the legal labor market, ex-offenders must make a decision whether to remain in legal employment at reduced earning power or to spend at least some time in the illegal sector. Ethnographic evidence and in-depth interviews suggest that individuals do indeed make cost–benefit analyses about whether to engage in crime based on how much they can earn in the legal and illegal markets (Sullivan, 1989). Evidence also suggests that a considerable number of individuals are involved in both legal employment and illegal activities concurrently (Sullivan, 1989; Sviridoff & Thompson, 1983). Over 25% of Sviridoff and Thompson's sample of prison releasees in New York reported generating income through crime while also working legally. It is possible that time in prison not only decreases earnings power in the legal sector but increases earnings power in the illegal sector, due to increased "crime skills" and criminal networks. This would make a return to crime even more likely in response to diminished opportunities in the legal sector.

Over 60% of the 600,000 inmates released each year return to crime, are caught, and return to jail, most within 3 years of their release (Langan & Levin, 2002). Other ex-offenders return to crime but are not rearrested. I can only speculate about how many of those who return to crime, if any, would have returned to crime regardless of their earning power in the legal labor market, and how many returned to crime due to their lower earning power. This is an important gap in the research literature and makes it difficult to estimate the impact of the earnings gap on increased crime. I assume, for the sake of this analysis, that some ex-offenders return to crime at least in part due to their lower earning power.

To be convinced that this is a possibility, we would have to believe that crime is a viable alternative to generate earnings. This is certainly conceivable for those ex-offenders who return to urban areas, particularly low-income neighborhoods, where there is ample opportunity to generate earnings through crime. According to my estimates, for the average African American male ex-offender to make up for the estimated earnings loss, he would need to make $8400 illegally. For example, it has been estimated that drug dealers in Washington, D.C. net an average of $38 an hour (Reuter, MacCoun, & Murphy, 1990; inflated to current dollars). At that rate, it would take 221 hours to make $8400 or seventy-four 3-hour days per year, certainly a conceivable amount. An individual who would earn the median income for African American male ex-offenders that I estimate to be $13,000 could do better through full-time drug selling, which netted about $30,000/year in the late 1980s (Freeman, 1996; Reuter et al., 1990; inflated to current dollars). These estimates provide an approximation of what could be earned through crime, but a complete analysis would need to take into account the probability of being caught and the costs of that eventuality.

Of the roughly 147,000 African American male inmates released each year who return to crime and are arrested and imprisoned, we can assume that there are *(1)* those who would turn back to crime for reasons other than their reduced earning power, *(2)* some who turn to crime just enough to make up the lost income, and *(3)* some who turn to crime exclusively due to lost earning power because they can earn more full time in the illegal sector. For the sake of this analysis, I assume that a third, or about 49,000, would turn back to crime anyway, another third turn to crime to supplement legal income, and a third turn exclusively to crime because their ex-offender status prevents them from getting legal employment. I then add 10,000 to each of those numbers for those who turn to crime but we cannot measure because they do not get caught and thus do not appear in recidivism statistics.

The roughly 59,000 African American men who turn to crime simply to supplement their legal income (i.e., to earn an additional $8400) need to generate a total of almost $500 million annually in crime. What is the cost to society of $500 million in crime? Freeman (1996) suggests that the economic costs of crime include not only property loss in many cases but also medical costs and lost work time. Estimating that the full cost is twice the initial financial cost implies an almost $1 billion annual cost to society from the increased crime due to the earnings gap for at least the 3 years until most of these men are rearrested and sent back to prison. However, those who are not caught continue to add to the societal cost through increased crime.

The estimated 59,000 African American men who support themselves and their families solely through illegal earnings because they can make more from "full-time" engagement in the illegal sector need to generate about $768 million in crime each year (to earn at least the median African American ex-offender income of $13,000). Applying the multiplier I developed above for additional economic costs results in an estimate of $1.5 billion annually in increased crime for the period until these men are caught. This makes a total of well over $2.5 billion in increased crime from those who turn to illegal means of making up lost earnings.

Recidivism due to lost earnings creates direct costs to society not only through increased crime but also through increased prison costs. Assuming, as I did above, that there are about 82,000 men who turn to crime due to the earnings loss and are caught and reincarcerated, then at DiIulio and Piehl's (1991) estimate of $25,000 in annual prison costs per inmate, the cost to the corrections system of recidivism caused by the earnings gap is almost $2.5 billion a year.

What is the cumulative implication of these societal costs? These cost estimates summarized above in Table 17.1 are extremely speculative, and thus it does not make sense to try to compute the total societal costs of the earnings gap that results from incarceration. Nonetheless, these estimates make clear that the economic implication of the earnings gap is likely to be huge. Of course, there are also benefits from incarceration. At the very least, it reduces crime that would have been committed by the men who are in prison, at least for the duration of their prison stay, and, though the evidence is inconclusive, it might serve as a deterrent

Table 17.1 Summary of Estimated Economic Costs of Incarceration for African American Men

Description	Estimated Amount
Lost individual earnings	$8400 a year
	$136,000 over the lifetime
Family costs (lost child support)	$154 million a year
Neighborhood costs (North Lawndale, Chicago)	$45.6 million a year
Social costs	
Crime	$2.5 billion a year
Recidivism (prison costs)	$2.5 billion a year

Note. See text for assumptions and calculations.

to crime by others. My objective in this analysis is not to calculate the precise cost-effectiveness of incarceration, but rather to point out that reducing the earnings gap due to incarceration could generate significant economic gains.

Potential Means of Reducing the Ex-Con Earnings Gap

How might we reduce the size of the earnings gap? My empirical findings about the causes of the earnings gap can also be used to suggest what policy makers might focus on if they want to reduce the size of the gap.

SOCIAL ATTACHMENT   One of the more intriguing findings in my analysis of the PSID was the importance of social attachment with spouses and children in mediating the earnings gap. I found that marital and parental status differences explain the largest proportion, about 24%, of the earnings gap between ex-offenders and others. According to my analysis, ex-offenders and nonoffenders have similar rates of paternal status, but they have a 30 percentage point difference in their marriage rates. I thus infer that a key form of social attachment might be paternal involvement: since parental rates are the same but marriage rates are different, the issue may be not having children but being engaged in their lives. Greater engagement with one's children might promote greater motivation and accountability to generate legal earnings (this proposition is confirmed by other research studies; see Travis & Waul, 2003).

Although we know little about what would actually increase paternal involvement among ex-offenders, we can think of a number of ways to help strengthen marital relationships or even postseparation paternal involvement, including expansion and protection of visitation rights, visitation assistance (i.e., transportation assistance for families, particularly to rural prisons), postrelease family counseling and reunification assistance, tax-based marriage incentives, and forgiveness of overdue child support payments.

HUMAN CAPITAL   My analysis suggests that human capital differences, such as education and work experience, make up as much as 20% of the earnings gap between ex-offenders and others. Through an increase in prison educational programs and vocational programs, which have been significantly cut over the last two decades, it may be possible to close this human capital gap. The average prison stay is only 2.5 years, which leaves little time for human capital acquisition, even if inmates dedicated most of their prison sentence to it. But for those ex-offenders with longer prison stays, there is more potential that in-prison vocational programs, if they can be demonstrated to effectively increase postrelease earnings, could cause reduction in the size of the gap. To the extent that postrelease educational and employment training programs can build human capital among ex-offenders, they present another important means of reducing the earnings gap.

RACE   I estimate that racial differences account for about 12% of the earnings gap between ex-offenders and others. In other words, some of the difference in earnings between ex-offenders and others is due to factors associated more directly with their race than with their incarceration status. To the extent that the race variable is picking up preference-based discrimination by employers on the basis of skin color, stricter enforcement of racial discrimination laws may reduce differences associated with race. To the extent that the race variable is picking up statistical discrimination by employers who are making assumptions about productivity based on skin color, then perhaps screening and referrals by an intermediary organization that can reduce uncertainty and information costs might also reduce differences associated with race.

EX-OFFENDER DISCRIMINATION   Another form of discrimination, certainly correlated with racial discrimination, is employer discrimination against ex-offenders. To the extent that this is driven by lack of information and uncertainty in the hiring decision, the impact of stigma might be attenuated through audits and prosecution (under Title VII of the 1964 Civil Rights Act) for "inappropriate" discrimination (e.g., where the type of crime is not relevant to job responsibilities), the aforementioned role of an intermediary organization providing screening and referral, subsidized bonding (to reduce employer liability), and the expungement of criminal records for nonviolent crimes.

PREVENTING A RETURN TO CRIME   The relationship between return to crime and the earnings gap is a difficult one to sort out: the size of the earnings gap likely influences a return to crime, and a return to crime influences the size of the earnings gap. Either way, if ex-offenders can be prevented from returning to crime, there will be a social gain. How might this be achieved? To the extent that the return to crime is caused by lack of success in the legal labor market (see Chiricos, 1987; Freeman, 1996) any effort that improves ex-offenders' ability to find legal employment would reduce the likelihood of a return to crime. Efforts such as prerelease employment counseling and work readiness and postrelease employment support and placement may accomplish this. A more direct way to control the return to crime would be closer postrelease supervision, including innovations such as electronic monitoring or place-based parole systems that assign parole officers to specific neighborhoods for greater engagement with the parolee's environment.

Conclusion

One important implication of the significant and sustained earnings gap for ex-offenders is that while we consider incarceration as a means for ex-offenders to pay their debt to society, we continue to extract retribution long after the ex-offender is released from prison. The debt to society, rather than a one-time prison sentence, is a life of reduced opportunity and barriers to self-sufficiency, particularly punitive to African American males.

To the extent that this cumulative disadvantage only impacts ex-offenders themselves, the policy implication could simply be to better calculate the full costs of incarceration to an individual as their sentences are determined to help the sentence better match the crimes. However, to the extent that this disadvantage has repercussions throughout society, then the lifelong penalty paid by ex-offenders is actually a burden borne by us all. Thus, our current corrections policy likely has significant unrecognized net costs to society.

This analysis has policy implications for each of the stages of the corrections process. Regarding sentencing, corrections policy should be closely examined to see whether those with a role in sentencing are encouraged to take postrelease earnings loss into account as a component of the punishment. If not, how might projected lost earnings be incorporated into sentence determination? Regarding time during prison as well as post release, there may be policy interventions that can reduce the size of the earnings gap. With many states facing fiscal shortfalls, the current policy trend is to reduce funding for prison programs. High-quality research is needed to determine whether there are prison-based and postrelease programs that can be shown to increase earnings and, given the ripple effects that I outlined here, would result in net savings for states. Given that marital and parental attachment may play a positive role in boosting earnings, there may be prison-based and postrelease family support programs that can help strengthen the bonds between ex-offenders and their families. Finally, to address stigma on the part of employers, employer-focused education, support, and accountability may help reduce unfavorable hiring practices due to preference-based or statistical discrimination.

NOTES

1. This is in comparison to an incarceration rate that was quite stable at around 110 per 100,000 for several decades up until the 1970s and increased to 458 per 100,000 by 1990.
2. For additional comparison, among Hispanic men the rate is 1231 per 100,000, and among African American women it is 185 per 100,000.

3. In this chapter, I use the term "ex-offender" to refer to an individual who has been incarcerated. Technically the term usually includes any individuals convicted of a crime, regardless of whether they serve prison or jail time.
4. As Levitt points out, this is average cost; marginal cost is certainly lower.
5. For a full discussion of methodology, econometric models, samples, and results in this analysis, see M. Joseph, unpublished data, which is available upon request from the author.
6. This estimate is in line with studies that have used other datasets to examine the relationship between incarceration and earnings; Western (2002) found a 19% decrease in earnings, Grogger (1995) found a decrease of 22%, and Kling (1999) estimated a decrease in the range of 23% to 31% for those serving over a year.
7. Where necessary, all dollar values in this chapter are discounted using a 5% interest rate.

REFERENCES

Blumstein, A. (1995). Prisons. In J. Q. Wilson & J. Petersilia (Eds.), *Crime and public policy* (2nd ed.). San Francisco: Institute for Contemporary Studies.

Bureau of Justice Statistics. (1997). *Lifetime likelihood of going to state or federal prison, U.S. Department of Justice report.* Washington, DC: U.S. Department of Justice, Bureau of Justice Statistics.

Bushway, S. (1998). The impact of an arrest on the job stability of young White men. *Journal of Research in Crime and Delinquency, 35*(4), 454–479.

Chiricos, T. (1987). Rates of crime and unemployment: An analysis of aggregate research evidence. *Social Problems, 34*(2), 187–212.

Chicago Tribune Editorial. (2001, March 17) *The risk of erasing the past.* Chicago Tribune. Section 1, 18.

Currence, P. L. J., & Johnson, W. E., Jr. (2003). The negative implications of incarceration on Black fathers. *African American Research Perspectives, 9*(1), 24–32.

Dale, M. (1976). Barriers to the rehabilitation of ex-offenders. *Crime and Delinquency, 22*(7), 322–337.

Darity, W. A. Jr., & Mason, P. L. (1998). Evidence on discrimination in employment: Codes of color, codes of gender. *Journal of Economic Perspectives, 12*(2), 63–90.

DiIulio, J.& Piehl, A. (1991). Does prison pay? The stormy national debate over the cost-effectiveness of imprisonment. *The Brookings Review, Fall,* 28–35.

Finn, R. H. & Fontaine, P. (1985). The association between selected characteristics and perceived employability of offenders. *Criminal Justice and Behavior, 12*(3), 353–365.

Freeman, R. B. (1992). Crime and the employment of disadvantaged youths. In G. Peterson & W. Vroman (Eds.), *Urban labor markets and job opportunity* (pp. xx–xx). Washington, DC: Urban Institute Press.

Freeman, R. (1996). Why do so many young American men commit crimes and what might we do about it? *Journal of Economic Perspectives, 10*(1), 25–42.

Granovetter, M. (1995). *Getting a job: A study of contacts and careers.* Chicago, IL: University of Chicago Press.

Grogger, J. (1992). Arrests, persistent youth joblessness, and Black/White employment differentials. *The Review of Economics and Statistics, 74*(1), 100–106.

Grogger, J. (1995). The effect of arrests on the employment and earnings of young men. *Quarterly Journal of Economics, 110*, 51–71.

Hagan, J. (1993). The social embeddedness of crime and unemployment. *Criminology, 31*, 465–492.

Harrison, P. & Beck, A. (2004). *Prisoners in 2003. Bureau of Justice Statistics Bulletin.* Washington, DC: U.S. Department of Justice, Bureau of Justice Statistics.

Hill, M. (1992). *The panel study of income dynamics.* Newbury Park, CA: Sage.

Holzer, H., Raphael, S., & Stoll, M. (2004). Will employers hire ex-offenders? Employer preferences, background checks and their determinants. In M. Pattillo, D. Weiman, & B. Western (Eds.), *Imprisoning America: The social effects of mass incarceration.* New York: Russell Sage Foundation.

Kirschenman, J. & Neckerman, K. M. (1991). "We'd love to hire them, but . . .": The meaning of race for employers. In C. Jencks & P. Peterson (Eds.), *The urban underclass* (pp. xx–xx). Washington, DC: The Brookings Institution.

Kling, J. (1999). *The effect of prison sentence length on the subsequent employment and earnings of criminal defendants. Princeton University Discussion Paper in Economics #208.* Retrieved November 5, 2009, from the Princeton University Web site: http://wws.princeton.edu/econdp/pdf/dp208.pdf

Kling, J. (2004). *Incarceration length, employment and earnings. Princeton IRS Working Paper #494.* Retrieved November 5, 2009, from the Princeton University Web site: http://www.irs.princeton.edu/pubs/pdfs/494.pdf

Langan, P. & Levin, D. (2002). *Recidivism of prisoners released in 1994. Bureau of Justice Statistics, special report.* Washington, DC: U.S. Department of Justice, Bureau of Justice Statistics.

Levitt, S. (1996). The effect of prison population size on crime rates: Evidence from prison overcrowding legislation. *The Quarterly Journal of Economics, 5*, 319–351.

Lott, J. R. (1990). The effect of conviction on the legitimate income of criminals. *Economics Letters, 34*, 381–385.

Mukamal, D. (2000). Confronting the employment barriers of criminal records: Effective legal and practical strategies. *Journal of Poverty Law and Policy, Jan-Feb*, 597–606.

Mumola, C. (2000). *Incarcerated parents and their children. Bureau of Justice Statistics special report.* Washington, DC: U.S. Department of Justice.

Nagin, D. & Waldfogel, J. (1995). The effects of criminality and conviction on the labor market status of young British offenders. *International Review of Law and Economics, 15*, 109–126.

Nagin, D. & Waldfogel, J. (1998). The effect of conviction on income through the life cycle. *International Review of Law and Economics, 18*, 25–40.

Needels, K. (1996). Go directly to jail and do not collect? A long-term study of recidivism, employment, and earnings patterns among prison releasees. *Journal of Research in Crime and Delinquency, 33*(4), 471–496.

Pager, D. (2003). The mark of a criminal record. *American Journal of Sociology, 108*(5), 937–975.

Pattillo, M., Weiman, D., & Western, B. (2004). *Imprisoning America: The social effects of mass incarceration.* New York: Russell Sage Foundation.

Reuter, P., MacCoun, R., & Murphy, P. (1990). *Money from crime: A study of the economics of drug dealing in Washington, DC.* Santa Monica, CA: Rand Drug Policy Center.

Sampson, R. J. & Laub, J. H. (1993). *Crime in the making: Pathways and turning points through life*. Cambridge, MA: Harvard University Press.

Sullivan, M. (1989). *Getting paid: Youth crime and work in the inner city*. Ithaca, NY: Cornell University Press.

Sviridoff, M. & Thompson, J. (1983). Links between employment and crime: A qualitative study of Rikers Island releasees. *Crime and Delinquency, 4*, 195–212.

Travis, J. (2005). *But they all come back: Facing the challenges of prisoner reentry*. Washington, DC: The Urban Institute Press.

Travis, J., Solomon, A., & Waul, M. (2001). *From prison to home*. Washington, DC: Urban Institute Press.

Travis, J. & Waul, M. (2003). *Prisoners once removed: The impact of incarceration and reentry on children, families and communities*. Washington, DC: The Urban Institute Press.

Waldfogel, J. (1994). The effect of criminal conviction on income and the trust reposed in the workmen. *The Journal of Human Resources, 29*, 62–81.

Watts, H. & Nightingale, D. S. (1996). Adding it up: The economic impact of incarceration on individuals, families, and communities. *Oklahoma Criminal Justice Research Consortium Journal, 3*, 55–62.

Western, B. (2002). The impact of incarceration on wage mobility and inequality. *The American Sociological Review, 67*(4), 526–546.

Western, B., Kling, J., & Weiman, D. (2001). The labor market consequences of incarceration. *Crime and Delinquency, 47*, 410–427.

PART V

Conclusion

18

The African American Male

The Social Policy Challenge of the Twenty-First Century

EARL S. JOHNSON, III AND WALDO E. JOHNSON, JR.

> What every Black American knows, and Whites should try to imagine, is how it feels to have an unfavorable and unfair identity imposed on you every waking day.
>
> —Andrew Hacker

Recently, we were sitting with a friend who has worked in the social policy setting arena for over 35 years. He was on the Republican side of the aisle during the debate and passage of the Civil Rights Act of 1964, legislation that he and his boss took great pride in getting passed. He said, "If Black people don't do something real soon, you will be irrelevant." He then went on and said, "I'll give you 10 years, after which nobody is really going to care what happens to Black people." That was 8 years ago.

The aftermath of Hurricane Katrina in New Orleans, and the disproportionate number of Black people adversely affected, arguably made our friend's 10-year prediction seem credible. Without resources to evacuate the city, unable to seek shelter and safety on higher ground, and largely abandoned by public agencies whose duty it was to serve its citizens as well as media who failed to raise public consciousness, residents of New Orleans, particularly poor African American residents of the Lower Ninth Ward, were in fact, made to feel irrelevant, or worse. How did this happen? First of all, the media stripped them of their U.S. citizenship status by referring to them as "refugees." In addition, initial news reports often portrayed them as looting stores and businesses in New Orleans. The media were so confused about what was happening that they initially portrayed—and the public envisioned—young and old African American men and women as criminals. Images of African Americans running down the streets with commodities in their hands led to public condemnation and revilement. On September 1, 2005, then Louisiana Governor Kathleen Blanco authorized U. S. National Guard troops to "shoot and kill" rioters and looters, which followed President Bush's statement that looters in New Orleans and elsewhere in the chaotic aftermath of Hurricane Katrina should be treated with "zero tolerance." At the same time, those in New Orleans who were not immediately impacted by Katrina and the breaking of the levees were in many respects continuing their lives as usual. Later, however, revised news reports showed that the "looters" were not taking televisions and luxury items but basic necessities for survival in a city that was completely devastated. Many were without clean water, electricity, or gas for weeks, or even months in some instances. What does my discussion with my friend have to do with social policy? The answer is: Everything.

U.S. governmental leaders, both elected and appointed, failed at the district or ward, municipal, county, state, regional, and national levels. Furthermore, the various institutional arrangements these leaders create and oversee, ostensibly to protect and serve the welfare of their respective constituents, is central to framing a social policy critique of the historical and contemporary social status of African American males in the United States. While there are arguably public policies that appear to be aimed at African American males which negatively affect their well-being, perhaps more profound are the unintended or nuanced negative effects of policies that have a deleterious impact on the urban poor, the unemployed, and the ex-offenders of which African American males are disproportionately overrepresented.

Social science research scholars have led the vanguard of those who document the social status of American citizens and critique the impact of various social policies. Social work research scholars are prominent among those. As the chapters in this volume have shown, the state of African American males in American society is both precarious and delicate. Larry Gary stated in his keynote address at the University of Chicago that Jewelle Taylor Gibbs may have overstated the problem in her book *Young, Black and Male in America: An Endangered Species* (1988). However, his comments and observations definitely do not indicate that all is healthy and well with regard to the current and future state of Black America, especially the economic, social, and health status of African American males in the United States.

Since the publication of the volumes by Gary and Gibbs, several social work research scholars have published volumes that document the increasingly ominous status of African American males in U.S. society. Larry E. Davis has published extensively on African American families in context. In particular, he has explored theories, problems, and issues within the social, economic, and political environment and their impact on adolescence and youth, clinical interventions on the social problems of youth, and group work and social problems of minority youth. In his volumes *Working With African American Males* (1999), *Ethnic Issues in*

Adolescent Mental Health (1990) with Arlene Stiffman, and *Race, Gender and Class: Guidelines for Practice With Individuals, Families and Groups* (1989) with Enola Proctor, Davis provides empirical and clinical evidence of the challenges that face African American males and other minority adolescents and youth. When these volumes are examined as a body of scholarship, however, Davis also provides a progressive account of the declining developmental and psychosocial statuses that have become emblematic of far too many African American males over their life course in the United States. In fact, from a developmental status perspective, it is not surprising that the increasing developmental issues and social problems experienced by African American males during adolescence would severely limit the opportunity structures for human and family development, and paternal involvement in adulthood.

In addition, Janice Matthews Rasheed and Mikal N. Rasheed in their volume *Social Work Practice With African American Men: The Invisible Presence* (1999) examine policy, research, and practice issues with African American men and clinical implications of historical trauma response in African Americans. Similarly, Rasheed and Rasheed document empirically and clinically how the needs of African American men have been largely ignored as a client base in need of the assistance offered by social work as a profession. In addition, they also show how African American men's diminished stature as a client base in social work practice has resulted in the profession's inadequate response to the needs and future development of African American families and communities.

In related scholarship on African American males, Ronald B. Mincy, Sr. presents a progressive timeline in which he documents the declining status of African American males. He initially examines the developmental difficulties of young African American males in his volume *Nurturing Young Black Males: Challenges to Agencies, Programs and Social Policy* (1992). Subsequently, Mincy focuses on the declining role and involvement of African American men in the lives in their children in his volume *Black Fathers in Contemporary American Society: Strengths, Weaknesses and Strategies for Change* (2003) with Obie Clayton and David Blakenhorn. He observes that at an earlier period, the declining role involvement was due to marital break-up but that contemporaneously, a disproportionate number of African American children are the products of out-of-wedlock parenting relationships in which their fathers have limited or no involvement at all. In *Black Males Left Behind* (2006), Mincy thoughtfully links together these two bodies of scholarship in order to demonstrate how the breakdown and disintegration of societal institutions like the African American family, both nuclear and extended, and social institutions like the formal and informal educational systems, have affected African Americans.

In *The Minds of Marginalized Black Men: Making Sense of Mobility, Opportunity and Future Life Chances* (2006), Alford Young, Sr. sheds light on the worldviews of ten African American men residing on Chicago's Near West Side by chronicling how they see themselves position in American society given their various social statuses. Young's poignant description of the lives of these men affirm that these men, like so many of their African American peers, have dreams and aspirations that are socially normative but often lack the opportunity to achieve them. For these men, social mobility is stymied not as a result of individual agency but more accurately, limited opportunity to enact their dreams and aspirations. While a number of issues emerge as descriptive of current statuses of the individuals profiled, education, work preparation and labor market participation are among the most prevalent.

In *Reconnecting Disadvantaged Young Men* (2006) by Peter Edelman, Harry Holzer and the late Paul Offner, grapple with the enduring public policy concern surrounding the out of school and out of work statuses of American youth ages 16-24, of which a disproportionate number are African American males. The authors recommend public policies and interventions that enhance educational and work opportunities to build individual and collective human capital. Similarly, William Julius Wilson in *When Work Disappears: The World of the New Urban Poor* (1996) links the effect of "growing joblessness and dwindling work opportunities, particularly in inner city neighborhood on family formation and stability, and crime. He posits that this phenomenon has racial implications given the disproportionate inner city communities populated by African Americans. Like Edleman, Holzer and Offner, he also offers policy recommendations to address this massive problem.

As each of the chapters in *Social Work With African American Males: Health Mental Health and Social Policy* highlight, there are assets among African American males. But what the research is highlighting is that those assets are often overshadowed by socially constructed barriers and obstacles that preclude African American males, as a group, from being able to fulfill the mythical quest of "pulling oneself up by one's bootstraps." This is not to say that, as Gary articulated, African American men and young African American men are not doing better as groups. The question is: Better than what?

From these chapters it is clear that African American males are challenged from before birth until the day they die. And not all of those challenges are directly the result of their own doing, especially at the earliest stages of their lives. For example, the health status of African American males (and African Americans in general) emerges at risk at birth. African American people have a disproportionately higher infant mortality rate and instances of low birth weight (which contributes to significant health outcomes and concerns) than any of their peers in the United States. Once they are born, African American children are more likely to live in poorer neighborhoods. Typically, the parents of African American children have lower paying jobs than their peers, and they are more likely to be underemployed or unemployed longer than their peers. Thus, starting off, African American children have a longer duration of living at or near the economically defined level of poverty as well as being in poor health in the United States.

Addressing the issues that African American males face in the United States through a social policy lens is challenging in that it is difficult to focus and articulate the specific issue or issues that impact them, thus making it more difficult to understand and then solve these "problems." Identifying the myriad of issues facing African American males makes the situation rather daunting if not overwhelming for policy makers and practitioners alike. Yet perhaps as the Katrina aftermath showed most dramatically, issues facing African American males in the United States have not gone away and are unlikely to disappear very soon. Therefore, we must find both the will to intervene and then develop strategies to improve their overall status in the United States.

The chapters presented in this book and other recently published works on African American males in America, such as those of Edelman, Holzer, and Offner (2006), Holzer and Offner (2006), and Mincy (2006), reopen a window into the lives of African American males that was opened in the late 1960s (Burton and Tucker, 2009; Edin, 2009; Liebow, 1967), middle 1980s, late 1990s, and 2000 but was then abruptly shut during the economic downturn at the beginning of the century (Pager, 2008). Funding for programs targeting African American males virtually dried up (see *Why We Can't Wait*) by 2004, and of those in existence, only a few programs were not focused on African American males in jail. This new window gives us a chance to see not only that the status, health, and economic well-being of African American males has not improved but also that they are faced with extraordinary obstacles in gaining access into mainstream U.S. society. It is clear from the works of Edelman et al. (2006), Mincy (2006), and the set of provocative essays from the recently published book *The Covenants with Black America* (2006) that the economic and social challenges that all African Americans—and for the purpose of this volume, African American males—face are complex and systemic.

The social and economic story only captures a portion, yet a significant portion, of the story facing African American males. Another part in the story of African American males has to do with their health and well-being. As Christopher's (2006) and Barrington's (2004) work indicates, African American males are vulnerable to a variety of physical and mental illnesses. The findings of Christopher (2005), Barrington (2004), and Wilde (2005) add support to the increasing evidence that health disparities are growing in the United States, as are the detrimental impacts that health disparities have on racial, gender, and ethnic groups' ability to navigate toward economic and social integration. The significant negative health disparities the African American community faces in comparison to other ethnic and racial groups is quite dramatic. Figure 18.1 reflects these concerns.

Photos and obituaries represent the challenges facing African American males during economically troubled and environmentally challenged times. As one reads the obituaries, it becomes evident that the males who died during Katrina died of preventable diseases such as hypertension and stroke. If they were to have received proper medical attention (or even their medicine), there is a likelihood that they would not have died. In contrast, older White residents of New Orleans died of natural causes.

These trends have been persistent for decades. They are having a deleterious impact on the way that African Americans in general and African American males specifically traverse through society in their quest to live "normal" and productive lives.

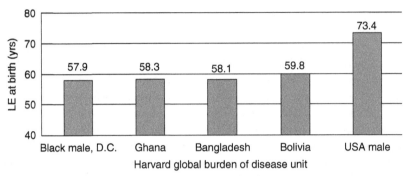

Figure 18.1   Average male life expectancy (LE) at birth.

The social policy responses to address these complex and convoluted issues do not come instinctively to the policy-making public. However, in terms of financial and societal investments needed to pursue and implement a successful social policy strategy to improve the outcomes of African American males, this consciousness is imperative. To make matters more challenging, should policy makers find the will to address some of these issues, the solutions will not be inexpensive. Failure to address these health and economic disparities and how they affect African American males in particular is to consciously ignore a segment of our society. If African American males are ignored, which the literature implies that they are, then they truly have become irrelevant and are destined to be further excluded from participating in the development of our society.

Today we run the risk of having both young and old African American males feel that they are expendable and irrelevant. The comment by the musician Kanye West, during a telethon to raise money for victims of Hurricane Katrina, that "Bush don't care about Black people" echoes the sentiment felt by many African American males. While Mr. West's comments were directed at the George W. Bush Administration, it can be inferred that his words were also addressed to past administrations—and to all federal government. The government's failure to identify, acknowledge, and address the issues that face African American males in the United States was brought to light in the aftermath of Hurricane Katrina, which many believe to be the single largest failure of the federal government to provide for its citizens.

So as social workers, advocates, and policy makers, the fundamental concern becomes what to do if we are interested in including all members of society in moving the nation forward. The first question we have to ask is, What can be done to improve the lives of African American males?

The answer to this question may be easier than the process of getting to the solution(s). First and foremost, we have to agree to change our attitudes about African American males. We must get present and future generations of the United States to acknowledge and accept the notion that African American males are integral and important members of our society. The research of Ravenell et al. (2006)

demonstrates why this is the case. In his study, gay African American males fared better on certain dimensions of status and well-being than straight African American males, posing the question of why "society" is more comfortable and accepting of African American males who are gay than those who are straight. This question does not imply that either group of African American males has it easy; rather it raises the question of question of why one group does better economically than the other, given that their primary difference is their sexual preference. Next, couple this with other statistics such as African American males are disproportionately dropping out of high school, being incarcerated, committing suicide at younger ages (Joe, 2006), and are more susceptible to being exposed to and dying by violence than their peers of different ethnicities, genders, and age. Taken together, all of this research begs the question of where African American males fit in or have a place in our society.

The challenges start at an early age for African American males, as a recent Yale study on expulsions shows. The study highlights the fact that young boys (4 years old and younger) are more likely to be expelled from preschool than any of their peers because of behavioral problems (Gilliam, 2005). In fact, the report claims that African American children are twice as likely to be expelled and that boys are nearly four and a half times more likely to be removed from classes. Yet the most damning statistic is as follows: "The increased likelihood of boys to be expelled over girls was similar across all ethnicities, except for African Americans where boys account for 91.4% of the expulsions" (Gilliam, 2005).What does this say to young African American boys at a very early age about their worth, value, and importance? Quite simply, it implies not too subtly that they are expendable, even at an early age, if they do not conform readily.

The level of disparity at such young ages is heart-wrenching, as it sets the tone for years (and greater intolerance) to come. What happens is that these children get thrown out of kindergarten and then eventually get thrown out of or drop out of high school. As spectators (policy makers, academicians, practitioners), we watch these children become chronically ill, drop into the criminal justice system, or die, sometimes violently (Joe, 2006; Johnson et al., 1999; Pate, 2005). The data are pretty clear on what we have been watching over the past 30 or more years.

Statistics so clearly and convincingly highlight the obvious story facing African American males in the United States: they are not part of the economic engine driving our society. As our society ignores, neglects, and imprisons many of these males, some still do more than survive. They thrive and become part of the "mainstream." Yet for those men who struggle to become part of the mainstream there must be some strategy or effort to keep them believing that there is hope and real opportunity available to them and to their less fortunate brothers to fully participate in this society with meaning, dignity, and respect.For this to happen we as a society have to willingly bring them into the system. The door of opportunity must be opened to them. The only way to ensure that African American males have a better chance of succeeding is to care, as a society, that they are as well attended to (or perhaps even better attended to) than the disadvantaged in our society.

The remainder of this chapter proposes a three-step policy process that would greatly improve the well-being, social integration, and potentially the economic status of African American males in the United States. These options are by no means easy to implement or even to agree upon, but they are designed to provoke discussion and to implement action—before things get worse.

The Plan for Success: Step One

Step one of the policy objective called The Plan for Success recommends the establishment of an Independent Education and Wellness (IEW) Plan for every African American male born in the United States (and eventually every child). This plan would start before the child is born and follow him or her until graduation from high school or college. This plan would help families and their children at an early age to chart, plan, and strategize for *their* futures with the assistance of other professionals (e.g., social workers, medical practitioners, day care providers, social and public health administrators, relatives, and educators). It would force the systems that usually intervene in a child's or adult's life to change the way in which they do business to guarantee the objectives and outcomes that they have all set for this child and this family.

Through this process at a very early stage of life, the child develops an expectation that the investment is going to materialize into something positive. For African American male children, this formal expectation may be something that their predecessors have never experienced. With this process in place at the beginning of a child's life, African American male children may now begin to realize that they are part of the "social contract" and that society has real and positive expectations for them as contributing and valued individuals. Their role in society begins to change and so do their values and the values of others. This process can happen at any stage in the child's life course. However, the earlier in the child's life the intervention is started the more "champions" and partners there will be to see that he progresses positively. For example, as Pate (2004, 2005), Waller (2002), Johnson (2001), and Johnson and Levine (1999) and others point out, many noncustodial/absent fathers are not always absent from their children's lives, but they lack real opportunities to be fully engaged with their children because of a number of mitigating circumstances (incarceration, ex-wife/girlfriend has another partner, not knowing that they have a child).As a result, there is disassociation, distancing, and or a degree of resentment that develops and grows between the child and the absent parent. In an IEW plan, the mother of the child, unless absent or unavailable, would work with social services, child support, public health, her family, his family (the absent/ cohabitating parent), and the father of the child to devise a plan for the child to succeed despite the parent's living or relational situation. What would make this different from what currently exists are two major things. First, the conversations among the parties would not be based upon obligations and antagonism but on a desire to see the child succeed. Second, the social service and public health systems would have to change the way that they interact with each other to see that progress is made on the child's behalf because they are partly responsible for the child's progress. These are seemingly small changes, but they would be dramatic in the implementation and delivery of social services and public health, particularly to African American males.

Implementing this process would require, as mentioned above, that the public social, health, education, and criminal justices systems change, and change dramatically. Public support systems like labor, social service, public health, child support, and the judicial system, rather than taking a role only when problems develop, would be involved on the front end of a child's life. Working with the parents, they would help figure out the best strategy to support the child's needs, as well as recognizing the needs and challenges of the respective caregivers. The comprehensive nature of this process is truly a fundamentally different manner of "doing business" for the public support systems. However, there are measurable outcomes and real checks and balances that would be put into place that would allow all parties to know that the child is positively growing up and that the child's existence is not a burden but a valuable and important part of the society at large. And perhaps for the first time, African American males may see that their success is as important as anyone else's.

Under no circumstance are the authors of this chapter naïve enough to believe that this could or should happen overnight. The fundamental question becomes whether there is a desire for these young men to have the support from the full society to succeed as a group. If the answer to that question is yes, the integration of public systems has to be in the design. Today African American males are far away from being systematically included in an integrated public support system, except for the criminal justice system. Yet it should not be discounted that our systems can be changed. If our government believes that it can change foreign governments that it has relatively little power over, the question becomes, Why is it not possible to change the way our public social systems interact with the public here in the United States? When the United States makes a commitment to do something, it usually does it. For example, when the former Soviet Union went into space, the United States became determined to be the leader in the aerospace sphere and put a man on the moon. During the economic downturn of the 1950s, it still had the will to put men to work and build its interstate highway infrastructure. Most recently, the United States' desire to change a repressive regime resulted in the country going to war in Iraq, with determined resolve. To take any of these steps or actions, the United States had to be committed to a result. As is evident today in its war on terror, the United States has to dedicate the appropriate resources (both money and people) and it has to affirmatively state, as it did with the space projects in the 1960s, exactly what the goals are to get people to support those goals. In the end, the people are paying for those goals to be implemented. The first success from such a process might just be that men, especially African American men, gain access and acceptance to other systems than the judicial/criminal justice system. If the IEW plan could be implemented and followed through, the African American male would be prepared to enter into the labor force ready, willing, and skilled. Next they will need real jobs and real work.

The Opportunity to Work: Step Two

Changing the social and public health delivery systems is insufficient if it does not produce both social and economic opportunities. In today's world there is a need for jobs and work that provide the means to live, not just to survive. Like the early intervention that would move them along positively on their educational and health trajectories, early access to work for African American males is a necessity. A working society is a healthy society. A better working society, where jobs are healthier, safer, and show the opportunity for growth and advancement, will mean a healthier society and a healthier worker. Therefore, to reduce the persistent and significant work disparities that exist between Blacks and Whites during any economic period, the government must play a more active role in hiring and providing employment opportunities. The government can do the hiring or it can encourage and demand that those that it contracts with have a diverse workforce, with a focus of improving the representation of African American males in respective organizations. The data are clear that African Americans and African American males have been disproportionately, and some (Waldinger, 1996) would argue structurally and systematically, excluded from meaningful, gainful work. Mishel, Bernstein, and Allegretto's work *The State of Working America 2006/2007* also highlights the economic challenges that African American males face. African American males as they go up the economic ladder are constantly undervalued as employees and are thus less likely to be compensated for their work.

In order for African American males to be able to participate more fully in society, and to reap some of the economic advantages that mainstream society has to offer, the government must engage and support the development of young African American men. The IEW plans, which has them focused on fulfilling their end of a social contract, explicitly state that there is an expectation that these young men will be positively productive (educated, trained, and ready for meaningful employment) and able to work (healthy, living in a safe environment). These are part of the social contract and the assumption in each IEW plan. Therefore, if the IEW plans are to be successful, the government has an obligation to see that there are good jobs available to people, especially those people who have traditionally not benefited from meaningful opportunities. Its responsibility becomes filling those jobs with people normally excluded from those opportunities, namely making these opportunities available to African American males.

Some may argue that this will interfere with the role of business and commerce as well as the free market. Others might argue that this is affirmative action of the kind that is now unpopular, if not against the law. That is an argument for another time. While private business obviously plays an important role in employment in the United States, government should take the lead, setting standards for fair employment practices or providing incentives to the private sector to encourage employment for the groups of underemployed, including African American males. The challenge here is to help society and to provide opportunity and meaning to a group of individuals who have not received many of the benefits that society has to offer.

This should be the government's role. And the government is in a unique place to make available such opportunity. The United States is a constantly growing and evolving place, with an infrastructure that is in constant need of revamping, refurbishing, and developing to keep up with the changing times and the environmental and economic pressures that we place on it. Many times these changes or fixes do not get implemented because of claims of lack of resources or prohibitive costs to improve or fix a system or structure that is decaying or broken. These situations can go unattended to and when they do, we end up with situations such as New Orleans or other preventable environmental or preventable economic disasters. Another example is the public schools that poor children attend. A community engaged in IEW plans would not allow for its children to go to school in overcrowded, unhealthy, and unsafe (physical and environmentally) environments because these children would then not be able to meet their respective IEW plans. Failures such as dilapidated or overcrowded schools would lead the community to devise a plan and implement it quickly so that these children could meet their obligations. At the same time it's possible to imagine that the government might join into a community benefits agreement with the residents of the community to ensure that its people were part of the planning and building of these new schools, which in turn would go a long way toward improving the economic and possibly the actual health environments of these low-income communities.

This process does not replace the role of the private sector. It augments the private sector's ability to meet the demands of society. This strategy also clearly separates the mandates of government from the driving principles of the private sector. Yet under this strategy the private sector has a vested interest in seeing that African American males succeed because it will eventually cause greater competition in the marketplace, as well as raise the bar on innovation and ideas once African American males become full participants in this sphere.

While there are some that argue that it is not the government's role to provide economic opportunity, they would be hard-pressed to argue against government's obligation not to perpetuate a permanent excluded group from the opportunities available to others in this society. If government does not do something to raise the chances for young and older African American males to work and move up the economic and social ladder, the ramifications for African American people, and more specifically for African American males, could be even more devastating. If the research presented in this book is any indication of the coming crisis, it would be dangerous for policy makers not to begin strategizing on how to implement a progressive and thoughtful work opportunity plan.

Access to Public Housing: Step Three

The third step of this strategy is the need to rethink public housing policies. The general policy of not allowing single men to live in public housing sends a signal of negative value and worth to men, particularly to economically challenged

African American men. The message is that they are not worthy of public support despite having or being part of a family that resides in the public facility (married or not). Many argue that there is a scarcity of public housing and that the available housing stock should go to women and children, or that the cost of expanding the stock of public housing to men would be too costly and potentially disruptive. Is this true? In those theoretical perspectives, the question becomes, What is the cost to society for excluding them from public housing opportunities? As a society, we make costly choices all the time. Why would we not choose to invest in decent public housing so these men could begin to stabilize their lives? One just has to drive through any local public housing development and realize that men are there. The question becomes, Why not permit them to live inside public housing, rather than exclude them? Would it not be better for the community and better for these men to have public housing available to them? If they are able to attain consistent shelter/housing, they are more likely to attain employment; and with employment begins the process of better health and safer communities. As the literature indicates, the better one's living situation, the healthier the individual. Those that are relegated to living in substandard environments are more likely to be ill (Kawachi & Berkman, 2003), which also makes it difficult to maintain employment.

How can this be a healthy and successful outcome for the individual or system? Our social policies need to be devised to serve those most in need to be successful social policies. They cannot be devised to exclude the very populations that need them the most. Our public housing policy must change to be more inclusive. Otherwise our already crowded cities and suburbs will have these men roaming the streets searching for warm and safe places to rest. At the same time, these men will cause a general uneasiness for those that must navigate to either avoid them or remove them in the name of safety and economic vitality. If we look closely in our cities at those who are doing this now, we see many African American male faces. This cannot be a successful outcome for U.S. housing social policy. Yet if phase one of this strategy is implemented, the need for and cost of revising our housing policy will diminish because as a society we will be watching closely how these men start transitioning from adolescence to adulthood, and if we see them falter we will be in a position to intervene. This will result in African American men becoming valued, incorporated, and understood in our society as opposed to being left behind and out.

In the introduction of the book, *The Covenant With Black America*, Professor Cornell West describes the importance of the Covenant:

> Our Covenant is neither a contract nor a compact. A contract is too selfish and a compact is too seasonal. Now is the time for us to keep faith with our spiritual, moral, and political covenant bequeathed to us by great foremothers and forefathers that simply says: stand with grace and dignity and take action with courage and compassion, with malice towards none yet a righteous[ness] against injustice, so that every day people—especially their precious children—can flower and flourish as the sun shines and the stars shout with joy.

Our challenge today as practitioners, policy makers, and members of the community is to create and then seize opportunities to help African American males move forward in the United States. It is here that we must depart from the concept of the Covenant and with a focused and unrelenting purpose include the African American male in the social contract twith the United States of America. We must be selfish today in our purpose if we are to address the situations that these men face. For without making the system and ourselves value African American males with the same level that we see bequeathed to others, it will not be possible to achieve the goals of the Covenant. The result is that African American males will be further isolated and left behind, where mere survival is success. This would ultimately fulfill the doomsday scenario for African American men: that they are an endangered species on the verge of irrelevancy to the future progress of the United States and the larger global community. Implementing the actions outlined in this chapter is the first step toward crafting policies and generating political will to make sure that another generation of African American men are not lost to hopelessness and the criminal justice system. Instead, they should be treated as valuable participants in medical, business, and law schools and important contributors to the arts, sciences, and literature. These men need and should experience the spirit and joy to which Professor West alluded. But this can only be accomplished through a comprehensive approach.

REFERENCES

Barrington, R. (2004, April). Poverty is bad for your health. Discussion paper, Dublin, Ireland: Combat Poverty Agency.

Berkman, L. & Kawachi, I. (2006). *Social epidemiology: Social cohesion, social capital and health*, pp. 174–190, New York: Oxford University Press.

Brown, J. R. (2005). Community health strategies to improve the life options of young men of color.*Poverty and Race, 14*(5).

Brown, M. K., Carnoy, M., Currie, E., Duster, T., Oppenheimer, B., Shultz, M., & Wellman, D. (2003). *White-washing race: The myth of a color-blind society*. Berkeley: University of California Press.

Burton, L. & Tucker, M. (2009). Romantic unions in an era of uncertainty: A post-Moynihan perspective on African American women and marriage. In The Moynihan Report Revisited: Lessons and reflections after four decades. *The Annals of the American Academy of Political and Social Science, 621*(1), 132–148.

Christopher, G. (2005). Towards a "fair health" movement. *Poverty and Race, 14*(5).

Christopher, G. (2006). *A way out: Creating partners for our nation's prosperity by expanding life paths for young men of color*. Washington, DC: The Dellums Commission Report, Joint Center on Political and Economic Studies Health Policy Institute.

Clayton, O., Mincy, R., & Blankenhorn, W. (2003). *Black fathers in contemporary American society: Strengths, weaknesses and strategies for change*. New York: Russell Sage Foundation.

Collins, J. W., Jr., David, R. J., Handler, A., Wall, S., & Andes, S. (2005). Very low birthweight in African American infants: The role of maternal exposure to interpersonal racial discrimination. *Poverty and Race, 14*(5).

Davis, L. (2008). *Working with African American males: A guide to practice.* Newbury Park, CA: Sage Publications.

Davis, L. & Proctor, E. (1989). *Race, gender and class: Guidelines for Practice with individuals, families and groups.* Needham Heights, MA: Allyn and Bacon.

Edelman, P., Holzer, H. J., & Offner, P. (2006). *Reconnecting disadvantaged young men.* Washington, DC: The Urban Institute Press.

Edin, K., Tauch, L. & Mincy, R. (2009). Claiming fatherhood: Race and the dynamics of paternal involvement among unmarried men. In *The Moynihan Report revisited: Lessons and reflections after four decades. The Annals of the American Academy of Political and Social Science, 621*(1), 149–177.

Gibbs, J. T., (1988). *Young, Black, and male in America: An endangered species.* Dover, MA: Auburn House.

Gilliam, W. S. (2005, May 4). Prekindergarteners left behind: Expulsion rates in state prekindergarten systems. www.childstudycenter.yale.edu\gilliam.html

Hacker, A. *Two nations: Black and White, separate, hostile, unequal.* New York: Charles Scribner's Sons.

Holzer, H. J., & Offner, P. (2006). Trends in the employment outcomes of young Black men, 1979–2000. In R. Mincy (Ed.), *Black males left behind* (pp. 11–39). Washington, DC: The Urban Institute Press.

Holzer, H. J., Raphael, S., & Stoll, M. A. (2006). How employer perceptions of crime and incarceration affect the employment prospects of less-educated young Black men. In R. Mincy (Ed.), *Black males left behind* (pp. 67–87). Washington, DC: The Urban Institute Press.

Joe, S. (2006) Explaining changes in the patterns of Black suicide in the United States from 1981 to 2002: An age, cohort and period analysis. *Journal of Black Psychology, 32*(2), 262–284.

Johnson, E., Doolittle, F., & Levine, A. (1999). *Fathers' fair share: Helping poor men manage child support and fatherhood.* New York: Russell Sage Foundation.

Johnson, W. (2001). Paternal involvement among unwed fathers. *Children and Youth, 23*(4/5), 459–482.

Kawachi, I. Berkman, L. (2006). A historical framework for social epidemiology. In L. Berkman, I. Kawachi (Eds.), *Social epidemiology.* New York: Oxford University Press, 3–12.

Littles, M., Bowers, R., & Gilmer, M. (2007). *Why we can't wait: A case for philanthropic action: Opportunities for improving life outcomes for African American males.* New York: Ford Foundation.

Mincy, R. (1994). (Ed.). *Nurturing young black males: Challenges to agencies, programs and social policy.* Washington, DC: Urban Institute Press.

Mincy, R. (Ed.). (2006). *Black males left behind.* Washington, DC: The Urban Institute Press.

Mishel, L., Bernstein, J., & Allegretto, S. (2006). *The state of working America 2006/2007.* Washington, DC: The Economic Policy Institute.

Pager, D. (2008). Blacklisted: Hiring discrimination in an era of mass incarceration. In E. Anderson (Ed.) *Against the wall: Poor, young black and male,* Chapter 5. Philadelphia: University of Pennsylvania Press.

Pate, D., Johnson, W., & Tuarner, M. (2004). Strengths and vulnerabilities of low-income married parents. Commissioned paper for the ACF/HHS Strengthening Healthy

Marriage Initiative, published by the Manpower Demonstration Research Corporation.

Pate, D. (2005). Deadbeat dads or fatherhood in poverty?. In J. Berrick and B. Fuller (Eds.) *Good parents or good workers: How policy shapes families' daily lives*. New York: Palgrave McMillan.

Pouncy, H. (2006). Toward a fruitfull policy discourse about less-educated young men. In R. Mincy (Ed.), *Black males left behind* (pp. 293–310). Washington, DC: The Urban Institute Press.

Primus, W. (2006). Improving public policies to increase the income and employment of low-income non-resident fathers. In R. Mincy (Ed.), *Black males left behind* (pp. 211–248). Washington, DC: The Urban Institute Press.

Rasheed, J. & Rasheed, M. (1999). *Social Work practice with African American men: The invisible presence*. Thousand Oaks CA: Sage Publications.

Ravenell, J., Johnson, W. & Whitaker, E. (2006). African American men's perception of health: A focus group study. *Journal of the National Medical Association, 98*(4), 544–550.

Rodgers, W. M., III. (2006). Forcasting the labor market prospects of less-educated Americans. In R. Mincy (Ed.), *Black males left behind* (pp. 39–66). Washington, DC: The Urban Institute Press.

Smiley, T. (2006). *The covenant*. Chicago: Third World Press.

Stiffman, A. & Davis, L. (Eds.). (1990). *Ethnic issues in adolescent mental health*. Newbury Park, CA: Sage Publications.

Waldinger, R. (1996). *Still the promised city: African Americans and new immigrants in post-industrial New York*. Cambridge, MA: Harvard University Press.

Waller, M. (2002). *My baby's father: Unmarried parenthood and paternal responsibility*. Ithaca, NY: Cornell Press.

West, C. (2006). A call to action. In (Ed.), *The Covenant* (pp. 239–240). Chicago: Third World Press.

Wilde, J. (2005). Taking the Social Determinants of Health Seriously. Dublin, Ireland: Institute of Public Health Inequality.

Wilson, W. (1996). *When work disappears: The world of the new urban poor*. NewYork: Random House.

Young, A. (2006). *The minds of marginalized Black men: Making sense of mobility, opportunity and future life chances*. Princeton, NJ: Princeton University Press.

INDEX